Methodism
and the
Southern Mind,
1770–1810

Methodism
and the
Southern Mind,
1770–1810

CYNTHIA LYNN LYERLY

New York   Oxford

Oxford University Press

1998

Oxford University Press

Oxford   New York

Athens   Auckland   Bangkok   Bogotá   Buenos Aires   Calcutta
Cape Town   Chennai   Dar es Salaam   Delhi   Florence   Hong Kong   Istanbul
Karachi   Kuala Lumpur   Madrid   Melbourne   Mexico City   Mumbai
Nairobi   Paris   São Paulo   Singapore   Taipei   Tokyo   Toronto   Warsaw

and associated companies in
Berlin   Ibadan

Copyright © 1998 by Cynthia Lynn Lyerly

Published by Oxford University Press, Inc.
198 Madison Avenue, New York, New York 10016

Oxford is a registered trademark of Oxford University Press.

Library of Congress Cataloging-in-Publication Data
Lyerly, Cynthia Lynn, 1960–
Methodism and the southern mind, 1770–1810 / Cynthia Lynn Lyerly.
p.   cm.—(Religion in America series)
Includes bibliographical references and index.
ISBN 0-19-511429-9
1. Methodist Church—Southern States—History.   I. Title.
II. Series: Religion in America series (Oxford University Press)
BX8241.L84   1998
287'.675'09033—dc21   97-27780

1 3 5 7 9 8 6 4 2

Printed in the United States of America
on acid-free paper

In memory of my grandparents

Preface

IN EVERY SOUTHERN METHODIST'S life, there was a moment when class, gender, race, and status were stripped away as the believer stood alone before God, who judged solely by the purity of the human heart. When southerners converted to Methodism, they entered a world fraught with external and internal dangers, where they struggled against enemies desperate to seduce them from the "narrow way" of Wesleyan holiness. In spite of steady and powerful opposition, white women, slaves, free blacks, and plain folk men remained faithful to Methodism and promoted a worldview in which an individual's devotion and piety were all-important.

This book tells two interrelated stories. The first is the history of how marginalized southerners advanced an ethic vastly at odds with southern secular mores. Methodists, sustained by their belief that every convert was the master of his or her own fate, denounced the white male culture of honor, the gentry's greed, and slavery, and held up an ideal of human relationships based on love and mutual respect. Early Methodists created a public sphere in which southerners at the margins of power could advance to leadership and earn the esteem of their fellow believers, a public sphere in which southerners from all walks of life were welcomed and valued. This is also the story of a South resistant to change, of southerners who zealously guarded their hegemony against any and all comers. Critics of Methodism perceived the church as a threat to white supremacy, slavery, gender conventions, patriarchy, parental control, and gentry rule. Battles between Methodists and their opponents took place in private, especially between wives and husbands, children and parents, slaves and masters, and in public, as white men, especially elites, contested the assertiveness of their erstwhile "inferiors" and fought to retain control of their world. Historians of the South know much of how the stories end. Those living through the contested rise of evangelical Protestantism did not.

Early southern Methodism represents one of the rare movements in southern history that held out the promise of a just world, one in which each individual had agency, worth, and dignity. The promise was largely unfulfilled; the ideal remained hopelessly out of reach even for many who dreamed of it. Nonetheless, these pages are filled with poor and lower-class white men, slaves, free blacks, and white women who did not simply take the world as they found it, who fought hard and well, and who nurtured and sustained each other in their struggle. Methodists' opponents were actors, too, who made conscious, deliberate choices to defend their power and their hegemony. When these worlds collided in the late eighteenth and early nineteenth centuries, neither side was certain of victory.

Scholarship is a collaborative effort, and many people nurtured and sustained me and this book. My gratitude for the team at Oxford—especially Cynthia Read, Will Moore, and Daphne O'Brien—is unbounded. I wish to thank the staffs and archivists at Duke University's Special Collections, the Southern Historical Collection at the University of North Carolina at Chapel Hill, Lake Junaluska, the Maryland Historical Society, and the Baltimore-Washington United Methodist Historical Society at Lovely Lane Museum. Betty Ammons of Lovely Lane, Jennifer Geran at Rice University's Interlibrary Loan department, John White at Chapel Hill, William R. Erwin, Jr., at Duke, and David K. Himrod of Garrett-Evangelical Theological Seminary were especially helpful. The Reverend Edwin Schell went above and beyond the call of duty. This work was completed with the invaluable assistance of a National Endowment for the Humanities Doctoral Dissertation Fellowship and a Boston College Research Expense Grant.

Various people have assisted me by reading parts of this work or by discussing concepts and arguments. My colleagues at Boston College let me think out loud and offered intellectual and moral encouragement at critical stages of this book's life. I am tremendously fortunate to be in a field and a university where established scholars encourage and mentor novices and where collegiality is more than superficial. Andrew Bunie, Joan Cashin, Jane Dailey, Elizabeth Hanson, Anya Jabour, Gerald McKenny, and Mrinalini Sinha offered astute advice and criticism of parts of this manuscript. Sylvia Frey, Rachel Klein, and Betty Wood made perceptive comments on conference papers relating to this work; they and numerous other historians have inspired me beyond the ability of footnotes to acknowledge. Thomas Haskell read the dissertation on which this manuscript was based with care and thoughtfulness and improved the work more than he will ever know. And finally, I owe a tremendous debt of gratitude to the best of advisors, John Boles, who has been critic, reader, teacher, and mentor. His example continues to awe, inspire, and humble me. Any errors that remain are, of course, my own.

Like the early itinerants, I am indebted to those who sheltered and supported me as I worked. Patricia Bixel, for her friendship, wit, brilliance, and patience, has my lasting thanks. My friends in Houston and Boston have emotionally sustained me. My aunt and uncle, Rachel and Gene Childress, graciously put me up on a research visit. My largest debt is to my parents, Anne and Mark Lyerly, who fed and sheltered me during research trips, who patiently listened to hours of conversations about the late eighteenth century, and who have encouraged and inspired me from the start. This book is dedicated to the memory of their parents and my grandparents, where my personal historical memories begin.

Boston, Massachusetts   C. L. L.

Contents

Methodism
and the
Southern Mind,
1770–1810

Introduction

When Worlds Collide

I will stop you from going to hear these Methodists; they are
turning the world upside down and setting people crazy.
— Thomas Hinde, to his wife, Mary, 1788[1]

THOMAS HINDE FAILED TO make good on his threat to keep his wife from Methodism, and later this same year, his world was indeed turned upside down by the church. Before his conversion, Hinde was a quintessential Virginia gentleman. Born into privilege in England in 1737, Hinde received training in surgery and medicine in London. Ambitious and proud, he emigrated to Hanover County, Virginia, at the age of thirty, where he married Mary Hubbard and became the commanding patriarch of a wealthy family. In Virginia Hinde moved in the "gayest circle of society" and lived ostentatiously, extravagantly, and immersed in the culture of honor. Like many well-educated Virginia men, Hinde imbibed the secular spirit of the enlightenment, prided himself on his rationality, and became a "confirmed deist." But in the late 1780s, the Methodists converted first his daughter Susanna and then his wife, and after his numerous desperate attempts to reassert patriarchal control had miserably failed, finally the doctor himself.[2]

Methodism disrupted Thomas Hinde's worldview and his predominance within his home. Thomas came to have three strong-willed, assertive, and zealous Methodist women in his family. His daughter Susanna was "fearless and undaunted on all occasions," and "possessing naturally a strong mind and great energy," she "became a bold, intrepid, and courageous soldier of the cross." His precocious younger daughter Hannah converted at age eleven and "was so gifted in prayer at that early period of life, as to excite the attention of her friends and strangers." Thomas's wife, Mary Hinde, all of the biographers agree, was the family's spiritual head. When the Hindes moved to Kentucky in 1797 and found Methodists there backsliding, "the old lady, always the more indefatigable and persevering of the two, now led the way," organizing a local society and arranging for an itinerant to serve them.[3] Mary was also intrepid in advancing the cause of Methodism outside her family; she was said to have "carried the war into the enemy's camp."[4]

Although he had previously been a man who delighted in "the fascinating allurements of the fashionable society," Thomas Hinde attempted to live by Wesleyan standards after he became a Methodist. Following his conversion he "released a tenant from a pretty considerable rent" on the sole condition that the man open his house for Methodist "preaching and class meeting."[5] Hinde refused to collect his debts, and some said he became benevolent to a fault. When he was paid money for his medical services, "it was likely that he would throw it into the lap of the first female member he passed in reaching home."[6] Hinde's personal transformation is most evident in the Methodist values he adopted after his conversion. Hinde renounced the pride, ostentation, and stature of his class and cultivated instead the Wesleyan posture of humility. As a Methodist, he became known for being "the humblest of the humble," and his son later recalled how the doctor had once compared himself unfavorably to a family pet: " 'The humble look,' said he, 'of the dog driven out from the room, pierces me to the heart. I envy the dog his humility.' "[7]

Thomas Hinde was merely one of many who were transformed by Methodism in the South.[8] Although the typical Methodist convert was not, like Hinde, a well-educated, elite white man, Hinde's story illustrates the vast gulf between secular southern mores and the Methodist worldview. Few southern men, Methodist or not, would have claimed that pride was the ultimate virtue, but rare indeed would be the white man outside evangelical churches who would have envied "the dog his humility." And in an era in which women's religious leadership was still extremely controversial, Hinde had three female leaders in his own household.

This study explores the psychological, social, and intellectual changes that Methodism made in its early converts and analyzes the confrontations between Methodists and southern society in the years from 1770 to 1810. Methodists in these four decades were often fearless social critics and embraced a worldview genuinely at odds with the dominant secular mind-set. While evolving and expanding, however, Methodists were changed by their experiences in the South and by their southern converts. Dating the evolution of white southern Methodists away from social criticism and toward social conformity is, like dating any evolution in ideas and values, a tricky business. This study ends with the year 1810, when clear signs (discussed in the epilogue) existed that the church had changed in some ways and was changing in others, but it would be erroneous to see this year as an absolute divide.

The sources used in this study are primarily published and unpublished memoirs, journals, and correspondence. Unpublished correspondence, memoirs, and manuscript journals present several interpretative problems. As is common with such sources, they privilege the literate. Literate ministers and lay people often recorded the testimony and life stories of Methodists who could not read or write, as well as their encounters with people outside the church, and these accounts are not without biases. One major bias was the Methodist worldview. Although Methodists could be extraordinarily compassionate, they could also be moralistic, self-righteous, and intolerant of other faiths or beliefs. We cannot, for example, take at face value Methodists' claims that this or that man was a "drunk," for their own policy of abstinence from hard liquor colored their view to the point that a man they termed a "drunk" might have been only a man who drank. Methodists tended to put things in religious—especially biblical—terms, and so in order to acknowledge their predispositions and biases, we must understand the scriptural conventions within which they interpreted experience.

The many extant journals of preachers present special problems. Methodist clergy kept journals in part to record the "rise and progress" of Methodism in America. Many seem to have believed that their journals would be read by others, some shared their journals with other ministers and lay people, and a few assumed their journals would later be published in some form. James Meacham, to take one example, occasionally addresses an imaginary reader in his journal and expected his journal to be read. When he began courting a woman he wished to marry, he put her name in a simple code to protect their privacy.[9] Many preachers protected the names of members who violated the rules and the names of nonmembers as well by using initials or dashes. Itinerants, it should also be remembered, were very busy men who sometimes recorded events or conversations days after they occurred. Preachers were not always unified in their opinions and attitudes. The idiosyncratic Jeremiah Norman, for example, tended to be more conservative than his fellow clergymen. Although a majority of ministers condemned wealth and ostentation, Norman did not, and he even believed that Methodist preachers needed to be more respectful when dealing with the gentry. His attitudes toward women and slavery were more traditional than those of most of his counterparts. While he was atypical, he does show that there existed a range of opinions among the clergy.[10]

White preachers and members were part of the larger Anglo-American world, and they partook of its racial and gender biases. Even antislavery clergymen occasionally made racist remarks.[11] One preacher who championed women's leadership in the church prefaced an exhortation to a lay woman's activism with the words "women are weak,"[12] and many referred to women by their husband's first and last names preceded by "Sister." The minority of well-to-do members is overrepresented in the extant correspondence while there are only a handful of accounts authored by African Americans who were members in this era. Preachers, most of whom came from poor or yeoman families, were predisposed to believe that wealth was equivalent to ungodliness, and thus we must read their comments about elites with this in mind. The more we understand the Methodist worldview and the prejudices of its literate members, the better we are able to interpret their comments.

Published sources present an even greater interpretative challenge. Because of the diligence of historians such as Robert Drew Simpson and Edwin Schell, we know that the published memoirs of Freeborn Garrettson and Francis Asbury were edited in such a way as to minimize conflicts over slavery and race relations between Methodists and their opponents.[13] Moreover, published antebellum church histories erroneously attribute early Methodist opposition to slavery to overzealous "English preachers."[14] In fact, the most zealous and influential antislavery ministers were men such as James Meacham, southern born and bred, and Freeborn Garrettson, son of a Maryland slave owner and, before his conversion, a slaveholder himself. I have therefore been cautious in using published sources to evaluate the actions of ministers and members on this front. Published memoirs also tend to glorify the clergy, leave out names of people being criticized, and minimize conflicts between Methodists. Some published histories, written when the church was no longer a suspect and despised sect, tried to downplay the plebeian origins of their church by overstressing the contributions of the minority of elite members.

One of my findings reinforces the historians' conceit that written histories shape the future by reinventing the past. After consulting manuscript sources and correspondence, I discovered that the memoirs and histories published by the church obscured not only some of the attacks on slavery but the radicalism of early Methodist women as well. One church historian writing in 1909, for example, made the claim that in early Methodism, women "were expected, even required, to 'keep silence in the churches,'" a statement belied both in almost every manuscript source and in the author's own pages.[15]

Published sources are critical to understanding the transformation of Methodism, however, precisely because of these biases and revisions. Beginning slowly in the era covered in this study and increasing in intensity in the antebellum years, Methodists tried to deny the class composition of the early church and its earlier radicalism on slavery and gender roles. Before the turn of the century, the efforts to obscure were largely defensive; the church was under attack because of its antislavery views, its expanded public roles for women, and its lower-class majority. In later antebellum years the effort to revise the Methodist past coincided with the transformation of the southern wing of the church into a consciously regionalized body that defended southern institutions. By reinventing the past, antebellum southern Methodists obscured the radicalism of their predecessors and blurred the distance between their views and those of the founders.[16]

Although I have focused in these pages on Methodists in the South, my analysis should not always be read as making exclusive claims for southern Methodists. Some of the values and conflicts described herein were unique neither to the region nor the sect. Battles between husbands and wives over religion, for example, were commonly reported by northern Methodists, American Baptists, and others. Methodists were not alone in their beliefs about the salutary effects of suffering, either. Southern Methodists were certainly not the first people to be condemned for their enthusiasm, and they were not the last. And Methodists did not stand alone in their opposition to slavery.[17] This study is not, however, an institutional history of Methodism in the South. For important events in denominational history, such as the Fluvanna conference and the O'Kelly or Hammet schisms, readers should look elsewhere. This study concentrates on what was common among southern Methodists and not on local variations. Yet the experiences of members in Charleston, South Carolina, were not identical to the experiences of those in frontier Kentucky, and at times I have been explicit about variations within the region. The strength of Methodism in Delaware, as historians of Delaware remind us, set that state apart from its neighbors in the Revolutionary and postwar era.[18]

There are several reasons that, despite these warnings, a study of one sect in one region is valuable. The Methodist system of itinerancy—rotating ministers as frequently as every six months and by 1810 at least every two years—meant that a preacher like Thomas Morrell, who spent most of his career in New Jersey and points north, served a tour in Charleston. Many preachers, such as Freeborn Garrettson, Francis Asbury, Richard Whatcoat, John Kobler, Jesse Lee, and Benjamin Lakin, were not limited to a southern ministry, and worked, as did Garrettson and Lee, in New England, or like Kobler and Lakin, in the Old Northwest, or like Asbury and Whatcoat, throughout North America. Because of this rotation system, ministers were often thrust into unfamiliar neighborhoods, and on their first rounds they noted in their journals the state of Methodism in the area. They based this judgment not on local opinions but on their previous experiences, the church's book of *Discipline*, and the admonitions of their superiors in the ministry. Methodists everywhere did not behave the same, but itinerants tried to exact some degree of conformity to their preconceived notions and the ideals laid down in the doctrinal literature. They considered their church as transcending city, county, state, and national boundaries.

The rotation of ministers and their predisposition to keep journals allow modern-day analysts to compare Methodists in various areas. By far the largest issue that divided some Methodists from others was slavery, with a chasm between those who owned slaves and those who did not and between those who were slaves and those who were not. When American Methodism began, slavery was a continental institution but as slavery became increasingly regionalized, Methodists themselves—for reasons I will discuss in subsequent pages—became more regionally polarized. A regional analysis enables us to see common threads in the experiences of Methodists. Conflict between Methodist wives and non-Methodist husbands, Methodist slaves and non-Methodist masters, Methodist children and non-Methodist parents, for example, was a regional phenomenon. In plantation belts, of course, different resources could be mobilized against Methodist slaves than in cities or on the western frontier. But the persistence of conflicts within households between "superiors" and "subordinates" in diverse localities alerts us to look for those values within Methodism that, first, might encourage a "subordinate" to challenge a "superior" and, second, might provoke reaction by a "superior" against a dissenting "subordinate."

Pioneering work by many historians enables us to compare Methodist values with those of other southerners. Studies by T. H. Breen, Edmund Morgan, Lacy Ford, Jr., Kenneth Greenberg, Stephanie McCurry, and J. William Harris, for example, have shown that white men of the South tied their own freedom and independence to the enslavement of blacks and dependence of women and slaves. Class conflict between white men was muted by their common mastery over their households and dependents.[19] White men also had in common, as Bertram Wyatt-Brown and others have shown, a code of honor. Although the characteristics of the code varied by class, it, too, revolved around each white man's ability to govern his own affairs free from outside interference. The code of honor emphasized outward appearances and the evaluations of others, and not a man's inner sense of himself.[20]

Methodism challenged these southern values and practices on a number of levels. Methodists cultivated an inner-directed morality in opposition to the other-directed ethic of honor. Methodists prized meekness, humility, and docility in a society in which meekness, humility, and docility were associated with slaves, women, the poor, and children. They ranked people by their piety and holiness rather than by their race, gender, class, or status. They refused to show deference where, by secular standards, deference was due. Although they did not mount a sustained assault against patriarchy, they did not accept patriarchal authority unquestioningly. Methodism supported and bolstered pious men, women, and children who were in conflict with impious patriarchs. For a few decades, Methodists challenged slavery as well. Their attack ebbed and flowed, they alternately advanced and retreated, and they frequently changed their strategy, but nonetheless they were the most persistent and vocal critics of slavery among the evangelical sects. Among all religious groups, they were second only to Quakers in their opposition to human bondage. Unlike the Quakers, however, Methodists actively recruited slave and free black members, a more indirect, but no less real, attack on slavery. Many disputes between Methodists and their opponents revolved around this more implicit challenge to slavery, for whites outside the church were frightened that a sect so identified in their minds with antislavery would have such influence on slaves and free blacks. Conversely, non-Methodist whites were equally horrified by the influence blacks, especially black male preachers and exhorters, had within the church, particularly over white women.

One of the temptations for historians of the post-Revolutionary South is to read backwards from the Civil War, and this study frequently succumbs to that temptation. Yet it is equally clear that early southern Methodists were qualitatively different from their antebellum successors. In the church's first decades, its members were cultural critics—not in response to southern secular mores, but as a result of their Wesleyan heritage. Their notions of women's proper roles were often at odds with dominant southern views, for Methodists promoted women's vocal participation in public spaces and women's religious leadership. They proffered an ideal of manhood vastly at odds with secular norms. Early Methodists refused to accept the republican defense of slavery; they claimed that slavery was an evil in itself as well as a system that bred other evils. Their views about hierarchy differed radically from secular views, for they denied that wealth, power, and status were measures of excellence. Methodists' failure to sustain their critique of southern values, their gradual modification of their oppositional worldview to a more accommodationist one, and their growing acceptance of and later acquiescence to slavery and patriarchy does not alter this fact.

Several historians have emphasized how evangelicals differed from other southerners. Rhys Isaac's insightful study of Virginia Baptists explored one important aspect of this challenge—evangelical attacks on gentry customs, mores, and habits. As Isaac shows, Baptists prized humility and in their churches valued piety over property, status, and wealth. Donald Mathews's classic study of southern religion revealed how attitudes toward slavery and black converts were equally important in dividing evangelicals from other southerners.[21] The role of gender in early southern evangelicalism has been less explored than the issue of slavery. Mathews perceptively raised the issue of women and gender conflict in his work, but few, with such notable exceptions as Jean Friedman and Richard Rankin, have followed his lead. But along with class, race, and slavery, gender was a pivotal factor in the conflicts over religion and religious authority in the Revolutionary and early national South.[22] Southern evangelical women and the gender conflicts that evangelicalism provoked, however, cannot be understood apart from the other conflicts that arose over values, race, class, and slavery. I have therefore integrated discussion of women into all aspects of this work. Women were the bearers of the word, keepers of doctrine, and—black women consistently and white women occasionally—the defenders of the rights of slaves. To omit women from an analysis of Methodist doctrines or practices would be more than uninclusive, it would be historically inaccurate.

A word must be said about the nature of power. Historians, either implicitly or explicitly, have often portrayed power in early southern churches as flowing from the ministers (assumed to be the most powerful) down in ever-diluted fashion to parishioners. The more I progressed in my study the more inadequate this conceptualization became. John Wesley sent preachers to America because Methodist immigrants requested that he send them. As the first Methodist itinerants fanned out into the South, they had no church buildings, no licenses to marry, no authority to baptize or administer the sacrament, and no money or land in their "treasury." In the post-Revolutionary era, when American Methodists officially organized as a church, fierce competition for converts raged between the sects, denominations, and various forms of nonchurch belief. With the disestablishment of the Church of England, church membership became voluntary and financial support of churches became voluntary as well. When itinerants came into a new neighborhood, they most often held services in private homes of men and women who volunteered to host such services. Itinerants' salaries were too meager to support them without donations of free food, lodging, and services (like shoeing horses and tailoring). If no doors were opened to them, circuit riders would move on to neighborhoods where they were more welcome. On the southern and western frontier, the situation was often more precarious, for even men and women who were supportive of the church were frequently unable to contribute much toward its ministers' upkeep.

The power that these men had lay primarily in their ability to persuade others—to reach their audiences, to change the hearts and minds of their listeners, to keep their members together and zealous. When men and women became Methodists, they voluntarily ceded religious disciplinary authority to lay and clerical leaders, but at any time they could withdraw from the church. Had the pews not been filled, the money not been given, the homes not been opened, and donations in kind not been made, the church would have died. Moreover, the itinerant system was only one part of the church administration. Local lay leaders—class leaders, exhorters, local preachers, and unofficial but no less influential pious men and women who acted in these roles from time to time—ran the church when itinerants were on their rounds. These leaders were black and white, male and female, and they as much as the itinerants were responsible for keeping the church alive and thriving. Often the most powerful member of a local society—the one who commanded the most influence and respect—was a woman.

The evangelistic nature of Methodism also made every member a local missionary; mysticism made each a prophet. Indeed many (perhaps most) conversions were initiated by ordinary lay men and women. Methodists were relentless in pressing, or more accurately hounding, their relatives, friends, and strangers to convert. Members remembered their conversions and recited the circumstances of them throughout their lives in the church and this testimony, in turn, reinforced the role of all members in proselytizing. Methodists also believed in the possibility of direct and individual revelation from God. God could strike believers unconscious, speak to them via dreams, visions, or signs, and apprise converts directly of actions to take or avoid. Preachers are best known for believing themselves under divine inspiration, but lay men and women all across the South reported similar interaction with God. Letters and memoirs of lay men and women show how thoroughly immersed most of them were in Methodist doctrine and culture, and how supernatural their faith was. For all of these reasons, power was not concentrated in the hands of ministers, much less in those of stewards or trustees.

The Revolution ushered in a climate in which many inherited traditions and "truths" could be questioned. The success of Methodism in the postwar era is one indication that dissent and change were possible in such a climate. But the growth of evangelicalism was not merely a product of the Revolution; it constituted a revolution in itself. To understand the multifaceted aspects of this revolution, I have organized this work topically rather than chronologically. I will begin with the earliest American Methodists and explore the unique conflicts between them and their opponents in the Revolutionary era. Next I will turn to the inner world of converts, for without an understanding of the beliefs, psychology, and mentality of Methodists, we cannot hope to understand their response to conflicts or their critics' response to them. Core values and doctrines made Methodists who they were and united them despite social, economic, racial, and gender differences. Equally important, however, is how race, gender, and class intersected with Methodism, and chapters 3, 4, and 5 explore the church's attitudes, converts' behaviors, and the unique concerns of poor, black, and white female Methodists. The central moral conflict in the postwar era—the conflict over slavery—was pivotal to southern history as well as to how Methodists were perceived. Finally, I will analyze the collision of worldviews between Methodists and their opponents, integrating the battles over values, race, class, gender, and slavery as well as analyzing the response of critics to the church. Some critics, like Thomas Hinde, were conquered; when they converted to Methodism, they entered a radically new world.

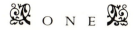

ONE

Revolutions Civil and Religious

Methodist Beginnings in America

A FAILED AND PERSECUTED Irish farmer and a bold, pious woman are credited with founding Methodism in America, a fact less coincidental than it would first appear. Robert Strawbridge, a Methodist who fled his native Ulster because of religious persecution, emigrated to America in 1760, settling on a farm near Baltimore, Maryland. Strawbridge was not successful "as a man of business"; his farm, "had it not been for the toil of his wife and the charity of his neighbors, would have failed to keep himself and family from want." Better at preaching than farming, Strawbridge soon raised a small society of Methodists that met and worshiped at his home.[1] Another immigrant band of British Methodists landed in New York in 1760—only these men and women began to forsake Methodist ethics in the New World. When Barbara Heck, "a woman of piety, persistence, and genius for affairs" encountered her male friends and relatives playing cards, she became outraged, "seized the cards, threw them into the fire, and gave her friends a solemn warning against sin." To return the group to Wesleyan piety, Heck entreated her cousin, Philip Embury, who had been a Methodist preacher in England, to begin holding services. Word soon spread that Embury's home was the scene of strange goings-on, where "women often prayed, and even stood up and made speeches just like the men." Heck was likely one of these women.[2] From these modest beginnings, the Methodists grew into one of the most successful religious movements in American history.

Because more and more Methodists made the journey to America, British founder John Wesley dispatched missionaries to guide them and to seek out new souls to bring within the fold. Methodists came to the New World with distinct doctrines, values, and practices (discussed in the next chapter), a new vocabulary, and a unique method of organization. Their vision of America was colored most of all by the Wesleyan imperative that the people of God should separate themselves from the people of the

11

world. In the South, the division between the "godly" and "worldly" largely matched the division between the powerless and the powerful. Methodism proved especially popular with slaves, white women, and poor or struggling white men, while elites looked on the movement with contempt and suspicion. When the crisis between England and the colonies erupted into rebellion and war, the Methodists were perceived by some and labeled by many as enemies of the Revolution. To Methodist preachers, the most important "freedom" was found in religion, the only meaningful war was the one against sin, and the real revolution came when men and women converted. In part because of a few Methodist Tories, in part because Methodists challenged southern hierarchies of gender, race, and class, southern officials and vigilantes proscribed members and leaders of the fledgling movement. When the gunfire stopped, Methodism was firmly planted in the new nation and its preachers were poised to carry their war into every byway of the South. Methodists' experiences during the Revolution, like the experiences of Heck and Strawbridge in forming the first Methodist societies, were pondered, interpreted, and woven into the fabric of Methodist identity.

To write about Methodist beginnings in America (a past northern and southern Methodists shared) is to enter a world of both fact and myth.[3] The men and women in the movement were grand interpreters who shaped moral lessons and discerned profound meaning in the everyday stuff of life. When Methodists interpreted the stories of their origins, they affirmed their central belief that the "world" was the enemy of God and his people. The lesson of the New Yorkers' experience was simple. Without the close-knit fellowship of other members and a clear sense of separation from the world, even the faithful could be seduced from Wesleyan piety. And as was often the case in Methodism, the one to point the group back to righteousness was, by secular standards, the least powerful. Strawbridge's story also exemplified movement values and inverted worldly expectations. Harvesting souls was a higher calling than harvesting crops. When Methodists described his business failure, it was not to remind other men of their duties as providers but to show that God could make great things from the least promising of people. In admiring a failed farmer and an outspoken woman, Methodists reiterated their central belief that God's ways were not those of the world.

The experiences of ordinary men and women could be used didactically because the people of God had a special role in the grand drama of life. Methodists, like other Protestants, believed in the providential course of history. All past and present time was oriented to the end time—the second coming of Christ on earth. Other Protestants saw the New World as God's chosen site for the unfolding of his plan, but to Methodists, America was a mission field, not a New Eden.[4] Francis Asbury, the preacher most responsible for church growth in America, had no sense of the New World as a "city upon a hill"; his purpose in emigrating was to "live to God, and bring others so to do." He was not overconfident: "The people God owns in England, are the Methodists. The doctrines they preach, and the discipline they enforce, are, I believe, the purest of any people now in the world. . . . . If God does not acknowledge me in America, I will soon return to England."[5] Although a few Methodists, like Robert Strawbridge, fled persecution, the vast majority were not seeking a spiritual refuge. Other Protestants shaped their myths around America as a promised land; Methodists fashioned theirs around the battle between the "worldly" and the "godly."

Another component of Methodist mythmaking was the lurking fear of decline. Because the world was so corrupting and evil, preachers constantly warned Methodists to "be ye separate" in order to lessen temptation. Satan interfered, in Methodist views, in human affairs, but Satan had help from worldly people. Before his conversion in 1778, Joseph Everett was plagued by the devil, who nourished the evils of "pride, self-will, and anger," and "the children of the devil," the "wicked" who joined him in "carnal and forbidden pleasures," especially drinking. After the first pangs of conviction, Everett began to withdraw from "evil company" and spend more time with other Methodists. The exclusiveness of the sect was designed to help keep people like Everett from the world. Business, politics, and even simple conversations with nonbelievers could draw a member's heart from God. Complete isolation was neither possible nor—for such an evangelistic sect—desirable, but the church's long services and variety of spiritual gatherings offered a number of ways for members to come together without risk of outside contamination. The fear of spiritual decline was a central part of American Methodisms' founding myth—witness the fate of Barbara Heck's male compatriots—and served to remind members that only watchfulness, piety, and community could help members stay righteous.[6]

Perhaps the most important part of Methodism's founding myth was the sect's self-image as a despised, outcast group.[7] Methodists wanted to be despised; the Bible said that the righteous would be persecuted by the ungodly. As long as Methodists were persecuted, they were assured they were doing God's will. Their critics' derisive comments and actions thus ironically helped Methodists define themselves as pure. In one sense, of course, Methodists in the South were outcasts: their converts were predominantly the powerless and marginalized. But Methodists were not dismayed at their lowly following. Wesleyan values and the British experience had prepared them to expect opposition from elites. They were proud of their humble beginnings and of their appeal to the very people secular society deemed inferior.

In numerous ways, the first American societies resembled their British forerunners, although Methodism started in a more auspicious setting in the mother country. John Wesley and his friends began to hold special prayer meetings and Bible studies at Oxford. Influenced by Moravian pietism on his earlier trips to America and Germany, Wesley felt that all Christians needed to experience conversion, and then lead a pristine and introspective life aimed at perfection. Because of their strict self-monitoring, he and his followers were derisively labeled "Methodistic." Wesley's small group grew into a splinter movement in the Church of England, especially attracting women and the working classes.[8] British Methodists, too, had poor heroes and brave heroines in their founding myths, but John Wesley's towering presence was by far the most central.[9] In America, Wesley's sermons and essays were avidly read, studied, and memorized; most members knew him through his doctrines. Lay men and women, however, "founded" Methodism in the colonies. Wesley decided to send missionaries to America largely because colonists wrote urging him to do so.[10]

Women and the lower classes flocked to Methodism in America as they had in England. But a third group became a key part of the pioneer societies in the New World. In Maryland and New York, the first Methodist societies had black members—both slave and free. Strawbridge's efforts in Maryland "became the center of attraction to large numbers of people, both white and black."[11] Mary Switzer and Jacob Toogood were among Strawbridge's black converts.[12] In New York, Betty, the servant or slave of

Barbara Heck, and Peter Williams, the slave of a tobacconist, were two of the founding members.[13] Black New York Methodists contributed money to help build the first church. A sister society formed from this group on Long Island around 1768, and after six months, its members numbered twenty-four, "nearly half of them whites—the rest [N]egroes."[14] Methodism was born in America as a biracial lay movement.

Methodists used a new religious lexicon to describe their unique organizational features. The smallest organizational unit in the church was the *band*. Bands were composed of a handful of members of the same sex and marital status who met weekly to "speak . . . freely and plainly" of the "true state" of their souls. In the South, far more central than bands were *classes*, the most important and, in some sense, defining units within Methodism. Classes were composed of a dozen or so members who met once a week under the direction of an appointed layperson. When Methodism was new in an area, a class would include all the local members. As the membership increased, classes were divided by sex, marital status, age, and race, for church leaders believed that class meetings would be more edifying if the members shared similar concerns. The weekly meetings consisted of devotions, hymn singing, and discipline, but their central purpose was for members to share their religious experience. In class, members' most private thoughts and feelings were probed by leaders who asked "searching questions" and conducted "a free inquiry into the state of the heart." Methodists were to "confess [their] faults one to another"—including those "committed in tempers, words or actions." They were urged to "desire" that others "should come as close as possible" and "search" their hearts "to the bottom." Methodists were to keep no thought hidden from the group, to become, in effect, transparent to each other.[15]

Classes combined to make the local *society*. Other sects and denominations called similar units congregations, but to Methodists, a "congregation" was the group of people who came to services, some of whom were not members. Congregations included children too young to join the church, those people interested in religion but not yet converted, members of other sects, and the curious. Most services, including prayer meetings, funerals, and regular worship services were open to all, but Methodists conducted certain kinds of meetings where only members of the society were allowed. The most important of these were the *love feasts*. In love feasts, Methodists were served bread and water and testified about their religious experiences. The goal of a love feast, as the name implies, was to unite the membership in love through this communal sharing. A "good" love feast was one where the spiritual passions of the society were rekindled, where the emotionally and physically demonstrative ritual of conversion was revisited.

Methodism's unique features and organization nurtured lay leadership and local talent. In band and class meetings, love feasts and services, members related their religious experience and yearned to testify with what their brothers and sisters would call "eloquence" and "power" and "influence." The most respected lay Methodists were those who could raise a "shout," revive zeal, or make their listeners weep. These eloquent speakers were young and old, male and female, enslaved and free, well-read and illiterate. During testimony, they were judged by their pluck, sincerity, creativity, and above all, their capacity to touch the hearts of their audiences. The democracy of voices in church gatherings was unequaled in other public spaces of the South. Special services and meetings also created strong, cohesive, and supportive communities of believers, creating out of many I's the Methodist *we*. During the years in which Methodists were an outcast sect, these gatherings were critically important, for they reinforced the separation of the group from the world and spiritually buttressed those members who faced the most hostility from family and friends.[16]

Members whose relatives rejected them found new families in the movement. Women in the church became "sisters" and men, "brothers," language that fostered intimacy and helped to bridge gaps of class, race, and status. The importance of the familial concept to Methodists is hard to overstate. Peter Pelham's daughter Sally had "[received] a letter two days past from Betsy Hicks in which she mentioned the death of 'Mrs. Ross,'" Pelham remarked in a letter to a friend, adding that "we expect it is Sister Betsy Ross."[17] To Pelham, "Mrs. Ross" and "Sister Ross" were not the same woman. Witness, too, the journey of a man named Goodlow. William Ormond first preached at "Mr. Goodlow's" home on July 29 when "Mr. Goodlow" was awakened "in a powerful manner." On the second of September, Ormond returned to the home to preach and noted that "Mr Goodlow seem[s] very desirous to serve God." On October 7, Goodlow joined the Methodists. When Ormond returned again on December 16, it was to "Bro. Goodlow's."[18] Goodlow had passed from a distant "Mister" to a familiar "Brother."

The brothers who were preachers were organized into the *itineracy*. Methodists were not the first to make preachers responsible for more than one local group or to designate certain people as roving evangelists. But the "itinerant plan," as Methodists called it, was institutionally unique. Itinerants traveled a *circuit* that took three or four weeks to ride; along the way, they stopped and held services, met classes, and evangelized. As membership in larger cities increased, some itinerants were assigned to "stations" that encompassed multiple societies in and around those cities. Itinerants were frequently rotated among different circuits, among stations and circuits, and in the eighteenth century among regions. Many early preachers served both above and below the Mason-Dixon line during their careers. When a circuit rider became "worn down" or when he married, he could "locate," that is, become a local preacher. Other sects used itinerants as an expedient when there were not enough ministers to fill every position. For early Methodists, the itineracy was not temporary, but permanent, not an expedient, but an ideal.

Until 1784, when the American Methodists organized as a church (thus making official the separation from the Church of England), preachers were not ordained ministers.[19] They could bury the dead and conduct worship services, but could not administer the sacraments, baptize, or perform the marriage ceremony. Even after 1784, the name "preacher" was the one most Methodists used. The choice was a meaningful one. Terms like "clergy" and "ministry" had, in Methodists' eyes, the taint of worldliness. The "ministry" was educated, part of the establishment, esteemed by the rich and powerful. Preaching—bringing people to Christ—was a Methodist's principal duty. Like other evangelicals before them, Wesleyan preachers considered their sermons and exhortations moments of high drama, when listeners' eternal fates depended on the speaker's ability to make hearts melt and sinners repent. "Preaching" was thus not limited to the clergy; as a verb, it was used when lay men or women who were not ordained and not licensed melted hearts with oral testimony and brought others to Christ. Slightly more official than these lay preachers were local preachers—men who were licensed but not ordained and who did not have all of the privileges of their traveling brethren.[20] Above them were the licensed and ordained itinerants. Even the highest-ranked leaders in the new church—its bishops—were specifically commanded by the *Discipline* to travel.

The itinerant system served multiple purposes, some intended and some incidental. Circuit riders reached a wide audience on their three- to four-week rounds. Through the itineracy preachers shared the wealth—no itinerant was stuck for very long in a poor area. The itineracy inhibited alliances between preachers and particular members, thus keeping the message and church discipline freer of local interests and more uniform as a body. And critical was the itineracy's fostering of local lay leadership; these men and women carried on the work of Methodism while preachers were on their rounds. Less obviously, the itineracy conveyed an ideal of the Methodist church as a dynamic body unrestricted by borders. Methodism, like its ordained preachers, was constantly on the move, ever expanding both in numbers and in amount of territory covered. The itinerants, weaving in and out of local societies, knit these small, insular, and sometimes provincial families into an "imagined community"[21] of American Methodists.

Methodists, like other evangelicals, believed that the church should nurture and watch over its members, but Methodist and Baptist polity differed in several important respects. Baptists organized congregationally, and these local bodies wrote church covenants that outlined the fundamental doctrines and rules by which their members were governed. Methodism allowed no local variations; *The Doctrines and Discipline*[22] was the rule book for all. The *Discipline* broke down Christian obligations into three categories. First came the duty to do no harm "by avoiding evil of every kind," such as breaking the Sabbath, violating the Golden Rule, drinking liquor, marrying an unbeliever, fighting, buying and selling slaves, wearing "costly apparel," and "laying up treasures on earth." Second came the duty to do good. Methodists were to care for the "bodies" of others by tending to prisoners, the poor, and the sick. To care for others' "souls," Methodists were to reprove, exhort, evangelize, and set a good example. Third came the duty to obey "all the ordinances of God"—to attend church, take the sacrament, pray as families and as individuals, read the Bible, and regularly fast.[23] The inclusion of "shalls" with "shall nots" was important. The ideal Methodist was not simply a person who did not swear; the ideal member reached out to the less fortunate and regularly participated in church rituals and activities.

Discipline was central, literally and figuratively, to the church. The reproof, suspension, or expulsion of members served as a model for what the self must daily accomplish. Ministers often used one of two metaphors to describe expulsion. One was medical with religious overtones—"purging." In this era, purgatives were common treatments for illnesses and were used to purify the body by removing "bad" fluids. Thomas Chew noted "an increasing declension of Religion" in his circuit and believed the solution lay in greater discipline: "it is high time to purge the Classes in general, for unless the rubbish is remov'd out of the way we shall travel slowly." As the church tried to keep pure as a body by purging "bad" members, individuals tried to purify themselves in body and mind by purging bad thoughts and habits. The second metaphor preachers used for expulsion was "sifting," again a process of eliminating the bad so the good could flourish. For the self and for the local Methodist society, this "purging" was essential to a healthy spiritual life. Besides, as Methodists knew all too well, outsiders were watching for every slip members made, seeking opportunities to denounce them as hypocrites.[24]

Opposition was a fact of life for the early movement. The reason was partially unfortunate timing. Methodists entered the South almost on the heels of the gentry's conflicts with the Separate Baptists and on the eve of the American Revolution. The battle between the gentry and the Baptists in Virginia had resulted in two largely antithetical and competing worldviews.[25] In some ways, Methodism entered this setting on the side of the Baptists. Like Baptists, Methodists considered a conversion experience a prerequisite for membership. In conversion, the individual recognized his or her prior sinful life and unworthiness of redemption (termed conviction), sought revelation of God's grace (mourning or seeking), and in a typically dramatic and eventful manner, received evidence that their sins had been pardoned (conversion). Also like the Separate Baptists, Methodists held values that sharply contrasted with those of the ruling elite and of the Anglican ministry. Evangelicals put subjective experience at the center of their beliefs, while Anglicans drew spiritual strength and sustenance from the shared recital of prayers and liturgy. There was no place in Anglican worship for members to relate subjective experience. Potential Anglicans were catechized, taught a common curriculum of doctrine in question and answer form. To become a Methodist or Baptist, an individual needed to give unique (albeit with conventional aspects) testimony of his or her conversion and promise to obey the rules and adhere to the doctrines of the sect.[26] In terms of rules, Baptists and Methodists were somewhat similar. In terms of doctrine and the way doctrine affected individual psyches (explored at length in the next chapter), Methodists represented a new and unique breed of southern Protestant.

Although Methodists were quite distinct from Anglicans, Methodism was still a reform movement within the Church of England when Wesley's missionaries began their work. Because these preachers were not ordained by the king's church, members were supposed to turn to Anglican clergy for communion, baptism, and marriages. Methodist loyalties to the Anglican church in America were not strong, however. In the South, some evangelical Anglicans, most notably Devereux Jarratt and Charles Pettigrew, for a time welcomed the Methodist itinerants, their message, and their methods. In a few parishes, a spirit of genuine ecumenism seems to have prevailed, at least until the Methodists officially formed a separate church. But hostility was the more common response of Anglican parsons toward the unlettered itinerants.[27] Having been weakened by the Baptists, Church of England clergy did not welcome yet another competing sect.

The Reverend Archibald M'Robert penned a vituperative attack on Methodists in a letter to Jarratt, denouncing them for their "misguided zeal," allegiance to "Pope John" (Wesley), and embrace of "illiterate creatures void of all prudence and discretion." His elitist remarks illustrate two different conceptions of the "ministry." For Anglicans, learning, erudition, and distinguished deportment were critical, while for Methodists, oratorical skill, evidence of conversion, and a "calling" to the ministry were far more important. Methodists disapproved of parsons' lifestyles and their cozy relationships with the wealthy. They found Anglicans guilty of the sin of "formalism," a term that encompassed liturgical services, rote learning of the Bible, slow singing, sermons or prayers delivered from a written text, and in general, a focus on something other than experiential religion. M'Robert thus correctly observed that Wesleyans lacked a "catholic spirit," for Methodists believed most priests were unconverted and hence, were not saved. Perhaps dealing with such accusations himself, M'Robert called Methodists a "designing people" whose "professed adherence to the church [of England] is amazingly preposterous and disingenuous, and nothing but policy." It is doubtful that Methodists were "designing," but M'Robert's belief that Methodists were not firmly attached to the church was borne out by their actions.[28]

A far more serious problem for the Methodists was the one presented by the Revolutionary War. In some ways, Methodism made a good fit with the Revolutionary mentality. A number of American-born men entered the itinerancy in the 1770s and early 1780s, and these men, like their followers, were steeped in Revolutionary ideology.[29] Because the concerns of the two discourses were similar, American-born preachers readily shifted between religious and republican idioms in their sermons and writings. Evangelicals shared with revolutionaries a fear of corruption and a sense that extravagance, profligacy, and immorality characterized their society. Like the revolutionaries, Methodists prized virtue and liberty, and despised oppression and tyranny.[30] But for Wesleyans, there was ultimately no fusion of religion and republicanism; the Methodists did not espouse a civil religion.

Thomas Ware's experience is illustrative of the way Methodists viewed the Revolution and appropriated its rhetoric without coupling their movement to the rebellion. Born in 1758, Ware came of age during the crisis. He praised Patrick Henry's speeches "in defiance of the sovereign who was endeavouring to crush us" and believed the colonists "justified in resisting [the British government], and throwing off the yoke." Filled with patriotic fervor, Ware joined the continental army, trusting that if the rebellion were victorious, "tyranny and oppression would be overthrown throughout the world."[31] Although Ware believed in "the justness of our cause in the sight of Heaven," he did not further meld providence and the war. After he recovered from a debilitating bout of camp fever that followed him into civilian life, Ware turned his thoughts to God. Hearing of the victory at Trenton, he wrote: "From this time I considered my country safe, nor ever after sickened at the thought of wearing the chains of civil bondage. But, alas! I wore chains infinitely more galling than any ever forged by an earthly tyrant. My soul was in bondage to sin. Civil freedom I thought I understood, and gloried much in it. But the perfect law of liberty, promulgated by Jesus Christ the Son of God, I understood not." Though Ware employed the language of the Revolution to describe his spiritual quest, he retained the Methodist division between the divine and earthly realms. And significantly, Ware prized the freedom of his soul above civil freedom, even insisting there could be no true freedom until Americans threw off the bondage of sin.[32] Although he was a Revolutionary War veteran, he saw the real revolution as one in which the individual found liberty in Jesus.

Wesleyans merged best with Revolutionary ideology in their embrace of the era's definition of virtue. In late colonial America, virtue had been associated with civic participation; white male freeholders were to keep vigilant watch over government and cast their votes for leaders who were themselves virtuous. During the war, virtue was further wed to masculinity through emphasis on martial valor. But another definition of virtue, one associated with women, the home, and Christian piety, became predominant in the 1780s.[33] Methodists and other evangelicals helped revive the notion of private Christian virtue by recruiting women and emphasizing inner piety. Even when Methodists linked public and private virtue, the stress was on the private. In March of 1777, preacher John Littlejohn chanced on a tavern where people were dancing and playing cards. He first proffered religious reasons for them to desist, but addressing a stubborn group of card-playing men he resorted to a blend of patriotism and religion: "I reminded them of the Countrys being at War of the battle of Bunker Hill and West Plains, saying your Fathers, Brothers or Sons have moistened the soil of the Country with their own Blood, and you are bringing the vengeance of God upon your selves and your Country." Personal Christian virtue, in Littlejohn's mind, could sway the outcome of battles.[34] God would not reward with victory a people who gambled and danced.

Littlejohn's invocation of the war was atypical. For most Methodist preachers, the Revolutionary War was not an opportunity to exercise virtue but a distraction from God. Preachers frequently complained that members were too preoccupied with the war. Francis Asbury noted in 1776 how "many had so imbibed a martial spirit that they had lost the spirit of pure and undefiled religion."[35] Battles remained on the periphery of ministers' consciousness; instead of preaching against monarchy or for the continental army, Methodists continued to preach of the need for salvation and holy living.[36] The war increased suffering and death without a concomitant increase in access to souls. For some colonists, Methodist indifference to the cause was a form of treason. But preachers merely had a different set of priorities. From Wesley (and the New Testament), American Methodists inherited a belief that obedience was due to civil authority. This obedience was not, however, absolute. Preachers felt they had a higher calling, and any law or official that stood in the way of saving souls was to be disobeyed, any war that interfered was a hindrance to God's work. As exemplars for the flock, preachers were supposed to be "dead" to the world, and that meant, in practice, a single-minded focus on bringing others to Christ and keeping the converted in the narrow way of Wesleyan holiness.

How successful preachers were in shutting out the world is evident in their unpublished writings. Lapses were noted, and required penitential anguish, but preachers, judging by the things they chose to record, viewed events and people through a Wesleyan lens. One would be hard-pressed to learn anything of substance from these sources about the crisis between England and its colonies, the formation of the republic, or politics in the new nation.[37] After the Revolution, the preachers continued to see the state as an entity they were bound to respect but as one that they wanted as little to do with as possible. The Baptists tried to enlist Methodist aid in their effort to have former glebe lands sold, a measure that seems quite uncontroversial. But Methodist preachers decided to remain "Neuters," as one diarist termed it.[38] Glebe lands were not their concern. To take a position would needlessly entangle them with secular matters. Preachers had their own revolution to make, their own battles to fight. Benjamin Abbott "never meddled in the politics of the day," he recalled about the Revolutionary era, for his war was against the "works of the devil."[39]

Methodist reluctance to link the Revolution with their movement derived from their hostility to the world, but it was also influenced by the widespread belief that they were Tories and Tory sympathizers. The leaders of the church were Wesley's missionaries, and they were Englishmen, recent immigrants whose loyalties were assumed to lie with the British. Because they had no settled parishes, circuit riders were certainly in a position to spread war news and critical military information. And the charge that early Methodists were Tories was not without some basis in fact. John Wesley, unfortunately for his followers in the New World, published a tract denouncing the rebellion. A Methodist preacher distributed copies of King George's Proclamation in the colonies. And some Methodists were admitted Tories. Captain Webb, a popular Methodist preacher in the North before the war, was an English officer. A Methodist lay man of Maryland, Chauncey Clowe, raised a band of 300 Tories and brought much persecution on Methodists as a result.[40]

The pacifism of many Methodist preachers and lay men also contributed to beliefs that they were Tories. Unlike the Quakers, American Methodists had not openly espoused pacifism prior to the war and some colonials suspected that Methodist claims of conscience were opportunistic or, worse yet, indicated disloyalty to the Revolutionary cause. American Methodists indeed took no official position on military service. They were equivocal about the war itself. Wars, in general, most agreed, were bad things. Even many of the American-born preachers who valued Revolutionary ideals such as freedom and liberty saw war, in principle, as an offense against God. Rather than linking military service or conscientious objection with duty to God, as other sects did, Methodist leaders left the decision about whether to serve up to the individual and supported with prayer both those who refused to fight and those who served, watching over the wives and children of both groups. The pacifists who believed "shedding human blood" (in the words of one objector) was sinful did not attempt to enjoin other men to follow their lead.[41] Methodist neutrality on this issue, even from men with absolutist positions on bearing arms, keenly illustrates how the movement saw secular matters. The war was not their business. If a member could remain a good Methodist in uniform, if serving would not wound his conscience, the sect did not interfere. The nuances of the Methodist position were lost on Revolutionary officials. Enough Methodists chose pacifism to cast aspersions over all men in the movement.

Methodists' opposition to oath taking further contributed to suspicions of Methodist disloyalty. Because the Revolution was a civil war, states drew up loyalty oaths to determine citizens' allegiance. Many Methodist preachers and lay men refused to swear and sign these oaths; some were taken to court in Maryland as a result.[42] The church did not prohibit oath taking, although pietistic sects in general were hostile to oaths. The Maryland oath linked allegiance to bearing arms, and pacifists thus had double reason not to sign. Military and civil authorities looked with rightful suspicion on men who had refused to swear allegiance to the Revolution and yet persisted in traveling about the country and drawing large crowds. Oath taking, moreover, was one of the privileges that separated white from black in the South; a white man who refused to give his word was seen as a man of questionable character.[43]

During the war, the Methodists would face some of the fiercest opposition from civil authorities that they had to endure in America. Fined, imprisoned, beaten, and constantly threatened, Methodists—for both religious and military reasons—were openly viewed as enemies. Freeborn Garrettson was twice attacked and beaten.

William Wrenn and Jonathan Forrest were among those Methodist preachers arrested during the war. Joseph Hartley was imprisoned more than once. Francis Asbury, who alone of the British missionaries remained in America through the war, believed his life to be in danger on several occasions. Some pacifist members were placed under military guard, others were beaten, and a number were imprisoned. Nelson Reed visited pacifist Methodist lay men who had not been fed during their two days of imprisonment. Philip Gatch was attacked several times. Caleb Pedicord was so severely beaten in Dorchester County that he never fully recovered.[44]

A careful analysis of wartime persecution shows that suspected Toryism was only one of many reasons Methodists were harassed. Garrettson's beatings and imprisonment were due as much to his antislavery stance and his conversions of slaves as to his association with a church tarred as Tory.[45] Methodists also challenged the South's gender ideology, especially expanding the public roles open to women. Class conflicts were equally central to the tension between Methodists and civil authorities.[46] In branding itinerants who interfered with southern hierarchies as traitors, opponents of Methodism were not necessarily lying. The southern elite's commitment to revolution was conservative. They never intended for the rhetoric of liberty to threaten their leadership or the ideology of equality to extend outside the circle of white property-holding men. While they were fighting a war against British tyranny, they did not relish meddlers who interfered with patriarchal households and who had the temerity to call slaveholders tyrants in their own neighborhoods. To the ruling gentry, violations of cherished southern mores may well have seemed treasonous during the war.

The charges that Methodists were disloyal, except in the localities with active pro-British Methodists, were also convenient ways for civil and military authorities to discredit the sect. Whether authorities believed that Methodists were pro-British is another question entirely. With the populace in a war mood, officials could prejudice audiences against Methodism by accusing them of treason. Many leading men seemed to have used charges of Toryism as a convenient way to silence troublesome itinerants. Jesse Lee, himself a conscientious objector, suspected as much. "If a person was disposed to persecute a Methodist preacher," he later wrote of the war years, "it was only necessary to call him a Tory, and then they might treat him as cruelly as they pleased."[47] Other evidence suggests that charges of loyalism were sometimes brought merely to thwart Methodist progress. Joseph Hartley was imprisoned twice for being a nonjuror, but other preachers suspected this was a ruse. One wrote, "All that the opposers wanted was to prevent his preaching in the country."[48] When in jail, Hartley attracted large crowds to the prison and "frequently preached through the grates, or window," until some people began to fear that "if the preacher was not turned out of jail, he would convert all the town."[49] When officials saw the unintended result of their actions, Hartley was promptly released. Evidently, the "nonjuror" accusation was less important than stopping Hartley from gaining converts.

Rivalries between sects also came into play. William Watters, an American-born itinerant, was assigned to Fairfax Circuit in Virginia in late 1775 and early 1776. On a congressionally appointed fast day, he went to hear the Anglican priest give a sermon. The minister spent most of his time denouncing the Methodists, telling his audience that they were "a set of Tories, under a cloak of religion." He pronounced that "the [Methodist] preachers were sent here by the English ministry to preach up passive obedience and non-resistance." In a patriotic frenzy, the parson finished "by declaring that he would, if at the helm of our national affairs, make [the Methodists'] nasty stinking carcasses pay for [their] pretended scruples of conscience." Perhaps under some suspicion himself as part of the king's church, and certainly under pressure because of Methodist successes, this parson appealed to popular opinion by raising the specter of English conspiracy. Whether he believed the Methodists were Tories or instinctively conflated religious apostasy with disloyalty is unclear. But one additional charge he leveled against the Methodists was patently untrue and indicates a good deal of dissimulation on his part, considering how well off Anglican ministers were in comparison to their Wesleyan foes. He told the crowd that money, and not souls, was the Methodists' "real object."[50]

Another form of rivalry involved Methodist challenges to secular ideals of masculinity. Pacifism was an extreme violation of the male code of southern honor. Honorable men fought for their families and their communities; they did not flee from sacrifice, even from death. The Revolution intensified the association between masculinity and fighting. Manly, martial virtue was glorified and celebrated in war-era political gatherings.[51] In such a climate, there is little wonder that pacifism was stigmatized. Jesse Lee, a Methodist who refused to bear arms, was assigned to drive a wagon for the continentals. Many officers tried to persuade Lee to fight, but he refused. Near Salisbury, North Carolina, Lee's unit passed "roads thronged with people, men, women and children, with their property, flying from the face of the enemy." Thinking that such a scene would naturally stir Lee to battle, his colonel asked him, "don't you think you could fight now?" Lee answered in the negative. We can easily imagine what the colonel thought when Lee's honor could not be roused even to avenge the suffering of women and children.[52]

Other wartime persecution resulted from Methodists' conflicts with southern patriarchs. Freeborn Garrettson preached a sermon in 1778 so powerful that it caused "a great shaking among the people. Among the rest, a woman was struck, and cried aloud for mercy, till she fell to the ground. Her husband was much offended, and I was informed that he threatened me, as he said, for killing his wife."[53] The murder was metaphorical, not literal, but as we will see later, the husband who threatened Garrettson was not entirely mistaken. Preachers had many such confrontations with irate men. In the fall of 1775, Philip Gatch had an appointment to preach at a Maryland widow's home but noted in his journal that a "large man met me at the door, and refused to let me go in. He claimed some connection with the family, from which he imagined his right to act as he did."[54] Secular gender conventions gave male relations "rights" (they might have called them "duties") to interfere in the lives of women who lacked the guiding hand of a patriarch. Although Gatch was born and raised in Maryland, he did not recognize male authority when it was invoked to persecute Methodist women. Soon after this incident, Gatch was met on the road by a man "whose wife had been convicted under the preaching of Mr. Webster" (a Methodist itinerant) and who with some friends "intended to revenge himself" against this affront by attacking the next preacher he saw. In a clear effort to publicly shame a man who did not respect a husband's prerogative, the mob tarred Gatch, with the last stroke of tar applied across Gatch's naked eyeball, permanently impairing his vision.[55] His crime was not Toryism but subverting patriarchal authority.

These small-scale domestic rebellions were cause enough to see the Methodists as traitors to the southern way of life, but the Wesleyans went further. They meddled with slaves and spoke against slavery. Freeborn Garrettson was one of the southern-born preachers who waged war against oppression during the Revolution. Soon after his conversion in 1775, the Lord spoke to him and told him to "let the oppressed go free." Garrettson promptly emancipated all of his slaves and began causing trouble for his neighboring slaveholders, proselytizing to slaves and denouncing slavery as a sin. Compounding his treason by being a pacifist, Garrettson refused to join the army, pay the objector's fee, or take state oaths. Accused on more than one occasion of being a Tory, Garrettson was finally imprisoned in Maryland in February of 1780 and charged with being a "Fugitive Disaffected Person" because he refused to take a loyalty oath. Despite what his arrest warrant said, Garrettson himself never believed his arrest was solely due to the war. He once noted that "for a cloak they charged me with Toryism" and later reflected that the reason he was released after only sixteen days was that his jailing had the opposite of its intended effect—he, like Joseph Hartley, attracted larger crowds around the jail than he did before he was imprisoned.[56]

In 1791, Garrettson's memoirs were published for the church and either Garrettson or his editor carefully removed some of the most controversial passages that dealt with slaves and slavery. A comparison of Garrettson's printed memoirs and his manuscript journals shows why leading men (most likely slaveholders) might have wanted to silence this preacher.[57] The 1791 version, for example, tells of a meeting Garrettson held in June of 1775 where "the power of the Lord came down in a wonderful manner," many were "struck to the floor," and the cries of these mourners "were heard at a great distance." The next morning, the printed memoir recounts, "a gentleman . . . came to the house to beat me: soon after he entered he began to swear, affirming I would spoil all his negroes." The slaveholder repeatedly struck the preacher.[58] The excerpts from the manuscript journal make the context of this beating much clearer. Garrettson originally wrote of this meeting that "about forty people (mostly Black people) came together."[59] Again, the same year, the printed version tells of a Sunday service where "a company of Belial's children gathered to prevent the meeting" and "raged and threatened."[60] The manuscript journal supplies the missing explanation for the threats. In it, this day's events begin with this clause: "One Lord's Day whilst I was holding a meeting among the poor blacks."[61] There are even more glaring omissions in the 1791 text, including an excision of an antislavery sermon Garrettson preached.[62] On September 21, 1778, Garrettson helped shelter a badly beaten slave runaway,[63] an incident that is not even alluded to in the printed journal.

The two causes of Garrettson's persecution—the war and slavery—are more closely related than they first appear. The Revolutionary War was a triagonal war,[64] with slaves forming the third force. British policy and slaves' longing for liberation combined to frustrate the southern colonial war effort, especially in coastal South Carolina. At this time, Methodism had no foothold in the Palmetto state, but was strong in Maryland and Delaware, where Lord Dunmore's Proclamation created fear and panic among slaveholders. Antislavery men such as Garrettson might well have seemed a threat to the war effort because they regularly met with blacks and were known to speak against slavery.[65]

Several Maryland runaway ads of the war era support this hypothesis. In July 1778,

George Fitzhugh advertised for the return of two slaves. One, named Jack, he described as "an artful fellow" who "professes himself a Methodist." In November of the same year, another slave owner of Kent County, Maryland, advertised a runaway named Betty, who he said was "very vicious, yet assumes the marks of uncommon piety, which enables her to impose on the credulous." Betty had run away in July, when perhaps not coincidentally Freeborn Garrettson was preaching in and around Kent County. A Baltimore slave owner sought the return of a different Jack in 1782 and noted that his slave "pretends to be a great Methodist."[66] The mention of religion in these ads is curious. Unlike scars, weight, height, or clothing, religion cannot be seen on a person. It is possible these masters believed their slaves could be caught at a religious meeting, yet they insisted their slaves were feigning piety. A more likely explanation is that these owners suspected Methodists and other sects had somehow convinced their slaves to run away. Mentioning the church in these ads would alert other owners to the dangers of the Wesleyans.

Two incidents in particular serve to illustrate exactly how opposition to both the war and slavery combined to make Methodists a frightening body, events that never seem to have made it into any of the histories printed by the early church in America. The first involved Thomas Rankin, who arrived in 1773 and initially took charge of the American Methodists. Nineteenth-century church histories usually described Rankin's mistake, for which he had to escape to England, to have been support of the British. Reverend John Lednum, writing in 1859, claimed that Rankin "had declared from the pulpit of St. George's [a Methodist church in Philadelphia] that he believed God's work would not revive until the people submitted to King George."[67] Preacher Jesse Lee, writing in 1810, lumped Rankin with all the British missionaries who returned to England and wrote that "some of them were imprudent in speaking too freely against the proceedings of the Americans."[68]

There is no reason to doubt that Rankin was a Tory sympathizer. Yet on two occasions he went beyond mere opposition to the rebellion. The first was in July of 1775 in Gunpowder Fork, Maryland. Congress had called for a day of fasting in the colonies, and Rankin tried in front of a large audience "to open up and enforce the cause of all our misery." Rankin informed the crowd that "the sins of Great Britain and her colonies had long called aloud for vengeance and in a particular manner the dreadful sin of buying and selling the souls and bodies of the poor Africans, the sons and daughters of Ham." If Rankin believed the colonies should suffer more than the mother country, he did not record mentioning it this day.[69] A month later Rankin was in Philadelphia and noted privately in his journal that he was opposed to the rebellion and yet not to the colonists. Here he "had frequent opportunities from the first general congress that was held . . . till now; to converse with several of its members; and also with many members of the Provincial Congress, where I travelled." Once again he linked the rebellion to slavery, only this time he explicitly condemned the contradiction by which the American nation was born: "I could not help telling many of them, what a farce it was for them to contend for liberty, when they themselves, kept some hundreds of thousands of poor blacks in most cruel bondage."[70]

There is little wonder, then, that Rankin had to flee the country and that numerous Methodist preachers and lay people in the Upper South were persecuted in the war years. The slaveholding elite had long before the Revolution grounded the freedom of whites in the enslavement of blacks. The ideological edifice that muted conflict between vastly divergent classes of white men was almost a century old, but material inequality was pronounced enough that elites had reason to fear its structural soundness.[71] In the Upper South, where lower-class whites were divided in their loyalties, slaveholders faced additional pressures. The gentry knew that the rhetoric of liberty could be used to contest their rule and their hegemony.[72] Perhaps the fact that over thirty-five Maryland Methodist lay men were indicted for preaching as nonjurors is explicable in light of these fears.[73] As a biracial church that particularly appealed to lower-class whites, free blacks, and slaves, and that contained some known Tories, Methodism was undoubtedly perceived as a threat. When preachers began pointing out logical inconsistencies in the discourse of liberty, the threat had become treasonous reality.

Modern historians have noted how the Revolution and its rhetoric brought the paradox of a war for liberty in a land of slavery to the fore. Pioneering Quaker abolitionists had exposed the paradox, yet the Quakers were not an evangelistic sect. Elites certainly had more to fear—at least in potential numbers—from Wesley's followers.[74] The Methodists had, after all, just swept across the mother country decades before, converting thousands away from the Church of England. In the colonies, the Anglican church was weaker in numbers, clerically understaffed, and attacked as part of the English conspiracy to make Americans dependent. The forecast for Methodist success in such a setting had to have seemed positive. If, as many Methodist preachers claimed, their opponents' charges that they were Tories were a ruse to thwart their progress, the strategy of their foes was sound. Antislavery Methodists were thereby painted as enemies of (Revolutionary) liberty, and as part of the British conspiracy to enslave white colonial men. Methodism's appeal to slaves, free blacks, women, and poor white men, moreover, probably enhanced the sect's reputation as dangerous to white male freedom, linked as it was to slavery, white supremacy, and patriarchal control.

For decades after the Revolution, Methodist leaders were proud of their unjust suffering during the war.[75] The "dark days" of the Revolution became part of the Methodist founding myth. Methodists viewed this era as the trial by fire of the fledgling church, with the church emerging, like the gold in the scripture, purified. A Virginia minister in 1871 cast the matter in such providential terms: "Sore and great were these afflictions; the infant church was in the midst of the fire. Yet she stood firm, trusting in God, and praying for deliverance. When the storm swept away it was seen that the tree of Methodism, though torn and broken, had struck its roots deeper into the soil, and again budded and brought forth fruit."[76] The persecution of the war years became a Methodist legend. What is striking, however, is the fact that church chroniclers, almost to a man, attributed the wartime persecution to the taint of Toryism. In so doing, Methodists obscured the true beginnings of the church and, in effect, severed themselves from earlier church radicalism, especially on slavery. It is of crucial importance that most church chroniclers before the Civil War neglected to mention Rankin's antislavery arguments against the rebellion. It is likewise important that Freeborn Garrettson's controversial ministry to slaves and opposition to slavery became toned down in the published version of his memoirs. By rewriting the multifaceted causes of their persecution into a simple tale of political and wartime rivalries, Methodists also learned the wrong lesson. The fact that they had survived the war intact despite charges of Toryism could have been interpreted to mean that their message and style were strong enough to overcome political opposition. The lesson they in fact seemed to draw from their Revolutionary experience was just the opposite— do not interfere with civil government.[77] This credo, of course, fit perfectly with the Wesleyan imperative to "be ye separate."

The implications of the "dark days" myth were far-reaching. Southern Methodist historians of the nineteenth century used remarkably similar language to describe two of the most controversial aspects of early Methodism—loyalism and antislavery. Tory statements by Wesley, Rankin, and others were deemed "unfortunate." So too were early Methodist measures against slavery.[78] One late nineteenth-century minister and historian called the wartime denunciation of slavery "unfortunate" and "unwise," although he conceded that the authors of the statement "certainly were sincere men" who "believed in their hearts that slavery was a great wrong." Compare this with his assessment of the pacifism of some members: "However we might condemn their principles, we must admire the firmness they displayed in refusing to do what they believed to be wrong." Significantly, he attributed both Toryism and antislavery to the "zeal" of the "English preachers," ignoring the fact that Garrettson was only one of many American-born preachers who were ardent foes of slavery. As a rhetorical ploy, however, his move was brilliant. In this subtle linking of antislavery and loyalism he could discount both as English imports, and could continue the tradition of denying southern Methodists access to their radical past.[79]

From modest beginnings with Robert Strawbridge and Barbara Heck, the membership was nearly 15,000 strong by 1784. In the Christmas Conference of that year, American Wesleyans organized as the Methodist Episcopal Church, with an official hierarchy and a consciousness of themselves as a body tied to, but distinct from, British Methodists. Methodists' experiences in the Revolutionary era helped foster their sense of separation from English Methodists and from other American Protestants. The "dark days" myth also reinforced Methodism's stark division between the worldly and the godly, further binding the members to one another in support and comfort.

The persecution of Methodists did not abruptly end with the armistice. But as the Tory epithet lost its edge, southerners hostile to the church began attacking other equally troubling aspects of Methodism. Although Methodists were no longer enemies to the nation, they remained, for many in the South, enemies to regional values and ideals. For their part, Methodists expected opposition to continue because they expected to stay religiously pure. Organizationally, they were prepared for the new nation. The itinerancy enabled the sect to spread west with American settlers; the nurturing of lay leaders ensured that the work of the church was always performed at local levels. Yet becoming a Methodist was far easier than being a Methodist; the sect's unique doctrines made the self a work always in progress. As the founding myths so clearly emphasized, spiritual decline was ever possible in a corrupt world. Methodists had to keep vigilant watch over one another and each member had to keep watch over his or her own heart. Early Methodists had believed they were waging a war within a war. Each convert also had to wage war with the self.

✖ T W O ✖

The Marrow of the Methodist Self

Doctrines, Values, and Practices

> Extatic raptures would creep through my heart, and Heaven
> slide through my crimson life. I set in the pomp of self-
> abasement, a-kin to nothing, a-kin to dust, and yet en-
> gulphed in love to Christ.
>
> —Sarah Jones[1]

SARAH JONES, LIKE MANY Methodists, ascended to heights of rapture and sank to
depths of self-loathing as she strove to live in what Wesleyans called "the narrow
way." Methodists so diligently explored their inner selves that even a single day's soul-
searching could cause them to both soar and plummet in tortured self-examination.
Jones, in a letter to a friend, described her thoughts on a typical day. During an hour
of prayer in which she suffered "accute agony," she "plunged in a sea of self abase-
ment, and self abhorrence; and groan[ed] . . . for the deepest measure of profound
humility," but later, when recalling that Christ was "ointment" "for every sore," she
became "buried in wonder, swallowed up in extatic joy and gladness."[2]

Sarah Jones's psyche, like those of her fellow Methodists, can scarce be understood
apart from the church's doctrines, values, and practices. Views about the self, about
obligations to others, and about humanity's relationship to God formed the core of
Methodist identity and shaped the way members viewed the world around them.
Church practices and rituals reinforced these identities and provided models for men
and women in the church to follow as they refashioned the self and built communities of like-minded believers. Although factors such as race, civil status, gender, class,
and age render analysis of "the Methodist psyche" problematic, Methodists shared a
religious identity that transcended these differences. Much of the remainder of this
work will explore how religion intersected with these other key variables, and we will
occasionally note those differences here. Yet these diverse people with varied experiences also had at least one important characteristic in common—they were all Methodists.[3]

In the decades surrounding the disestablishment of the Church of England, sectarian affiliations were better predictors of behavior and values than they are today. To
identify someone as a Methodist in the late eighteenth century meant to describe a

way of life and thinking that was relatively distinct. Doctrinally, Methodists believed in free will, falling from grace, and sanctification, beliefs that expanded the human role in salvation and that exalted human will. Methodists engaged in torturous examination of their psyches in the attempt to live godly lives, alternating between euphoria and melancholy with each success or failure. Ideas about the salutary effects of suffering and the importance of asceticism also shaped church members. So too did Methodists' valuation of the heart over head, enthusiasm over "formality," emotion over reason, love over authority. To critics Methodists appeared monkish, self-absorbed, insane, or despondent, but the exclusive and tight-knit community of the church provided succor and comfort for converts struggling to mold themselves in their image of God in a hostile world.

Conversion to Methodism brought with it a change in perception, which members described as a revolution of their consciousness. Some spoke in terms of seeing "things in a new light from what I had ever had before."[4] One even claimed that "every thing appeared new," "as if I had got new eyes."[5] Most evangelicals described conversions in similar terms, for all believed they had in a sense died to their former selves. But it is just as important to ask what sort of people converts became *after* the new birth, and here sectarian differences are important. When men and women called themselves Methodists, they were both distinguishing their beliefs and ways from others, and signifying their acceptance of certain values and practices, some of which were unique to the church. When men and women chose to become Methodists, they assumed an identity that affected their behavior inside and outside chapel walls.

The church did not arise in a vacuum, and the changes Methodism wrought on people's perceptions must be placed in the context of some broader religious and intellectual currents. One of these is the long-term trend in Protestantism toward increased human responsibility for salvation.[6] A related broader trend is that toward "boundlessness," the nineteenth-century stress on the glory and power of the individual. A third is the psychological transformation that resulted in a new valuation of inner life and the cultivation of emotions.[7] Methodists did not invent the boundless self, but they were tireless promoters of it. Despite the fact that we share a belief in individual agency, the inner world of early Methodists is alien to us, in large part because they viewed human ability to shape the self (with God's help) as almost unlimited. They believed it possible to control passing thoughts and feelings and thus did not recognize what we would call the subconscious or unconscious mind. The closest they came to such a notion was their belief that Satan could infiltrate a true believer's mind if he or she was not vigilant.[8] The practices of Methodists are equally foreign, in large part because they believed that God could reveal himself to humans in direct and immediate ways and could take possession of the body and soul if the believer was faithful.

To explore the impact of Methodism on the self and society, we should begin with converts' religious beliefs. If we may judge by what Methodists said, doctrine was critically important to their sense of a unique religious identity. Methodism did not allow societies leeway in interpreting scripture, as Baptists did with congregations, and thus there was remarkable unity among Methodists on doctrinal issues. Standard texts by theologians such as John Wesley provided the basis of Methodist Bible interpretation. Although theirs was a piety based more on experience than theology, the evidence indicates that Methodist lay people and clergy were well aware of their unique beliefs. The shorthand terms that Methodists used for the triumvirate of doctrines that formed their spiritual core were free will, falling from grace, and perfection. All were critically important parts of the whole; all expanded Methodists' sense of human agency.

As the first evangelical sect to espouse a free will doctrine, the Methodists were in a good position to capitalize on the growing sense Americans had after the Revolution that men and women could influence and even control the future. The delicate balance that evangelical Calvinists had hoped to maintain between human and divine responsibility for salvation was never an issue for the Arminian Methodists (who in fact seemed to have rarely sought and little valued balance.) God, in their view, had sacrificed his son in a spirit of free grace and love for humanity, and all those who acknowledged their sins, repented, and accepted Christ into their hearts were candidates for salvation. The emphasis in Methodism was on the human role in the process. God's desire for men and women to be converted and his mercy were constants; humans were the ones who had to be moved to acknowledge their sinfulness, repent, and accept Christ.[9]

Free will doctrine was the most obvious difference between Methodists and other evangelicals. Eighteenth-century Baptists and Presbyterians professed to be predestinarians, to believe that God had foreordained who would be saved (the elect) and who would not (the damned). By the early nineteenth century, Baptists and some Presbyterians, in effect, preached and lived an Arminian gospel; calling people to convert "now" was implicitly, at least, a nod to human agency. Methodists, however, *espoused* an Arminian doctrine and lived an Arminian gospel, and thus never had to reconcile, as other sects did during the Great Revival, the apparent contradiction between aggressive revivalism and predestination.[10]

The difference between predestinarian and free will doctrines was so stark that it was easy for both sides to caricature one another and ignore their common emphases on God's mercy, human sinfulness, and the importance of holy living.[11] Methodists simplistically alleged that the doctrine of election encouraged moral laxity. If God had foreordained who would be saved, Methodists claimed, then there was no reason to live a moral life. Preacher Thomas Ware made a typical attack in his memoirs. He told of a young man raised as a Presbyterian whose father and minister caught him playing cards on a Sunday. The two "sharply rebuked" him, but the young offender, according to Ware, "boldly took refuge under the doctrine taught him from the pulpit," telling his minister that his crime was "from all eternity decreed."[12] Such a story bears none of the subtlety of eighteenth-century Calvinist theologians' views on agency and responsibility. Methodists also caricatured predestination as a doctrine that led to intense psychological despair—occasionally causing suicide, some claimed—as people fretted over whether or not they were among the elected. Predestinarians, of course, could be just as simplistic. Calvinists sometimes inverted the charges, accusing Methodists of believing in "works"[13]—of holding that people could win salvation by doing good deeds. Methodists no more believed this than Calvinists believed that morality was irrelevant.

At the heart of such mutual enmity was a vast difference of opinion about human agency and the nature of God, a difference muted when other sects leaned toward Arminianism but stark in Methodism's first decades in the South. A correspondent of preacher John Baldwin, Major John Overstreet, described what separated Methodists from other evangelicals. Overstreet, a Presbyterian critic of Methodism, congratulated Baldwin for preaching a sermon on "the depravity and inability of human nature to do the will of God without the grace of God." Overstreet rued that he had "heard so much of the powers of nature extolled," for he believed that "our hearts are so deceitful & desperately wicked" that it was "rank Pelagianism" to "take part of the credit of our salvation to ourselves!" Those who would do so, Overstreet claimed, "speak of the Almighty as a vile mortal." In raising up humanity, Overstreet felt, Methodists had lowered God. Adam Rankin, a Presbyterian clergyman, was even more direct. For him, free will doctrine was the view that "God has loved us, and put all power into our hands, to govern and dispose of ourselves, both in this world and that which is to come, and that it behoves Christ to humble himself unto us." The rhetoric was overdrawn, but there is a kernel of truth to the charges that Methodists both humanized God and exalted the self.[14]

Although Methodists never lost sight of the awe and majesty of God, they did not have the same sense of his inscrutability that characterized even evangelical Calvinists. Wesleyan clergy would certainly have denied that they reduced God to a "vile mortal" or that they "extolled" the "powers of nature," but they did proffer new images of God that made him seem far less intimidating. Methodists, for example, often described God as a mother or a friend. In one of "Dr. Byron's" poems printed several times in Methodist periodicals, the following comparison was made:

> What is more tender than a mother's love
> To the sweet infant fondling in her arms? . . . .
> Now, if the tenderest mother were possest
> Of all the love, within her single breast,
> Of all the mothers since the world began,
> 'Tis nothing to the love of GOD to man.[15]

Sarah Jones once depicted Christ as a nursing mother, envisioning herself and her prayer partner as "both spirits on Jesu's breast as twins, swallowing the streams of Love."[16]

Others described Christ as a spouse, as Freeborn Garrettson did in a sermon. William McKendree entered a poem in his journal describing Jesus as a close confidante:

> Did Christ expire upon the cross,
>   And is he not your friend?
> Your Saviour is your real friend
>   To tell your secrets to . . .[17]

Although the Methodists' God could be a stern, demanding, and damning one, when men and women wrote about their relationship to God, they most often described it as loving and very personal. To Christians who stressed God's omnipotence and majesty, the image of Christ as a mere "friend" came close to blasphemy. Although critics did not say it openly, one suspects that part of the reason they denounced this familiar image of the Almighty was that the relationship between God the Father and humankind was seen as the model and rationale for all forms of hierarchy on earth. If the distance between the divine and his creatures narrowed, what might this mean for other unequal relationships?

Overstreet had also alleged that Methodists exalted human nature, a charge that was in large part true. If we may judge by the way Methodists thought of the self, they indeed believed nature to be quite powerful. Methodist preacher Thomas Ware acknowledged that early opposition to Methodist doctrine centered on their notions of human ability. Methodists, Ware noted, were charged with "enthusiasm." "Our opposers did not blame us for not living up to our profession outwardly," he continued, "but for professing too much—more than is the privilege of man in this life, in speaking with Christian confidence of the knowledge of a present salvation by the forgiveness of sins and the witness of the Spirit." Betsy Goodwin clearly was confident. "[L]et me inform you without boasting, and in the fear of God," she wrote to William Spencer, "that I have enjoyed the perfect love of God for near two years."[18]

Christ as a pal, God as a tender mother: to non-Methodists, these were bad enough. But far worse was the assurance, even smugness, Goodwin expressed. Explicit in free will doctrine was the notion that anyone could choose God and be certain of salvation. Faith in the individual's ability to shape his or her own future was an Enlightenment legacy, too, but the majority of southerners' lives belied this notion of freedom. What the secular Enlightenment had brought to the educated southern elite, the Methodists promoted to all who would join them. Equally significant, Methodists taught men and women in rituals, testimony, and communal gatherings precisely how to go about molding their own futures. The self-confidence that free will doctrine engendered in ordinary men and women like Betsy Goodwin was further nurtured by the doctrines of falling from grace and perfection. Although predestinarian sects were by the late eighteenth and early nineteenth centuries moving toward a tacit acceptance of human agency in the conversion process, they had no equivalents to the remaining two controversial doctrines. Other sects encouraged their adherents to avoid sin— some even talked of holiness—but none of Methodism's major competitors believed that perfection was possible on earth. Similarly, a Baptist and a Presbyterian could "backslide," but so could a Methodist, and backsliding connoted a *temporary* loss of zeal and confidence. A Methodist who fell from grace and died before he or she converted again was destined for eternal suffering in hell.

Conversion, Methodists believed, was only the first step in a lifelong struggle. Converts could, if they were not diligent, "fall from grace"—that is, so estrange themselves from God that they would be barred from heaven. Calvinists might despair of their salvation, but they at least had the succor of the "final perseverance of the saints"—the doctrine that the elect could not fall.[19] A Baptist of King and Queen County summarized the Methodist position as being that "a Man might be in heaven to day & in Hell tomorrow." When asked if he had ever heard a Methodist preach such a doctrine the Baptist responded "no, but they preech falling from grace." Adam Rankin, ever the bluntest of critics, once more condemned the Methodists for raising up humanity and reducing God. According to Methodist doctrine, Rankin declared, the "covenant" could be "broken and ratified, and ratified and broken, as often as the caprice of the creature suggests," thus "render[ing] the whole oeconomy of redemption, as void as if it had never been." In place of the everlasting promises of an Almighty God, Rankin suggested, Methodists had substituted human whim.[20]

Countless debates revolved around these very issues of the nature of God and the extent of human capacity. Jesse Lee disputed with a Calvinist lay man named Woodruff on perseverance. Woodruff displayed "a good deal of anger" when he "found out that [Methodists] believed a person might fall from grace and be lost" and insisted that "after a man is converted . . . he is obliged to be saved whether he will [or] no." Woodruff's deterministic language underscores the gulf between the two men's beliefs. Woodruff told Lee he would rather hear Methodists "curse God at once, as to hear us say that God would give his love to a person and then take it away again." Lee clarified that he was not saying God would revoke a blessing, but that men and women, as responsible agents, "might cast it away." Only Methodists, in Lee's mind, comprehended the responsibility that came with having free will. The doctrine of "perseverance" did not invite the level of spiritual vigilance Lee believed was necessary.[21] Significantly, Jesse Lee did not describe falling from grace as a passive act. One "cast away" God's blessing.

Even some Calvinists reluctantly agreed that the doctrine of perseverance encouraged moral laxity. William Hill, a Presbyterian clergyman who left a journal of his 1790s ministry in the Northern Neck of Virginia, made the following observation: "I find that it has a very pernicious effect, especially among ignorant people to be continually preaching up, the doctrine of the perseverance of the Saints without enforcing christian duties, or having it clearly understood that the perseverance of saints taught in the bible is a perseverance in holiness & not in sin. This is the error of too many of the Baptists now a days, which brings bible calvinism into contempt, & gives currency to the doctrines of arminianism so industriously circulated by some others."[22] We need not conclude that predestinarians were more likely to "sin" but need merely note that, for Methodists, salvation explicitly depended on constant self-monitoring. If Hill, despite his denominational and elitist bias, was correct, this was not as obvious to the average predestinarian, who regardless of his or her views about conversion, gave God the larger role in salvation.

The dangers of falling from grace forced Methodists into a perpetual battle for self-mastery and a constant quest for zeal, introducing into the Wesleyan worldview the uncertainty they had condemned in predestinarian doctrine. Methodists did have a balm for those who did not wish to be poised forever on the precipice of falling from grace. After conversion, Methodists were urged to seek the "second blessing" of sanctification, also called "perfection" or "holiness." Francis Asbury even told one audience "that the only security pointed out by the apostles against apostasy, is to go on to perfection." Methodists who became "sanctified" were often said to be in a state of "perfect love." Freeborn Garrettson described Sister Bassett in just such terms. Bassett was "one of the happiest women I have met with," he wrote, and a "living witness of sanctification. Her soul seems to be continually wrapped up in a flame of divine love." Richard Graves was sanctified on July 2, 1799, and wrote that his heart had been "all love" since then.[23]

Methodists prepared themselves for holiness through self-denial, prayer, scriptural study, and fasting, but experienced sanctification much as they had conversion, instantaneously. They were certain that they were to strive for sanctification and believed it was possible to achieve. In an incidental comment to a Presbyterian correspondent, Sarah Jones made clear the difference between the two sects. According to Jones, the man confessed to a "hard heart": "He said, whether it is God's will, or his own indolence, he could not tell." "What can you think of such blindness?" Jones asked a fellow Methodist. "I intend through grace to give him one bill of exchange, and lash him with my *God's will*, which is, santification [*sic*]."[24] Sanctification, as Jones's comments reveal, was a Methodist duty.

Her indignant remarks also show how Methodists abhorred spiritual passivity. The three doctrines were complementary and mutually reinforcing and necessitated that Methodists actively work at their religiosity. The cycle began in conversion and was repeated throughout a believer's life: people would feel their wretchedness and depravity only to soon experience the fulfilling joy of God's blessing. Once converted, they strove for sanctification, or if they were not careful, they fell from grace. Those who had fallen from grace could restore the cycle with another conversion and the sanctified could restore the cycle by being, as Wesley put it, "moved from their stedfastness."[25] These beliefs had a profound effect on Methodists' sense of the possible. In Methodists' views, it made eternal difference whether they died in a fallen state or in a perfected state, and thus they often waged daily psychic warfare.

Sarah Jones knew the dangers and rewards of self-mastery full well, and she admitted that "every day is a day of wrestling agony and tears with me." Her great fear was to commit Christian "treason," which she succinctly defined as "to grow dull" (not to *become* dull). Elizabeth Anderson believed that if she had the proper mind-set in prayer, she could literally be with God: "this night I feel determined to try & get to heaven although I waid thrugh many trying scenes yet Daniels god is able to deliver." With many Methodists, the "agony" they subjected themselves to resembled a military battle or a long, perilous journey. "The good Lord knoweth," Jones wrote on another occasion, "the war is perpetual while here, and I would not give six pence for a soldier that cannot stand bullets; no matter what size." Daniel Grant agreed, and counseled his children that there would be many trials in this life, "all tending to turn you aside from the strait & narrow way." In another letter he declared that they would all need "steady & constant watchfulness if we desire to injoy the smiles of heaven." John Littlejohn reminded some members in a letter that "our life is a continual warfare." Methodists saw themselves as soldiers in God's army and expected to war with internal (and external) enemies.[26]

It is not necessary—or accurate—to claim that Methodists alone faced psychological struggles as they worked to become good Christians. Many Calvinists, if they did not rise and fall as often as Methodists, did undergo times of spiritual despair and rapture.[27] The important difference is that Methodists were taught to believe that they could, should, and indeed must take control of their hearts and minds and bend their own wills into the shape that God desired. When they were unsuccessful, they faulted themselves for being "poor worms." When they succeeded, they believed they could do almost anything to further the cause of God.

Sarah Jones showed how the weak self and the boundless self formed part of a psychic whole, revealing the paradox of the perfectible convert striving to submerge the very will that made attaining perfection possible. "I am imprisoned," she wrote, "Love with golden chains hath bound my head, my heart and hands, and I can truly say 'tis a pleasing pain.—I feel my widening soul a sacrifice to love.—What can relieve the throbbing heart, or slack the glowing flame? Whole oceans cannot quench it."[28] The language seems conflicted, but for Jones there was no tension between her prison of love and a soul that was capable of producing an unquenchable flame. A favorite Bible verse of members and clergy was "In Him, all things are possible." When Methodists fully submitted to God by bending the self to his will, they became, as clergy often described them, "living flames" who feared no mortal man or woman and believed themselves capable of "all things." The effect, however expressed, was a self that, once mastered, could then master any cause. The tenets of free will, falling from grace, and sanctification were instrumental in forging a sense of human ability among church members.

Doctrines formed the theological core of Methodist distinctiveness, yet there were other factors that contributed to sectarian identity. In reading descriptions by Methodists of other sects and descriptions of Methodists by nonmembers, it is impossible not to sense something we might term a Methodist *style*. Those outside the church certainly thought the Methodists had peculiar, often strange, ways. Methodists just as frequently indicated how out of place they felt at services conducted by other sects. Wesleyan values and practices combined to create patterns of interior and exterior life that set Methodists apart. The key components of this style were emotionalism, mysticism, asceticism, enthusiasm, and evangelism. These characteristics often overlapped, as they might when a convert awoke from a visionary trance with loud shouts of praise. It is nonetheless useful to analyze them separately as much as possible, to discern what comprised Methodist identity.

Methodist religiosity was intensely emotional. Faith was to be experienced—more precisely, to be felt—not rationalized. Methodists had little confidence in reason, and although they saw the reasoning faculty as a gift of God, they did not seat religion in the head. Benjamin Lakin faulted himself for having "given way to Philosophy, . . . seek[ing] therein what alone is to be found in Christ." Ezekiel Cooper argued that reason was not "a standard against revelation," for he believed "revelation" was "true reason itself." He cautioned that "there is a danger, very great danger to substitute reason in its depraved uncertain state as a standard by which we account for things relative to religion."[29] Many scholars have noted how groups like the Methodists prized emotion over reason, the heart over the head, feelings over ideas. The contemporary critics of early Methodism were not as kind. They charged Wesleyans with fanaticism and irrationality. In the Age of Reason, it is understandable that expressive evangelicals would seem out of place, for not only did they appear to exalt feelings and impressions, they even, like Cooper, claimed that reason was more "depraved" than emotion.

Methodists had words for their critics as well; most often labeling less demonstrative denominations and sects as "formal" or "cold." When clergy detected a lack of zeal in their own members, they used the same terms. Nelson Reed called an audience of 1779 "very formall." James Meacham believed that "if it was not for Class Meeting our dear people would soon become as formal as the old Episcopalians." Spontaneity, which was most often manifested in emotional outbursts, became in many ways the test of true religion for Methodists.[30] On one level, of course, Methodists were simply intolerant. They refused to acknowledge that liturgical, scripted services could evince deep religiosity from parishioners. But on another level, Methodists were more "tolerant" than their critics. Lakin had spoken of "Philosophy" as reason's creed. Because of their class, race, or gender, most Methodists had no access to philosophical education. A religion based on emotion or feeling was a democratic faith.

Yet it is misleading to say Methodists courted "emotions" or "feelings," because only certain kinds of feelings and emotions were desirable. Consider the case of John Littlejohn, whose horse became restless while Littlejohn was trying to wash it: "I was fretted & tempted to Anger, I cried O Lord from anger set my spirit free. It worketh not thy right[eousnes]s, Cleanse thou me from secret faults[.] I do not remember haveing felt anger since my conversion to God before, may I feel it no more. O may I be all love & joy & peace." Littlejohn's prayer is especially significant, first because his anger was directed at an animal and not at a human being, and second because he seemed to associate conversion with an absence of anger. Littlejohn condemned himself not for his behavior but for his state of mind. Other Methodists also chided themselves when they felt anger, jealousy, and hatred. John Wesley, as one scholar has noted, saw "anger to be a form of madness."[31]

Happiness was, on the other hand, desirable, and in Methodist services, meetings, and private devotions, happiness often reigned supreme. When a class meeting went well for preacher William Ormond, he claimed that "several got happy." Thomas Mann frequently noted that "all appear happy" or "appeared very happy." Methodists used the word "happy" so often that modifiers became important in distinguishing degrees of the emotion. After a successful service, William Ormond noted that "Sinners trembled & the Christians were uncommonly happy." Isabell Owen, too, got "uncommonly happy" as Thomas Mann looked on in an 1805 meeting. Sarah Jones romantically described her mood in similar terms: "My soul is unspeakably happy— Every day is Spring, and every month May." These happy folk provide a useful corrective to scholarly views that evangelicals were always (or primarily) sour and grim.[32]

But the emotion that Methodists prized most was love. John Wesley had written that the "whole nature" of Christian zeal was "the love of GOD and man," and American Methodists believed that the essence of God's will was love. Joseph Pinnell described love as "the most noble [passion] of the mind[.] Its sof[t] influence is spread over the believers soul— & makes every duty sweet—Its rich perfume fills Heaven[.]" Sally Eastland was almost overwhelmed with love, and in a letter to a minister wrote: "dear brother the topic is JESUS and his Love, but oh my feeble pen—it fails, it fails; my unskillful hand falls short here; I cant tell much,—but one thing I can tell I love to be hearing of him; and when I hear from Him, some times all my poor [Eastland drew a figure of a heart here] desolves in love."[33] Methodists' halting or effusive attempts to describe feelings of happiness and love underscore how seriously they took Wesley's injunctions to heart.

Love was also the standard for Methodists' interactions with one another; they were supposed to be "of one mind and heart." In a class meeting John Kobler presided over, he noted that "our hearts melted and ran together." Benjamin Lakin described his feelings about his fellow Methodists in similar terms: "my heart felt united to them in love. . . . I felt the bonds of love uniteing my heart to the Lords peopel."[34] It is tempting to stress the limits of these "bonds of love." Methodists fought among themselves and did not love all equally. But there were also times when this "uniteing" love pushed back the world and its hate. Preacher David Smith, a freedman who equated slavery with the Devil, described a service of "dear uniting love" where "the slaves and their owners . . . seemed to be one in Christ Jesus" and were "melted into sweet communion with the spirit and united in Christian fellowship."[35] For a few brief hours, Smith believed, seemingly insurmountable barriers had been breached and harmony achieved. Such moments may have been rare but they were nonetheless significant in a world where divisions and rankings were all in all.

Inexpressible joy, uniting love, and unspeakable happiness were a far cry from the emotional temper of the nonevangelical, much less the secular, South. One need only think how out of place such feelings would have been at other public venues. Love was not the motive force in the wider southern world that it was in Methodism. The gap between Methodist ideals and realities notwithstanding, the fact that evangelicals held up love as an ideal was innovative enough. The counterhegemonic force of such an emotional ideal is easy to overlook in our era, when we take for granted that love and happiness are universal goals. Such was certainly not the case in the eighteenth century, not even among all evangelicals. William Hill, the Presbyterian who was called too "methodistic" by his brethren, referred far more often to "peace" in his journal than to happiness or love.[36] What the Methodists' emotional style represented was a reordering of their members' experiences on a profound level.

Mysticism was another important and controversial component of the Methodist style. Methodists who claimed knowledge of their salvation or sanctification were viewed as presumptuous. More presumptuous still was the way they also purported to know God's will. The injunction to lose self-will and pursue only the will of God was central to Methodist practice. Wesley exhorted his followers repeatedly to "do every thing in the spirit of sacrifice, giving up your will to the will of GOD."[37] In his widely distributed essay "The Character of a Methodist," he again stressed that a Methodist's "one desire" was "not to do his own will, but the will of him that sent him." A Methodist was to have a "single eye": "There is not a single notion in his heart, but is according to his will. Every thought that arises points to him, and is in obedience to the law of Christ."[38] Of course, to be able to pursue God's will, Methodists had to be able to discern it.

God's will was revealed in the Bible and explicated in the Methodist *Discipline.* But Methodists had a more controversial way to discern God's will. Methodists believed that God could and often did speak directly to men and women through signs, dreams, and visions.[39] Although the meaning of God's communications was sometimes difficult to determine, Methodists did try to interpret them. John Littlejohn's experience with dream revelation began when he was under conviction. This dream, he remarked, was "afterwards almost literally fulfulld" and "its interpretation to me was easy." It probably came as no shock to Littlejohn when later a Quaker woman who had been attending Methodist services told him her dream. A messenger, she said, had revealed that she must continue with the Methodists despite the opposition of other Friends.[40] Other Methodists had waking visions and saw signs that they tried to understand. Benjamin Lakin was working outdoors in 1799 when a small bird "came and sat on a saplin" near him and looked attentively at him. Suddenly, Lakin recounted, "A thought struck my mind that if the Bird should light on my head I should see trouble." Soon the bird did just this, and Lakin reported his "feelings [were] awfull and my thoughts [were] various." Francis Asbury told of a woman who believed her death was imminent because a whippoorwill passed close by her head.[41]

Mysticism could threaten the social order, for through direct revelation, God bypassed earthly and ministerial authority to speak directly to the believer. A Methodist boy provoked heated controversy when he related a vision of death that challenged local hierarchies. The boy emerged from a twenty-four-hour trance to claim that Christ had taken him "by the hand" on a tour of heaven and hell. In heaven, the boy claimed, he had seen very few people he knew. The boy wanted to stay in paradise, but Christ said "not yet." In hell, he found many people from his community, including one man everyone thought had gone to heaven but who instead had been condemned for "lightness and trifling." Some of the damned sent warnings to the living. When the boy related his vision, non-Methodists called him a liar and some threatened to whip him, for one of the men he had claimed to see in hell was not yet dead. The boy solemnly predicted that if the man was not yet dead, he would die soon. The man in question died within a week, undoubtedly lending more credence to the boy's claim.[42]

Dreams and visions seem to have been a common part of Methodists' contact with God, and as illustrated in this boy's story, Methodist beliefs permeated the nonwaking hours of converts. As preachers so frequently told their audiences, more southerners were going to hell than to heaven; even professors could fall from grace and go to hell, like the light and trifling man, whom the boy alone was able to "see" for what he really was. Also significant is the fact that the boy was given messages from "inferiors" to "superiors." In his dream, children told him to warn their fathers and guardians yet living to repent or be damned. Methodist views about death, which I will explore shortly, likewise infused this dream, for the pious child longed to stay in heaven, and the quick, predicted death of the neighbor reminded all that life was short. Methodists attentively listened to what had been revealed in trances, visions, or dreams, thus allowing even a child the ability to reveal the mind and will of God.[43]

Clergy found dreams and visions problematic when they conflicted with Methodist doctrine and belief. But most preachers did not doubt that God could speak through these supernatural means. As should be apparent, a belief in immediate and direct revelation conferred a great deal of power on lay people, for they could bypass ministerial and, more significantly, patriarchal or gentry authority and interpret God's communications for themselves. For the most powerless members of southern society, this interpretive and moral autonomy had special significance. To critics and outsiders, Methodist mysticism was at best odd and at worst a usurpation of divine power by ordinary mortals. Mysticism, like emotionalism, helped set Methodists apart and carved out a space within Methodism that individuals could shape for themselves.

If we had to isolate the most distinctive aspects of the Methodist style, however, enthusiasm and asceticism would take first and second place. Both were complementary aspects of the Methodist self. Ascetic self-control characterized one side of the Methodist psyche—the side that usually brought despair and self-loathing. Complete abandonment characterized the rapturous side. Unlike the private despair and self-loathing asceticism caused, enthusiasm was public and visible. It was also the most criticized aspect of Methodist worship. More than any other evangelical sect, Methodists were identified with the way their converts behaved in services—the loud shouting, clapping, falling, and weeping.[44] In these early decades, preachers overwhelmingly supported and encouraged enthusiasm. Physical and emotional outbursts were not the goal of worship but were evidence that God was touching men and women in direct and immediate ways. Clergy actively sought evidence of God's presence in services, and most defended the enthusiasm of their audiences. Many felt it was better to allow some excess than to dampen the spirit. John Littlejohn was representative. He observed in 1778 that "it is more and more clear to me that it is best to bear w[i]th what we judge to be out of order, than to check it abruptly."[45]

Methodism was theater, and many—both sympathetic and hostile—came to watch what must have often been the best show in town. Some aspects of enthusiasm were entirely conventional. Most commonly, one Methodist would become "struck" with the power of God during a hymn, prayer, sermon, or testimony and would shout aloud or fall. The contagion would then spread throughout the house or chapel, and others would fall, weep, and cry out. A service George Wells led in 1792 was rather typical. He was talking with a woman under conviction when "it affected hir I got happy the flame spread to the other preachers. Bro. C. began to sing and the love of God began to flow like a river of oile we then went to prayer the power went from breast to breast and it laid hold of a black girl and shee cried [Amen] for mercy."[46] Wells's description is revealing. First, he interprets the enthusiasm positively, using the words "love" and "happy." Second, he attributes the events to God's "power." Third, he uses the metaphor of fire, as many Methodists did, to describe how God's power spread in the group. Once someone got "happy," it was seen to be almost inevitable that the contagion would, like fire, spread.

Another course that enthusiasm often took was to infect people who had no religious inclinations. After a Methodist would cry out or fall, a few of the men and women who had come to observe or to criticize would try to flee the scene—but not before one or more of them were also "struck." As reports spread in the area, the numbers attending services would increase. Criticism and opposition would increase as well, as would the number of scoffers who would mysteriously be drawn against their will into the vortex of enthusiasm. In a love feast that John Kobler attended, "the Lord broke in upon a dear woman" who "arose and with a loud voice gave praise to the Lord." According to Kobler, "this set the whole house on one flame." Several more women shouted and fell, and soon Kobler could not hear above the ensuing din. The noise alarmed the crowd outside the building, and "the wicked broke the door open and all came in some laughing others crying." Before the service ended, Kobler proudly observed, "the Lord humbled some" scoffers.[47] Each stage in the process confirmed that God was a real presence on earth. When God touched men and women, Methodists believed, the experience could overwhelm the body and result in physical, emotional, and verbal outbursts.

Throughout the South, scenes like these served to strengthen Methodists' reputation and self-identification as enthusiasts. Because enthusiasm was so controversial outside the sect, the fact that Methodists persisted in physical and emotional displays was, on at least an unconscious level, an act of religious assertiveness and certainly a form of religious self-expression. Perhaps more important, enthusiasm, like mysticism, enabled the ordinary believer to have direct and unmediated contact with the divine and further expanded personal agency. It may seem contradictory to claim that a sect that believed its members should subsume their will in God's and that exalted the loss of self-control in possession rituals or ecstatic visions increased the autonomy of many converts. And for the minority of Methodists who were legally and financially independent, the surrender of control to God did represent a check on autonomy. For men and women who were dependent on others (most white women and all slaves), possession and direct contact with God had different implications. God could and often did compete with earthly superiors for authority. In subsequent chapters we will see how "God's will" affected the balance of power in various relationships. Here we need only observe that in mysticism and enthusiasm, converts could know the heart and mind of God.

A caveat is in order. The boundless self of dreams and shouts was not the only side of Methodist personality. Methodists frequently lamented that they were unworthy creatures. When comparing themselves to God, Methodists called themselves poor worms, vile, or "mean."[48] Sarah Harrison, for example, believed herself "one of the weekest [sic], and one of the unworthiest, that ever set out in the service of God."[49] The language of self-abasement was so pervasive among Methodists that it is at times tempting to see the human self as shriveled and small next to the Wesleyan God. Yet self-loathing was only one side of the Methodist personality; the other side, the boundless side, was able to achieve complete self-mastery and even to touch the infinite. Sarah Jones was "called on to pray" in front of her "wicked relations" one evening, and felt overwhelming power: "God stept in me; and they [her relations] universally melted. . . . Thus Hell gave back, and devils were subject to me." Jones's claim that God "stept in me" might have been heretical to other Christian groups but was quite normal among Methodists.[50] Through mystical and enthusiastic contact with God, converts gained immediate, significant power.

Asceticism, the fourth characteristic of the Methodist style, should be viewed not as a reduction of self but as a different way of marshaling and manipulating individual willpower. Within the larger spiritual pattern of conversion-sanctification-falling came the daily ascetic effort to master the self that the church taught was possible and necessary. Historians have certainly appreciated the extent to which the outward behavior of Methodists, like that of Baptists, was observably ascetic.[51] Dress was one of the ways evangelicals set themselves apart from others; their plain dress signified a renunciation of the world and diminished the distance between members of different classes. Clergy disapproved of high headdresses, ruffles, laces, gold, and "costly apparel" in general. Non-Methodists of Delaware even joked in 1783 that wool would be cheap that year because Methodist women were burning their headdresses. Many Methodists showed this change immediately, as did an Army captain who cut off his long hair and the ruffles on his shirt right after conversion.[52]

Abstention from worldly habits also distinguished evangelicals like the Methodists from other southerners, especially from those immersed in the culture of honor. Drinking liquor, playing cards, racing horses, gambling, attending the theater, dancing (both in frolics and balls), and cockfighting were punishable offenses. Had members simply avoided such pursuits, they would have occasioned less criticism. But they took it upon themselves to seek out evil and condemn it, and often boldly imposed themselves and their reproofs where they were unwelcome. Two Methodist women, for example, persuaded preacher Nelson Reed to accompany them to a harvest dance in order to rebuke the dancers.[53] By such means, the reputation of Methodists for avoiding the pleasures of the world was further enhanced, as was their reputation for zeal in the cause of their religion.

But Methodist asceticism was more than a pattern of outward behavior. It was above all part of the effort to master the self. God, Wesleyans believed, wanted his followers to avoid sins of omission and of commission, to try to cleanse themselves from all impure thoughts and desires, and to subsume themselves in him. Methodist beliefs about the need for self-mastery are most evident in their attempts to control unconscious behavior. No sin was small enough to be ignored. Methodists felt guilty for what they called variously "levity" or a "light triffling spirit." Daniel Grant chided himself for "coldness" and "formality in my devotions" on one occasion and "listen[ing] to the failings of others" on another. Methodists faulted themselves for laughing, "murmuring," "wrong tempers," "worldly conversation," and "impatience." They were ashamed when they committed these "sins" because they signaled a loss of self-control.[54]

Let us briefly look at two of these offenses—levity and laughing. We would be wrong to conclude that Methodists were against joy or happiness, for they heartily approved of ecstatic emotions and behavior in worship, private prayer, or devotions. Levity and laughing were only wrong when they were secularly inspired or symptomatic of a loss of control. The church taught, and members seemed to have believed, that it was possible to bend the self and mold the will into a pure spiritual force. A burst of laughter signaled that the convert had not achieved self-mastery. Without understanding the subconscious mind, church leaders (from the bishops to class leaders) urged Methodists to examine their minds and hearts and control passing thoughts as well as behaviors. Individual Methodists seemed to have internalized these injunctions to an extraordinary degree.

Methodists' dual focus on actions and thoughts is most evident in attitudes toward sins of the flesh. The ideal for all Methodists was what they tellingly called "mortification"—to completely bring the flesh and the mind's focus on the flesh under subjection. Sins of the flesh, such as gluttony, pride in appearance, and lust were to be avoided, and the most serious ones could bring expulsion from the church. Even thinking about the flesh, moreover, was seen as impious. This is one context in which the (bachelor) itinerancy of the Methodists should be placed, for traveling ministers served as living examples of men walking by the spirit instead of the flesh. Clergy often ate what they could scrounge or beg, and not infrequently went without meals. Even those with generous donors ritually fasted, as did their parishioners. Preachers' clothes were simple, common, and usually in need of repair. And ministers were single men committed, while they remained in the itinerancy, to celibacy.[55]

Young itinerants' struggles with the flesh and with thoughts of the flesh help illustrate how asceticism involved the mastery of both mind and body. Preacher William Ormond, for example, found desire in and of itself a problem. "My flesh is an enimy to my soul," he noted on several occasions when dreams or thoughts troubled him. So too did Freeborn Garrettson, who one night suffered a temptation, or as he termed it, "the enemy of my soul assaulted me": "For a few minutes I sensibly felt the power of darkness. I rose out of my bed, wrapped myself in my great coat and slept on the floor." "This body must be kept under . . . ," he added. "I am determined to mortify the deeds of the body." The prize for asceticism in the pursuit of a spiritual mind, however, goes to Jeremiah Minter. Because he wished to live in perfect "purity of mind" and "as a self-denial," Minter, "with the aid of a surgeon became an eunich for the kingdom of heaven's sake."[56]

Minter's drastic action illustrates how some Methodists took asceticism to extremes. One couple, desiring to fulfill the biblical command that "old things must be done away, and all things must become new," began to burn all their possessions, including "a large bundle of paper money." Benjamin Abbott wrote of a man ready to cut off his right hand, because scripture said "if thy right hand offend thee, cut it off." Some Methodists slipped over into more pietistic sects; some fasted excessively. And it was not uncommon for men and women, in the throes of conviction for their sins, to think about suicide.[57] Ascetic church leaders were not the best guides in these matters, for the line they drew between the proper self-denying spirit and improper zeal was quite fuzzy. Minter was expelled from the itineracy for castrating himself, but the officials who expelled him ended up calling his offense only "a sin of ignorance." (In fact, there was no rule in the *Discipline* against what we might term sins of excess.) The church was better at encouraging asceticism than in defining its limits, and even readmitted Minter later for a short time as a local preacher.[58] For every Jeremiah Minter there was probably a man or woman who continued to secretly drink liquor or gamble in spite of church rules. But if these represent the extremes that could be found in Methodism, they also show how ascetic the typical Methodist was. The body was merely a "tenement of clay" that temporarily housed the soul and distracted the mind from God.[59]

Nowhere can Methodist views about the body, asceticism, and self-mastery be better illustrated than in Methodist attitudes toward sickness, suffering, and death—some of which were shared by other evangelicals. Pain, sorrow, and misfortune were used by God, Methodists believed, to remind the unconverted of their mortality and the converted of their Christian duties. Freeborn Garrettson, for example, visited a sick woman in 1780 who "lay under the afflicting hand of providence." Upon her conversion, "her bodily disorder was suddenly removed." When Garrettson himself was stricken with fever and ague, he prayed that "this occasion of confinement may be sanctified to me."[60] All "afflictions" were really for the good of humanity. Ezekiel Cooper told an ill man that his sickness was the "hand of correction." A woman named Milley was in an "afflicted state of body," but a fellow Methodist remarked that he had "hope that it will in the end prove as blessings in disguise."[61]

When God punished his flock with illness or misfortune, he was attempting to bring them closer to him. Suffering was a reminder that all must be ready for death. If the body was afflicted, converts were to remember that the flesh was temporary and the spirit eternal. Many Methodists tried to be content with bodily pain or illness, hoping to heighten the spirit by transcending the flesh. Richard Whatcoat, for example, strived for a "thankful heart a truly resigned will in all things" when he was plagued with an inflamed eye. When Rebecca Ridgely was having trouble with a disrespectful nephew, she, too, tried to turn the situation to spiritual advantage: "the Lord I trust will bear me up through Lifes uneven way, and Bring me at Last to Glory, for this I know is Scriptureal, that thro' [many] tribulations and trials we are to be made perfect."[62]

A poem published in the *Arminian Magazine* in August of 1790 was only one of many that extolled the blessings of suffering. In "A Funeral Hymn," verse after verse pointed out how men and women were "chasten'd by sharp affliction's rod" and how their "sharpest suff'rings flow'd" from "love divine":

Long in the fiery furnace try'd
    With salutary pain;
In suff'rings to thy Lord ally'd,
    With him triumphant reign!
GOD brought thee low, to raise thee up,
    He kill'd to make alive:
Go, bless him for the bitt'rest cup
    Thy Saviour's love could give.

As the poem indicates, affliction—"salutary pain"—united believers most of all with Christ, the Suffering Servant. Henry Boehm noted as much when he saw Edward Callahan dying. Although cancer had eaten away much of Callahan's face, he still praised God. "Like his Master," Boehm noted, "he was made perfect through suffering."[63] Persecution was similarly seen as a blessing. Some Methodists courted persecution, for they believed that in order to be pure, they had to suffer, or, as one of their favorite Bible verses put it, to be "as gold tried by fire." John and Charles Wesley had practically urged Methodists to seek out the enmity of others in the *Discipline*. Members were encouraged to do good in part by "submitting to bear the reproach of Christ, to be as the filth and off-scouring of the world: and looking that men should *say all manner of evil of them falsely for the Lord's sake.*"[64]

Tales of persecution were such an important part of Methodist testimony that we may well ask if the church's belief that persecution was a sign of proper Christianity predisposed Methodists to exaggerate or invent opposition. These stories bear remarkable similarities—the slave persecuted by his or her master, the wife by her husband, the child by its parent, and the poor by the rich. Should their conventional character cause us to question their accuracy?

Although Methodists do seem to have at times exaggerated opposition, the evidence indicates that criticism, vandalism, and to a lesser extent violence against Methodists were common. Enough of these accounts were corroborated by newspapers or by the "persecutors" themselves to show that Methodists need not have fabricated these tales to have felt persecuted. The conventional character of stories in which godly Davids battled ungodly Goliaths does prove, however, that Methodists had a formula that they used to interpret such incidents. This formula enabled those Methodists who were the least powerful in the world's eyes to bear up under all sorts of harassment, for it allowed them to invert earthly rankings and to view persecution, like all suffering, as a purifying force. The result was that because persecution was a positive sign, some Methodists were emboldened to risk criticism and bodily harm for their religion, which in turn resulted in more of what they called "persecution." Although the extent of opposition may have been at times exaggerated, the Methodist worldview practically guaranteed that they would be opposed.

Sickness, persecution, and suffering, if turned to advantage, provoked moments of absolute spiritual clarity for believers who could "humbly kiss the sacred rod."[65] In their most lonely, confused, and trying times, they stripped all away but God. But these temporary afflictions were merely training for the most important moment of self-denial in a Methodist's life—death. Regardless of the physical pain and emotional anguish that the dying endured, the church set great store in converts experiencing a "happy death."[66] Mrs. Woods of Baltimore, for example, was described as being in "exquisite pain of Body" from an "incurable cancer," but, as her fellow Methodist Maddox Andrew observed, "her soul is happy in God." Andrew's wife Pamela concurred, adding that Woods's "love is so strong, and her faith so triumphant, that she longs to be disolved and to be with Christ."[67]

To triumph over pain and death was to have complete self-dominion, to fully sublimate the flesh to the spirit. Mrs. Moore, another Baltimore woman, was "like a living flame" on her deathbed, so "filled with GOD, that every word she spoke was peculiarly weighty." Her minister described her as martyrlike, for "what else," he asked, "could enable her to triumph over all the decays of nature, and in the agonies of death!" Moore, it was reported, faced death "without either sigh or groan," which confirmed her mastery over "nature."[68] Another reason Methodists were supposed to face death like Mary Foyns, who "Died without a strugle sigh or gron," was that death represented the moment of transition to a heavenly state and was a believer's last chance to evangelize. Preachers made special efforts to attend the dying, to pray, counsel, sing, and witness the victory over death that normally followed. William Adams, whose deathbed ritual was enacted over the course of several weeks, had time to warn all the unregenerate around him of the need to convert and to testify that he was "so happy at times that he thought he had rather die" than live.[69] In the deathbed ritual, Methodists both affirmed the victory possible over mortality and drew witnesses near to God. It was deemed especially significant if the dying could help the unconverted realize the need for repentance. To this end, men and women like Adams paid special attention to those who had not yet professed religion and reminded them that their turn could be next.

Ministers, too, tied death to both victory and conversion. Clergy performed burial services over corpses shortly after death, but more important was the funeral sermon, often preached days or weeks after burial. Rarely did ministers center these sermons around the lives of the deceased.[70] Typically, preachers briefly eulogized the dead and then moved to their more urgent messages. Deaths of the faithful were something to be celebrated, for they represented the ultimate triumph of the soul over the body. Preachers used the text "O death where is thy sting, O grave where is thy victory," a verse also shouted by people in their final moments of life. Death was something to be conquered, as other funeral texts showed. "The last enemy that shall be destroyed is death" was one such sermon; "I have fought the good fight," another.[71]

Survivors' behavior was equally important; they too were supposed to exhibit self-mastery amid grief. It was not appropriate, the church believed, for Methodists to grieve excessively or for a long period of time. "Why mourn?" one poem in the *Methodist Magazine* asked, "since death presents us peace, and in the grave our sorrows cease." Ministers often gave advice to the bereaved that seems, to an outside observer, callous. Ezekiel Cooper consoled a new widow with this warning: "Ah Sister let this teach us the uncertainty of all things under the sun. Our life is as a dream or a vapour soon passing away."[72]

Methodists did mourn, of course, and the vocabulary of feeling and emotion they learned in the church helped them express their grief. Yet they also tried to use grief (another form of suffering) to become better Christians. Edward Dromgoole, at the time an itinerant preacher, returned from his circuit in 1784 to find his young son dead. "O mighty woe[;] how can I sustain the load . . . ," Dromgoole confessed to his journal. He sadly recalled his son's "dear face," "black eyes," "pretty lips," and "innocent ways," until "the Torrent rises too high for all the bounds and breaks out. Now all the springs of sorrow are open in my heart while my distress is unutterable: Groans and cries must supply the place of Speech." Dromgoole placed this death in a Methodist context: "How vain is all that is under heaven: how uncertain all that we are fond of in this vale of tears." After imagining meeting his son in heaven, the grieving father inscribed a prayer reiterating the lesson God had taught him through his son's death: "thou hast been pleased to touch me in the tenderest part and to give me a striking instance of the frailty of human life." Like many Methodists, Dromgoole tried to use this death in a positive way. He begged God to "[sanctify] this visitation of thy Providence and may it be a means of loosening my heart from every thing that is earthly and of drawing my willing soul to the blessed Regions of everlasting felicity. . . ." Dromgoole closed his prayer by contrasting the bliss of heaven with the "pain or sickness or death or crying" of earth.[73]

Dromgoole's effort to control his grief, to use his grief as a means of achieving closer communion with God, was just one of the many sides to Methodist asceticism. The ascetic convert sought to master his or her mind, body, and emotions. In hymns, poems, sermons, and class meetings, Methodists were urged to exert control over the self so that when death did come they could face it without a struggle or groan. Methodists certainly experienced physical and emotional pain; the church merely taught them to try and manipulate sorrow and suffering for positive ends. At this distance it is impossible to measure the extent to which Methodists actually suffered pain and anguish on their deathbeds. What we can observe with regularity is the extent to which the dying claimed to be free of pain and anguish. The convention of the happy death is emblematic of the success of Methodist asceticism. Transcendence of the flesh by the spirit was enacted most vividly on deathbeds.

The final component of the Methodist style was aggressive evangelism. Again and again, people outside the Methodist church noted (and frequently complained about) the incessant proselytizing of the Wesleyans. The *Discipline* required converts to reprove, exhort, and evangelize; abundant evidence shows that Methodists took this command to heart. Evangelistic methods varied drastically even in the pulpit, so it should not surprise us that some converts boldly told their friends they were bound for hell while others tearfully confronted them with the joys of salvation. Methodists were, in any event, sure about the "true" (i.e., the Methodist) path to heaven. In their diaries, letters, and conversations, members frequently sized up the chances of others' salvation. Methodists were predictably pessimistic about the chances of Episcopalians, divided on a case-by-case basis over Baptists and Presbyterians, and certain that the unchurched and the lukewarm of whatever faith would perish. Surrounded by so many who were spiritually dead, Methodists worked aggressively to convert—so aggressively that the sect's lay members were as well known for evangelism as their preachers.

Methodists' unecumenical views help explain why the dying paid such attention to converting those around their deathbeds. Methodists sought comfort in the idea that heaven would restore the family circle, but they were not sanguine about the heavenly family reunion.[74] Because of their evangelical creed, Methodists had to convert all their relations if they wished to be with them in the afterlife. Elizabeth Anderson was none too gentle with her unconverted brother John Owen. In her letters, Anderson used high-pressure tactics with great skill. "What joy it would afford to heare that you had experiancd the forgiveness of your sins," she began, but warned Owen that he "must be in good earnest it is not a matter to be trifeld with." Next she employed guilt, begging Owen to "let not the prayers of all your friends be lost upon you." Anderson also tried to strike at his fear, reminding Owen that "life is uncertin and death is shure." Finally, she commanded him to get religion: "I charge you to meet me in heaven where distress and all confution will end." As her strident appeal shows, a family reunion in the afterlife was contingent upon her family members' conversions.[75]

Evangelism was necessary, Methodists believed, because judgment was certain. Consequently, funeral sermons emphasized the conditional nature of salvation. Preachers proclaimed "it is appointed unto men to die, but after this the judgment." Over children's graves, they reminded their listeners that "except ye be converted, and become as little children, ye shall not enter into the kingdom of heaven." Or, as another sermon text pointed out, at death, "they that have done good" would have "the resurrection of life," while "they that have done evil" would have "the resurrection of damnation."[76] Although the Methodist idea of heaven as a family reunion was important, the idea of heaven as judgment was more so. Individual believers would be rewarded; the wicked would be punished.

Methodist views are well illustrated by a dramatic incident in Benjamin Abbott's ministry. While in Maryland during the Revolutionary War, Abbott sat through an Anglican funeral service and was not pleased with what he heard. The sermon was "short, easy, smooth, soft," Abbott said, and when the parson invited him to add a few words, Abbott readily agreed. Amid a chorus of lightning and thunder, Abbott "set before them the awful coming of Christ, in all his splendor, with all the armies of heaven, to judge this world and to take vengeance on the ungodly!" To emphasize how precarious life was and hence the need for his listeners to convert immediately, he added, "It may be . . that he will descend in the next clap of thunder." Both the storm and Abbott raged for about an hour, during which time many "screamed, screeched, and fell all through the house."[77]

Not all Methodist preachers had Abbott's showmanship (or his fortunate timing), nor did they all center on hell and judgment in funeral sermons. Yet the thrust of Abbott's effort—"warning and inviting sinners to flee to Christ"—was at the heart of Methodist evangelism. To this end, Methodists exhorted and harangued, reproved and harassed those about them. The self-confidence and sense of agency Methodism had nurtured came in especially handy when members evangelized. To the extent that Methodists had a social mission that reached outside of their own circle, it was evangelistic. Rather than trying to remake the environment outside their loving communities, they sought to draw more and more individuals into the circle.

The Methodist style, with its emphasis on emotionalism, mysticism, enthusiasm, asceticism, and evangelism, set Methodists apart in both their own minds and the minds of non-Methodists. Church doctrines of free will, falling from grace, and sanctification helped forge individual Methodist identities. Converts believed that they were the masters of their fate and that this fate was daily in the making. Methodism held out the hope of a perfected self and the danger of a fallen self, and charged men and women with negotiating the territory between the two. To successfully complete their journeys, Methodists had to reform their outward and inward behavior to conform with what they believed to be God's will. As every choice was meaningful, every action significant, and every thought controllable, even those Methodists most powerless in the secular world were vested with agency. Methodists believed in the power of all individuals to achieve their own salvation and to mold their own psyches. In order to master the self, they tried to sublimate the body to the soul, to heighten spirituality by denying the flesh. Methodism turned the trials of mortal life into sources of possible triumph by viewing suffering as salutary, persecution as chastening, and death as victory.

Individual believers had direct contact with the divine in stylized and public enthusiastic behavior and more personalized contact with God in mystical experience. By encouraging emotional expressions of religion, Methodism proffered an ideal world of love and happiness that sharply contrasted with the secular world of the South. Through evangelism, converts attempted to bridge the gap between themselves and others by drawing more people into the church. While men and women wound their solitary paths to heaven or hell, the church offered solace and comfort along the way. Methodists shared their trials and triumphs with one another and tried to urge each other on in their lone journeys. Their destiny as individuals and as a group was otherworldly, but in order to get to heaven, they had to first remake themselves on earth.

Members shared a common identity as Methodists, but their race, status, class, and gender helped forge subcommunities within the sect's larger group identity. Sarah Jones had perceptively noted that "the war is perpetual while here." Thus far, I have shown how this warfare was waged internally and displayed in public services. Now I will turn to the very real external enemies that Methodists faced, for these external enemies often shaped experience in ways that divided, rather than united, southern Methodists.

THREE

Slaves and Free Blacks
in the Church

IN METHODISM SLAVES AND FREE blacks found a God who did not see differences in color, caste, gender, or status. In Methodist doctrine, oppressed and victimized African Americans found a value system that prized individual choice and agency in a world where they had few choices and where their individuality was often not respected. In Methodist rituals, slaves and free blacks affirmed their sense of self-worth and humanity and openly challenged the racist ideology of their oppressors.[1] By registering support for Methodist values, slaves could express their disdain of their owners' lifestyles, morally invert secular rankings, and proclaim their faith that God would avenge the wrongs done to them. And when the misery and pain of bondage taxed the human spirit, Methodist slaves found comfort and hope in their religion.[2]

Historians of slave religion often focus on the late antebellum period, in part because of the rich source material contained in the Works Progress Administration interviews with former slaves. In these interviews, freedmen and -women revealed many white ministers to be among slavery's staunchest defenders, men who advanced slave obedience from the pulpit and who often reduced the Bible to a proslavery manifesto. In the late antebellum era, southern ministers, Methodists included, spearheaded efforts to religiously justify slavery and to ground the proslavery argument in a Christian framework of benevolence and stewardship.[3] But such was not always the case. In the late eighteenth century, and to an lesser extent the early nineteenth century, when Methodist ministers preached on slavery, they usually denounced the institution. Far more ministerial effort went into convincing masters to free their slaves than in urging slaves to obey their masters. We cannot hope to understand the nature of black Methodism in the late eighteenth century unless we distinguish preachers' attitudes in this era from the proslavery stance of later antebellum years.

There were decided limits to early Methodist egalitarianism, but in the midst of

47

what many historians believe to be the nadir of slave treatment, sects like Methodism offered more respect for slaves' humanity, more attention to their physical and psychological needs, and more emphasis on what blacks and whites shared than slaves could find in any other arena. The public nature of evangelical activity, moreover, offered slaves and free blacks a forum for expressing their sense of community, worthiness, and pride. Methodists' antislavery policies, sermons opposing slavery, and the church's stands against cruelty and neglect of slaves surely made Methodism more attractive to slaves and free blacks. Methodists also opened some leadership positions to African Americans; black men became respected preachers and leaders of black and biracial groups.[4]

Uncovering the experience of slaves and free blacks in the church and what Methodism meant to them is no simple task. The vast majority of early Methodist sources are white-authored, and the attitudes of white Methodists ranged from extreme empathy with slaves to thinly veiled contempt. Part of the story of slave and free black Methodism was indeed one of race relations: how whites in the church acted upon blacks and how blacks acted, reacted, or resisted. Yet there was certainly more to the religiosity of African Americans than their interactions with white southerners, and we must seek to explore and analyze these personal and communal meanings of black religious experience. To begin sorting out these multiple layers, let us first turn to an interpretive case study: the career of Henry Evans.

Henry Evans, a free black shoemaker from Virginia, converted to Methodism at an early age. At some point in the late eighteenth or early nineteenth century, Evans decided to open a shop in Charleston, South Carolina. On his way south, he stopped in Fayetteville, North Carolina, and was reportedly appalled with the lack of religious worship and instruction for the city's blacks. He began holding services, and as one white minister recalled, "no ordinary preacher was he." Despite much persecution, Evans eventually formed a society and became known as the founder of Fayetteville Methodism. Evans and his followers, "out of rough-edged materials," built a church twenty by thirty feet large that was financed, except for a five dollar gift from a white man, entirely by black Methodists. A few years after the meetinghouse was constructed, the crowds had grown, forcing the society to enlarge the building.[5]

Interpreting the significance of black leaders is complicated by the fact that many of the sources describing them were written after the Methodists abandoned their earlier antislavery thrust and more fully embraced southern racial mores. The ministry of Henry Evans is a case in point.[6] The details of Evans's career that are most often cited come from the 1859 autobiography of white minister William Capers. Capers, who was highly critical of early Methodist antislavery efforts, spoke at length of Evans's benignity. No black preacher, Capers claimed, "was more remarkable for his humble and deferential deportment towards the whites than Evans was, . . . never speaking to a white man but with his hat under his arm; never allowing himself to be seated in their houses; and even confining himself to the kind and manner of dress proper for negroes in general." Also according to Capers, whites stopped persecuting Evans when "One after another began to suspect their servants of attending his preaching, not because they were made worse, but wonderfully better." Proof of this, Capers said, could be seen by Fayetteville blacks' new respect for the Sabbath and habits of temperance.[7]

Capers made a series of assumptions about Evans, his followers, and his ministry that bear further analysis. To Capers, Evans's outward performance of the rituals of the southern caste system was a sign of deferential acquiescence, if not acceptance of racial hierarchy, but his behavior is better seen as an example of what a free black leader in the early national South had to do to survive. Whites in the late eighteenth century were no less diligent than their descendants at searching out "pride" and "impudence" in African Americans. Despite his efforts to portray Evans as humble, Capers must have been somewhat divided about the black preacher's personality, for he also claimed that "Henry Evans was a Boanerges; and in his duty feared not the face of man." "Boanerges," meaning "sons of thunder," was the surname Christ gave to James and John after selecting them as apostles. The Evans who was a "Boanerges" and who "feared not the face of man" does not fit well with the humble, deferential Evans who seemed never to have challenged racial conventions. Nor does the humble preacher of Capers's fancy fit with other evidence about Henry Evans.[8]

Fayetteville authorities saw Evans as a dangerous menace and refused to let him preach in the city limits. Evans resourcefully began holding services in Sandy Hills, an area just outside town. Mobs repeatedly "tried to stop him; but he preached on, and worried them out by continually changing his meeting place." After Evans had attracted enough of a following to build a meeting house, whites trickled in, beginning with a "schoolmistress" who was expelled from the Presbyterian church for shouting.[9]

While the fears of Fayetteville masters that Evans would promote rebellion and dissension proved groundless, the absence of rebellion does not mean that Evans or his members accepted white supremacy. Their loyalty to Evans and Methodism is evident in their secrecy: Evans's followers did not reveal his meeting places. Capers is best read as a man torn between his respect for Evans, his paternalistic racism, and his desire to distance himself from earlier antislavery Methodists. His blindness to slaves' own motives in choosing to follow a preacher who was proscribed by white authorities is not surprising. And what of the "son of thunder" himself? Evans's courageous efforts to keep a venue for black worship open despite threats and official proscription indicate that he was not the tool for white authority that Capers implied he was. And finally, we may remark that Henry Evans, by dressing like the men and women he first served in Fayetteville, was fulfilling standards established by John Wesley.[10]

Our understanding of Evans is also complicated by the fact that modern scholarship, while rejecting Capers's racism, sometimes shares his reductive view of black religious experience. Slave religion is too often linked with either resistance or acquiescence, as if a slave's relationship to his or her master were the only aspect of life that religion helped explain and govern. Capers's reductionism is all the more striking because he belonged to a sect that required all members to give up a host of "vices," yet he interpreted slaves' decisions to abide by Methodist rules solely in terms of how masters were affected. Slaves were parents and children, husbands and wives, neighbors and friends, members of churches and individuals who formed opinions. Religion helped explain and order all of these experiences and roles; religion demarcated, even within slavery, a portion of the world that slaves and their God controlled. The decision of Fayetteville slaves to give up drinking could have easily been (and probably was) unrelated to their masters. We should not accept Capers's suggestion that slaves abandoned drink in order to be *"wonderfully better"* (i.e., more productive) *slaves.*

Whether or not sobriety influenced work performance, whether or not masters wanted them sober (or like one of Frederick Douglass's owners, periodically drunk), slaves who believed that God and their chosen faith demanded sobriety might have seen that as sufficiently compelling.[11]

As the case of Henry Evans shows, many white Methodists were racists, but how this racism influenced their attitudes towards slave and free black members has been a matter of historical dispute. Some historians have emphasized the racial conservatism of evangelicals, finding more continuity than change between the early and antebellum eras. These scholars see white evangelical Protestants as supportive of slavery and the racial caste system and emphasize the inequality in evangelical churches. Other historians emphasize the radicalism of evangelical views on slavery and race and argue that white evangelicals created in their churches an environment far more egalitarian than the world outside.[12] Although we will examine white Methodist views on slavery and blacks in depth in a later chapter, we should at least begin our discussion of them here since these issues were important to black members.

The typical views of white Methodists in the early church differ markedly from those in the antebellum era, largely due to the erosion of antislavery radicalism over time. The church increasingly bowed to southern racial mores in the nineteenth century, and antislavery stalwarts died or moved to free states and territories.[13] While there are a number of radical antislavery preachers from early Methodism who could be cited as evidence of change over time, the views of a man who was atypically more conservative will also illustrate the difference between the early and later eras. Jeremiah Norman was one of the least radical eighteenth-century preachers. He did not approve of the immediatist abolitionist views of some of his fellow ministers and was himself noticeably lukewarm about emancipation. His racism was also more pronounced than that of most preachers. Nonetheless, Norman enforced Methodist rules against buying and selling slaves, rules that required members to write emancipation deeds freeing newly purchased slaves after a period of service and that called for expulsion of members who sold slaves. On March 16, 1799, he required a slaveholder to sign a writ eventually emancipating a slave he had purchased (or face expulsion). On September 23, 1799, October 9, 1799, and March 15, 1800, Norman calculated—using guidelines in the *Discipline*—the manumission dates for slaves purchased by several Methodists. And on February 25, 1800, he expelled a member for selling a slave.[14]

As short-lived as early Methodist antislavery efforts were, they must somehow be differentiated from overt promotion of slavery. Methodists' opposition to slavery, however limited, was clearly greater than that of most southern whites. Did Jenny, one of the slaves whose manumission deed Norman recorded, see Norman as a man who supported slavery? Surely slaves, despite their resentment of the racism and segregation in the church, were sophisticated enough to appreciate the difference between proslavery attitudes and attitudes of preachers like Norman. And Norman admitted being exceptional. In his journal he bemoaned the fact that the vast majority of preachers were zealous opponents of slavery.[15]

Church leaders and preachers also opposed cruelty and neglect of slaves. Methodist clergy often noted how slaves were inadequately clothed, overworked, underfed, and cruelly used, which confirms historians' assessments that the eighteenth century witnessed some of the worst abuses of slaves in American history. Clergy and members denounced such abuses from the pulpit, privately reproved members for maltreatment, and disciplined some slave owners for physically abusing slaves.[16] The rhetoric of "brotherhood" and "sisterhood," so prominent in Methodism, must have rung truer in a sect whose leaders were in the main against slavery and who spoke out against physical abuse and neglect. In an era when other whites were debating whether people of African descent were human, and when racists were emphasizing the inhumanity of blacks as a justification for slavery, white Methodists viewed blacks as a part of the human family whom God had created and whom, once they had been converted, God would redeem in an eternity without racial distinction. Some African Americans found these views appealing.

White Methodists' racial attitudes, while more progressive than many others of their day, were still rooted in Anglo-American prejudices. In most areas of the South, black Methodists belonged to biracial societies, but they did not usually worship on terms of complete equality. The extent of segregation was often related to the age and size of the Methodist society in a locale. The formation of classes shows this development. When Methodists were new to an area, all the members would be put into a single class, as were the twenty white women and one "African" man in a Kent circuit class in wartime Maryland. As a society expanded, classes would be divided, sometimes first by race, other times first by gender. In long established areas, it was not uncommon to have a white women's class, a white men's class, and a black class. It does not seem, however, that during the years under study there was any division of black classes by slave or free.[17]

In services, the extent of segregation also varied. The common open air services—in groves, fields, or barns—did not allow rigid segregation, and in these services a fluid color line seems to have existed.[18] In a Virginia service held in a barn, for example, a minister who spoke to "a stout company of whites and blacks" reported that "several sinners were much convicted and one poor backslider was reclaimed. Some lay on the floor from about dark till midnight like dead persons." Jesse Lee, in his history of the Methodists, told of a meeting in the woods at which "many scores of both white and black people fell to the earth." During this same revival in 1787, Lee recalled that "It was often the case that the people in their corn-fields, white people, or black, and sometimes both together would begin to sing, and . . . pray . . . till some of them would find peace to their souls." Before the camp meeting era, when a special area of the campground was set apart for black worshipers, outdoor meetings were the least segregated of Methodist services.[19]

In services in private homes, no single system prevailed. Benjamin Abbott preached in a home where blacks were in the kitchen and whites in the parlor. John Kobler, however, did not mention such separation when he described preaching in a widow's house to a "very lively little company of both black and white . . . some prostrate on the floor and others [weeping] out loud."[20] In chapels built by Methodists, segregation was more rigid, and services were normally segregated either spacially or temporally. Spacial segregation was enforced by relegating black worshipers to balconies or rear areas of the church; and in some cases, with blacks outside and whites inside.[21] On at least one occasion, whites met outside while blacks met inside the church.[22] Another common mode of segregating black and white worshipers was for special services to be held at different times. Henry Boehm and others regularly reported holding black love feasts inside churches an hour or two before white love feasts. Other services were held at night specifically for slaves whose owners did not allow them to attend daytime meetings. Black members may even have preferred temporally segregated to mixed race meetings, for they could worship with other slaves and free blacks in their area without owner supervision and also without the stigma of being relegated to pews farthest from the pulpit.[23] Whether spatial or temporal, the existence of racial separation in Methodist churches warns us against portraying early white Methodists as twentieth-century egalitarians even though they seemed radical to others by the standards of their time. The task for historians is to appreciate both their radicalism and its limits.

While segregating black and white members undercut the Wesleyan notion of a common redemption for all, other practices and rituals reinforced it in ways that might have had special appeal to slaves. Antislavery Methodists extensively dwelt on the theme of the color-blind redemption in their efforts to convince slave owners to emancipate. One clergyman reminded a slaveholder that "a Soul as precious as his[,] Bought by the same price[,] redeem'd by the same blood[,] and an heir of the same Kingdom" should be emancipated. The communion ritual strengthened this claim, for as he served the bread to each member, the minister paraphrased the New Testament words of Christ "The Body of our Lord Jesus Christ, which was given for thee, preserve thy soul and body unto everlasting life" and when serving the wine, the minister intoned "Drink this in remembrance that Christ's Blood was shed for thee." In such rituals and language, southern Methodists asserted that free blacks and slaves were, in the eyes of God, equal to all other believers.[24]

The sermons preached to slaves constitute particularly compelling evidence that the attitudes of early Methodist preachers were different from those of the antebellum period. Although most sermons to slaves (as to all audiences) centered on the need for conversion or holiness, some reinforced the idea that slaves who were Christians had a special place in God's heart precisely because of their unjust suffering on earth. In July of 1797 William Ormond preached to blacks on the text "disallowed indeed of men, but chosen of God, and precious." All Methodists would appreciate the distinction in this verse between man's evaluation and God's evaluation, but black worshipers, suffering the oppression of slavery and a racial caste system, had even more reason to feel "disallowed indeed of men."[25] Slaves also closely identified with Old Testament heroes whom God stood by and kept safe through slavery and other persecutions, and some Methodist sermons stressed Old Testament stories with themes of deliverance. In Warrenton, North Carolina, William Ormond preached to a predominantly black audience from David's fortieth psalm: "I waited patiently for the LORD; and he inclined unto me, and heard my cry. He brought me up also out of an horrible pit, out of the miry clay, and set my feet upon a rock, and established my goings." Freeborn Garrettson spoke to a black audience on the travels of the children of Israel. One of James Meacham's sermons to blacks was on Daniel's delivery from the lion's den. Black minister David Smith linked his conversion with his emancipation in his exhortations, telling "how God had delivered me from the devil and slavery."[26]

Some sermons to slaves dealt more closely with the idea of divine retribution for crimes against the innocent. Meacham preached to a black audience on Luke 20:

1–18, Christ's parable of a man who planted a vineyard and then "let it forth to husbandmen." The landowner later sent three servants to receive some of the harvest. The husbandmen beat the servants and gave them nothing. The man next sent his son, whom he thought would command their respect, but they killed him. Christ revealed the fate of the unfaithful: "[The lord of the vineyard] shall come and destroy these husbandmen, and shall give the vineyard to others." Meacham's sermon text closed with a related parable. Builders reject a stone that becomes the cornerstone, and "whosoever shall fall on the stone shall be broken; but on whomever it shall fall, it will grind him to powder." Not only might his slave listeners have identified with the abused servants and with Christ (the son), but also with the retribution meted out in both stories.[27] A related sermon theme was that of Judgment Day. At a funeral sermon for a slave in Virginia, the sermon text centered on millennial judgment, when the dead "come forth." "They that have done good" are resurrected for Heaven; "they that have done evil" are cast into "damnation." A funeral sermon for a slave in 1792 centered on the inverted world of the Second Coming, when "those who have wives be as though they had none," and "they that weep, as though they wept not," and "*they that buy, as though they possessed not.*" The special meaning this might have had for slaves in the audience is self-evident.[28]

Emancipation was not only promised in the afterlife; a number of sermons addressed slavery and freedom in less metaphorical ways. In one of the most direct antislavery sermons delivered by a white preacher before a black audience, slaveholding and judgment were linked. Henry Willis preached the dedication sermon for a black Baltimore church on the text Acts 7: 7: "And the nation to whom they shall be in bondage will I judge, said God: and after that they shall come forth and serve me in this place." This text was not the standard Methodist dedication sermon for new meetinghouses, and thus was probably chosen with the black audience in mind. No whites, it seems, were present with the "nearly five hundred colored people" in this ceremony, except for Willis and his bishop, Asbury.[29]

Ezekiel Cooper's Fourth of July sermon preached to a crowd of blacks and whites stressed the hypocrisy of a freedom-loving nation that allowed slavery in its borders. Brother Chalmers reinforced this message with an exhortation designed to show that God might choose to judge slaveholders at any time. He told an anecdote about a slave auction to convince whites present that "he was certain God would send some judgment upon those who were obstinate."[30] In Chalmers's tale, a slave up for auction had a free black friend who was determined to buy and emancipate him, but an evil slave owner, who wished to move him to Georgia, kept outbidding the friend. As the situation looked hopeless for the slave, the evil slave owner was "on a sudden . . . struck with a judicial stroke from God and fell dead on the spot." Slaves in the audience undoubtedly appreciated both the sermon and the exhortation. In such ways, Methodist preachers could appeal to slaves and attack slavery (and slaveholders) in one bold stroke. It is not difficult to understand the attraction Methodism held for slaves who were exposed to radical antislavery preachers.[31]

It has been possible thus far to discuss the attitudes of white Methodists without extensive comparison with those of other whites. Yet such a comparison is essential to understanding early black Methodism. Non-Methodists viewed the church as subversive of racial hierarchy, one of the many reasons masters outside the church tried to stop their slaves from attending services. To elite whites in particular, sermons and exhortations condemning slavery and suggesting that republican values were incompatible with slave owning were evidence enough that Methodists were dangerous. Chalmers's story of instantaneous punishment for the slave buyer alienated most of his white non-Methodist audience. Although one slave owner resolved to free his slaves after this service, many area whites were horrified and felt such talk might encourage slaves to revolt. For slaves, the disapprobation of their owners and the courage of the Methodist preachers despite local sentiment must have made Methodism even more attractive.

Hostile whites often associated Methodism with fears of slave rebellion. It is extremely unlikely that any white Methodist minister ever encouraged slaves to revolt against their owners, although many noted privately in their journals their hopes that God would end slavery soon and mete out just punishment to slaveholders. John Kobler, after disciplining a master and his son who had burned a runaway slave with hot irons, noted that he was "awfully made to fear they will be sick of hot irons in a coming day." Later, upset that slaves were not allowed to attend services and instead were forced to work in the fields, he prayed privately for what he called the "revolution": "O merciful God when will the time and revolution commence to roll away this our reproach[?] [H]asten, —O hasten it merciful God I most earnestly entreat thee."[32] Such thoughts, we may safely conclude, were not normally aired in public, but Kobler's meditations illustrate the depth of some preachers' hatred for slavery.

Slave owners seem to have often assumed that their slaves, if exposed, would be drawn to Methodism, and once exposed to a church that opposed slavery, would want to rebel. John Littlejohn heard his first Methodist sermon in Norfolk in the early 1770s. Robert Williams, whom Littlejohn believed at first to be a "Crasy fellow," climbed to the top of the courthouse stairs and began singing hymns. The sermon Williams delivered was not preserved, but Littlejohn heard the mayor of Norfolk tell a friend during this event that "If we permit such fellows as these to come here we shall have an Insurrection of the Negroes."[33] In the early 1790s, several insurrection scares were blamed on the Methodists. James Meacham, in 1792, noted how after one such scare, "the cursed venom began to fly against the poor Methodists and Quakers . . . [;]some was for hanging the Preachers on a Tree." In 1793, Jeremiah Norman, puzzled at a light crowd for a Sunday service, discovered that whites "had made avow [sic] against hearing the Methodists any more" because of "the notion of the insurrection of the Blacks."[34]

In 1800, as word got out about the testimony of one of Gabriel's coconspirators that Methodists were among those to be spared (with Quakers and Frenchmen) because they were "friendly to liberty," Methodists were again seen to be dangerous to slavery. One of the white men accused of harboring the fugitive Prosser was a Methodist, and this may have increased slave owners' fears. Ben Woolfolk, the confessing conspirator, also linked rebellion and slave religion by reporting that he had spoken to the conspirators of the parallels between their planned revolt and the delivery of Moses and the Israelites from bondage under Pharaoh.[35] An editorial in a Virginia paper on Gabriel's revolt described slave insurrections as inevitable because of "the doctrine" of "liberty and equality" that the writer claimed "has been, and is still preached by the Methodists, Baptists and others, from the pulpit without any sort of reserve." South Carolinians, who in their press met Gabriel's Plot with "virtually complete silence," in December of 1800 barred all slave and free black gatherings before sunrise and after sunset whether for "mental instruction or religious worship."[36]

Such proscriptions on black worshipers help explain the context of one preacher's sermons urging slaves to obey their masters. In 1798, Methodist bishops Coke and Asbury published an edition of the *Discipline* with explanatory notes. Although they deemed slavery a "great evil" and an "enormous evil," the bishops counseled preachers when visiting from house to house to enforce the "relative duties," a reference to the passage in Ephesians that includes the words "Servants, be obedient to your masters." As both Asbury and Coke were in 1798 ardent foes of slavery, this focus on slave obedience would seem inconsistent. Yet it was part of a two-pronged strategy designed to alleviate slave owners' fears while encouraging emancipation—urge slave owners to free their slaves and urge religious slaves to obey their masters while in bondage.[37] After being physically threatened with violence several times because of his vocal opposition to slavery, Coke developed this tactic: "I bore a public testimony against slavery, and have found out a method of delivering it without much offense, or at least without causing a tumult: that is, by first addressing the Negroes in a very pathetic manner on the Duty of the Servant to the Master; and then the Whites will receive quietly what I have to say to them." We have no record of the reception Coke received by black listeners on this occasion. Perhaps they were outraged; perhaps they knew of Coke's abolitionism and figured out his strategy. If any of the other antislavery Methodist clergy tried Coke's plan in the pulpit, they left no record of it.[38]

Although sermons to slaves on obedience were rare, there were at least two other preachers who spoke on this theme. Jeremiah Norman preached on the relative duties, "and was unusually pointed on the duty of servants," in June of 1800. Asbury preached to a black audience in 1807 on the Ephesians verses on obedience. Two other sermons to black audiences might also have included references to slaves' "duty" to obey their masters. That the passages on obedience in the *Discipline* and these few sermons alleviated masters' fears of Methodism's pernicious influence on their slaves is doubtful. As late as 1818, after the church as a national body had stopped denouncing slavery, a Methodist minister was tried in Maryland for allegedly inciting slaves to rebellion.[39]

The fact that sermons to slaves and free blacks were far more likely to condemn slavery than encourage obedience goes a long way toward explaining the attraction of Methodism for black southerners. Overall, the church's record was mixed, with clergy expelling members who sold slaves and condemning bondage from the pulpit yet at the same time segregating blacks and whites in meetinghouses. When white Methodists are compared to their contemporaries, however, it is easy to see why they were viewed as radical. Methodist ministers were among the most vocal white opponents of slavery in the early national South. For slave and free black members, the Methodist church offered the single best hope (slender as it may have been) for manumission. In rituals and rhetoric, Methodists promoted an ideal of Christian brotherhood and sisterhood that they themselves did not always live up to but that differed dramatically from the racist ideology undergirding slavery.

To assume that slave and free black Methodists were passive recipients of white policies and beliefs is as misguided as it is to assume they joined the church only because of its stand on slavery. Religion helped explain life, death, the self, and the world as well as bondage and freedom. Black religiosity involved personal and communal identity, moral values, theological beliefs, and the outward manifestations of all of these. In the public spaces of evangelical churches, slaves and free blacks asserted their humanity and worth. Through religion, slaves resisted the definitions racists tried to impose upon them. By creatively exploiting Methodist policies and positions, slaves obtained a measure of autonomy and some even obtained their freedom.

Many slaves and free blacks identified themselves as Methodists and in some societies African Americans dominated the membership. The church began giving separate membership statistics by race in 1786, when black members made up 9 percent of all American members. Between 1786 and 1810, the number of black as well as white Methodists climbed steadily, and so too did the ratio of black to white members. In the early national era, the percentage of Methodists who were black remained at about 20 percent (see the appendix). By 1810, 30,000 blacks were members of the Methodist church, and they were overwhelmingly southern slaves. Yet these numbers, as significant as they are, do not tell the full story of black Methodism, for they do not represent black "seekers." Evangelical churches had stiff entrance and membership requirements, and thus some blacks (like whites) affiliated with the church for a number of years before joining. Small children were not counted as members, even if their parents regularly brought them to services. A larger problem with these statistics is that some non-Methodist owners forbade their slaves to join the church. Over 300 slaves, for example, who converted at a Virginia revival in 1787 wanted to become members but were prevented by their "lordly" masters.[40] The aggregate membership counts also do not reflect regional variations. In 1790, Broad River circuit, South Carolina, reported that almost 1 in 4 Methodists there were black. In western North Carolina's Yadkin circuit, however, only 8 out of 304 Methodists were black. The society in New Bern, North Carolina, had 390 black and 30 white members in 1807. There were only 3 black members reported in Savannah circuit, Georgia, in 1790, probably because several all-black, black-led Baptist congregations were well established before the Methodists arrived in the Savannah area. Many of the predominantly black Methodist societies were in urban areas, but some were rural. One western piedmont society had 50 black and 2 white members.

The decision to become a member rested with the slave—up to a point.[41] Some non-Methodist masters prohibited their slaves from joining the church. A few Methodist slave owners, moreover, seem to have forced their slaves to attend services. Slaves were "called in" to hear Thomas Rankin and "were collected" or "called together" twice to hear Francis Asbury. To join the church, however, was another matter. Even if some Methodist masters had wanted to force slaves into the church against their will, the admission process would not have allowed it. All potential members had to give convincing oral testimony of their conversions, show an understanding of doctrines and rules, and agree to abide by church discipline. Methodist preachers in this era, do not seem to have required slave owner authorization before admitting slaves as members; at least in the contemporary accounts examined for this study there is no trace of such a policy or practice. The extant evidence indicates that slaves, apart from those whose owners forbade them to attend or join, united to and withdrew from the church of their own accord.[42]

Blacks made up a significant percentage of members but perhaps an even greater proportion of Methodist audiences. White ministers' journals do not, of course, shed much light on what Albert Raboteau has called the "invisible institution"—the secret services blacks conducted away from whites and without consent of their masters. Jeremiah Norman was once stranded in an area without Methodists on a Sunday and was directed to an all-black worship service, but even here, whites knew of this meeting. What the sources do clearly document, however, is the extent to which black Methodism was *visible*. African Americans were a vocal and prominent part of Methodist services in the South. They were present in homes, barns, chapels, and groves where Methodists met. In cities, towns, and the countryside, they could be seen and heard at Methodist worship.[43]

Most blacks were in the pews or aisles of Methodist meetinghouses, but some could be found in pulpits. Methodists, like the Baptists, opened a number of leadership positions to black men in the years before 1810. Black male leaders did, however, face a glass ceiling until they formed the separate African Methodist Episcopal church. The top of the Methodist hierarchy—the offices of bishop, presiding elder, and elder—was white. Although the positions of trustee and steward were normally filled by white men as well, there were exceptions. In Wilmington, North Carolina, to prevent a defection of the members from the Methodist Episcopal church, blacks were appointed stewards.[44] But the central clerical leadership role in Methodism was that of preacher, and a surprising number of black men became well-known for their skill at preaching the gospel. The most famous of those who worked in the South was perhaps the itinerant Harry Hosier, who traveled with white Bishop Asbury, minister Freeborn Garrettson, and others. Hosier was more popular with audiences than many of his white counterparts, for several reported him as the main attraction when they preached together. Henry Boehm described Hosier as a "very eloquent" speaker with a "musical" voice, whose "tongue was as the pen of a ready writer." Blacks especially enjoyed Hosier's sermons and some "came a great distance to hear him."[45]

Hosier traveled with white clergy; Henry Evans built his ministry in a city. Yet even in remote and rural areas a number of men rose to prominence. A Tennessee preacher named Simeon was another black Methodist leader who achieved a degree of regional fame. Simeon had joined the church as a slave in 1790 and soon felt the call to preach. His skills as preacher and "the purity of his life so won the affections" of his master that he freed Simeon and gave him a small farm. Simeon's ministry was primarily to other blacks, and with them "he enjoyed a popularity that belonged to no other man in the community." He also, a white minister wrote, "commanded the respect" of whites for his stellar preaching, "countenance full of the expression of benevolence," and "mind far above ordinary." White families must indeed have admired this man, for Simeon was often called to minister "at the bedside of the sick and dying" whites, to orchestrate the most important Methodist ritual.[46] Jeremiah, a black minister of unknown civil status, enjoyed great popularity in rural western North Carolina in the early nineteenth century. He preached throughout his region at black, white, and biracial services.[47] Other black preachers make brief appearances in the historical record. In 1806, an African American named John preached in a Georgia service.[48] An unnamed black man preached at Brother Morris's home in 1795; another at Brother Crawford's in 1800.[49] A black minister named Joe preached in Currituck County in

1799. These and other men occupied positions of public authority that were rarely open to blacks.[50]

Black women, like white women, were not licensed as preachers or exhorters in this era, although they did evangelize, testify, reprove, pray, shout, and exhort. One remarkable woman whose story appeared under the name of "Old Elizabeth" felt a call to preach soon after her conversion in slavery around 1779. In 1808, as a free woman, Elizabeth appointed prayer meetings for black women, and around 1810 began unofficially to preach. She was discouraged by many white Methodist leaders, but she described this discrimination almost solely in terms of gender and not race. Elizabeth persisted in her ministry and eventually even preached against slavery in Virginia. She was in many ways exceptional; few black women before 1810 were able to follow in her footsteps.[51]

Black ministers played important roles in the free black and slave community as well as in the church. Often they seemed to have acted as intermediaries between the white ministry and the black community. Black preachers also had the respect of religious whites, a fact that would not have automatically raised their esteem among African Americans, but that did mean they had freedom of movement and speech not normally allowed blacks in a slave society. Because of their positions as itinerants, these men were able to travel and thus could brings news or information about long lost relatives and friends. Even before Gabriel's Plot was discovered, the climate could be hostile, especially in the lower South, for black preachers. In 1785, Francis Asbury tried to persuade Richard Allen, then a free black Methodist preacher, to accompany him on a tour of the South. Allen was warned that "in the slave countries, Carolina and other places, I must not intermix with the slaves, and I would frequently have to sleep in his carriage, and he would allow me my victuals and clothes." Allen declined going, for he feared that if he fell sick, he would have no one to care for him. Asbury, though for his time a progressive man on race and slavery, showed the limits of his empathy with those suffering under the racial caste system, and countered that he, too, received only food and clothes for a salary. Allen repeated his reasons: "[Asbury] could be taken care of, let his afflictions be as they were . . . but I doubted whether that would be the case with myself." Allen chose to remain in the Maryland-Delaware area for his ministry.[52] The ideological climate improved somewhat for black Christians when northern states enacted gradual emancipation and some southern states eased manumission laws.[53] Preaching was, it should be emphasized, the only calling a black man could pursue that gave him access to large slave audiences.

By their very existence, African American preachers challenged white supremacist views, infused black members with racial pride, and testified to Wesleyan beliefs in the distinction between God's and humanity's rankings. All Methodist preachers rose to their positions by demonstrating an ability to persuade the unregenerate to convert and the converted to persevere. All had to show signs that God had set them apart for ministerial work. The black ministry, by bringing others of both races to God, bore witness to Methodist beliefs that God did not order his world by status, race, education, or wealth. The persuasiveness and oratorical skill of black preachers gave them tremendous influence and even power—in the Methodist sense of the term—over the souls and bodies of blacks and whites. James Finley reported that a slave minister named Cuff preached "with an eloquence and power none could resist. Often have the hearts of proud and wicked masters, from adjoining plantations, who had been attracted out of mere curiousity to attend the meetings, been made to tremble, while the falling tear from proud and haughty mistresses, who would wonder at the audacity of the negro, would betray the emotions his eloquence had produced."[54] Where else could slaves see their mistress bathed in tears at a black oration or their master trembling for mercy before a black man? It takes little historical effort to imagine how it must have felt for slaves to see their owners so affected by a black minister. For a few precious moments, it must have seemed that the world was right side up.

For all their power and authority, black preachers had to be, as Methodists might have said, "wise as serpents and harmless as doves." Black ministers walked a tightrope in a slave society, and black Methodist preachers were no exception. They were suspected by white authorities of fomenting insurrections or fostering discontent among slaves. Their visibility and freedom to travel made them conduits for possibly subversive information. The crowds of slaves and free blacks they attracted alarmed slaveholders and nonslaveholders alike.[55] Even from white clergy, black ministers faced racism. All Methodist ministers were urged to be humble and meek, and to avoid pride. A common lament of white clergy was that members had complimented them to their faces, a situation they feared would inflate a minister's ego and cause him to improperly value himself above God. White clergy seemed especially sensitive to the sins of pride and vanity in black preachers. Francis Asbury linked Harry Hosier's ego to his power over white audiences: "I fear his speaking so much to white people in the city has been, or will be, injurious, he has been flattered, and may be ruined." James Jenkins, writing in a later era, remembered "some difficulties" as he put it, with "an influential coloured man, who desired further promotion in the church" in 1802. Jenkins unabashedly claimed next that he had "generally found that these people cannot bear promotion: like too many white people, they become proud." For Jenkins, then, pride was a danger to "many" whites, and to most blacks.[56]

Despite such attitudes, a number of black men became leaders of classes or societies. Blacks were officially appointed class leaders and exhorters in Baltimore, Maryland, and Charleston, South Carolina.[57] Sancho Cooper, who died in 1865, was a class leader in Columbia, South Carolina, for more than sixty years.[58] Numerous black men exhorted or led prayers in Methodist services. In his journal, Thomas Mann mentioned numerous black exhorters, among them Pomphy, two slaves belonging to Brother Taylor, George, Jeremiah, and several men whose names were not given. A black Virginia boy, according to Freeborn Garrettson, "exceeded all the youths . . . for a gift and power in prayer."[59] Blacks ran a society in Oxen Hill, just opposite Alexandria, Virginia, on the Potomac. The Oxen Hill Methodists built a meetinghouse, ran their own affairs, and handled the same routine disciplinary proceedings that other local Methodist leaders did. They also voluntarily and regularly contributed to the support of white itinerants.[60]

Some black men led groups of both whites and blacks. Near Wayne County, Kentucky, a Methodist society was headed by an extraordinary slave named Jacob. One white preacher remarked that "every member had been awakened under his preaching." Jacob and two young white women had organized the society in this area, and he was appointed leader at the behest of one of these women. Jacob both preached and handled discipline for this group, and was successful, for the white itinerant "found his society in excellent order." Jacob, an exceptional preacher, was illiterate. On Saturday nights, his master would read him the Bible, and "when a text was read that suited Jacob, he would ask his master to read it again and would "memorize the text, book, chapter, and verse" for his sermon the following day.[61] Jacob's experience illustrates both the repressive nature of slavery and how one man struggled success- fully to maintain some autonomy within that system. Although he was neither al- lowed nor taught to read, he did not automatically choose the first verse his master read to him as a sermon text. His master had the power of literacy, but Jacob had a preacher's "power" to choose a text that inspired him. Unfortunately, we know very little about the relationship between Jacob and the white women who entrusted him with their spiritual welfare, but we may assume, from the itinerant's judgment, that Jacob enforced Methodist rules among his followers. Jacob ascended to a position of leadership that—in church meetings—reversed the hierarchies of race and slavery.

Jeremiah, the aforementioned preacher from western North Carolina, was also the leader of his society. His society was composed of fifty blacks and two white women who united with Jeremiah because there was no white Methodist group in their area, and they would not join the Baptists.[62] Even in the relatively new settlements of Ken- tucky or the white majority west of North Carolina, a black man who had disciplinary and spiritual authority over whites—especially white women—must have been an anomaly outside the evangelical churches. Considering the intimacy of class meetings, in which members were encouraged to bare their souls and tell every sin of thought and deed, the relationship between these black male leaders and white female follow- ers is extraordinary. In the context of a common faith, demonstrated ability, and evi- dence of divine blessing, a few white southerners deferred to black authority by choice.

The church's encouragement of some black preachers and leaders was undoubt- edly important to rank-and-file black members. To understand the other reasons that so many blacks found Methodism appealing, we must try to recover their religious ac- tions and beliefs and place them in the context of the times. There were practical rea- sons that slaves might have been attracted to Methodism. At services, they could meet relatives and friends from neighboring plantations, find spouses, and spread family and neighborhood news. Camp meetings, which drew owners and slaves from great distances, must have been especially useful in this regard.[63] Visiting and worship were not mutually exclusive. It must have been especially meaningful to worship with old friends or distant family members; such reunions would be a foretaste of the ultimate reunion in heaven.

Blacks may also have been attracted to the church because Methodist views about the human family were more inclusive than those of other southerners. Methodists' familial rhetoric corresponded to that already prevalent in slave communities. In Methodist churches, every female member was a "Sister" and every male, a "Brother." The church community formed a Christian "family." Herbert Gutman and other scholars of slave families have noted how slaves, deprived of legal authority to keep their biological families together, creatively responded by forming "fictive kin," a practice that Methodist forms of address closely emulated.[64] Sometimes these "fami- lies" were inclusive. William Colbert referred to the black society at Oxen Hill as "my black friends" or "my good black brethren." Mrs. Bassett, the wife of an antislavery legislator from Delaware, when at camp meetings, was said to have been as likely to "embrace a pious dusky daughter of Africa, in her rejoicing as a white sister." Richard Allen felt a familial connection to some of his fellow Methodists who were white. He called Benjamin Abbott a "father and friend to me" and lauded a white couple who had "bathed [his] feet with warm water and bran" when he was suffering from rheumatism. On numerous occasions, black and white members related to each other as fellow Methodists and through their common values and rhetoric were able to briefly transcend differences of race and caste. In a Virginia service, Myles Greene was delighted that "a certain negroe Man appeard to be very happy. I spoke to him [and] he began to praise God with such sweet expressions that I think I immediately felt the affects of the same." When whites and blacks shared intense religious experience, the sense of the church as "family" was surely more palpable.[65]

A third reason that slaves might have been drawn to Methodism was that church values and ideals allowed them to condemn their owners, and feel morally superior to masters and mistresses. Church polity, which allowed any member to report on any other member, opened up a space where blacks could monitor (and implicitly judge) the behavior of whites. A black Methodist of North Carolina, to cite one example, informed his minister that a white member drank and swore. Even when slave owners were not members, church condemnation of pride, ostentation, gluttony, and greed—"sins" their owners so frequently indulged in—must have appealed to slaves. Methodists inverted the values of a slaveholding society by lauding the virtues of the weak and powerless. Instead of status, competition, material success, and honor, they prized humility, charity, simplicity, piety, and love. To become a Methodist was thus a way for many slaves to reject the lifestyles and values of slave-owning whites.[66]

It could be argued that in accepting Christianity, slaves were in effect accepting the worldview of their owners, even if their owners were not Methodists. Yet such an argument would not account for the narrow-minded way Methodists construed "true" religion. Methodists saw Catholicism as a horrid mutation of Christianity and thought Quakers were too quiet in meetings. They drew clear dividing lines between sects that taught that conversion was needed for salvation and those teaching that faith and church attendance were enough. The greatest nightmare preachers could imagine was for their members to become like Episcopalians. Baptists and evangelical Presbyterians were riddled with doctrinal errors; Congregationalists had stone hearts as well as bad doctrine. In short, Methodists were as sure of the rectitude of their beliefs as they were that all who believed differently were dreadfully wrong. If there were Methodist slaves who believed that they were accepting their masters' faith by accepting Christianity—and there is no evidence that there were—those slaves would have had even more reason to feel morally superior to their masters. Being Methodists, they would have seen themselves as "true" Christians and their masters as "false" ones.

The fact that so many slave owners derided the Methodists may also have made the church attractive to slaves. We can see evidence for this best in the breach. Francis Asbury frequently commented that slaves held by professing Christians were the least receptive to Methodism, and he also tried whenever possible to meet slaves separately because slaves often were not responsive to his message if their owners were present. James Meacham found the same dynamic at work among Brother D's slaves (probably Edward Droomgoole). Meacham blamed the slaves' "hardness and inattention to the things of eternity" on the fact that "their Lordly Master is a [local] preacher and has been for this many years and holds them in slavery."[67] The tale of Major Martin's efforts to bring his Kentucky slaves to Methodism is also illustrative. According to a friend (who seems especially blind to the irony in the account), Martin took a "wagonful" of slaves to a camp meeting and they "professedly converted." Once home, however, "finding their lives by no means a practical comment upon the Scriptures which he daily read for their instruction, he watched the opportunity for sending them all to another camp-meeting to be converted over again." Most slaves, the evidence suggests, showed no interest in joining a church that had admitted their masters.[68]

On very rare occasions, slaves followed their owners into the church. Richard Whatcoat told of a slave who was touched by the "narrow way his Master was walking in and also the way his Mistress was in." Many slave owners rejected Methodism, but those who joined the church were far more often brought to faith by their slaves than vice versa. The slave preacher Cuff brought his owner to Methodism, as did Richard Allen; both were freed after their owners' conversions. Two members of the prominent Gough clan of Maryland were influenced to convert by slaves. As with white wives who brought their husbands into the church, slave evangelists who conquered their masters' disbelief had the satisfaction of being the moral leaders of their owners. Since Methodists frequently told the stories of how they were converted, the leadership of such slaves was therefore publicly asserted and reasserted in each telling.[69]

It is not surprising that slaves were also attracted to the church because of its antislavery stance. The creative ways that slaves exploited Methodist positions deserve special attention. There is much evidence that slaves both in and outside of the church knew about Methodist antislavery efforts and policies on slavery. A shrewd bondswoman named Alley ran away from her owner in 1790. In his advertisement for her return, her master noted that she had thus far eluded her captors by claiming that "her mistress had married a methodist preacher and set her free."[70]

The story of Richard Allen's emancipation is likewise instructive. Allen, later famous as the head of the separate African Methodist Episcopal church, was in early life a slave in Delaware. He converted to Methodism before the Revolution, when as he described it, "all of a sudden, my dungeon shook, my chains flew off. . . . My soul was filled." Allen, like all Methodists, saw church values and the world's values as antithetical. He called slavery a "bitter pill" even though his owner "was what the world called a good master." Allen and his siblings were allowed to attend Methodist meetings even though their owner was not converted. This aroused the attention and ire of neighbors, who "said that Stockley's negroes would soon ruin him" with such behavior. Allen and his brother "held a council together," and decided that if they were to ensure the "privilege of attending meeting once in two weeks," they would have to allay white fears "that religion made us worse servants." The Allen brothers decided to work "to keep our crops more forward than our neighbors," and soon Stockley "boasted of his slaves for their industry and honesty."[71]

After thus easing his owner's mind about Methodism, Allen took a bolder step. He convinced his owner to host Methodist services. After some months of doing so, noted antislavery minister Freeborn Garrettson preached in Stockley's home on the text "thou art weighed in the balance and found wanting." According to Allen, Gar-rettson "among the rest weighed the slaveholder." After this sermon, Stockley "could not be satisfied to hold slaves, believing it to be wrong." The indebted Stockley agreed to let Allen and his brother purchase their freedom for sixty pounds gold.[72] Richard Allen was a gifted preacher and an able leader, as we know from his later accomplish-ments. If we closely examine his life in slavery and the circumstances of his manumis-sion, we also see that Allen was quite shrewd. For one, he was aware of the white gos-sip about his "good" master and chose to be a conspicuously diligent worker so as to protect the limited privileges his owner allowed him. Most Methodist slaves left no autobiographies, yet if we learn from Allen's story, we must revise our notions about religion's effect on slave productivity.

More than one scholar has noted how some masters claimed that evangelical slaves proved "good" workers and that slave owner distrust and hostility to churches like the Methodists often receded when masters realized that religion did not hinder slave productivity. These circumstances led one historian to conclude that Methodist clergy unintentionally increased slave owners' profits.[73] Yet such analysis leaves slave motiva-tion and slave self-interest out of the equation. As human beings trying to adapt to a repressive and harsh system, slaves may well have sacrificed in one area to improve their lives in another. The Allen brothers calculated that better work performance would lead to more religious autonomy but certainly evinced no desire to enhance their master's profits for his sake, and Allen's wording that he and his brother "held a council" suggests that the two carefully considered the consequences of their actions.

Allen provides one example of how religious slaves' decisions about work perfor-mance might be interpreted. Other slaves may have made similar calculations. Black preacher David Smith, when traveling for the Methodists in rural Maryland, observed that "many of the slaves were converted to God, and naturally they became better ser-vants, and afterwards obtained their freedom." Smith linked conversion and emanci-pation, with becoming "better servants" being the intermediate step.[74] Yet his use of the word "naturally" forces us to probe deeper. It is not surprising that certain Methodist rules, such as the prohibition on drink, might lead to better work perfor-mance. As evidence from later decades shows, some slaves took pride in their work; historians have not concluded that these slaves were seeking to enhance their masters' profits. It is problematic to assert that slaves who found religion and became better workers were being duped into supporting their oppressors. What religion provided all converts, it provided Methodist slaves: a personal relationship with God. Decisions slaves made in the context of accountability to God may well have had nothing to do with their owners whatsoever.

Allen, though, had freedom in view. Like the bondwoman Alley, he surely knew of Methodist efforts against slavery. His initiative in bringing Methodism to his owner was probably related to the church's antislavery stance, for it is more than happy coin-cidence that the sermon Garrettson preached was against slavery and that Allen's owner agreed to let Allen and his brother purchase their freedom as a result. The Methodists by the turn of the century had made what historians term a "retreat" on antislavery. But for several decades they were the most persistent antislavery evangelis-tic body in the South; only the Quakers exceeded their efforts. Quakers, however, were less expansionist and less interested in (and sometimes hostile to) blacks joining their church. A majority of slaves freed in Caroline, Talbot, and Dorchester counties of Maryland, one historian has shown, were freed by Methodists, with a number of these emancipation deeds bearing Garrettson's name as a witness.[75]

In Methodist churches across the South, though more heavily in the Upper South, slave members worshiped alongside blacks who had been freed by Methodist owners. Despite segregation, despite the fact that few blacks were appointed stewards, despite the racism of Methodist clergy, and despite the all-white upper tier of Methodist leadership, Methodist slaves had some hope for freedom, and this fact alone accounts in large part for blacks' receptivity to Methodism. For many Methodist slaves, this hope was not to be realized. Francis Asbury's frequent comments about how slaves belonging to Methodist owners were unreachable are once again illuminating. When owners preceded their slaves into the church, the Methodists had, however unwillingly, put their imprimatur on slavery.

Slaves and free blacks found other church rules and policies advantageous. Some African Americans sought ministerial help to stop slave-owner abuse. A free black Methodist woman complained to preacher James Meacham that her child, who was a slave, was being "striped" by the child's Methodist owner, and "she could not bare it." Meacham confronted the man, who took refuge in his slave's age and claimed that all children needed stern discipline, and that he "was more severe with his own [white children]" than slave children. Meacham "begged her to strive to be patient" and told her that he did not think "bro. S. would treat them out of Christianity."[76] The mother was determined to have some justice done, however, and countered that this master had also "whiped severely" an adult bondman (who was enrolled for freedom when he had "repaid" his purchase price via labor). "Bro. S" then "confessed he did whip him for which he was convicted and felt much distress." Meacham lectured the slave owner about beating "a man, that was a man as well as he was," told him not to "Lord it now as formerly," and "begged him to give himself to God." Without recourse in any other forum, slaves and free blacks with slave relations could at least make limited appeals for humane treatment through the church.[77]

Slaves and free blacks also had intellectual and psychological reasons for joining the church. Methodist doctrine emphasized the agency of individuals who could freely choose salvation and were personally accountable to God for leading a moral life. Under the shadow of slavery and racial injustice, slaves and free blacks had little opportunity to shape their own destiny. In Arminian religion, they at least were able to make a free choice, and exercise free will, and for some slaves this might have been a compelling reason to choose Methodism. One need not argue that all slaves were inclined toward free will doctrine or that there was a natural affinity between a yearning for civil liberty and a belief in human agency to recognize that the rhetoric of Arminianism and the rhetoric of liberty were quite similar. Richard Allen described his conversion as a liberation, and other black Methodists spoke of conversion as an experience of "power," "liberty," or "freedom." Predestination implied that whatever was, was God's will. Just as some slaves may have found this doctrine comforting because it explained their bondage and put events beyond their owners' control, others may have found Arminian doctrine comforting both because it explained slavery as the willful sin of their masters and because it allowed them to believe that even within the constraints of slavery they were moral agents who had the will to control their lives and make moral choices. In conversion, slaves had spiritual autonomy and could psychically redefine themselves as people worthy of God's love and concern. Whites and blacks alike saw conversion as the means to become, in the words of "Old Elizabeth" a "new creature in Christ." The exhilaration that all Methodists felt upon conversion must have been even more intense for slaves, defined by law and society as property.[78]

"Old Elizabeth" described her early life as a slave as a series of assaults upon her will. When eleven years old, she was separated from her mother and father (both Methodists) and sent to work on a farm miles away from them. There, "so lonely and sad," she finally asked permission to visit her parents and was "positively denied." She went anyway, and was "sent back" the next day and bound and beaten for her disobedience. Depressed and unable to eat, Elizabeth reported that "still I was required to do all my duty." Only in religion was Elizabeth able to do as she pleased. Her free will was made clear in the form of a question that God asked her in a vision: "Art thou willing to be saved?" Although she lived in an area "where there was no preaching, and no religious instruction," Elizabeth continued communing with her God.[79]

The rhetoric of conversion was infused with language that would have had deep resonance for slaves: liberty, power, freedom. In one service a black woman was "struck down under the power of God" during a prayer meeting. Other black worshipers "got round her on their knees and cried out to the Lord for her" until God "set her soul at liberty." At the meeting's end, her clergyman reported, this woman left "praising God as far as I could hear her."[80] David Smith also used the language of freedom. His conversion to Methodism as a bondman so enraged his Maryland master that he tried to sell Smith into Georgia. Anguished and fearful, Smith recalled "the power [God] had exercised in freeing me from sin. . . . [If] God was able to deliver me from the corrupt influence of the world and the power of Satan, that he was able to deliver me from this slave-holder." When Smith indeed was liberated, he rejoiced in being "free—both soul and body." Consider also antislavery minister James Meacham's description of two slaves who were hoping to be converted. These bondmen belonged to a Brother Howard, who himself had just converted to Methodism, and were described by Meacham as "seeking for a better world."[81]

The ideas of liberty and deliverance were not merely abstract, otherworldly concepts for slaves. But we risk oversimplifying slave religion if we ignore the otherworldly meaning of conversion. Smith spoke of two forms of freedom—that of the soul and that of the body—and two forms of deliverance—from worldliness and from bondage. Both forms of freedom and deliverance were important to religious slaves. The "power" to choose or refuse that Arminian doctrine ceded to the individual provided slaves the opportunity to shape their futures in a realm over which their masters had no control. The "freedom" slaves experienced upon conversion was palpable despite their earthly bondage. A "better world" was possible for religious slaves even in the context of enslavement. Because the Methodist rhetoric of conversion drew so heavily on the language of slavery and freedom, slaves' religious experience had a depth and complexity of meaning that whites might have intellectually appreciated but would not have emotionally shared. Even though slaves who converted, like David Smith, felt "free" from sin, they still prayed to be "free" from slavery.[82]

Conversion allowed slaves to redefine and remake themselves in ways that differed substantially from their owners' opinions of them. The gulf between slave owners' views of slaves and slaves' views of themselves was sometimes immense, which helps explain why when "Black Harry" Hosier told his African American audiences "that they must be holy," "certain sectarians" were described as being "greatly displeased with him." Several runaway ads underscore how slaves contested their masters' definitions of them. George French advertised for the return of Charles, who ran away on Christmas Eve, 1790. According to French, Charles "pretends to be a Methodist, and can deliver many texts of Scripture, which he is fond of doing, but is a sly hypocrite." French did not allege that Charles engaged in activities forbidden by the church, and it is reasonable to assume that for his master, Charles's "hypocrisy" was to steal himself. Slaveholder Thomas Love made more specific allegations about his runaway slave named Jem. Love wrote that the "chief of [Jem's] conversation will be on Religion, as he hath, for some time past made, affectedly, zealous declarations in the Methodist profession." But Love also claimed that Jem was "fond of gambling, and will get drunk"—activities forbidden by Methodists.[83] Both owners believed their slaves' religion to be affected, but both slaves had made professions of religion to their masters, and in this era, such professions were as apt to anger as to appease slave owners. The slaves had identified themselves as Methodists, and their owners accused them of hypocrisy, an accusation frequently leveled at all kinds of Methodists in this era. We should rightfully be suspicious about these masters' claims, for slaves who violated Methodist rules, like all members, were subject to punishment.

Nor was Methodist discipline solely imposed by whites on blacks. Evidence suggests that some Methodist slaves monitored one another and reported violations of the *Discipline*. At least two black Methodist women brought charges against black men for sexual assault, and in the trials, evidence was presented on both sides. One of these women, in her testimony, "gave such strong proof of her Chastity" and used "language so modest" that the man she accused was expelled. The other accused a man of "makeing to[o] free" with her; in this case both accuser and accused were suspended after their testimony. As these two cases show, Methodists could hold all members to a standard of behavior that would condemn "sinful" conduct. Slaves who were members had voluntarily joined the church and accepted Methodist morality.[84] The allegations of the two women reveal yet again how some Methodist slaves chose to define themselves in terms radically different from white racist ones. In later antebellum years, a well-articulated planter paternalism encouraged some slave owners to respect slave marriages and to promote monogamy.[85] But in this earlier period, the slaves and free blacks who became Methodists were advancing their own vision of proper conduct, and this vision contradicted white racists' assessments that blacks were sexually promiscuous or prone to immorality. Like the runaways whose masters deemed them "affected," these two women were in their own way proclaiming the right to define themselves.

In conversion, blacks were able to become "new creatures," human beings worthy of God's love and concern. In sanctification, black Methodists could build on these newly constructed selves to create positive gender identities. A bondwoman told Freeborn Garrettson the story of her sanctification. Shortly after her conversion, she became "powerfully convinced of the necessity of sanctification and earnestly sought it by day and night." This woman was extraordinarily faithful to her church. As a slave who "hire[d] her time of her master," she spent many hours in worship—Garrettson

claimed to have seen her often "at five sermons running." She lived alone in a board-
ing house, but evidently her religion helped stave off loneliness, for "she rises several
times in the night to pray." Her prayers for sanctification were answered when God reportedly told her to "Be clean."[86] "Old Elizabeth" had a similar experience. Converted
when a slave, Elizabeth had been free twelve years when, she said, it was "revealed to
me that the Lord had given me the evidence of a clean heart, in which I could rejoice
day and night, and I walked and talked with God, and my soul was illuminated with
heavenly light."[87] In an era when black women were commonly called "wenches"
and the white press unabashedly referred to black women as lascivious, the testimony
of sanctified Methodist women takes on special significance.[88] In seeking and attaining holiness, these women rejected white society's opinions.

While Methodist doctrine encouraged slaves to use their agency and allowed them to
contest racist views on their own terms, the ascetic practices of Methodism helped
slaves cope psychologically with the trials of bondage. Methodism taught that the body
was a vulgar shell that housed the immortal soul, and through such beliefs slaves could
psychically distance themselves from labor and abuse. Old Elizabeth claimed that "many
times while my hands were at work, my spirit was carried away to spiritual things."
Richard Allen reported similar feelings. When working for his self-purchase, he testified, "while my hands were employed to earn my bread, my heart was devoted to my
dear Redeemer." Even free black Methodists, forced by law and custom into unskilled
manual labor or monotonous service jobs, likely found this ability to separate mind and
body in religion a coping mechanism.[89] Psychic distancing was crucially important in
Elizabeth's life as a slave, and this seems to have been passed in her case from mother to
daughter. According to Elizabeth, "At parting, my mother told me that I had 'nobody in
the wide world to look to but God.'" At first, her mother's parting words merely deepened her sense of loneliness, but in time, she reported, "I betook myself to prayer, and
in every lonely place I found an altar." In her world of sorrow, Elizabeth's time with God
was her only comfort. In prayer, she "was filled with sweetness and joy" or even when
working, she "was often carried to distant lands."[90]

In addition to Elizabeth's poignant testimony, we have the story of a slave man
named Cuff, who through religion was enabled to survive horrid brutality and assert
his will. Cuff was sold to a master who despised religion and forbade Cuff to pray or
go to Methodist services. Cuff reportedly replied that while he could obey most of his
master's demands, he could not obey this one, for "My Massa in heaven command me
to pray." Cuff's earthly master was incensed, and after saying "we shall see whose authority is to be obeyed in this matter," he administered twenty-five lashes to Cuff's
"bare back." Still Cuff refused to quit praying, and the master gave twenty-five more.
After this, the bleeding Cuff continued to insist that he would pray, and was beaten
until his master had to "give over from sheer exhaustion."[91] In this dramatic contest
of wills, Cuff cited God's preeminence over his owner as reason to disobey, using language that directly challenged his master's authority over him. His defiance in the face
of his beating and his continual statements to his owner that "you may kill me, but
while I live I must pray"[92] bear witness to his courage and to the strength he found in
his religion. The comfort that religion provided slaves in these dark moments gives us
an idea of how important it was for slaves to have choice in religion, and how their
Methodism enabled them to endure, to survive, and to retain hope.

Certain church rituals seem to have been especially important to black members. Baptism (the only rite besides communion that Methodists viewed as a sacrament) was one of the many ceremonies that emphasized the common humanity of all and the redemption open to all. A slave woman presented herself for baptism at the Hopkins home in the fall of 1790. During the ceremony, "she wept and cryed out for Mercy" and the minister urged her to seek close communion with God "that Jesus might Baptise her with the Holy Ghost and with fire." By the spring of 1791, the Hopkinses had freed their slaves, perhaps in part because they had observed rituals that affirmed slaves' connection to God.[93] Slaves had special reasons to treasure the baptism of their children, for this was the only public ceremony in which their parental role was acknowledged. Methodist clergy seemed to have commonly spoken to mothers before baptizing black children, for one noted that when "asking where the Mother" of an infant was, he had his "poor heart touched" when he found that she had been "sold from the child." A New Kent slave mother was so affected during her child's baptism that "the power struck her as also many others then present." A group of slaves witnessing a baptism of black children heard a short exhortation on "the duties of parents" afterwards and "there were several tears shed" before the minister had finished. Slave parents, especially mothers, affirmed their own sense of obligation to their children through such rituals. And such rituals were dramatic illustrations of slaves' worth before God.[94]

Methodist meetings served many public as well as private purposes for slaves. There were few public arenas in the South where blacks were welcome as participants and not servants, and fewer still that allowed and respected black self-expression. The voices of black worshipers were routinely heard in Methodist services. In love feasts across the South, black members "gave in wonderful experiences," spoke "sensible and feelingly . . . of the work of grace on their hearts," or made a "mighty noise."[95] Black rejoicing and impassioned testimony often emphasized the living power of the Holy Spirit, an emphasis also central to many African religions. Slaves, like all church members, experienced revelation, inspiration, and possession and shouted, fell, or were overcome when touched by the Holy Spirit in services. Phrases like "some of the blacks were much effected," "great shout among the d[ea]r black people," "Believers praisd Jesus with their tongs, Hands, and feet, Particularly among the poor opresd Africans," "great shakeing among the Blacks," or "a wonderful move among the Blacks" are common in the clergy's manuscript journals from this era.[96]

For slaves these periods of inspiration or possession fulfilled many functions. On a personal level, divine contact helped ease earthly burdens. Many slaves were described as being "happy" or "carried away with raptures of joy" in services.[97] All Methodists had reason to cherish releases from worldly sorrow, yet we still must consider the context of slavery as a unique one. The precariousness of life in bondage, with slaves' fate dependent on the good or ill will of their owners, made the Methodist idea of earthly existence as a "vale of tears" a palpable reality. Those moments when slaves could be "happy," whether through religion or otherwise, were thus crucially important to psychological survival. On a communal level, Methodist rituals helped reinforce a sense of separateness and a sense of a special destiny that historians have also found in later antebellum slave testimony and slave spirituals.[98] Henry Boehm reported many happy and emotionally moving love feasts among black members, yet one of July 19, 1800, stood out. It had begun at sunrise, and when Boehm arrived later, "the Dear people was shouting and praising, that God [had] maid them, and redeemd them and converted them, bless the Lord it apeart to me as if the power could sensible be feld as far as sound reacht[.] I dont no, that I ever had such feelings before[—]it apeared as if glory was opend upon earth." Many black members were "over come with the power of God" and fell unconscious—so many that even though some were "hoisted out through a window" and laid outside, only half of the whites, when they arrived for their meeting, could get inside the church. The whites were forced to hold their love feast in the woods.[99]

Boehm had long been exposed to Methodist enthusiasm, so his assessment that he had never felt such power before must be taken quite seriously. So too must the testimony of the blacks that God "maid them, and redeemd them and converted them." Their sense of being God's people, God's creation was real and powerful and they publicly proclaimed it for all present to hear. Though few whites in the South would have denied that African Americans were divinely created, the treatment slaves and free blacks received in the non-Methodist world constantly assaulted their humanity; in communal shouts, black Methodists asserted that they were both human and blessed.[100] Methodist beliefs about the bifurcation of all human experience into the "world's" and "God's" reinforced and, for some slaves, defined this sense of special Christian destiny. Methodist beliefs that slaveholding was inimical to Christianity, when superimposed on the worldly/godly dichotomy, led to the conclusion that slaves would enjoy God's favors while their masters suffered his wrath. One preacher's vision of the afterlife, a vision likely shared by most slaves, was so ordered: "I hope to see most a poor Slave [wrapped] up in God and Heaven [;] their cruel bloody oppressive Masters will sink and burn in Hell fire for ever and ever." This inversion in the afterlife also implicitly conferred moral superiority on earth to slaves—at least to slaves who had converted.[101]

A final aspect of black Methodism that is of central importance is the way slaves and free blacks drew strength from religion to resist slavery and racism. Eugene Genovese, in his seminal study of slavery, defined the two contradictory impulses of Christianity as quietism and revolution. Although there were few slave rebellions in the American South, the three major insurrections and scares all had a religious component. Most Methodist slaves seem to have pursued a course between resignation and rebellion, at least as the terms are secularly construed. In an ideological sense, however, their faith was rebellious, for in Methodism slaves refused to see themselves as property or beasts of burden, and instead saw themselves as a people whom God loved, for whom God had sacrificed his only son, and whom God had destined for a world where their suffering would be avenged. Slaves who converted against their masters' wishes made the act of becoming a Methodist a rebellious one. David Smith had belonged to a family of Catholics who were violently opposed to the Methodists; for Smith, then, becoming a Methodist was at least an act of independence. One obviously exasperated slaveholder chose to rid his household of religious conflict by freeing a slave woman "*because she had too much religion for him.*" When slaves chose a church that their owners despised, they conspicuously rejected their masters' values.[102]

Some Methodist free blacks and slaves were openly assertive; a few were even prepared to fight for their church. A "negro woman, armed with a hoe" rescued preacher

Richmond Nolley from a mob planning to "duck him." Another incident occurred in a Methodist service of 1788. An opponent of Methodism had hired a "fighting man" to beat preacher John Young. One of Young's black followers "would have floged [the hireling] if it had not been prevented."[103] "Old Elizabeth" likewise stood up to white authority. Around 1808, when holding a prayer meeting for black women in Baltimore, she confronted a city watchman who had come to "break up" her meeting. He told her that "people round here cannot sleep for the racket." Elizabeth "soon grew warm and courageous" and boldly asked the watchman why he did not stop the "ungodly" when they were making noise in "dancing and fiddling." She "laid [her] hand upon him and addressed him with gospel truth," asking him not to persecute people worshiping God. He "turned pale and trembled, and begged my pardon," she related, and he promised never to disturb a religious meeting again.[104] A number of black Methodists, like "Old Elizabeth," fought against slavery after they had been emancipated. Richard Allen preached against slavery, and as an African Methodist Episcopal bishop, refused slaveholders admittance to his church, one of the few revisions the African Methodist Espiscopal leaders made in the *Discipline*. Daniel Coker issued a wringing indictment of slavery and of proslavery arguments in 1810.[105]

Running away was another way to protest slavery, and numerous Methodist slaves did just that. The runaway slave Will, his owner claimed, "frequently resorts among the people who call themselves Methodists." Jack, who ran away from George Fitzhugh, was "an artful fellow, and professes himself a Methodist." Solomon Stocksdale's escaped slave Jack, according to his owner, "pretends to be a great Methodist." Another runaway slave named Allick was also said to be "an artful fellow" who "affects to be a Methodist."[106] In his journal William Ormond recorded an extraordinary event involving runaways, although he gave exceedingly few details. In 1800, Ormond was awakened from his sleep by three whites seeking runaway slaves. Ormond recounted that "they attempted to take one, but he cleared himself and gave one of the Men a bad wound." Whether these runaways were being harbored at this Methodist home is unclear. What is striking is that to these slave catchers, the logical place to look was at a Methodist home, where this night slept a noted antislavery Methodist preacher.[107]

We should perhaps leave the general assessment of Methodism's effect on slaves up to a man who had converted while still a bondman. In 1810, Daniel Coker, who would become a bishop of the separate African Methodist Episcopal Church in 1816, authored an antislavery pamphlet, *A Dialogue Between a Virginian and an African Minister*, which was published in Baltimore. Besides being a tour de force of African American antislavery literature, and one of the first works by a black leader in the new nation to promote pride in origins by choosing the name "African," this pamphlet also addressed white fears about Methodists. Coker organized the work as a conversation between a Virginia slaveholder and himself and at one point had the Virginian saying that the Methodist preachers "are forever preaching against slavery (as I understand) and have been instrumental in bringing about the freedom of some thousands in the United States."[108] Coker carefully refuted proslavery arguments based on the Bible, expediency, and fear, and touted the justice of emancipation. But in one dialogue, he urged the Virginian, if he refused to emancipate his slaves, to at least treat them as human beings and to permit them to attend church services. Those masters who kept their slaves from religion, Coker's African Minister said, "do it in order to keep them in a state of ignorance, lest they should become too wise to answer their selfish purposes and too knowing to rest easy, and satisfied in their degraded condition."[109] In Coker's view, Methodism made slaves "too wise" and "too knowing" to wish to remain in bondage. Coker himself, it should be noted, escaped from his Maryland owner to New York soon after his conversion.[110]

As we will see, slave and free black Methodists often came to services at their peril. We must, as a result, take their loyalty to their religion seriously. For thousands of slaves belonging to Methodist owners, the end of the eighteenth century would bring freedom. For many others, the new century would see their hopes of liberty dashed. Slaves and free blacks who joined the church found solace, comfort, and self-worth in its doctrine. Methodism's denunciations of gentry behavior and its inversion of values meant for slaves and free blacks that at least in God's eyes, they were superior to their oppressors, and in services, slaves found one of the few places they could endorse values antithetical to the lifestyles of their owners.

Some free black and slave men rose to leadership positions over black and mixed race societies, further bearing witness to how Methodists differed from the larger slave society. Despite the segregation in some services by race, the church offered more equality and more respect for the personhood of slaves than slaves received from their owners or other whites. Churches were also one of the few public places where slaves could assemble together and speak much of what was on their minds. In Methodist rituals like conversion and sanctification, free blacks and slaves could define themselves as people worthy of God's love and humane treatment, and could publicly assert in these rituals and in testimony their own sense of worth and importance. For those Methodists in bondage, religion provided psychological release from the sorrow, toil, and abuse of slavery.

For some slaves with Methodist owners, the church actually helped procure better treatment. Yet Methodist ministers could not or would not prevent some of the most horrific abuses of slaves. Even when the church did not take action, slaves found in religion consolation and hope for eventual justice. James Meacham witnessed the separation of a slave family in 1789. Their owner had died and the mother and father were willed to a family in the Carolinas, while the children—"one of which a sucking child"—were willed to people in Virginia. Meacham was so horrified that the owner had willed "away with his Sheep and Oxen, the dear purchase of Christ['s] blood" that he lapsed into stream of consciousness later when recording the scene in his journal:

O the crys of the poor captive woman is enough to move the heart of the most obdurate, on her Taking leave of her Children, [']O my Children, my children no more to see my children,['] with her little ones around her crying [']Mamma my Mamma is a going away, I never shall see my Mamma no more['] at last Trembling in the Melting streams of Tears extorts the cry, [']I hope I shall see you again at Judgment Day, whether I am prepared or not I hope to see my children['] and so turned her back upon her tender Plants, for Carolina with her heartrenting screams and cryes, without the least shadow or hope of ever seeing them again while life should last.

This mother's parting words contain both comfort and warning—comfort for her family at the idea of a reunion in heaven and warning for those who would not be so lucky at Judgment. That she spoke in front of white witnesses of "Judgment Day" instead of "heaven" is in itself significant. In her grief and anger, the afterlife became a place of retribution as much as a place where parting would be no more.[111]

Here we see both the Methodist universal and the slave Methodist particular. All Methodists shared the idea that heaven would be a place of family reunion. And it was not unheard of for white Methodists to expect their persecutors or enemies to be found wanting at the bar of Judgment. But no white Methodist ever had to face the horror that this slave mother confronted. Her final words to her children illustrate better than membership statistics, white testimony, and scholarly assessments the importance of religion to Methodist slaves.

✿ F O U R ✿

The Poverty of Riches

Methodists and Class

At Colonel Robert Carter's Nomini Hall, December 24, 1789:
"I exhorted in the Evning the famaly how *hardly Shall a Rich Man
Enter the Kingdom*."

Near Baltimore, Maryland, July 12, 1793: "Visted Mary Davis
poor in circumstance rich in grace."[1]

—Richard Whatcoat

SOUTHERN METHODISTS privately and publicly made numerous comments about the sinfulness of riches and the riches of grace. In these two terse entries of Richard Whatcoat's journal, we see laid bare one of the Methodists' inversions of values. In the stately mansion of Nomini Hall, perhaps provoked by the grandeur and display around him, Brother Whatcoat warned one of the oldest wealthy southern families that their salvation would be well nigh impossible. Far less is known about Mary Davis, who might never have entered the historical record had it not been for her piety. By gender and class a more typical early Methodist, Davis represents the many plain folk converts who found meaning and worth in the church.

Methodists fashioned an ethic that contrasted sharply with the gospel of wealth. They condemned the ostentation and pride of the gentry, and denounced the accumulation of riches as an evil in itself. Methodism taught that men and women must seek to do good in all aspects of their lives and that every choice was vested with moral consequences. Methodists thus faulted the rich for what they did with their money as well as for the good they failed to do with it. In a church that prized righteousness above all else, poor and struggling Methodists viewed themselves with self-respect and dignity even though they lived in a world where poverty was deemed a failure. By praising industry, thrift, and modest living, by finding virtue in poverty, Methodists ordered their world so that southern elites were morally suspect. When surrounded by their predominantly plain folk members in Methodist services, itinerants ignored the code of honor and lashed out at the wealthy, their lifestyles, and their values. In their churches and meetings, Methodists created a place where secular rankings were set aside and where mutual respect characterized the interactions between people of different classes. Instead of focusing on the exterior, on display, and on the opinion of others, Methodists focused on the inner quality of the individual's heart. A person's worth, to Methodists, was divorced from what they owned and how they were perceived by the "world." A "poor" but pious Mary Davis was the superior of an impious gentleman, both in the eyes of God and in the eyes of her fellow Methodists.[2]

Attitudes toward wealth and poverty, class and hierarchy were in flux during the Revolutionary and early national period, and Methodists, like their contemporaries, participated in the effort to overthrow traditional notions about status and rank. Historians profoundly disagree about the nature of evangelical moral economy. Scholars looking at the Arminian thrust of northern nineteenth-century revivalism argue that petty capitalists and the rising bourgeoisie, frightened by their loss of control over workers, embraced and promoted a theology of self-control and self-restraint. Arminianism, with its individualistic thrust, allowed the bourgeoisie to surrender responsibility for their workers' well-being and encouraged workers to see themselves as responsible for their fate. The doctrine of free will thus functioned to place the onus of success or failure in the nascent capitalist economy on the individual. If a man were sober, industrious, and self-critical, he expected to prosper—at least in the afterlife.[3]

Historians of the American South have wrestled with different issues. Most agree that evangelicals offered some criticism of gentry values, but the nature of the critique and the extent to which gentry hegemony survived the evangelical challenge is a matter of intense debate. Those scholars who see the postwar South as precapitalist argue that despite harangues against ostentation, evangelicalism was, at its heart, compatible with planter hegemony. Other historians have emphasized the countercultural nature of evangelicalism and argue that it provided a significant alternative to the gentry's worldview. Southern historians have taken women and gender seriously, with the most compelling and sophisticated paradigm positing that evangelicals valued order and hierarchy in the household, an explanation that aptly links gentry dominance with patriarchy and slavery.[4]

The southern Methodist experience casts serious doubt upon the characterization of Arminianism as "bourgeois." The values of sobriety, industry, and thrift, as well as the belief that every convert should master the self and control his or her behavior, were all part of the Methodist message from the sect's first forays into the pre-Revolutionary South. Long before Charles G. Finney began to copy the successful rituals and theology of Methodist revivalists, southern Methodists had set much of the South aflame with religious fervor. Plain folk of the early American South (precious few of whom could be considered "bourgeois") embraced Arminianism in a context far removed in time and place from concerns about unruly wage laborers. The southern Methodist experience also shows that, in this early period, planter hegemony and Methodist values were decidedly at odds. Gentry opposition to the Methodists was repeated and vocal; elites certainly did not perceive the Methodists as allies, but as enemies at worst, as a nuisance at best. Elite scorn was, in many ways, predictable. In a culture that viewed success as a testament to familial standing and personal character, where status, power, and wealth were intrinsically connected, where self-mastery was deemed possible only for those who mastered others, the Methodists' strong denunciations of elite display and pride were bound to provoke wrath.[5]

Methodists based their views of wealth, industry, and poverty on Wesley's writings, on their reading of the Bible (especially the New Testament), and on their observations and experiences in the South. Methodists brought Wesley's theology to the New

World; they did not fashion their views of wealth in reaction to southern elites.[6] Wesley wrote copiously about wealth and its bearing on salvation, and many of these writings were reprinted in America and quoted by southern members. The inaugural 1789 issue of the American Methodist periodical the *Arminian Magazine* published a Wesley sermon on the text "They that will be rich, fall into temptation and a snare, and into many foolish and hurtful desires, which drown men in destruction and perdition" (1 Timothy 6: 9). Wesley strictly defined riches as "more than food and *coverings*," although he considered this verse particularly aimed at those who "*lay up treasures on earth*."[7] Wealth, in Wesley's eyes, led to three sorts of sins—sins of the flesh; sins of the eye; and the greatest sin of the three, pride. After denouncing gluttony, "elegant epicurism," and those who took "supreme delight" in learning, Wesley devoted most of his sermon to the sin of pride. To seek the "esteem, admiration, and applause of men" was to turn from God. The proud rich, in Wesley's view, missed out on the trials by which God chastened humanity. In "avoiding every cross, every degree of trouble, danger, difficulty," men and women could not be made perfect. Wesley cautioned the rich that wealth insulated them from suffering, and thus from the spiritual blessings that came with suffering.[8]

For Wesley, though, the temptations to sin and ease were merely by-products of a greater evil. Wealth was intrinsically wrong because it led to an imbalanced distribution of God's material gifts and encouraged people to choose a worldly path. Wesley believed that life presented a series of choices between good and evil, and he urged faithful Methodists to make every decision—even the most routine ones—carefully and introspectively, with the good and God's will in mind. In his essay on dress (which was often reprinted in America), he stressed that even ordinary choices had moral consequences. In condemning ornamentation and "superfluity" of dress (such as "gold and costly apparel," "high heads, enormous bonnets, ruffles, or rings"),[9] Wesley was little different from other pietists who shared his view that finery and fashion engendered pride, vanity, and lust. But Wesley's most passionate and original arguments linked plain dress to benevolence, and posed the issue in terms of an absolute choice: "the more you lay out on your own apparel, the less you have to clothe the naked, to feed the hungry, to lodge the strangers, to relieve those that are sick and in prison, and to lessen the numberless afflictions to which we are exposed in this vale of tears."[10]

To illustrate, Wesley dramatically recounted an incident from his days at Oxford. His college maid was working in a thin cotton dress and winter was fast approaching. Wesley reached in his pockets for money to give her for a coat, but none was there—he had spent it on pictures for his walls. He imagined a conversation at the bar of Judgment about this very incident. The Lord, in Wesley's vision, berated him: "'Thou hast adorned thy walls with the money which might have screened this poor creature from the cold!'" Wesley enjoined his followers not to make the same mistake: "Are not these pictures the blood of this poor maid! See thy expensive apparel in the same light: thy Gown, Hat, Head-dress! Every thing about thee which cost more than Christian Duty required thee to lay out, is the blood of the poor!"[11] Using such dramatic imagery, Wesley hoped to revise Methodists' assumptions about moral agency and self-conscious action, to reformulate their notions of direct and indirect causation. Just as God had causally linked the maid's suffering to Wesley's unthinking decision to buy pictures, the wealthy were responsible both for the direct suffering they might cause others and for the indirect consequences of their possessions and spending. Wesley's justification for such causal thinking rested on a radical notion of property. Everything on earth, in his view, belonged to God: "he only *lends* them to us: or to speak more strictly, *entrusts* them to us as stewards."[12]

The stewardship Wesley envisioned was much more than disinterested gifts to charities; the ideal Methodist would ascetically refuse to accumulate wealth. God allowed men and women to feed, clothe, and shelter their own household, to retain enough funds to carry on their businesses, and to leave a modest inheritance for their children. All else of this world's goods, in Wesley's ethic, were to be given to others. He counseled Methodists to "look upon yourself as one of a certain number of indigent persons, who are to be provided for out of that portion of his [God's] goods, wherewith you are entrusted."[13] The American *Discipline*, spelled this out in no uncertain terms: Methodists were forbidden from "Laying up treasure upon earth."[14]

Because of their founder's views, formulated decades before Methodists came to America, Wesley's missionaries were predisposed to be critical of the southern gentry. Southern elites, like those in Britain, with their conspicuous consumption, ostentation, idleness, code of honor, and pride, were a countermodel of Methodist piety. Horse racing, fancy clothes, mansions, imported luxuries, fox hunting, and the ubiquitous balls—those pleasures that set the southern gentry apart from their poorer neighbors—were deemed sinful by Methodists. The fact that most wealthy southerners depended on the labor of slaves for their lifestyles compounded, in Methodists' views, the danger. Slavery, which was for most preachers a sin in itself, encouraged idleness, pride, cruelty, and dissipation in masters. Methodists saw hard work (when done for oneself) as ennobling. Methodists' disgust with masters' lifestyles was most marked when they contrasted free states and territories to the slave South. In Ohio, James Smith remarked, all were "on an equality; pride and slavery are equally strangers; industry is seen in all."[15] Unlike Puritans, who saw material success as evidence of God's favor, Methodists encouraged "industry" in an ideological context in which accumulated riches were patently sinful, especially when acquired by slave labor.

This ethic of hard work, humility, unstinting benevolence, and hostility to wealth challenged values at the core of southern elite culture. Southern elites certainly did not invest every consumer decision with the moral weight Wesley recommended. More significant was the principle underlying the Methodist position on wealth: that people were to cultivate and then obey inner moral voices and to look only to God for confirmation of their worth. What plain folk Methodists and non-Methodist elites both seemed to understand was that conspicuous consumption and ostentation were in and of themselves less important than what they represented in southern culture. The southern gentry typically judged themselves by the way others of their class saw them, or as Wesley might have put it, sought the "esteem, admiration, and applause of men." The urge to *appear* genteel and honorable was so strong that elites even risked bankruptcy by importing goods they could not afford and death by engaging in duels. Methodists were not oblivious to the opinions of others; they were warned to behave in ways that did not bring reproach to themselves, their church, or the gospel. Yet such a standard was qualitatively different from the notion that one's worth was measured by what others thought. For Methodists, finery and ostentation were symptoms of the depravity of southern values; the other-directed culture of honor was the disease itself.[16]

To say that southern elites were a countermodel of Methodist piety is to examine the two mentalities from the Methodist vantage point. We might (as elites did) invert the formula: Methodists were a countermodel of southern elite values. The gentry especially despised Methodist preachers, who seemed to embody everything that was wrong with the sect. Usually landless, many times carrying what they owned, itinerants wandered about begging for donations among people who could little afford to give. Often disheveled, sometimes ragged, and usually dressed in simple clothes, Methodist preachers lacked erudition, spoke in rustic metaphors, and a few were even illiterate. In the pulpit, they shrieked, wept, stamped their feet, and thundered, totally disregarding the solemnity due God in worship. (The reactions of "weak" listeners, elites believed, were predictably grotesque.) Preachers, moreover, acted as if they were the equals of the gentry. If all these horrors were not enough, these ignorant preachers sermonized against pride, honor, finery, slavery, and riches to a mostly poor and plain folk, overwhelmingly female, and usually mixed-race audience. The Revolution had replaced a hierarchy of birth with a hierarchy of talents, leading to a quasi-religious belief that those who attained wealth were, in the new republic, deserving of it. This upstart sect, however, had the nerve to suggest that these deserving elites were going to hell. In short, Methodists trampled on or denounced most things elites held dear.[17]

Methodist preachers discounted elite criticism and echoed Wesley's ethos—many borrowing his exact language—in the South. Freeborn Garrettson, when collecting donations for a poor widow, told Methodists that those who "give to the poor lend to the Lord" and many ministers connected wealth, idleness, and ostentation with sin.[18] Two of preachers' more popular sermons in the South involved explicit condemnations of wealth. The first was the parable of Lazarus and the Rich Man from Luke.[19] This cautionary fable told how a man rich in life received hell's torment in death, while Lazarus, a sore-ridden beggar who ate crumbs that fell from the rich man's table in life, was "comforted" in "Abraham's bosom" in death. This passage in no way faults the wealthy man for indifference or lack of charity; it merely posits an afterlife in which earthly conditions are reversed. When the wealthy man cried to Abraham for water to cool hell's flame, the Patriarch replied: "Son, remember that thou in thy lifetime receivedst thy good things, and likewise Lazarus evil things: but now he is comforted, and thou art tormented." Perhaps the implicit sin was lack of charity, yet the explicit sin was having wealth.

For those rich listeners looking for a sermon a bit less condemnatory, there was always the moralistic New Testament query "What is a man profited, if he shall gain the whole world, and lose his own soul?" This sermon, which does not condemn gain per se, was preached throughout the South by various clergy.[20] There is evidence to suggest that this sermon was, on rare occasion, effective in reaching wealthy women. Jesse Lee spoke on this text on March 30, 1788, in Petersburg, Virginia. He noted that "a woman finely dressed" near the preaching stand "trembled and shook as though she had an ague." Several young women rushed to the wealthy woman's side, and prayed for her until she was converted.[21] At least one wealthy woman overcame her class prejudice against Methodism by recalling this verse. Rebecca Dorsey Ridgely, daughter of the wealthy Dorseys and wife of the rich and powerful Captain Ridgely, went to hear a Methodist preach in 1774. The sermon touched Rebecca, who found herself kneeling to pray, even though, she later recalled, "it then was a shame to kneel before the people" (especially, we might add, for the gentry). Yet Rebecca was so moved by the Methodists that she overcame her "shame to kneel," comforting herself with Christ's question: "But o I thought what is all the world to me if I must lose my soul[?]" Ridgely interpreted the popular sermon text precisely as ministers intended—earthly riches were meaningless without piety.[22]

Methodists had many other verses near to hand—including the one that claimed that it was easier "for a camel to go through the eye of a needle, than for a rich man to enter into the kingdom of God"—but just as important as sermons were clerical attitudes hostile to wealth, such as those Whatcoat evinced at Nomini Hall. Garrettson's wry comment in eastern Virginia was typical. He noted on March 26, 1782, that he had preached "to an audience of *what is called* the better sort," taking care, as many clergy did, to distinguish worldly terminology from religious. Five years later Garrettson offhandedly compared religion in Worcester, Maryland, where people were "poor, but blest" with that in the Sound, where they were "richer, and have less religion." In western Virginia, minister John Kobler similarly noted that in one audience were several well-dressed women "which called themselves [Ladies]," and later commented how in a group of wealthy Methodists "some of them has bowed greatly but not far enough yet."[23] Remarks like these were ubiquitous. In preachers' minds, southern elites were in the main haughty and irreligious.

Ministers often reminded the gentry that earthly wealth was transitory. Preacher William Chandler was staying at the home of a wealthy man named Major Kerr, who had shown unusual hospitality and kindness to the Methodists "though he was emphatically a man of the world." Walking with Kerr in his parlor, Chandler turned and told him, "'Well, major, this mansion is too beautiful to leave behind you, and yet you will soon have to leave it and go to that narrow house appointed for all living." Ezekiel Cooper, on a visit to the wealthy Captain Ridgely (Rebecca Ridgely's husband), found himself fearing for Ridgely's eternal fate: "How dangerous it is to possess such buildings and riches! Very apt to draw the mind from God—we had better be like Lazarith [sic], here to beg crums [sic] of bread, and hereafter go to glory."[24] It is unlikely that such strong disapproval went unnoticed by wealthy men and women.

Southern Methodists, as had Wesley, held the wealthy responsible for the direct and indirect consequences of their spending habits. Cooper once railed against ornate funerals with "parade, equipage, and pomp" attendant. Money would be better spent, in his view, to "cloath and feed a number of poor widows and orphans for some time; or school several poor children."[25] As in Wesley's college story, Cooper posited a stark choice—*either* funereal pomp *or* orphanages. Even southern elites who were committed to austerity probably found such reasoning absurdly ascetic. For Methodists, constantly urged to seek not their own, but God's will, every action involved such stark choices. And as Wesley and Cooper believed, God always wanted them to use their money to do good.

Lay people were also steeped in Wesleyan ideology. In a letter from a poor cousin, Eleanor Dorsey, to one of the wealthiest Methodist men in early America, Maryland's Harry Dorsey Gough, we can see many of the clergy's arguments put to use. Dorsey had moved to Lyons Town, New York, and wrote Gough for money to build a chapel there. Dorsey was a master of Methodist ideals and rhetoric, and she alternatively pushed and pulled Gough for a contribution. She began by asserting that she hoped to meet her cousin in heaven, a typical sentiment in letters between separated Methodist kin. "But," she cautioned, "let us first do all the good we can on earth."[26] "[T]he Lord has given you an abundance of this worlds goods," Dorsey reminded Gough, "and when I tell you your poor Breathren in this wilderness have need, hope you'll not shut up your Bowels of compassion." She appealed to the idea of an extended family of all Methodists ("your poor Breathren") and to New Testament teaching, paraphrasing Saint John's first epistle: "But whoso hath this world's good, and seeth his brother have need, and shutteth up his bowels *of compassion* from him, how dwelleth the love of God in him?" In the "wilderness," Dorsey continued, "money is very scearce and most of the people poor." She was apologetic, although by no means deferential, about asking him and the other "ritch Breathren" of Maryland again for money, but she was begging for God's work.[27]

Eleanor Dorsey had not yet exhausted her arguments. She lectured Gough on Christ's maxim that "it is more Blessed to give than to receive," and in language so close to John Wesley's that there is little doubt that she had read or heard read his sermon, she counseled "in those things it is only lending to the Lord." Unfortunately, we do not know if the bowels of Squire Gough and his rich Maryland Methodist brethren were shut up or not. What is clear is that Dorsey's language and reasoning closely followed that of Methodism's founder, an indication that Wesleyan views on wealth were accepted by American members. At least once prior to this, Dorsey had convinced rich Marylanders to donate money to their poor Brethren. Thus, we might conclude that she used arguments that she had cause to believe would work.[28] Her unabashed moralizing and her lack of deference suggests that she had largely internalized Methodist values. She was at least Gough's equal, and she implied that if he did not lend her the money, he was not a true Christian, which would make her his better.

In an era when property was an intrinsic part of liberty, it is questionable whether wealthy Methodists truly believed that they were merely borrowing their goods from the Lord. Few rich Methodists made the level of sacrifice encouraged by Wesley. Yet, as one minister noted, the early church's survival was heavily dependent on wealthy members, whose contributions were distributed among the poorer districts.[29] Because most of their members were slaves, lower-class or yeoman whites, and women, Methodists needed the minority of wealthy male members to keep the church, the publishing concern, and its few schools and charities afloat. The largest number of wealthy Methodists resided in Baltimore, and preachers often begged members there for money. In late 1792 and early 1793, Richard Whatcoat pleaded with Baltimore members for money to build a charity school—in addition to collecting donations for the poor and needy. In June of 1793, Whatcoat was again begging in Baltimore, this time for money to build a meetinghouse in Wilmington. South Carolina's James Rembert had it far worse than the Baltimore gentry. In 1794, he was the only Methodist steward in Santee circuit, South Carolina, and covered any debts the sect incurred out of his own pocket.[30] Clergy were uncomfortable about this dependence, which may in part account for the seeming rudeness they exhibited among the wealthy.

Methodists publicly warned southerners about the danger of conflating self-worth with the opinion of others. Jesse Lee delivered a sermon in Delaware that denounced both wealth and the gentry value of honor. He described those bound by honor as people desiring "the praise of men; to be esteemed, admired, beloved, or flattered." Honor was a special temptation to the rich, for "men may be bewitched by the world" and "those persons who are in affluent circumstances, are more likely to be drawn aside from following the Lord by the love of the world."[31] Similar denunciations of honor cropped up frequently when preachers compared their poor or slave members to the unbelieving rich. Writing in 1804 of Methodist progress in the Mississippi territory, Hezekiah Harriman noted that close to thirty blacks had "joined the society," while his white hearers (although "serious and attentive") kept their distance. "Some are like Agrippa, almost persuaded to be Christians," he wrote of Mississippi whites, "but pride, and the honour of the world, have hitherto hindered them."[32] Harriman may have oversimplified, but the routine jeers and mocking of hostile onlookers at so many services were surely vivid reminders of the price honor's defenders would exact from those who joined the Methodists. In Kentucky, John Kobler observed that some "hard sinners was brought to weep" in a service, but afterwards, their "wicked asociates . . . made sport and laughed at them."[33] To be caught weeping in public was bad enough; to become the object of ridicule was even worse.

Kobler thought there was biblical precedent for the attitudes he encountered. In 1795, he preached "to a very delicate congregation that strove harder to behave well" than "to worship God." "O how hardly can they that have riches enter into the Kingdom of God," Kobler lamented. His analysis of why this audience was not interested in Methodism shows his understanding of the code of honor: "it is too far for proud nature to stoop from the top of honour so high, down to the low degraded cross of Jesus." Kobler comforted himself with the thought that "Thus it was when the [Messiah] was upon the earth[;] while the nobility rejected the council of God against themselves—the common people heard him gladly." In Kobler's mind, Christianity inherently warned the "nobility . . . against themselves" while common people lived naturally more Christian lives. On New River circuit in the Blue Ridge highlands, when Kobler attracted some wealthy people to the church, he attributed his success to divine intervention: "God . . . is about doing [miracles] . . . even to the drawing of cammels thro the needles eye." "[T]he noble and the wise," he remarked, again alluding to the other-directed culture of honor, "have so many eyes upon them."[34] The contrast between the Methodist ethos and the southern code of honor was reinforced by both the church and its critics.

Methodist views about the evils of wealth and honor help explain why the church was unpopular among the gentry, but they do not fully explain why so many middling and poor people embraced the church. We cannot assume that plain folk seethed with such class resentment that they were ready to embrace any ideology that condemned elite ways. Moreover, republicanism offered a secular version of Methodists' views on wealth, one that did not require intense introspection or the renunciation of the code of honor. Part of the reason that Methodism was successful among the lower and middle classes lay precisely in the timing, for in the late eighteenth century, inherited values and traditional ways became open for discussion, among them the cultural and social hegemony of elites. Secular political rhetoric of equality and democracy dovetailed nicely with Methodist beliefs. For those living in the settled areas of the South, who had long watched wealthy neighbors parade in carriages, build elaborate mansions, dress in the latest European fashions, and lord it over them in courthouses, town squares, and Anglican churches, the leveling tendencies of the Methodists, much like those of the Baptists analyzed by Rhys Isaac, must have seemed an extension of democratic ways from the political to the religious world.[35]

It is perhaps worth comparing the customs of Anglicans with those of the Methodists. Anglican pews were filled by rank, with the wealthiest and most prominent families seated nearest the parson, and symbolically, closer to God; the rearmost pews were reserved for the parish poor. The gentry paraded into Sunday church services at the last moment and were also the first to leave. Local vestries controlled much of the content of the parson's sermon, as well as the distribution of charity to the "deserving" poor of the parish. Anglican clergy were separated from the poor by their education, salary, and clothing, with their black priestly gowns symbolizing their erudition and status in the congregation.[36] Early Methodists, in contrast, met as often in barns, private homes, or out-of-doors as they did in meetinghouses. Their churches, when built, were architecturally simple; windows were often a luxury. Preachers stood on makeshift tables or behind plain podiums. Inside church buildings, Methodists did often divide their congregants by gender and race, but white women and white men did not fill the pews in order of wealth. As Methodists, common whites could come together with each other and create a community free of the arrogance, ranking, and status-laden rituals of the secular and Anglican world.[37]

Poor and yeoman whites may also have been attracted to the church because its preachers articulated their values and represented their interests. Their ministers often engaged in debates and confrontations with the wealthy, and perhaps more important, acquitted themselves well in these encounters. When surrounded by plain folk members in services, Methodist preachers were not afraid to rail against wealth, ostentation, or pride. Jacob Young colorfully recounted a prolonged contest between poor parsons and the gentry in a Mississippi camp meeting. Preacher James Axley, with some "splendidly dressed" hearers in attendance, launched into a sermon "against superfluous ornaments, and the passions, pride, and vanity" that caused them. The wealthy "Madame Turnbull" (perhaps feeling Axley's eye upon her as he spoke) bid a hasty retreat under the insult, taking with her a "gay daughter" and her slaves. Axley caught up with Turnbull before she left, "made some apologies," and bid her return the next day, where, with her husband ("Esquire Turnbull," a justice of the peace) now in the audience, she was treated to an Axley sermon against "pride and vainglory." The stakes, we should note, had now been raised. It was one thing to insult a wealthy woman and quite another to insult both her and her husband, and to do so with her husband, who was obliged to defend her from public attack, according to the code of honor, present. Esquire Turnbull predictably rose during the sermon and demanded that he be allowed to reply. Minutes later, with Axley in tears and Turnbull shouting for another gentleman to help him remove the "insulting" Axley from the stand, the service was in disarray.[38]

Enter the indomitable and eccentric preacher Lorenzo Dow (who heretofore lay sick in his tent). Dow strode to the pulpit, quieted the audience, and proceeded to speak about the ostensibly uncontroversial subject of the American Revolution. Turning from his praise for the war's aims to the law, Dow extolled the virtues of a constitutional republic that guaranteed a host of freedoms to its citizens, including freedom of religion. His audience, including the Turnbulls, likely found all of this familiar and easy enough to approve. (The Methodists who had heard Dow before may well have held their breath, knowing that "Crazy Dow" had a method to his madness.) In a paroxysm of patriotic fervor, Dow even recited the "oath of office" that bound all government officials to support and defend the Constitution. And then Dow came to the point. Any man, he harangued, "who would interrupt a Methodist preacher" during a service was a "mean, low-lived scoundrel" and any official who did the same was, because he had sworn the very oath of office Dow had just repeated, a "perjured villain." According to Young, the "angry" Esquire Turnbull knew he had been bested and quietly left the camp grounds with his family.[39] Whether or not the contest went as well for the parsons as Young described, such dramas effectively shifted public power from wealthy southerners to the poor men denouncing them. Axley and Dow were able to critique the gentry in a public setting, perhaps saying much of what the Turnbulls' poorer neighbors and slaves had been thinking. Itinerants were not dependent on local credit networks or on the services wealthy planters provided their poorer neighbors; they could speak for their lower-class parishioners without fear of economic retribution. Common people—white and black, men and women—at this camp meeting witnessed a contest between two sets of values. In effect, Methodists carved out public spaces where such contests could be fought between the classes on terms closest to equality afforded in the South. It might even be argued that, surrounded as they were by their supportive members, poor parsons had the advantage.

Preachers were ideally suited to publicly represent the southern plain folk, whom they emulated in behavior, dress, and lifestyle. A majority of southern preachers came from modest backgrounds, and those who came from wealthy families voluntarily eschewed comfort and luxury to itinerate. Itinerants chose lives of poverty and depended on the donations of others for their food, clothing, and shelter. Ministers visited, lodged, and supped with plain folk far more often than they stayed in mansions. On the first round of a new circuit in central Kentucky, Jacob Young stopped at an isolated "little log cabin . . . with no stable or outbuilding of any kind." Sister Carson, her husband gone from home, was reluctant to let him stay until she realized he was a Methodist preacher. Then, her "eyes fairly sparkled" and she happily ushered Young inside and fetched "good sound corn" for his horse. In the small and sparsely furnished cabin, Young was treated to a supper of "corn bread, fried venison, and crop-vine tea." Countless plain folk like Sister Carson provided shelter, food, and company for itinerants. Such generosity and intimacy made for strong ties between preachers and common whites.[40]

In parts of the South, especially the low-country regions of the seaboard states, the membership consisted primarily of men and women for whom a season of bad weather could spell ruin. About fifteen miles north of Clarksburg, Virginia, itinerant Henry Smith discovered a society of what he called "backwoods people." These members "came to meeting in backwoods style—all on foot." One old man had on shoes and the local preacher had on "Indian moccasins," but "every man, woman, and child besides, was barefooted." Judging by Wesleyan standards, Smith found these "backwoods" people spiritually rich: "if there were no shoes and fine dresses in the congregation, there were attentive hearers, and feeling hearts, for the melting power of the Lord came down upon us."[41] Preacher John Kobler stayed with a member "of low circumstance" in Tennessee and in typical Methodist fashion Kobler used the event to remind himself that wealth without piety was meaningless. "Better to me is a dry morsel in the house of the poor," he remarked, "than the richest fattings in the apartments of the ungodly."[42]

Preachers sometimes complained of bedbugs and dirt, of homes filled with smoke or animals, but normally they were grateful for plain folk hospitality and companionship. Methodist preachers were specifically directed to avoid the arrogance Anglican parsons had exhibited toward their middling and lower-class parishioners. Preachers were urged to "Be ashamed of nothing but sin: not of fetching wood . . . or drawing water: not of cleaning your own shoes, or your neighbor's." Of profoundest significance was the distinction the church drew between religious and secular rankings. "Do not affect the gentleman," the 1784 *Discipline* cautioned, for "A preacher of the gospel is the servant of all."[43] For Methodists in this early era, the term "gentleman" was used almost solely as a pejorative; a "gentleman" embodied all that was sinful and worldly in the South. Preachers were respected, admired, and loved by their members. Unlike other eminent men, preachers led without patronizing.[44]

Methodist preachers also frequently refused to show deference to elites to whom by secular standards deference was due. Jeremiah Norman was the exception to the rule, but his attitudes reveal how most ministers behaved. Norman believed that his fellow preachers were not deferential enough or genteel enough to reach the wealthy. "There is a kind of humble politeness necessary for the accomplishment of a preacher—in this refined age," Norman wrote, "but there is few that attend to it and therefore offend unnecessarily which makes them unprofitable among the better sort in the world." It was probably easy for a minister risen from the lower class to "offend" in numerous ways, as, for example, William Ormond did when eating at a North Carolinian's. Ormond found his host a "curious Old Man!" because "you must not make a noise with your lips when you sup at his table."[45]

Preachers' private interactions with southern elites were sometimes delicate balancing acts. It was not easy to eschew the deference and humility required by secular culture, represent the Methodists in a favorable light, and adhere to Wesleyan ideas about the sinfulness of wealth at the same time. In 1806, Bishop Asbury had an encounter with a southern judge that illustrates his effort to craft polite relationships without bowing to secular customs: "I visited Charles Tait, a judge; I did not present myself in the character of a gentleman, but as a Christian, and a Christian minister: I would visit the President of the United States in no other character; true, I would be innocently polite and respectful—no more. As to the Presbyterian ministers, and all ministers of the Gospel . . . to humble ourselves before those who think themselves so much above the Methodist preachers by worldly honours, by learning, and especially by salary, will do them no good." Asbury's sensitivity to the disdain of competing clergy is self-evident, but there is far more than wounded pride at work here. He self-consciously tried to find a mode of polite interaction that would not merely replicate worldly notions of rank and status. For a moment, he even consciously set aside the high premium Wesleyans placed on humility, embracing instead the pride he so often denounced in others. And he was especially eager to avoid appearing obsequious. "I spent the evening with one of the great," he noted of another such encounter, "the Lord and his own conscience will witness that I did not flatter him."[46] While a middle ground between rudeness and deference was sometimes difficult to find, preachers' efforts to be dignified and civil without being deferential offered one model for their plain folk members to follow.

For poor and middling southerners, to join the Methodists would to some degree have meant registering dissent against gentry lifestyles, values, and standards of success. In the church, moreover, there were times when plain folk religion conquered unbelieving elites. A Sussex County, Virginia, revival of 1787 provided one such drama. In Sussex, hundreds, both blacks and whites, "fell down, and lay helpless on the floor, or the ground," a high level of participation indeed. The whole audience "roared and screamed" so loud during one service that the preacher could not finish his sermon. What deserved special comment in this revival, however, was the reaction of the gentry: "Many of the wealthy people, both men and women, were seen lying in the dust, sweating and rolling on the ground, in their fine broad cloths or silks, crying for mercy."[47] What a picture this must have made for their poor neighbors! How gratifying it must have been to see the great and powerful struck down by God, convinced of their wretchedness, and crying for mercy. As the minister observed, these wealthy men and women were wearing uniforms of class distinction, clothes that clearly identified them as rich. For the poor who observed this scene, the leveling judgment of God would have been made evident as bondman and master, bondwoman and mistress all gained awareness of their sinful state. Such a display would not, we should note, have compensated for the vast inequalities of wealth and power in a substantive way, yet in an important psychological sense, these hours of writhing and crying must have demonstrated that God's ways and Virginia's ways were not the same.

Another reason yeoman whites might have been attracted to the church was that Methodists tried to help their needy members, and did so in ways that allowed the poor to retain self-respect. Methodist charity was often handled informally, by gifts from preachers to needy members. Richard Whatcoat, who also worked tirelessly to raise money in the Baltimore area for the education of poor Methodist children, dispensed aid to Methodists on his rounds. For Sister Holmes and "Poor" John Beates, there was money, for Sister Deleaney, a "pare of Shoes."[48] Since the clergy frequently lodged with the poor, they could directly assess need. Henry Boehm remembered how whenever he and Asbury, who were traveling together in the early 1800's, were given money, the bishop quickly gave it away to the poor, as "he was restless till it was gone." When a grateful convert insisted that Freeborn Garrettson take eighty continental dollars for saving his soul, Garrettson that same day gave the money to a needy man. Sometimes lay members were just as benevolent. Doctor Hinde of Kentucky, we will recall, was charitable to a fault. He reportedly never tried to collect his debts, and if someone did pay him, he would give the money to the next female member he saw. These informal donations must have left the recipients with more self-respect and personal dignity than previous Anglican relief methods. Instead of pleading for help before a panel of the wealthiest local men, the Methodist poor could expect aid from those closer to their own class, or, in the case of Hinde, from rich southerners who had voluntarily abandoned the external trappings of wealth and adopted plain folk ways.[49]

What is even more striking is how often the poor contributed their meager monies to the church. A poor elderly black woman of Charleston who "support[ed] herself by picking oakum, and the charity of her friends" tried to give Bishop Asbury a French crown because "she had been distressed on [his] account." Slaves and free blacks near Cumberland, Virginia, "bestowed their presents of pears and apples" to one preacher. During a hot and barren 1796 summer, when many people in Sampson, Cumberland, and Bladen counties of North Carolina were "very near Perishing," one "kind sister" shared a "dunghill fowl" with her preacher for supper. These contributions strongly suggest that the poor of the church believed benevolence to be a universal duty; all could support God's work, each within his or her means. By sharing what little they had with the church, poor Methodists—who might some future day become the recipients of such charity—were able to become benefactors.[50]

Methodists saw virtue in poverty, a position that historians often associate with accommodation to the status quo. George Reed told his listeners in a sermon that if they were poor it was because God "sees poverty best for you; he sees prosperity might prove your ruin." Reed's analysis, taken alone, does seem to suggest resignation to existing inequalities. But preachers were just as earnest about "prosperity" proving ruinous as they were about the virtues of poverty, and thus where elites were concerned, their ethic was oppositional. Their experience confirmed a pattern that they believed traced back to Christ's era. In the South, the poor *were* more receptive to Methodism, so much so that some preachers began to feel they were specifically sent to the poor. Francis Asbury's attitude was typical. In 1789, he remarked that "to begin at the right end of the work is to go first to the *poor*; these *will*, the rich *may possibly*, hear the truth." Again in 1804, while observing an "elegant church" that the once outcast Baptists had built in Georgetown, South Carolina, he noted that the Baptists "take the rich; and the commonalty and the slaves fall to us: this is well."[51]

The equation of poverty with receptivity to Christianity, and its corollary—the equation of wealth with sin—did blunt Methodists' assault on the inequalities of wealth in their time. There was radical potential in the idea that every economic choice should be made with the good in mind, but southern Methodists did not exploit this potential beyond urging wealthy Methodists to alter their own behavior. Here, as elsewhere, Methodists believed that change began with the individual and his or her conversion. In their fully religious outlook, the contrast between poverty and wealth was almost synonymous with the contrast between converted and unconverted. While such a notion helped poor and struggling members feel worthier and more righteous, it did not address the social system that produced economic inequality and its attendant ills. It was only natural, Methodists believed, that the rich would ignore their message and the poor take heed. Despite the limits of their vision, Methodists proffered a clear alternative to gentry values, one that forced rich converts to alter their behavior in substantive ways and offered poor converts a measure of pride and self-respect.

Take the case of Jane Craig, whom James Finley described as a "poor old Irish woman." Craig insisted on donating regularly to the church. When Finley suggested she was "too poor" and "too old" to contribute, she practically rebuked him, saying: "Bless God for poverty. I have none of the world, and there is nothing to take my mind off of Jesus, my blessed Savior. I should feel very unhappy and ungrateful if I did not give something to help on the cause of my blessed Master." Her words echoed those of the clergy, who since their arrival in America had been preaching that wealth and the "things of the world" were impediments to true Christianity. It is distinctly possible that Finley exaggerated her response. But what were her options? Being poor, old, female, and probably widowed, Jane Craig had little chance for upward social mobility.[52] Most Methodist societies had members like Craig. Sister Row, who lived in or near Orange County, Virginia, was also "under many distressing circumstances." Row, a widow, had "seven small children . . . one . . . scarcely able to help another."[53] Members like Row and Craig could not aspire to independence or wealth; they faced a lifetime of struggling to survive. In Methodism, poor members rejected self-pity and resignation to their "lot." Instead, they redefined what was important in life, translating their earthly misfortune into a virtue. Having "nothing" to distract her, Craig could focus on her "blessed Savior." We might rephrase the sermon text so popular with Methodists: in losing the world, she had gained her soul.

Poor people who contributed to the church knew that their monies did not go to support ministerial estates or lavish church fixtures. Methodist leaders tried to ensure that surplus funds would not be used in such worldly ways. When ministers at year's end had collected more than their paltry salary, they were required to give the extra funds to preachers in poor districts.[54] Most important, however, the poor who gave to the church were exercising the same choice that Wesley had argued came with all such decisions. In their cases, the level of sacrifice was undoubtedly much greater, but in Methodist views, the greater the level of sacrifice, the greater the goodness of the choice. Even Jane Craig and Methodist slaves felt a responsibility to give something to others, and they obviously took pride in furthering what they saw as the Lord's work. In these many ways, Methodism enabled lower-class members to retain a sense of pride, self-worth, and dignity, and to at least rhetorically and ideologically turn their misery into victory.

We can better understand the attraction of the church for the yeomanry if we look at the way the church transformed the minority of rich Methodists. For elites, to become a Methodist was to in many ways reject the values of their own class, and to embrace values promoted by the plain folk. The case of William Weems is instructive, and suggests that instead of wealthy and middling members "civilizing" lower-class Methodists,[55] lower-class Methodists humbled and changed the wealthy. Weems was born into a Maryland family of "good circumstances" and as a young man, he became a naval officer. He returned from one of his tours of duty to find that his brothers and sisters were "turning fools" by joining the Methodists. Weems was horrified that his "relations shood so degrade themselves, as to Sociate with such [despicable] people." In 1784, Weems married, and he and his wife were "fully engaged in the Pomps and Vanitys of this world" until she converted. Weems refused to convert with the Methodists because he thought them too "mean a people for me to be advised by, as there preachers were men not acquainted with the Languages." When Weems eventually joined the church, the decision changed his perceptions about class and worth: "I praise God that My Lot is cast among the poor and Dispised [; surely] it was a [miracle] that I ever came from among the Rich and Honourable, to become a dispised follower of the Lord." Weems, who celebrated being "dispised," had come a long way from his earlier concerns about appearances, honor, and status. As his story suggests, for elites conversion signaled a rejection of the pretensions of class and a new mode of interaction with nonelites.[56]

Upper-class members rejected badges of status by joining the church, the clearest being dress. In Methodist services symbolic renunciations of rank were commonplace, with members ripping frills off their shirts or removing their elaborate hats immediately upon conversion. The church also denounced certain lucrative pursuits. Distilling, a common way to supplement income, was forbidden by the church. A Kentucky man had cultivated a "splendid orchard of peaches," intending to turn the fruit into brandy. After converting, "he turned a drove of hogs into the orchard." There is the case of John Ryall Bradley, who at his conversion had to part with "a stud of race horses." And finally, there were the Methodist masters who freed their slaves, sacrificing not only their investment in human beings but also their status and identity as slaveholders.[57]

As the attack on slavery shows, Methodism went below the surface to challenge ideals at the core of upper-class identity. Southern men of the Revolutionary era prized the peculiarly regional ideal of "independence." To be independent meant to control one's estate, white dependents, and slaves with as little interference from government and outsiders as possible. Francis Asbury perceptively remarked that for elites, "riches" even tended to "[produce] a spirit of independence towards God."[58] Wealthy men who became Methodists, however, faced immediate, persistent, and invasive interference in their life from the church. They were told how (and how not) to dress, what recreations were acceptable, what language was appropriate, and even under what circumstances they could go to court. They were repeatedly warned against pride or arrogance, and exhorted to be humble and meek. They might even be sanctioned for actions taken in their household, such as abuse of a slave or white dependent. And advice could be given by the poorest and lowliest fellow member.[59]

Richard Bassett's commitment to Methodism was deep and unselfish and shows how the church could effect behavioral change on a grand scale. Bassett was a wealthy Delaware planter with 6,000 acres of prime land, three homes, and many slaves. He had served in Delaware's constitutional ratification convention, and in the early republic became a senator and governor. Bassett's status and wealth were secure. Yet he converted to Methodism and voluntarily abandoned many of his old ways. Preachers noted that, "though princely rich, he lived plainly, without display or extravagance."[60] Bassett not only emancipated his many slaves, he also led the fight to make it illegal to sell Delaware slaves beyond state boundaries and tried (unsuccessfully) to abolish slavery in the state, positions that undoubtedly alienated him from most Delawareans of his class. There were a few gentlemen who joined Bassett in the church, but his membership also expanded his social circle to include Methodists of all classes. He regularly attended Methodist quarterly meetings, class meetings, and later, camp meetings. He frequently housed a number of Methodists who were attending nearby services; one minister remembered seeing over a hundred guests at Bassett's home on one such occasion. Bassett, as all this suggests, was not a nominal member, and his Methodism cannot wholly be explained by political, economic, or social factors.[61]

In renouncing the world, Bassett gained a spiritual community with other like-minded believers, and by all reports, he delighted in their company. He wrote fervent letters to Bishop Asbury describing services he attended, and these letters indicate that

Bassett's beloved community embraced both rich and poor, white and black members. In June 1801, he exclaimed, "glory to God, he has done wonders. About one hundred and thirteen white and black were joined in society yesterday." A year later he reported in detail the events of a five-day meeting in Dover. He lovingly recalled both "a precious time" he had while attending "the black peoples' love-feast" and a communion service where over 1,200 "white and coloured people" took the sacrament. During this extended meeting, several dozen people were converted in Bassett's home. Bassett the lawyer, senator, Revolutionary leader, and governor modestly signed his letter "Your brother in Christ."[62] Clearly, Bassett's decision to unite with the Methodists was a turning point in his life.

When elite men like Richard Bassett, William Weems, or Thomas Hinde (who after his conversion envied the "dog his humility") joined the church, they were rejecting the values of their own class and accepting the values of a predominantly plain folk church. Methodism did not erase all distinctions of wealth, but it did bridge the gulf between rich and poor by forcing a more modest lifestyle and more humble behavior on the wealthy who joined the church. The church required a new mode of interpersonal relations between elites and their poorer neighbors, a mode governed by Methodist views about charity, benevolence, humility, and the irrelevance of earthly rankings to God. Whether men like Bassett actually experienced what Methodists called a "heart" change is impossible to determine. And placed in context of the southern culture of honor, what they may have secretly felt is not important. Honor focused on the exterior, on what others saw, what others thought. Elite men listening to the Bassetts, Hindes, and Weemses of the church heard them praise meekness and rejoice at being "dispised." Elite men watching these converts saw evidence that they had abandoned the symbols and values of their class and delighted in the company of unlearned and rowdy common folk. To those outside the church, these external and behavioral changes would have been interpreted as a defection from gentry values.

The experience of the elite Methodist minority also suggests that the distinction between types of "social control" have not been drawn clearly enough by scholars. It is true that the Methodists had a strict set of rules and a vision of the proper social order. In their class meetings and disciplinary proceedings, Methodist leaders tried to control the social behavior of their members. Because of Methodist doctrine and values, however, elites who joined the church were subject to more "social control" than were poor and middling members. The issue is not one of control, but of who was controlling whom. The church's requirements, enforced by clergy predominantly from the lower classes, sometimes were just too demanding for southern elites. James H. Keys, a slaveholding Virginian and a Methodist since at least December 1806, left the church in August 1810 when his wife was expelled for wearing a gold ring. Keys was incensed that a lower-class preacher, John Early, deigned to correct his upper-class spouse. He described Early (who was later made a bishop of the church) as "an ignorant, stubborn coxcomb's [sic] whose place would be best filled at the tail of a plough, than as a guide or director of civilized people." Keys's insult was linked to both class and race, for on his plantation, it is probable that most plowmen were slaves.[63]

Keys's indignation is indicative of how most elites saw the Methodists. Freeborn Garrettson believed his preaching "was too hard for some of the rich" while Francis Asbury observed that the wealthy were "so soon offended." "Among the wealthy and refined very bitter opposition to the Methodists exist," another circuit rider commented; "consequently our homes are among the poor."[64] Indeed, the most common encounters between Methodists and elites were hostile ones. In or near Prince George County, Maryland, a slaveholding magistrate named Barns used his slaves to disturb the Methodists. A white tenant of Barns was hosting services in his home, services presided over by the antislavery preacher William Colbert. Barns rode up with a team of slaves and ordered them to begin "fixing blocks under the hous [sic]," and they made so much noise that Colbert was forced to stop the service.[65] As a master of slaves and landlord to poor whites, magistrate Barns had plenty of reasons to oppose a minister who often brought poor whites and slaves together in worship. His too coincidental arrival surely showed the tenant his strong disapproval of this Methodist preacher. Numerous men who were considered by the world to be "gentlemen" found great sport in attending services and laughing, mocking, or otherwise disrupting worship, as we will see. Whether this particular disruption had more menacing undertones, we can only speculate.

Sometimes poor Methodists won such battles. A wealthy lawyer named Smith was "fond of criticising religious people," especially the Methodists' "unskilled ministers and ignorant members." One of Smith's rich friends, Brother Browning, was a Methodist, and Browning asked Smith if he thought he could preach and pray better than "ignorant" Methodists. Smith replied that he "would be very sorry if he could not." Browning arranged for the lawyer's comeuppance by having a poor working-class Methodist, a man gifted in prayer, pray in front of Smith. As "a man of deep piety," the "force of [the poor man's] prayer was felt by all," but especially by Smith, who was duly chastened.[66] Methodists capitalized on stories like this one, for they seemed to prove that the pious poor could, with God's help, humble and best the unregenerate rich. These tales also served to bolster Methodists amid continual harassment and held out the hope that their persecutors would see the error of their ways. Most of the gentry living through these decades were not so easily won over; they considered Methodists enemies or troublemakers. In the minds of Methodists and their upper-class opponents, there was an immense and unbridgeable chasm regarding visions of the proper order. To the gentry, the Methodists seemed the epitome of *disorder*. In the elites' view, Methodists were "rabble" or at least "enthusiasts" whose "meetings were noisy, with wild displays of enthusiasm." For most upper-class men (and some upper-class women as well), Methodism was a lower-class religion, or worse yet—in their racist view, the Methodist church was a "Negro church."[67]

Not all opponents of Methodism were elites. Some lower-class southerners also joined Methodism's detractors. The differences between the kinds of criticism leveled by elites and by plain folk, however, illustrate how class helped define peoples' responses to the church. The contests between poor itinerants and poor "sinners" were sometimes comical. Preacher William Ormond was staying in a tavern in 1792 and encountered men he described as "drunks." After some harsh words were exchanged, Ormond realized no one wanted him to pray for them, and he went to bed. He awoke to find that his shoes had been "nastied" by the hooligans.[68] Typically, lower-class opposition came from men who were not willing to surrender their few pleasures of the world. "Drunks" and "drunkards," in preachers' descriptions, constituted a majority of such opponents, labels we should not take literally. Gamblers, amateur musicians, and people who enjoyed other amusements condemned by the church likewise found Methodists too preachy and otherworldly. With the Anglican and later Episcopalian church weak and understaffed, "sinners" who had not flagrantly violated the law had been tolerated by clerical and lay authorities. To some of these nonevangelical or unchurched common folk, the Methodist custom of publicly rebuking sin must have seemed intrusive and unwelcome, even if those rebukes came from preachers and lay people of their own class.

Just as Methodism offered the poor a standard by which they were superior to the gentry, it also offered poor converts a standard by which they were superior to the unconverted poor.[69] Methodists readily censured others or told them they were headed to Hell. We can easily imagine how self-righteous some converts, sure of eternal life, must have appeared to their neighbors. Conversion changed those who experienced it. People who only days before might have played cards, drank whiskey, or danced were, after conversion, refusing to do so. Even more annoying, they were rebuking their friends for such simple pleasures and proselytizing at every opportunity. The exclusiveness and insularity of certain Methodist rituals, which were closed to nonmembers, drew lines between Methodists and others. For love feasts, preachers stood at the door barring admittance to anyone who did not have a ticket from a Methodist minister. Like other Methodist services, love feasts were loud and demonstrative; thus, those who were shut out could hear the exuberance and camaraderie that they were not permitted to enjoy and participate in. Little wonder that so many tried to sneak inside or were caught peeking through the windows. To some lower-class observers, it undoubtedly seemed that their old friends were not just setting themselves apart, but setting themselves above, their neighbors.[70]

Plain folk and gentry shared in their complaints about ascetic Methodist standards, and they also often agreed that Methodism had a pernicious influence on women and sometimes, children. Leaving gender, race, and denominational disputes aside for the moment, a comparison of gentry and yeoman complaints against the church reveals one important difference. Lower-class opponents of Methodism rarely objected in principle to the church's style of worship; elites often complained of the noise, emotionalism, and physicality of Methodist services. While elites most feared that Methodists promoted disorder with their enthusiastic worship, poorer detractors seemed to have feared most the ascetic standards of the church. Elites, too, thought Methodist prohibitions on dancing, dueling, and gambling were excessive, yet most of their voiced complaints centered on the "vulgar" displays.

Methodists' hostility to wealth and the class conflicts surrounding the church tell only one side of the story. Methodists also had a vision of the proper model of economy. The perfect lifestyle was that of an artisan or yeoman household. On one level, such an alliance was natural, for the small farmer, craftsman, or merchant would have shared many habits and values with the preachers. Clergy, for example, were to rise at four o'clock, cautioned to "never be unemployed" or "triflingly employed," to "be serious," and always be punctual.[71] The church urged many of these same guidelines on lay people. Wesley's teachings once again formed the basis of these values. The *Arminian Magazine* reprinted a Wesley sermon on 1 Corinthians 12: 31, "Covet the best gifts and yet I shew you a more excellent way." Christians, according to Wesley, could chose two paths. One, the less excellent path, was to avoid sin, but otherwise conform to the world. The alternative way, and the one he urged Methodists to take, was to strive for perfection. The more excellent way began with self-denial. Methodist men were to sleep no more than seven hours a night; Methodist women, no more than eight. Next, Wesley counseled all members to pray sincerely and frequently. After this, Wesley noted, Christians must proceed to their earthly business, for "it is impossible that an idle man can be a good man." Yet he urged them to do so with diligence, prayer, and with no eye to their own will. At meals, Methodists were to avoid gluttony and conduct only "edifying" conversations.[72]

In the American South, preachers and the *Discipline* reiterated Wesley's rules for excellent living. This model corresponded to the lifestyles of common and middling folk better than to those of the rich, and consequently made yeoman households appear more Christian, to Methodists, than those of their wealthy neighbors. Although these values, divorced from time and place, may seem "bourgeois," they were being promoted and embraced by southerners who were not bourgeois and who were not concerned about free wage laborers. The case of the Ohio migrants is instructive. As the territory of Ohio opened for settlement, those lands became the American Methodist Canaan. As a free territory with fertile land, Ohio seemed a yeoman paradise. One lay preacher waxed rhapsodic upon his first sight of Ohio, calling it a land "where human blood is not shed like water by the hand of the merciless and unfeeling tyrant." "Here the honest and industrious farmer cultivates his farm with his own hands," he proudly noted, and "the young man (instead of a cowskin or some other instrument of torture) takes hold of an ax, or follows the plough." The yeoman wife of Ohio, he observed, trained her daughters in the "distaff and the needle" and "the ruddy damsel thinks it no disgrace to wash her clothes, milk her cows, or dress the food for the family." In Ohio, hard work was "no disgrace," and as a result, Ohioans "live happy and their end is peace."[73]

The southern Methodist men who moved to Ohio became not only yeomen, but also mill owners, storekeepers, lawyers, judges, and congressmen. They went to Ohio to establish a virtuous community, one free of slavery and free of the vices associated with slaveholding wealth. Already possessing Wesleyan attitudes, many of them prospered. Methodists believed in the power of their own agency and that their individual decisions had direct and indirect consequences—consequences that a reflective person could control. Such causal thinking, along with the Wesleyan habits of sobriety, diligence, frugality, and saving, constituted a recipe for success in the new lands of Ohio. These values were brought to the frontier by Methodists; they did not wait for the development of small manufactures and industry to adopt them. There was no sense of unease about free labor discipline when Methodists arrived in Ohio, for most Ohio immigrants worked for themselves. If these values became bourgeois values, it is because the men and women who held them ascended into the middle class. Even in the non–free labor South, it is highly likely that some yeoman farmers who closely adhered to Methodist values succeeded because those values coincided with the habits needed to gain wealth. Sobriety, thrift, industry, saving, and long-term causal thinking, for example, were certainly as useful for the cotton farmer as for the free northern laborer.[74]

While the industrious nonslaveholding yeoman household was the familial ideal, early Methodists also had regulations on business and credit that together constituted a loosely defined economic policy. The most quaint of these rules was designed to prevent fraud and haggling; the *Discipline* prohibited "the *using many words* in buying or selling," although members seem to have rarely been punished for this offense. Perhaps more important, in a society where most credit was extended in face-to-face encounters, Methodists had strict rules about borrowing and lending. The *Discipline* forbade "borrowing without a probability of paying: or the taking up goods without a probability of paying for them" as well as "the *giving or taking things on usury*, i.e. unlawful interest."[75] Methodists explicitly linked contractual obligations to morality and expanded the geographical area of moral responsibility to include, as we saw with Gough and Dorsey above, other Methodists living far from one's neighborhood.[76] Methodists were even responsible for the harm they did to strangers. Thomas Love, a Methodist in backcountry North Carolina, must have felt lucky when a stray lamb and ewe wandered onto his property, for he wasted no time in butchering and eating the lamb and selling the ewe. For doing so, however, he was expelled from the Methodist church.[77]

One final aspect of Methodist policy is worth noting. The church urged members to look out for one another, "employing them preferably to others, buying one of another, helping each other in business."[78] To what extent members followed this advice cannot be ascertained. Yet there would be some advantages in hiring and doing business with fellow members. A fellow Methodist would share the same ethic. He would more likely repay his loan on time, or work diligently, and not overcharge for services. And although the church did not allow members to take one another to civil courts, members did bring economic disputes to the church for arbitration. For Methodist laborers, artisans, employers, and merchants, then, the church disciplinary process supplemented the courts. An ascetic Methodist who disliked worldly conversation, cursing, and other "ungodly" habits would also be less exposed to such behavior from a fellow member.

Although Methodists did not think in terms of overturning economic structures, their values posed a clear alternative to the gentry's in these early decades. They condemned the wealthy and their lifestyles in sermons and writings, linking riches with sins of idleness, dissipation, and greed. They urged their members to see every consumer choice as vested with moral consequences, an ethic that allowed ordinary men and women to see themselves as agents of good or evil by choice. Despite the limits of Methodism's reformist vision, the church held ample attraction to the plain folk. By joining the church, common men and women united, as did the wealthy Richard Bassett, to a family of like-minded believers. Within the church, distinctions of class were much less important than in society at large. The leaders of the church visited and stayed in members' homes, ate what they ate, wore what they wore, and slept on the same rough beds. If members grew old or infirm, the church would provide for them and clergy and fellow Methodists would visit and care for them. In the church, members heard sermons proclaiming that as Christians their lives were important and that their pains and sorrows were shared by God.

In condemning gentry culture, warning that wealth was a bar to salvation, and urging charity, Methodists fashioned an ethic that was at odds with that of the southern gentry. The wealthy men and women who did join the church had to sacrifice many of their symbols of status to remain members and had to relate to poorer members on terms of mutual respect. Through sobriety, diligence, and thrift, and by long-term causal thinking, poor and middling Methodists improved their lot. In its rules, the church regulated credit and business between members in a way that mitigated conflict and encouraged economic cooperation between members. In their "alternative measures of the good (and the bad) life,"[79] Methodism helped the widow, the infirm, and those just down on their luck hold their heads high and retain self-respect.

Especially for the Methodist poor, church policies, doctrines, and ministerial behavior must have been a welcome change from Anglican practice. And if they were reduced by circumstance to a beggar's life or the poorhouse, they could be assured that their clergy would not shun them. When a "poor beggar, a traveling man" happened by where preacher James Meacham was staying, Meacham "joined hands with him" and they prayed together.[80] On a visit to a poorhouse in Maryland, preacher William Colbert "pray'd with one of the ghastliest looking objects that I ever beheld with my eyes: His face was much eat away with the venereal disease."[81] Perhaps here, too, is where we should locate Methodism's popularity with the poor and common folk—in such small but important acts of kindness.

F I V E

"Mothers in Israel"

White Women in the Church

THE SUNDAY IN 1798 that Mary Hinde rebuked Major Martin probably began much as others had. Following church services, the Hinde family returned home, where they gathered to talk with neighbors in their Kentucky parlor. The conversation, as was often the case with Methodists on the Sabbath, centered on religion. When the topic turned to the "resurrection of the dead," Major Martin, a deist and a man immersed in the elite culture of honor, "made quite light of the matter." Mary Hinde, the Major recounted, "set out zealously upon me respecting the reality of these things and the great necessity there was for a preparation for them. [H]er words went to my heart, in so sensible a manner that I sat the resolution before I left the house [that] if there was any such a thing as religion in the world I would seek after it."[1] Mary's son, who described this famous incident for an antebellum issue of the *Methodist Magazine,* supplied the gendered analysis missing in Martin's account: "Here a man who had gloried in his strength and courage, and would have conceived it a disgrace to take an insult, or to bear even a rebuke from any man, thus assailed by an elderly lady, is suddenly put to flight."[2] Mary Hinde, boldly defending her religion of the heart, conquered the masculine realms of both intellectualized deism and secularized honor.

When Methodism's first historians wanted to capture the spirit of the early movement, they turned to the romantic figure of the circuit rider—the lone male with his wide-brimmed parson's hat traveling over perilous mountains to spread the gospel to southwestern emigrants. The image of the itinerant on the mountain pass is a compelling one, but let us follow the parson a little farther. When he reaches his appointed preaching place, often the home of a pious white woman, he preaches to a crowd composed primarily of white women and slaves, and later meets the local society, where white men like himself are again in the minority. If he is new to the area, a white woman will often be the first to open her home for services. At the end of the day, before he retires to a bed in a modest farmhouse, he dines on a meal cooked by a white Methodist farm wife or widow, who also repairs the rips in his coat and, most importantly, edifies him with her spiritual conversation. When he mounts his horse for his next appointment, women like Mary Hinde carry on the work of the church in his (typically) three- to four-week absence. The Mary Hindes of early southern Methodism were as vital to the church as its traveling preachers.

White Methodist women assumed active roles in churches across the South, and many were informal and some formal leaders of other Methodists.[3] Before crowded audiences of men and women, rich and poor, black and white, women spoke, counseled, reproved, testified, and even preached. Methodists listened attentively to women's testimony, sought their spiritual advice, and respected their opinions. The public drama of white women's religiosity, vividly captured in contemporary sketches and paintings of camp meetings, should not obscure the equally important small-scale dramas played out in homes across the South. Debates over doctrines, values, and practices took place both in public—between ministers, essayists, and politicians—and in private—between husbands and wives, brothers and sisters, fathers and daughters. Many southern women violated customs, the wishes of male relatives, and southern norms of femininity in the service of their religion. White women openly rebuked "sinners" and were assertive and outspoken in their evangelism. A surprising number of these women were extraordinarily courageous in defending their church and clergy from attack. Southern women found self-esteem, a need for their skills, and most important of all, agency in the church. Methodist women expanded their friendship and support circle outside their families and kin groups and often won the admiration and respect of their religious communities. And the church, to put it simply, could not have succeeded in its first four decades without the support and zeal of southern women.[4]

The southern context made women's participation in the church more an object of contention than in other regions. In the South, white men saw patriarchy as both the ideal government for families and the ideal mode of governance for slaves. A distinct southern notion of manhood emerged that was based on honor, white male independence, and the subordination of white and black dependents.[5] A patriarch's control over his white family was inextricably tied to white supremacy and slavery. Many southern men viewed women's involvement with Methodism as a broad threat to their own hegemony. The weakness of the Anglican church and the debates over the support of Anglican clergy contributed to the absence in the South of a "pious male" ideal analogous to the Puritan legacy in New England. Much of what constituted southern manhood was antithetical to the notion of manhood promoted by southern evangelicals. The masculine world of honor, as Mary Hinde's rebuke of Major Martin shows, was in form and spirit opposed to the feminine world of heart religion. Martin's conversion story was designed to teach Methodist readers that Christians could defeat foes considered more powerful in secular eyes. But it also keenly illustrates the gulf between pious Methodist women and worldly men of honor. Methodist women, by embracing the church and its values, contested the ideologies of honor and independence and promoted a family ideal of harmony and mutuality.

White women found support for their defiance of secular gender conventions in the messages and beliefs of church leaders. The relationship was not one-way:

women's commitment to the struggling church influenced preachers' views of women just as the clergy's views of women encouraged women's commitment to the church. Yet in a community so conscious of its values, the question of what preachers and leaders expected of women and said to women is surely of central importance. The most striking aspect of Methodist messages to women is the absence of a prescriptive domesticity. Unlike their successors, early Methodist leaders devoted little time and effort to outlining and even less to dictating women's roles in the family.[6] Neither of the two Methodist periodicals published in America before 1810, the *Arminian Magazine* and the *Methodist Magazine*, had a women's column, and rarely was any space devoted specifically to women's obligations as wives or mothers. Duties of mothers, for example, were addressed in pieces that discussed parental or family duties. Most of the female exemplars whose lives were discussed in these magazines were noted for their evangelism, piety, and bold defense of Methodism—not for domesticity.[7]

The most intriguing discussion of women's roles in these early periodicals came in a Wesley sermon reprinted in the *Arminian Magazine* on Matthew 25: 36, Christ's commandment to care for the sick and spiritually troubled. Instead of restricting women to a domestic sphere, Wesley defended women's rights and duties to visit, and railed against the prevalent Anglo-American notion that women were only designed as "play things." He emphasized women's God-given "right" as "rational creatures" to perform Christian obligations, reminding his readers that "*there is neither male nor female in Christ Jesus.*"[8] Like Wesley, his followers in the American South accepted the prevalent notion that men and women were fundamentally different, yet here, as elsewhere, the Methodists' God judged by criteria of inner piety.

In the mid-nineteenth century, women's piety was domesticated and the dutiful Christian mother, reading her children the Bible before the family hearth, became the ideal in male evangelicals' writings on women. Early Methodists, though, had a range of female icons, among them the assertive female evangelist, the persecuted martyr to the faith, the rapturous enthusiast, the wise counselor, and the reprover of sin. None was more important or more revered than the "Mother in Israel." Unlike the antebellum Christian mother, the "Mother in Israel" was a spiritual leader whose "children" consisted of adult men and women she had brought to the faith. When clergy venerated extremely pious and devout men, they compared them to the New Testament figure of Nathaniel, of whom Christ said at first sight, "Behold an Israelite indeed, in whom there is no guile!" Little is revealed about Nathaniel in the Bible except that he quickly proclaimed Christ to be "the King of Israel." A John Wesley sermon on this verse was reprinted in the American *Arminian Magazine*, and Wesley's extended commentary fleshed out what it meant to be "an Israelite in whom there is no guile." Wesley's Nathaniel was the epitome of a selfless and meek Christian. He had an "humble, gentle, patient love of all mankind," abhorred "pride," and eschewed "the honour that cometh of men, in being beloved, esteemed, and applauded by them." Wesley's Nathaniel was, in short, the inverse of a southern man of honor. Clergy were most likely to be called "Israelites" without guile, but a few leading lay men were also thus memorialized by ministers.[9]

In contrast, "Mother in Israel" was the phrase used to describe the Old Testament character of Deborah. Had Methodists wished to emphasize women's subordination, silence, or domesticity, they could not have picked a biblical woman with fewer of those characteristics than Deborah. As one of the Hebrew judges, Deborah administered justice, exhibited martial courage, prophesied, and gave advice—even on military matters, to her people. Her "motherhood" is metaphorical: the Old Testament descriptions of her in Judges do not mention children at all. One "Mother in Israel," Maryland's Rebecca Ridgely, was childless in a region where female infertility was regarded as a shame and a disgrace. Bishop Asbury twice reassured Ridgely that although she had a "Dry Breast," she had "adopted children" in the church who would "comfort [her] in the setting hour of life" and that she would have "a place in the upper house of God far, far better than sons and daughters." Asbury's words went beyond compassion; the church enabled women to transcend home and family and the ideology of domesticity. Many Methodist women of the South became identified as "Mothers in Israel," among them Sisters Small, White, Yancey, Cobb, and Mabry to name a select few.[10] Nathaniel was respected for his personal temperament, Deborah for her wisdom, bravery, and actions. Southern Methodists may not have given much thought to comparing or contrasting the two ideal types, but they knew their Bibles well enough to know the essence of Deborah's story.

An even more striking rejection of domesticity as women's sole ornament can be found in a sermon text, Luke 10: 38–42, which Francis Asbury often used when speaking to all-female or predominantly female audiences. The verses contrasted the behavior of two sisters, Mary and Martha, when Christ visited their home. Martha "was cumbered about with much serving" while Mary "sat at Jesus' feet, and heard his word." The angry Martha asked Christ to rebuke Mary for not helping, but instead Christ criticized Martha for being "troubled about many things" and commended Mary for realizing that "one thing is needful." He pronounced that "Mary hath chosen that good part, which shall not be taken away from her."[11] The text was well suited to convey Methodists' ideal for women—duties to God were more important than domestic responsibilities.

The Bible provided role models, but a number of other female exemplars sprang from the rank and file of Methodism. Britons Susannah Wesley, Mary Fletcher, and Hester Ann Rogers were extraordinary church leaders whom American Methodists revered. The pages of the *Arminian Magazine* abounded with lesser-known British Methodist women who exhorted, evangelized, withstood persecution, died happy deaths, and reproved sin where they found it. Barbara Heck, the New York woman whose denunciation of a card game inspired the formation of the first Methodist society in the city, was the American counterpart to Susannah Wesley. Southern women who wished to find inspiration in the Christian and Methodist past had a wide variety of examples to choose from.

An astonishing number of women rose to become esteemed leaders in southern churches, and these women, too, became role models for their "sisters" in the faith. Women who behaved like Mary rather than Martha were not just given the title "Mother in Israel"—they earned it. Sarah Hinton, to take but one example, was termed the "cornerstone" of Methodism in Washington, North Carolina. A witness recalled that "[a]round her individual exertions—and they were neither few nor easy—clustered its most flattering hopes, its most prosperous experience." Other Methodist women surely admired her. One also suspects that itinerants new to the Washington area courted the favor of this powerful and respected woman. Descriptions of women like Hinton are also a useful corrective to early church histories, which most often paint the "rise" of Methodism as the result solely of the heroic efforts of itinerant clergy.[12]

Moreover, preachers were as likely to seek the counsel of "Mothers in Israel" as women were to seek preachers' help. Sister "I. M." wrote a "mortifying" letter to James Meacham that so inspired him he was not sure "what to do or which way to turn to run fast enough to overtake her on her way to heaven." "[F]ull oft hath she refreshed my spirit," Francis Asbury wrote of Sister Boydstone, one of his many female counselors. Nelson Reed, although he envied that Sister Grymes "seem'd to be more faithful to god than I was," still found that "it comforted my soul to hear of the dispensations of gods grace to her." Sarah Hagerty closed her letter to a preacher by reminding him of his obligations as a Christian and a clergyman: "I must conclud by exhorting you to watch in all things pray in all prayer be faithfull to the charge commited to your care." One of the most prolific and well-known women of southern Methodism, Sarah Jones, corresponded with dozens of ministers over the years and offered her advice and counsel—both solicited and unsolicited.[13] We know of the activities of many Methodist women only through a brief description appearing in a mid- to late-nineteenth-century church history, but these descriptions are sometimes quite revealing. Methodist Sally Gordon was said to be "a woman of strong mind, and great zeal, and influence." According to Jacob Young, Mrs. Whitten was also a woman of "great influence and authority." Southern women were certainly influential in their homes and families, yet in the public sphere, aside from in the churches, women had decidedly little "authority."[14] Women's religious authority was not the demure behind-the-scenes manipulation that is often the only recourse of the powerless and subordinate. Methodist women were assertive, commanding, strong, and at times fearless. They were respected by preachers and members alike.

Had Methodist leaders wanted to curb women's autonomy or influence, church discipline presented one avenue for doing so. But the evidence from early Methodism shows that discipline was not used in such a manner. Quantitative analysis of Methodist church discipline is severely hampered by clergymen's haphazard record keeping. Throughout most of the years under study (1770–1810), itinerants often acted as judge and jury in the administration of church rules. These were busy men with an evangelistic agenda, and they often left scanty records. A typical entry on these matters was "expelled four or five" with no mention of the race and gender of the members involved. Offenses, even when listed, were not recorded with the precision a modern analyst would desire, for such general statements as "expelled for immorality" could involve any number of actual infractions.[15] With these gaps in mind, the extant evidence shows clear trends about discipline and gender.

James Meacham seems to have disciplined a greater percentage of women than other preachers, but even his record indicates that the female majority was not proportionally represented in disciplinary cases. Meacham left evidence of 41 members he disciplined—of these 11 were men, 11 women, and 19 were not identified by gender. The gender-specific offenses in Meacham's record include slave trading (all men), immorality (all men), marrying a sinner (all women), and nonattendance (all women).[16] Richard Whatcoat recorded 60 disciplinary cases over the course of a decade of his ministry. Thirty-seven of the members involved were men, 6 were women, and 17 were not identified by gender. Of those cases for which Whatcoat reveals the disposition, 9 men were expelled and 4 suspended, 4 women were expelled and none suspended, and 15 not identified by gender were expelled and 2 suspended. Offenses that can be identified in Whatcoat's journal as gender specific include slave trading—all those punished for this were men—and marrying an unbeliever—all punished for this were women.[17] As this tally indicates, Whatcoat disciplined the members in his immense charge at a very minimal rate of six per year, and men were overrepresented as objects of Whatcoat's discipline. The records for whites in Edenton Methodist Church in North Carolina, although they extend past the date of 1810, also confirm that men were more likely to be punished by the church, despite the fact that at the apex of male membership, women outnumbered them by two to one (31 women to 15 men). In 1811–1812, Edenton saw a virtual explosion in all members with the addition of 11 men and 18 women. These same years, 5 men and 3 women were expelled. By the end of 1812, then, a combination of expulsions and admissions had resulted in a net gain of 6 men and 15 women. Edenton church leaders expelled on average one woman for each five admitted and one man for each two admitted.[18]

The combined data of Meacham, Whatcoat, and the Edenton records, as well as other sources consulted for this study, reveals several important things. Some offenses were linked to gender, such as slave trading with white men and marrying an unbeliever and wearing costly apparel with white women. The prohibition on "mixed" marriages was a bitter pill for Methodist women who desired to marry, for it was much harder for women to find a mate in the female-dominated church than for men.[19] For exactly this reason, the punishment was eventually revised; women violators were placed on trial for six months. The rule on dress affected upper-class women most, and indeed Wesley and his American clergy justified their rules against ostentatious dress based on class and not gender. Violations of dress rules were, however, normally punished with a private warning first, then if the behavior continued, a public reproof. Egregious violations (ornate jewelry seems to have been viewed as such) brought more serious censure. The rules on dress did attack pride, and female pride more often than male. Yet the rules on dress also indirectly attacked the shallow secular emphasis on women's outward appearance.[20] Methodism focused on the inner self and not on outer dress or beauty. When a woman who was termed "the beauty of Baltimore" converted, Ezekiel Cooper noted that she was "now beautified with the robes of piety and a happy soul."[21] In a world where women's interiors and intellects were seldom taken seriously, the Methodists prized these very qualities.

Women were also not the only members to be punished for sexual immorality. Unmarried women who became pregnant, it is true, were vulnerable in ways the fathers of their children were not, and several women were expelled because their pregnancies revealed they had broken church rules. Yet there is much evidence to indicate that men identified as breaking sexual prohibitions were treated just as severely. A South Carolina man was "expelled publicly for Adultery" in 1792. Thomas Mann was part of group that expelled a "coupple [sic] for fornacation [sic]." In James Meacham's charge, a young woman was expelled on July 25, 1794, "for letting a young man into her room and sleeping him there till the next morning." The following day, when Meacham met the men's class, the young man involved in the same incident was also expelled.[22] Although sexual violations accounted for very few of the known reasons for expulsion, these cases illustrate that women were not the only ones charged with sexual sins.

Discipline—other than private reproofs or rebukes—was a rare event. If, as some historians have suggested, evangelical churches were an agent of elite or patriarchal authority, then, for Methodists, discipline was not where this effort was concentrated. Women were disciplined at a lower rate in proportion to their percentage of the membership than were men. Put differently, the church intervened in white men's behavior far more often than in white women's. Preachers' perceptions of women as more godly than men was undoubtedly influenced by men's recurring misbehavior. For women in the church, the expulsions and chastising of men may well have seemed a welcome change from white male license. For all members, Methodist discipline is best conceived as a combination of self-restraint and official censure, with self-discipline being the more important of the two. The impact of Methodist rules on women's behavior is most evident in the infrequency of punishment. Women were better at being Methodists.

Women were central to the success of early Methodism. Most obviously, they were in the majority of the membership. Although there are no national, regional, or state breakdowns by gender, abundant literary evidence proves that women outnumbered men in Methodist churches just as they did in most Protestant churches of the era. One of the first Methodist preaching tours in the South, by Joseph Pilmore in 1772, attracted the attention of the *Virginia Gazette* for precisely this reason. A correspondent of the paper noted that "[a]ll the Ladies . . . are become Proselytes to Methodism; the [Anglican] church is quite deserted."[23] Women were still in the majority thirty years later. In 1803 Preacher Thomas Lyell opposed the Methodist rule that called for expulsion of members who married nonbelievers because the rule disproportionately affected women, who in his estimate outnumbered men five to one. Lyell probably overstated the percentage of women in the church, but many preachers noted how their audiences and their societies were composed primarily of women.[24] Those outside the church certainly noticed that among white Methodists, women predominated. An Anglican priest who came from England to a Maryland parish in 1784 was negotiating his salary with local vestrymen when he discovered, much to his dismay, that some of them financially supported both Methodist and Anglican clergy. He complained and was met with a (surprisingly tolerant) response by one of the vestrymen which reveals that defectors to Methodism were mostly female: "Pray sir . . . we cannot divorce our wives and turn our daughters out of doors, because they have joined the Methodists." Additionally, local records that have survived show that women normally outnumbered men.[25]

Several things should be said to place women's numerical dominance of the membership in context. Women's participation in Methodism was voluntary. Although some non-Methodist men prohibited their female relations from joining the church, church leaders did not force women to become Methodists. Women could join and leave the church of their own accord. In an age of fierce sectarian rivalry and religious voluntarism, the ultimate power in churches thus belonged to the laity, who if dissatisfied could withdraw their money, time, and attendance. And the laity was overwhelmingly female. The voluntary nature of membership should caution us, regardless of our interpretation of evangelicals' ideas about women and gender roles, against arguing that churches imposed their values on helpless female members. The decision to become a Methodist was not taken lightly. Prospective members were placed on trial for a period of time before they could become full-fledged members, and during the trial period they learned church rules and procedures, which were strict and demanding. Once admitted to full membership, women were subject to the prohibitions and were expected to perform the duties outlined in the *Discipline.*

White women also tended to precede men into the church—both in families and in neighborhoods. When Methodist itinerants first came into an area, women were often the initial converts and the main source of encouragement to the clergy. Sister McAlland, described by a contemporary as "emphatically a woman of prayer," was the first person to join the Methodists in Columbia, South Carolina. In 1776, John Little-john noted that there were only two Methodists in Winchester, Virginia—Sister Bush and Sister Conrad. Mary Ennalls was credited with bringing Methodism to Dorchester, Maryland.[26] Sally Gordon's home was the first meeting place open to Methodists in Wilkes County, North Carolina. Widow Triplett, the first to receive the Methodist preachers in Baltimore, was honored for her hospitality and faithfulness when she died. Francis Asbury preached her funeral sermon from Acts 16:13–15, a text that honored a New Testament woman, who, like Triplett, opened her heart and home to Paul and converted her entire household.[27]

Because early Methodists met more often in private homes than in meetinghouses, many women became the hosts for services, classes, and prayer meetings. In their journals, preachers noted their stops as regularly as they noted their sermons. Sprinkled among the Gunpowder Meeting Houses and the Bethel Chapels are such stops as "Sister Heath's," "Sister Edwards's," "Widow Lloyd's," and "Sister Andrews's."[28] Women who hosted regular services were honored with having their name represent a local society, and they also assured their connection to a world beyond the home. In the rural South, many Methodists rode (or at times walked) miles to attend the nearest service. Itinerants, rotated as frequently as every six months, brought news from afar and from their own connections to the wider body of Methodists. These near and distant fellow believers regularly converged on the houses of many women, expanding their friendship circle and sphere of interest outside the home.

Women provided crucial economic support to the church. Wealthier women, like Rebecca Ridgely, generously donated money to preachers. Lower- and middle-class women made donations of their time, labor, and goods as well, most often by feeding and clothing itinerants. Sister Walker made John Early a homespun coat in 1807. Thomas Mann received breeches and a homespun coat from various women in 1805. Many preachers, Jacob Young and Francis Asbury among them, noted how women kept them clothed, sheltered, and fed during their rounds.[29] For lower-class Methodists, feeding and clothing non–family members represented a significant economic commitment. Women's support, whether in opening their homes, being the initial converts, or in providing goods, services, and money, must be contextualized within the broader reality of early Methodist experience. These women were not maintaining an accepted church with a solid reputation—they were aligning themselves with a group that was ridiculed, feared, and harassed.

The experience of widowed Methodist women is instructive, for widows were the most economically and personally independent of southern white women. It was not uncommon for the first Methodist preaching place to be in a widow's home, for as heads of households, they did not have to answer to husbands or fathers for their religious choices. Yet widows were not free from community and familial harassment. Francis Asbury witnessed several incidents in which widows were subject to community intervention. During a service at Widow Triplett's Baltimore home "a company of men . . . came drunk, and attempted an interruption." Triplett asked for, but did not receive, "redress" from a magistrate because of the "late riot made in her house." One Methodist widow was even opposed by other women. Agatha Ball, a widow described by her minister as "a famous heroine for Christ," was approached by a neighboring lady, who "took [Ball] from her own house, and with tears, threats, and entreaties, urged her to desist from receiving the preachers, and Methodist preaching; but all in vain. . . . [H]aving now found the way, she would not depart therefrom."[30] Widows' support for the church, then, even in such seemingly innocuous ways as opening their homes for services, was often a sure way to provoke communal disapproval or outrage, and as such frequently was an act of autonomy. With the most independent of southern women encountering such opposition, the dangers married and young single women faced become easier to appreciate. In the years when Methodism was most suspect, women kept the church afloat by their membership, time, money, and commitment. Such support was not uncontroversial.

Methodist women did not pave the way into the church merely to become passive recipients of clerical wisdom. On occasion, women, like other members, defied preachers' authority. Although preachers were usually receptive to women's mysticism, they reprimanded several female members for their visions and prophecies. Susannah Williams was in her fifth "vision" when a committee headed by preacher James Meacham visited her. She informed Meacham that she had discerned through a vision that he "was in a good deal of distress" and that he "wrestled hard in prayer for happiness." Despite the fact that Williams's claims (as reported by Meacham) were so vague that they could probably apply to most Methodists, he began "correcting" her visions the next evening. John Kobler also met a woman who, he wrote, "undertakes to prophecy and tell others what state they are in." Although she "was very positive . . . it was the working of the spirit of God," Kobler was equally sure it was "enthusiasm" and "beged her to quit or she wou'd do imense harm." Another Methodist woman pointedly argued with a preacher who told her to call her husband "Mister."[31] While the relationship between preachers and female members was typically warm and harmonious, these cases show that women could and occasionally did contest ministerial authority.

That some women would find license in Methodism to challenge preachers is not unexpected. Women frequently defied men outside the Methodist fold and violated southern norms of femininity in the service of their faith. The roots of women's self-assertion and autonomy can be traced back to Wesleyan doctrines and practices that expanded converts' sense of agency. For white southern women, as for blacks, conversion wrought a significant change in perceptions of the self and agency. Methodist women's voices, values, and concerns were not subsumed by those of patriarchs. In politics, the family economy, and the courts, the prevailing fiction held that a white man spoke for his family and that a patriarch represented the interests of his wife, children, and other dependents. But for Methodists, each soul had to represent itself before God. The central ritual of the church—conversion—was one in which each woman (like each man) came to terms with her own sinfulness and God's love for her. Although southern preachers and lay leaders expected women who were wives and mothers to infuse these domestic roles with Methodist ideals, women were first and foremost believers. Methodist ideology enabled southern women to carve out a realm of emotional, intellectual, and psychological experience where they were not some man's wife or some child's mother, but individuals with talents, fears, hopes, and dreams.

It is difficult to overestimate the way Methodist beliefs infused women with purpose and power. Sarah Jones described "[running] through blood and fire, and friends and foes, and devils, principalities and powers" as she tried to follow "the more excellent way." Life was warfare for her, and she was undaunted before her enemies: "What gives us courage? A good conscience, and daring insults from Hell, weary marches, hot battles, and powerful combats. This, and victory, always inures us to *endure hardship as good soldiers.*" Jones's metaphors were more vivid and colorful than most Methodists', but her sense of agency, duty, and ability was typical. Numerous white women developed their skills and talents in the public forum of the church. Methodists required that each individual member speak for herself. Routine church activities gave women experience in expressing themselves before audiences large and small. Testimony helped the individual speaker come to terms with her spiritual state, and ideally moved others to greater zeal or, if they were unconverted, to God. Methodist women influenced countless southerners with their compelling and dramatic accounts. Prudence Blakey Mead's considerable talents were memorialized in print by her husband. She testified so poignantly in love feasts, classes, and prayer meetings, he proudly related, that "the awakening conversion, and sanctification of souls, high and low, rich and poor, male and female, have openly and instantaneously occurred before many witnesses."[32]

Women's initial experience with self-expression came when they decided to join the church. To be admitted to the membership, women had to describe their conversions in convincing ways before other members. Women's conversions followed the conventional Methodist plot line—the journey from a sinful and worldly life to piety and salvation. But there were important gendered nuances in conversion accounts. Methodists vacillated between feeling powerless and powerful in their lifelong quests for salvation and perfection. The church encouraged humans to see their wretchedness, to loathe the self, to be humble and meek. Methodism also taught that individuals were the masters of their fate, and that with God's help they could accomplish the impossible, defy insurmountable odds, and become saints on earth. Because they came from a culture with sharply dichotomized southern gender roles, men and women often emphasized different aspects of the Methodist experience.

Men describing their conversions usually emphasized their feelings of powerlessness before God.[33] Women, on the other hand, often emphasized the power they felt in converting. Milly Stith claimed that at a camp meeting in Georgia "it pleased God, in his infinite mercy, and all-redeeming love, to give me a glorious manifestation of his love and power." Two months after the meeting, she still had "great reason to thank the Lord that I have continued to feel much of the power of his love."[34] Even when women were physically overcome, they used similar language. Mary Avery Browder "was wrestling with God in prayer" when she "felt his power in so wonderful a manner, that it occasioned my trembling body to fall down befor[e] Him." Although Browder felt "weak as a little child," she also confessed that she "saw the shining Glory of God and my soul and body was fill'd with such love, for power I never knew before."[35] Women's conversion stories reflected a newfound sense of agency. In God, women believed, all things were possible.[36]

White women were active members whose passion for their religion and church was rivaled only by that of the itinerant ministers who so depended on them. The chief business of the church was gaining converts, and women were the best recruiters. Women's first priority was to evangelize others in their family. Martha Luallen of South Carolina converted during the Revolutionary War, "became intensely interested in the religious welfare of her family," and "often lifted up her voice to God in behalf of her husband and children." A young woman served as what George Wells called "the chaplain in a large family" and tried to convert her parents, siblings, and her father's "workmen."[37] Numerous Methodist women were neighborhood evangelists as well. Sally Helm of Kentucky was known for "presenting the claims and hopes of Christianity to others." Delaware's Prudence Hudson, after her conversion in 1779, "entreated all around, with flowing tears, to come to Jesus and taste the sweets of religion." Evangelism was a duty, women believed, and in this spirit, Margaret Anderson made a resolution to "tell my associates, in plain terms, that they must be converted or eternally lost."[38] Women like these served as community counselors for people seeking religious help and advice. Jacob Young was in turmoil after he became convicted for his sins but could not turn to his father, who was "violently opposed to the Methodists." He sought comfort from a neighboring Methodist woman who eased him from the despair of conviction to the joy of conversion by singing hymns and "delightful conversation." Mary Ann Peaco was eulogized for her "salutary instructions" to her fellow Methodists; she "poured the balm of comfort into their tempted and sorrowful minds." Kentuckian Sarah Bruce also had "a peculiar aptitude in directing the inquirer in the way of salvation, and inspiring the doubting and desponding with confidence and reliance."[39] Peaco, Bruce, and their peers gained status and recognition for their religious leadership.

Another duty of Methodists, one explicitly ordered by the *Discipline*, was to reprove sin, and many women were known for their outspokenness in this regard. Delawarean James Hemphill, traveling to Maryland in 1802, was invited to breakfast by his business associate, George Kennard, where he met Kennard's wife, Providence, and two of her sisters. An astonished Hemphill reported what transpired in his journal: "Before we had been long seated Mrs. K attacked in the most severe Methodist strain I ever heard, told me I was in the broad road to hell, & that when there I would recollect [the] conversation that was passing between us when I saw her seated at the right hand of Christ." Hemphill, "lost in surprise at such a salutation" from a stranger, grew even more perturbed when her sisters started to "assist her but of that she required none." Upon Sarah Jones's death, Bishop Francis Asbury fondly remembered that she "reproved with pointed severity."[40] Women named and unnamed assertively (and, it seems, self-righteously) told others to abandon drink, deism, card playing, slave trading, gambling, fine dress, and irreligion or suffer the consequences of eternal flames.

Providence Kennard and Sarah Jones, like other Methodist women, were sanctioned to speak the "truth" and condemn sin by the church; when women did so, they flouted secular standards of femininity. White "ladies" were to be modest, demure, and deferential to men. "Mothers in Israel" were to be warriors for the faith.

A remarkable number of white southern women excelled in the public sphere of the church. Methodist worship was normally open to the public, whether conducted out-of-doors or in barns, warehouses, private homes, and public buildings. Because of Methodists' reputation for enthusiasm, many non-Methodists attended, if only for entertainment or to make sport. In these services, women's voices were regularly heard. Women's speaking in public, moreover, was extremely controversial outside evangelical churches and Quaker meetings. As a rule, southern moderate and conservative denominations followed the same pattern that Laurel Thatcher Ulrich found in New England churches where "men preached and women listened."[41] But Methodist women frequently gave testimony or conducted a part of the service. Even during male preaching, women were not passive, silent listeners; preachers often measured their success by the cries, shouts, and moans they extracted from their listeners—female listeners in particular. Both white women and slaves were known for "shouting"— sometimes so loud and so ecstatically that the preacher could not finish his sermon.

Services often included time for members to testify, class meetings were structured around shared testimony, and love feasts provided women with opportunities to speak about their inner lives and personal experiences before entire societies or regional bodies. Women's testimony was normally religious in nature. At a love feast Francis Asbury attended, "several holy women spoke of the perfect love of God." William Colbert presided over a class meeting where Sister Hoye "gave an account of the work of GOD in her soul." Women's testimony was so common that Richard Whatcoat noted about one love feast in 1795: "the first I remember being at that not one of our white sisters spoke."[42] Each convert, Methodists believed, had unique experiences that, if shared, would edify the group. Women had ample opportunities to develop their verbal abilities in the church. On occasion women even ventured into controversial topics when voicing their religious concerns.

At an Anglican service in 1784 the parson, upset by defections to Methodism from the Church of England, denounced Wesley and other Methodist clergy as "babblers" and "enthusiasts" and claimed that "no stream can rise higher than its source; consequently the preaching of the Methodists can only kindle an enthusiastic flame—a mere ignis fatuus—in any one." A Methodist woman in the audience known for her "accomplishments and piety" shouted, "Glory to God! if what I now feel be enthusiasm, let me always be an enthusiast!" The parson was too embarrassed to respond to her "rebuke." The Methodist preacher who related this story was proud of this woman's public defense of the church; the parson undoubtedly felt otherwise.[43] Sister Whitehead of Virginia was even bolder when she rose to speak at a heavily attended annual conference in 1791. The theme of her moral lecture was her distress at Methodists' growing involvement with the world. She first condemned the laxity with which her fellow Methodists were obeying the sect's rules on dress, sparing neither "young sisters . . . catching after the modes of fashion of this world which passes away" nor preachers who "ought to be examples of the flock." But by far the largest source of her grief, she revealed, was the fact that her fellow Methodists were becoming increasingly involved with slavery. In her view, it was the depth of hypocrisy for Methodists to keep slaves "in the field and kitchens cruelly oppressed, half starved, and nearly naked" and she warned that slave owners would themselves be "slaves to the devil in Hell forever."[44] Where else could Whitehead have given such a speech? Although slavery was being debated in Virginia's legislature and press, women's opinions were unsolicited. The church offered one of the only forums for Whitehead to publicly express her views on the issues of the day.

Some women not only testified routinely but were assigned lay leadership roles in services that traditionally in Christianity had belonged to men. Methodist services normally consisted of hymn singing, testimony, a sermon, one or more exhortations, and a prayer. Prayer, in services, families, and in private, was essential to the Methodist experience. Members used private prayer to ferret out sin in their hearts and to become close to God. Family prayer was designed to unite relations in faith and love, and helped train the next generation of potential Methodists. Prayer in services served a myriad of functions. First, it helped new converts learn how to pray without a book and what to pray as a Methodist. Second, a prayer could be used to express group concerns. The prayer leader might plead with God to end a drought, to bring a revival, or to shut down a local distillery. Third, public prayers, which often closed a service, might summarize the events of the day. If there had been many converts, the prayer would thank God for them. If there had been a "coldness" in the society, the prayer might be a plea for more "vital religion" in the membership. In an oral culture, skill in public praying was highly valued.

Many southern women represented their societies to God in public prayers. In North Carolina, Elizabeth Carey closed a meeting with prayer. Minister Joseph Travis recalled that his mother, who died in 1808, was frequently asked to close Methodist services with prayer. Margaret Wilson of Augusta County, Virginia, was described as "a woman of fine talents in prayer," so much so that "few men could excell her." The obituary for Prudence Hudson of Delaware noted that she was "gifted in prayer, and frequently exercised that gift in public." Jesse Lee made a comment that reveals how common women's prayer was. Describing a Virginia revival of 1788, he wrote: "There are but few, either men or women, boys or girls, but what will pray when called upon, and sometimes without being asked." In Methodists' perspectives, these women, putting their own words and dramatic skills to work, were representing their fellow believers before God.[45]

The exhortation was also a pivotal part of Methodist services, for it reinforced key points made in the sermon and contained the most direct appeal for converts. The role of exhorter was both an official and unofficial position in the church. Young men being groomed for the ministry were licensed first as exhorters and if successful, next as preachers. Talented lay men—and lay women—who were not on the ministerial career track were also asked to exhort; members given this role were thus publicly recognized as leaders in their local societies and as having the requisite piety and skill. At a well-attended outdoor service, John Early's sermon was followed by an exhortation from a Sister P. Dawson, whom Early described as "a dear saint of God." Dawson's passionate appeal served its purpose, for Early remarked that "Glory to God, he blessed it to the heart." In an 1802 Virginia meeting, Francis Asbury recorded, a Sister Jones (not Sarah) "rose up and gave an exhortation: she spoke as if she were going home to glory—I felt it." Several women exhorted at services over which Jeremiah Norman presided.[46] Female exhorters were publicly recognized as able speakers and local exemplars.

Women occupied other leadership roles as well, such as that of class leader. As disciplinarian and religious advisor, the class leader had the duty of probing each class member's spiritual state. Most class leaders were male, for preachers often appointed men who showed potential ministerial talent to these positions. Still, a small but important number of southern women were also appointed to lead classes. In Baltimore, Maryland, a circle of strong women were class leaders, among them Sisters Owings, Fonarden, Moore, Hawkins, McCannon, Timms, and Chamberlin. Sister Shaeffer, who according to Henry Smith was "one of the most devoted and faithful leaders I ever knew," led the largest female class in the Baltimore area—so large that it had to be divided in 1807. In Loudon County, Virginia, the first class leader appointed was a Mrs. Rozwell. A "Mother in Israel" headed a class of young women in Talbot County, Maryland. Sister Mary White of Delaware led class meetings and religious services from time to time.[47]

In addition, there were unique local opportunities for women's leadership. Methodist women formed female charitable societies in Norfolk and Baltimore. Methodist leaders constantly urged their members to establish schools for children and to place the girls under the tutelage of pious women. A Charleston orphanage with 150 children in its care was under the direction of two Methodist women. Widow Bowlds taught the small children and Sister Robison was their nurse.[48] A number of women's prayer meetings were established in the South, with women at their head. Three were organized in Baltimore in 1792, under Sisters Keener, Owings, and Fonarden. In Charleston, a group of white and black women formed a weekly prayer meeting in 1793. Ezekiel Cooper came back from a men's class meeting in 1791 to find that the women, who met regularly on their own for prayer meetings, were still assembled. In Winchester, Virginia, Sisters Bowers, Wall, and Reid often led prayer meetings.[49] In these varied settings, Methodist women cultivated their abilities and widened their sphere of influence.

Although there is no evidence that southern women were licensed as preachers, many women acted as de facto preachers or were described as preachers. Sarah Jones, as we will see, filled in for ministers both at her local church and in neighboring societies. The first Methodist to preach in Queen Anne's County was a blind Sister Rogers. Many women were credited with "assisting" preachers in ways that suggest they acted as vice-pastors. Catherine Bruff, for example, "was very useful" in a Baltimore revival of 1800, according to preacher Henry Boehm. Francis Asbury wrote to a Maryland woman and actually used the term "preach." He urged her to "Speak to all the sisters, aged and young, rich and poor. Pray with them, preach to them powerfully in companies." Sarah Hinton of Washington, North Carolina, was said to have had "the best gifts" of a preacher. She "not only sang and prayed in public, but exhorted also in the presence of all conditions of men."[50]

In the fluid situation that existed when Methodism was new to an area, women sometimes found themselves with other pastoral opportunities for leadership. After the Revolutionary War, Bennet Maxey was appointed missionary to Georgia. As a lone laborer, he could not reach every Methodist. At one settlement lived two women who had been members in Maryland. As no services were nearby, these women met each

Sunday in the woods for a class and prayer meeting. They were discovered one Sabbath by a hunter, who was enthralled and touched by their solitary devotions. He invited them to hold a church service in his cabin the following Sunday and publicized the event throughout his neighborhood. Because of the novelty of women conducting a service, the crowd that attended was large. The women read from the Bible ("in a clear, strong voice"), sang a hymn, and prayed. The audience, already bathed in tears, then heard one of the women describe her conversion with "a majesty and power truly wonderful." A shout ensued, many fell to the floor, and a few ran away frightened. The word spread and more people flocked to the hunter's cabin; services went on almost continuously for two weeks. Bennet Maxey was miles away when he heard of the women's work, and he arrived to find them "fighting most manfully the battle of the Lord" with forty converts already to their credit. The man who recorded this story also saw fit to remark that critics would see the women's actions as "shocking to delicacy, for women to speak in public, especially in such a mixed assembly." To answer this charge he repeated a common Methodist refrain: "God's ways are not as our ways."[51]

Evidence survives that at least one white southern woman officially communicated to Methodist leaders her desire to preach. Sister Deborah Lynch Owings, a prominent class leader of Baltimore, believed she had a call to preach, and the reaction of her ministers reveals that the church did not foreclose the possibility of women preachers. Brother Shadford encouraged her to attend a quarterly meeting and practice there, but Owings "made an attempt to address the people, and failed." She fell into despair, thinking that God would desert her because she had disobeyed his call. Preacher John Littlejohn somewhat disapproved of Owings's preaching, referring to it as "enthusiasm," but he still encouraged her to make a second attempt at addressing an audience.[52] Placed in context, the two preachers' reaction to Owings's call was remarkably progressive. One minister seemed to wholly approve, the other disapproved, but both encouraged her to try, and neither lectured her on women's "proper" roles in the church or attempted to dispute her call. Women's preaching had been and would continue for many decades to be extremely controversial in America, yet these men had given Owings an opportunity at a regional gathering of Methodists.

Owings's experience raises an interesting question that is ultimately unanswerable—what was the official position of the church on women's preaching? Easier to answer is the question of ordination and licensing, for there is no evidence that any women were licensed or ordained.[53] Although it is unlikely that all Methodist preachers would have assented to the course taken by Littlejohn and Shadford, there are no indications that they were atypical clergymen. Stith Mead, for example, explicitly supported women's preaching in his memoirs. Probably a combination of custom, clerical sexism, women's reticence, and ministerial entreaties worked to limit the number of encounters like that between Owings and her preachers. John Lednum wrote of Mary White, who presided over services and class meetings, that "she would have gone further and preached, if Mr. Asbury had encouraged her."[54]

Methodists were nonetheless noteworthy for the roles they did open to women. British Quaker Dorothy Ripley came to America on a preaching tour in 1802, in part to campaign for the abolition of slavery. Ripley was shunned by many Protestants, finding her greatest support from American Friends and Methodists. In Washington, a

Methodist preacher who was unable to make his nighttime appointment asked Ripley to preach in his stead, and Ripley reported that many people from the capitol and neighboring Georgetown attended. Ripley became so well known for preaching in Methodist services that Quakers in the American North and in Britain feared she had defected to Methodism. In her autobiography, Ripley described an important meeting with the two American bishops, Asbury and Richard Whatcoat. According to Ripley, the bishops received her as a fellow minister, even giving her the names of Methodists whom she could turn to for support and helping her to appoint meetings among Methodist blacks.[55]

Women routinely led critical parts of services, but they were normally not placed in the positions of trustee or steward. There were rare exceptions, such as a group of women who acted as trustees for a church in Elk Ridge, Maryland, that had little white male support. Bishop Asbury made no negative mention of this anomaly, which seems to indicate that Methodists did not oppose women in such positions, although they clearly preferred to have male stewards and trustees.[56] Some state laws barred all women (and black men) from such positions, by requiring trustees to be white male citizens if a church wished to officially incorporate. Trustees and stewards registered deeds for church property, arranged to construct, improve, and maintain church buildings, and sometimes handled other financial matters, such as providing money for the poor or widowed in societies or supporting preachers and their families. Methodist ministers seemed to have preferred appointing members to these positions who had more experience with the courts, the law, and accounting. Also, trustees and stewards tended to be wealthier than the average member, and they were often asked to make up deficits from their own purses.[57] Some historians have suggested that since women were normally excluded from the financial-administrative end of church leadership that they were effectively rendered powerless in southern churches.[58] The evidence strongly indicates, however, that this was not the case. The primary business of Methodist churches was not conducted in dull Saturday afternoon trustee meetings but in the vibrant services themselves. Women were prominent in those services.

The majority of women who shout and pray and reprove in the pages of preachers' journals are obscure: some are never named. Snippets of stories of others tantalize without detail, leaving us wanting far more. Obituaries fill in many gaps, ironically bringing to life the very dead being memorialized, but because Methodists set such store on dying triumphantly, obituaries, too, leave much of women's pre-deathbed lives in shadows. There were, however, southern Methodist women who achieved such legendary stature that they were known throughout the region. The stories of their lives in the church reveal many of the familiar contours of women's religious experiences, as well as the distinct and varied contexts women operated within.[59]

The most remarkable white woman in the southern church was Sarah Jones of Mecklenburg County, Virginia. Jones was famous for her piety, her prose, and her assertive defense of Methodism. Like many other women, Jones became a Methodist over her husband's strenuous objections. Tignal Jones was known as a man of "violent passions and a most ungovernable temper," and true to this characterization, he tried to stop his wife from attending Methodist services, once threatening to shoot her if she went. Sarah defied him, saying it was God's will that she attend a service, and returned from the meeting to face "her infuriated husband at the door, with his gun in his hand." She told Tignal that if he wanted to shoot her he would have to ask God's permission, and then she disarmed him. Tignal eventually joined his wife as a Methodist but never became as committed to the cause as Sarah.[60]

Sarah Jones was a prolific letter writer, and her correspondence with numerous preachers and lay people connected her to the larger Methodist community. Jones's letters were cherished by those who received them, for she thoughtfully and vividly described, in a style all her own, her spiritual struggles as a Methodist. Her prose traced the angst and ecstasy of religious life; few converts were as eager to plumb the depths of their psyches as Jones was. When Jones was ecstatic, she soared to heights undreamt of by many. Asbury said of her that she "wrote to admiration—all in raptures." Thomas Mann, who read Jones's published letters more than a decade after her death, concluded from them that she was a "good and gerat [sic] saint." Jones wrote essays on religious subjects as well. One on "Fortitude" so impressed James Meacham that he took it with him on his rounds and read it to another woman, Sister P. G., noting his "hope it will spur her up to much Diligence as also myself."[61]

Jones was part of a local community of Methodists that nurtured one another and, evidently, encouraged Jones to use her talents. Sally Eastland, Sister Taylor, Sister K., Sally Boyed, and Nancy Smith were as much a part of her life as the preachers who praised her. When Jones fell ill in 1792, Nancy Smith came to care for her and although Jones refused to "visit" socially (she called visiting "insipid"), she believed it her duty to visit Methodists who were sick. The published collection of her letters offers other insights into the ways women formed intimate ties with fellow Methodists and simultaneously broadened each other's world. Religious letters seem to have been used much as devotional essays, for these letters were shared with other Methodists much as Meacham shared her essay on fortitude. Within a letter to Jeremiah Minter, Sarah mentioned that she was enclosing part of a letter from L. M., said that she had shared Minter's previous letters to her with Brother D. A., asked Minter to write to Sally Eastland, and described how she, Eastland, and Sister Taylor, while reading one of Minter's letters aloud, were "set on fire" with "shouting and adoring."[62]

Jones, Thomas Ware noted, was a "person of superior gifts," and her talents lay not only in writing. James Meacham noted that she was "an excellent singer." Francis Asbury, who concurred that Jones "sung with great sweetness," attended a quarterly meeting in 1786 where "the words of our excellent sister Jones, both in speaking and in prayer, were sweetly and powerfully felt."[63] Quarterly meetings brought all the preachers together in a region, and yet Jones's efforts, in Asbury's mind, stood out more than those of his fellow ministers. Jones's description of her activities at another quarterly meeting may help explain why Asbury was impressed: "God poured his spirit out upon me, and I was at liberty in presence of my foes,—Hell trembled; and a woman of note . . . , a Mrs. W——r, got converted; and many others were cut to the heart."[64]

From her published letters it appears that Jones's public "speaking" might properly be called "preaching." She reported, for example, that in a 1791 service, "God gave me a convert." Enoch George had been scheduled to preach, but Jones presided when "he was not there." She substituted for a minister at least once more in 1792: "Last Sunday we had no preacher, and I met a company, (some seekers,) about fifteen miles from home. . . . I began conversing, singing, and praying about 12 o'clock, and tears rolled, and a time we had. In the afternoon I met again for prayer, and a rich merchant roared out, through conviction; and my son in law wept, with my daughter; and the place was shaken with the power of God." "I have seen God's power in declaring Christ amid hundreds," she wrote later that same month, "some have been lately converted, I hope, with me." Except for administering church rites, Jones's role was the same as that of other local preachers.[65]

Mary Hinde, who was far more successful at getting her husband to adopt her values, had an equally difficult experience in her early life as a Methodist. Her daughter was the first in the family to convert, but Thomas, Mary's husband, so opposed Methodism that he sent their daughter to live with an aunt and told her that she must give up the Methodists or "never . . . see his face again." But before Thomas had banished his daughter, she had infected Mary with Methodism.[66] Thomas Hinde was a London-trained physician and may have been exposed to Anglo-American doctors' common wisdom that Methodist "enthusiasm" was a form of mental illness. He tried first to bar his wife from Methodism by "refusing to furnish her with a horse to ride to church," but Mary walked instead. He became convinced that Methodists made their followers "deranged." The solution, Thomas believed, lay in treatment, and he applied a blister plaster to his wife to cure her. Mary was undaunted by the large blister that soon appeared and went to church anyway. Thomas was so impressed with his wife's perseverance in spite of pain that he eventually followed Mary into the church, and, unlike Tignal Jones, he became noted for his piety.[67] Mary Hinde remained bold in the cause of religion throughout her life. Henry Boehm remembered her as a "noble woman" who "gave a reason of the hope within her, silenced infidels, and carried the war into the enemy's camp."[68] Everyone who knew the Hindes admitted that Mary was the more zealous and indomitable of the two. Her husband, by all accounts, was proud of and inspired by his wife's reputation.

Elizabeth Henry Russell was another Methodist woman known far and wide for her piety and assertiveness. Russell converted following a service in 1788 and, unlike most husbands, General Russell followed her example that same day. Russell came from an eminent Virginia family—she was the sister of Patrick Henry. Jacob Young believed Elizabeth to be Patrick's equal: "She was eloquent, like her brother; a woman of exemplary piety and great zeal." A woman who lived near Russell remembered her as "excellent but eccentric" and "extraordinary." Russell's eccentricities included wearing men's hats, eschewing carriages for horses she mounted from a stump in her yard, and her pronounced piety.[69] General Russell died, leaving Elizabeth a widow, and she soon freed all the slaves she owned outright, which reportedly shocked and angered her slaveholding neighbors. She also, according to her biographer grandson, so believed in Methodist exhortations against worldliness that she renounced the property she held for herself in dower (from two marriages) as "acts of self-abnegation and generosity." She moved into a modest cabin and devoted half of its first floor to a Methodist chapel.[70]

Russell was by all accounts a woman of firm will, as two famous incidents in her life reveal. The first occurred with her son-in-law, Colonel Preston, who was known in Methodist parlance as an "infidel." He held a party in her honor, and just before dinner, in front of numerous guests, Russell "ordered the Bible to be laid on the stand" and commanded "Colonel Preston, go to prayer!" The second involved James

Madison, who was then a candidate for president. Madison was a guest in Russell's home, and she reportedly placed a firm hand on Madison's head, "and gently pressing him to his knees, as she knelt by his side, with all her force and zeal she prayed for him." Afterwards she seems to have lectured him on the benefits of free trade. Other Methodists held her in high esteem; the first college Methodists established in western Virginia, Emory and Henry, was named for Bishop Emory and Elizabeth Henry Campbell Russell.[71]

The experiences of these three famous women help illustrate what some women achieved as Methodists and encountered as a result of their religion. In Methodism, Elizabeth Russell forged an identity of her own. Being the sister to one famous patriot and the wife of two respected military leaders, Russell's life story could easily have been lost amid the battles and speeches of the men around her. Instead, because of her experiences in the church, she emerges as a forceful woman whose various homes became centers of Methodist activity and whose dedication to her faith won her respect and, in Methodist circles, fame. Jones, too, carved out a space of autonomy within religion. In her church, she conquered rich merchants, battled sin, led services, and wrote so eloquently of her spiritual life that her letters generated a denominational name for her. Mary Hinde became the matriarch of a large spiritual family that stretched beyond kin. Intrepid and zealous, she, too, warred for the cross. One of Mary Hinde's lasting legacies is perhaps the least obvious. In the 1820s, her son would write an extremely popular account of the progress of Methodism in the West. While other authors were obscuring women's outspokenness in the early church and touting the conversions of scoffing men over steadfast women, Mary's son pointedly wrote of the racial, class, and gender inversions that were central to early Methodism. It was he who recalled that his mother was viewed as more "indefatigable" than the good doctor. His respect for his mother's accomplishments undoubtedly influenced his interpretation of early Methodism.

As the stories of Hinde and Jones show, Methodist women's first acts of defiance were often attending Methodist services. While not all "Mothers in Israel" were as brave or defiant, conflicts between pious wives and the male relations who opposed them were ubiquitous.[72] Tales of persecuting husbands and fathers became part of the Methodist canon; their power derived from their basis in real life. The responses of patriarchs varied from the violent to the humorous. A Miss Connor of Tuckahoe Neck, Maryland, converted despite her family's opposition. Their method of deterring her was unique; in order "to keep her from going to a Methodist meeting," they "locked up her best apparel." When Connor went to meeting in her "ordinary clothes," her parents were "so mortified" that they relented to her wishes. Other women faced angry and abusive men. In March of 1792 James Meacham had retired for the evening when he "was wakened by the odious noise of a poor man, who appeared furious; who was in pursuit of his poor wife, that came to prayers." The woman had fortunately left before her husband arrived; the man "went off in a rage."[73] Sometimes men objected to the Methodists so stridently that they attempted to control women's religiosity at all times. "Mrs. Roberts" was in tears while describing her trials to Meacham. Her husband had threatened that "if he found her at prayers he would pull her up and abuse her."[74]

Perhaps Mr. Roberts was a rationalist; perhaps he belonged to another, more traditional, church. Yet many white southern men of various backgrounds and beliefs acted with anger and hostility and the broad pattern suggests the causes went beyond particular men and their personal opinions. Indeed, white men had reason to believe that their Methodist wives and daughters were at war with them. The church attacked fundamental aspects of southern white male identity. Upper-class men had much to fear from evangelicals, who denounced greed, pride, and ostentation and proclaimed that "God is no respecter of persons." Yet white men of all classes found their habits and rituals under attack by the church. Many of the activities condemned by Methodists were overwhelmingly male ones—like gambling, brawling, lawsuits, horse racing, cockfighting, and dueling. Some actions defined as sinful by the church, such as drinking, fighting, slaveholding, and dueling, had a special meaning in the male world of honor, for they cemented bonds between men and united them in a culture in which women had little influence.[75] In such a context, white women's embrace of the church was also a challenge to men's ideological hegemony. Considering how often Methodist women reproved sin and how many of these sins were "male," Mrs. Roberts may well have prayed—loudly and earnestly—that her husband would abandon his evil ways (which she may even have enumerated.) Methodist values, in short, were easily seen as subversive of southern masculine norms and patriarchy.

Methodist gender ideology did not consist solely of negative prescriptions. Like other evangelicals, Methodists exalted virtues traditionally considered feminine and condemned those traditionally seen as masculine. The church advanced an image of the ideal Christian as meek, obedient, humble, and submissive. Some historians have suggested that by exalting such virtues, evangelical leaders were attempting to control women by offering a spiritual justification of their subordination. Yet men were expected to cultivate these same qualities and the church honored pious Methodist men who did. Henry Smith feelingly recalled the saintliness of his former colleague John Kobler: "He was always and everywhere the same humble, unassuming, sweet-spirited, heavenly-minded man. O how often we have retired together from some log-cabin to a lonely place for private prayer, and embraced, and wept over each other's necks, and sometimes shouted aloud for joy, that we were accounted worthy to suffer a little in the cause of Christ! I have known many of the excellent of the earth, both among the preachers and membership, but a more humble, guileless, holy man, I never saw than my friend John Kobler." The distance between the man described in this obituary and the man of honor was vast. In the South, obedience, submission, humility, and meekness were all qualities associated with ideal wives and slaves (and in his journal, Kobler empathized with slaves and despised their owners). To become a Methodist meant—at the least—to embrace a worldview at odds with secular masculine ideals.[76] When women chose a church so antithetical to southern masculine values, they challenged a patriarch's vision of the world. Placed in this context, it is easier to comprehend why Freeborn Garrettson was once accused by an irate husband of "killing his wife."[77] Garrettson had committed a figurative and not a literal murder—he had converted the woman to Methodism. To many men, it seems, the effect was the same.

Women could, moreover, promote their visions of morality by converting their menfolk to the faith. Women's overriding reason for family evangelism was, of course, their desire that their male relations be saved. But women had other, more practical, reasons for trying to bring their men into the church. Women who successfully converted male relatives gained a measure of influence over their economic and personal lives. Women had a vested interest in—but little control over—family finances. Gambling represented a risk to women's future security, and by bringing men to Methodism women could use church rules to stop their men from betting. Methodists' opposition to drinking as well may have benefited some women on personal levels, reducing the unpredictability of male behavior.[78]

Women could also hope to alter their relationships with patriarchs through the mediating influence of the church. Methodists promoted love as the ideal basis for human interaction and opposed violence against adults by household heads—whether against spouses or slaves. A John Wesley sermon reprinted in the *Methodist Magazine* stated Methodist views unequivocally. "I cannot find in the bible," Wesley wrote, "that a husband has the authority to strike his wife on any account: even suppose she struck him first." Wesley's wording went well beyond southern custom and law, for he not only denied the effectiveness of violence, he denied that men had any "authority" to strike their wives, regardless of the circumstances.[79] Some Methodist marriages were evidently as loving as church ideals recommended, although it would be spurious to claim that all marriages between Methodists were as happy and affectionate as that of John Young, Sr. Young had been married for 44 years (and "five months and five days," he added) when his wife died in 1813. He recalled that "we had one bed one table one purs [sic] and there was no secrets between us so we allso had one mind." James Meacham called his wife, Polly, his "second self." Of William Partridge, it was said that "industry, piety, peace, and harmony were the motto of his house."[80] Not every Methodist man was as committed to harmony, for we know of Methodist opposition to wife beating precisely because some men in the church were disciplined for beating their wives. The church did, however, offer women an alternative to the courts in seeking to restrain patriarchal abuses, and did establish—as an ideal—a harmonious, nonviolent, and loving household.

Women who converted male relatives to Methodism also seem to have found more support for their public roles in churches than those who lived with non-Methodists. Francis Asbury made a revealing comment about a North Carolina woman, Widow Argate, whom he visited in 1805: "here is a change; the man is dead: the widow was attentive, and the blacks crowded to prayers."[81] The career of a Mrs. Tamzey Causey even more vividly shows the advantages of marrying a fellow Methodist. Causey converted in 1775, at the age of fourteen, but her father despised Methodism and attempted to persuade her to join the church. This "unavailing, he proceeded to threats, resolved, as mild measures would not answer, to violent." Despite her father's threats—one of which was that he would disinherit her—Causey continued to attend as many Methodist services as she could, although her parents prevented her from joining the church. Causey married a man who was also "much opposed" to Methodism (she had become engaged before she converted), but after marrying she was at least able to become a member. Widowed in 1796, Causey remarried in 1797 but this time it was to another Methodist. This marriage was decidedly different. "Those graces which had been partially hid under a bushel . . . ," her biographer noted, "were now more than usually brought forth. . . . Freed from those trials and hindrances which had so thickly strewed her path from the beginning, she pressed forward with redoubled vigour." Causey, when unopposed by male relations, became a central figure in her society, counseling, advising, and comforting others. Not surprisingly, her constant advice to Methodist youth was to warn them of the "destructive evil" of marrying an unbeliever. Having a husband in the church, for Causey at least, brought more than religious harmony; it also brought her freedom to develop her skills as a leader.[82]

Domestic conflicts did not always pit unbelieving men against Methodist women. Because of Methodism's doctrinal peculiarities and reputation for enthusiasm, even men of strong religious bent but different denominations could find much to oppose in the church. One obviously exasperated critic wrote the Methodists in New Bern, North Carolina, in 1808 and asserted as biblical "doctrine that a man has by the law of God such dominion over his Wife that she is bound to become a member of any church he prefers."[83] The correspondent's resort to "doctrine" makes perfect sense in a patriarchal culture. When a Methodist wife challenged her non-Methodist husband on free agency, perfection, or falling from grace, she introduced conflict over basic beliefs into the household. Preachers were often allies of women at odds with relatives. John Early met a young woman who wanted to become a Methodist but was opposed by her Baptist family. She, however, "could not be reconciled to be a Baptist." "I commended her to Jesus," Early reported, "and told her to join the Methodists through every opposition if she thought it was the will of God."[84]

Early used a telling expression—the will of God. Methodists believed that God's will should preempt every earthly consideration and that all Christians could discern God's will by attending church, reading the Bible, and by properly interpreting dreams and visions. Wesley, known for his harsh regimen for breaking the wills of small children and subordinating them to parental authority, even exempted them from obeying their parents if their parents' desires contravened God's will.[85] Sarah Jones had taken refuge in God's will when she defied her husband and attended a Methodist service. Rhoda Laws, a twelve-year-old Methodist whose father was an Anglican priest, also refused to obey her father's wishes because, in her view, they ran counter to God's will. Before converting, Rhoda's favorite pastime was dancing. Hoping to lure his daughter away from the Methodists, Parson Laws gave a ball, and tried to get her to dance by telling her it was not sinful. But Rhoda, claiming dancing was an offense "against my God and my conscience," refused. Instead, she retreated to the kitchen and read the Bible to her father's slave cook, another act of rebellion for he feared she would thus "ruin" his slaves.[86]

Although it is unlikely that women became Methodists merely because they wanted to defy male relations in the guise of religion, it is still clear that Methodist doctrines, values, and practices supported some women in their quest for autonomy. Women communicated directly with God through their dreams and visions, and like all Methodists did not confine "God's will" to received clerical views about Scripture. For men involved in conflicts with these women, it was obviously frustrating that church beliefs and ministerial advice did not check but instead seemed to support women's independence. Religion holds the keys to the meaning of life and death, right and wrong.[87] We know little of the substance of the conversations or arguments that took place between pious wives and non-Methodist husbands. What we can do is place such disagreements into ideological and temporal context and note that women's religious values introduced tension over moral principles into the home that might never have otherwise surfaced.

Methodism's impact on women spilled beyond strictly "religious" situations. Many southern women found their lives expanding beyond the household in the service of their religion. Sarah Miller's schedule was crowded with church activities. On July 8, 1809, she attended a church service. She had a class meeting scheduled during the day on the 9th, and another service that evening. On July the 10th, she had a funeral sermon to attend, and was already looking forward to a camp meeting that was to begin on September the 8th.[88] For rural women, church activities were opportunities to assemble with neighbors and friends on a regular basis. Another way the church widened the sphere of southern women was a by-product of the itinerant system. In the South, unescorted women rarely ventured far from home. But preachers routinely traveled, and many women accompanied preachers to neighboring villages or regional assemblies. On July 22, 1778, to take but one example, two women rode with Nelson Reed to his next appointment and on the 27th of the same month, Sister Oliver and her daughter did the same.[89]

The church also expanded women's circle of contacts beyond the confines of class and race. During services and class meetings, distinctions of wealth and status were symbolically set aside. Some historians have noted that poorer white women were, at least in later antebellum years, less constrained by custom than elite women. Methodist sources cannot speak fully to this thesis, yet it does seem that elite women in the church were pulled on the one hand by church strictures against upper-class mores and on the other by expectations of other elites that they would maintain these mores. Rebecca Ridgely, for example, immediately after her conversion, was lectured by her husband's friend, Dr. Goodwin, that "it was a shame to kneel before the people." Goodwin told Ridgely that "if he was in my husband's place he would not lett me go again." Ridgely was unconcerned about appearances and was willing to "give all the world" in exchange for the "peace" of conversion.[90]

White women in church services met blacks on the terms closest to equality afforded in southern society. Numerous scholars have found that a basic component of later antebellum proslavery arguments was the premise that white women needed to be protected from black men. When Virginians protested Methodist antislavery petitions to their legislature, they specifically cited "Rapes, Murders, and Outrages" as the natural outcome of a general emancipation. In Lunenberg County, 161 citizens signed a petition that made a thinly veiled reference to rapes they alleged had already been perpetrated by recently emancipated slaves, warning of "Insolences, and Violences so frequently committed to and on our respectable Maids and Matrons." Even in the relatively more open society of the post-Revolutionary era, white women's relationships with black men represented a violation of social norms. Despite such mores, a surprising number of white Methodist women routinely violated racial etiquette in church settings. The first white to join the persecuted black Methodist society in Fayetteville, North Carolina, for example, was Sister Maulsby, who had been expelled from a Presbyterian church for shouting. James Meacham praised "some of the dear humble white sisters" who joined black worshipers in a nighttime service. A number of white women hosted services or class meetings for blacks at their homes. As these meetings took place overwhelmingly at night, the prime hours for slave patrollers, such a step was extremely controversial in some communities.[91]

Methodist women also found the courage in religion to defy communal norms. In the persecutions of the Revolutionary War era, women often came to the rescue of embattled itinerants. Philip Gatch was surrounded by a mob during the war and was fortunate to have a group of Methodists traveling with him. "My company was anxious to fight my way through," he reported. "The women were especially resolute; they dealt out their denunciations against the mob in unmeasured terms." John Littlejohn had finished his sermon at the Pomphrey home when a constable came with a warrant for his arrest for preaching. While the constable confused another Methodist man for Littlejohn, the women came to a window and helped Littlejohn make his escape. The next day, the constable came to a love feast with a posse, but "the Sisters shamed them [and] they departed."[92]

One of the most heroic acts ever performed by a Methodist involved a Charleston woman, Martha Kugley (also spelled Coogley), who braved a proslavery mob. In 1800, the church attempted a last-ditch effort to oppose slavery in its *Address*, which encouraged Methodists to petition state legislatures for immediate or gradual abolition of slavery. Copies of this *Address* were sent to Methodist preachers throughout the South, and some made it to Charleston. Methodism in the city was already identified with white women and blacks. Asbury revealed that the majority of Charlestonians who attended services in 1795 were "women and Africans" and that among whites, there were "few male members." When Charleston residents discovered that local Methodists possessed abolitionist and, in their minds, insurrectionary literature, a mob descended on the nearest Methodist preacher, George Dougherty. Dougherty was held under a water pump, and by reports he would have drowned had it not been for Martha Kugley. Kugley pushed through the crowd, took off her apron, "pushed it into the pump-spout, and commanded them to desist." Kugley's daring becomes even more evident when we recall the duration of hostilities against Methodists in Charleston, precisely because of their reputation as an antislavery church.[93] It should not be surprising that some women were as bold and brave as Kugley in defense of their church. Methodist leaders valued women's advice and support, offered them more leadership opportunities than were afforded in secular society, and respected their opinions, intellect, and piety.

In the early decades of southern Methodism, women formed the majority of members and supported the church with their time, money, and labor. They violated gender conventions in the service of their religion by speaking in public assemblies, meeting blacks on terms closer to equality than were normal, lecturing men outside their families, or disobeying the orders of husbands and fathers. Women were often the centers of their religious communities, and many occupied formal and informal leadership positions. Finally, women were entrusted with conducting coveted parts of Methodist services—testimony, prayer, exhortation, and even, on occasion, sermons. What is even more remarkable is that women did all these things amidst a chorus of non-Methodist opposition. To join a church that was in its early years despised and ridiculed, to support that church in spite of vociferous objections by men inside and outside their families, to voluntarily align with a group that was during the Revolution suspected of disloyalty and after the war associated with abolition was a decision that could not have been taken lightly.

White women found in Methodism a definition of self that was as individualistic as that found by men in politics.[94] For most women simply joining the church represented an act of autonomy and self-assertion, and as their religious lives progressed they were further able to speak their minds and follow their consciences. In the church they were valued for their advice, intellect, and courage and found a measure of public respect and affirmation of their individual dreams, goals, and worldviews.

We began our exploration with Mary Hinde's bold rebuke of a deist. It is fitting to close with a more private demonstration of Methodist women's altered sense of agency and power. Protestant Christianity was infused with masculine imagery and manly rhetoric; the King James Bible, like the Methodist *Discipline*, used "he," "him," "brethren," and "man" when discussing both genders. We might expect the masculine bias of biblical language to provoke little comment from eighteenth-century southerners, even from women, for the language of the King James Bible was revered and deemed authentic by most Americans. But by inserting two small words in the middle of a New Testament verse, words easily overlooked in the middle of a lengthy passage, Sarah Jones made a place for herself and southern women like her who had been persecuted by southern men. On September 10, 1792, Jones mused on the certainty of suffering in the world before quoting and amending the Bible: "But these are the days that all flesh shall be tried, I verily believe; and *blessed is the man, or woman, that endureth temptation, for when he is tried he shall receive a crown of life.*"[95]

S I X

Slavery, Racism, and the
Master-Slave Relationship

The Methodist preachers of that day believed if the heart
were made right, it would influence the life and conduct of
the individual.

—John M'Lean, *Philip Gatch*[1]

I N HIS BIOGRAPHY OF Philip Gatch, John M'Lean wrote these words describing early
Methodism. Gatch, a man M'Lean came to know in church, in politics, and in the
courts, was one of the Virginia Methodists who freed his slaves and who so abhorred
slavery that he emigrated to Ohio with his wife and children.[2] With them also went
four slaves whose manumission dates had not yet arrived because by Virginia law, any
freed persons under the age of twenty-one were their former owner's responsibility;
to leave them in Virginia might have put their freedom in jeopardy. Gatch continued to
work against slavery and for blacks in Ohio. As a delegate to the constitutional convention, he voted to keep Ohio a free state and supported black suffrage, although this
latter measure did not pass. In his will he left part of his land to his four former slaves,
by this time residents of Ohio.

At the close of the eighteenth century, Methodists like Philip Gatch challenged the
values of a slaveholding society, both explicitly and implicitly.[3] Preachers' work for
emancipation, their efforts to reduce the suffering of slaves, their critique of the
master-slave relationship, and their attacks on certain kinds of racial prejudice all represent part of their mission to change southern values. For these few decades, Methodists, vocal and visible throughout the region, were the largest organized group to
consistently make antislavery pronouncements. A number of southern-born converts,
like Gatch, came to believe slavery was a sin, and developed what scholars term a new
"humanitarian sensibility."[4] Methodist antislavery appeals drew on moral and Christian precepts of old vintage and infused them with new meaning and urgency. Their
vision of the ideal South was one where each person was free from sin and from slavery, where the Golden Rule governed human relationships, and where men and
women strived to emulate God's mercy and justice. White Methodists did not always
live up to their ideals, but in an era when whites who had power were linking eman-

cipation with black misrule and insisting that property in human beings was essential to their own freedom, unlettered itinerants and plain folk members were preaching and testifying against slavery in public. Methodists' appeals to empathy had limited effect outside their membership; their entreaties to politicians enraged slave-owning elites and stimulated a growing interest in an ideological defense of slavery. The story of Methodist antislavery is one of idealism and faltering courage, of optimism and naiveté, of the possibilities and the limits of dissent in the early national South.

The interdependence of racism and slavery, so obvious to modern scholars, eluded many Methodist preachers. Steeped in their own prejudices, idealistic about human ability to recognize moral truth, and overwhelmed by an entrenched and systemic evil, they fell back on "God is no respecter of persons,"[5] a Bible verse they repeated often when working with blacks. Yet as Methodists themselves were wont to point out, God's ways and southern ways were not the same, and merely because white Methodists believed that God did not see color did not mean that they themselves were color-blind. White preachers referred to African Americans in ways that show their consciousness of racial difference—in terms of color ("black," "colored," or less often "sable"), as "Africans," as "Negroes," or as the "sons and daughters of Ham."[6] Their stark separation of the "worldly" from the "godly," moreover, seems to have allowed them to countenance worldly prejudice even as they noted God was free of it. Some preachers were oblivious to their own bigotry. The antislavery stalwart, Richard Whatcoat, noted of one black preacher that "he speaks well for a Negro." Thomas Morrell, commenting on Virginians' penchant for "noisy meetings," singled out black Methodists, whose "noise appears too mechanical tho at times attended with power."[7] When a slave owner who rose to testify in an early nineteenth-century service began to cough, a local Methodist preacher even included an epithet within an antislavery remark, telling the master that if he would "cough up the niggers . . . you'll have an open time."[8] Methodist whites, sometimes crudely racist, were not as free of prejudice as their God.[9]

White Methodists did not, however, accept every racist assumption of the age.[10] When referring to enslaved blacks, most preachers used evocative and sympathetic language. Slaves were "captives weary and heavy ladend," "poor afflicted negroes," and "poor, oppressed, neglected Africans," rhetoric that stressed how slaves were victimized by their owners.[11] Preachers also rejected the prevalent notion that blacks were naturally less moral than whites. Slavery encouraged sin in both master and slave, but according to Methodists, masters were at greater moral risk because the law did not check the power of these fallible and worldly beings. "How the world destroys the happiness of white folks,"[12] William McKendree once remarked, after a joyous night meeting with blacks. His reasoning followed from Methodist views about the corrupting nature of wealth. Since slaves and most free blacks were poor, they did not have to overcome the hurdles of honor, status, and security to faithfully adhere to church standards. The contempt other whites had for African Americans was further proof that blacks were not inherently immoral. For Methodists, to be "despised of men" was to be right with God, and slaves were the most "despised" people in America. But the main reason preachers rejected the idea of black moral inferiority was that their own experience belied such a view. In many areas, blacks were more receptive to Methodism than whites; preachers thus often concluded that blacks were morally superior.

Certainly this was James Meacham's opinion in August of 1789, when he awoke to hear blacks singing hymns in a plantation kitchen while "proud whites . . . live in luxury and abomination."[13] Daily encounters like this one help explain why many preachers had little patience with the proslavery cant that bondage was justified because of blacks' innate immorality.

Because they did not share every white prejudice, because they preached and ministered to blacks, and because they spoke out against slavery, Methodist preachers often seemed like racial radicals to other whites. Frenchman Charles Janson complained that Virginia Methodists "do great mischief among the slaves, whom they receive into their congregation, and place among the most select part of their white brethren." His statement is fascinating for what it ignores as well as what it condemns, for his words "place among the most select part of their white brethren" were figurative. For Janson, the fact that Methodists allowed blacks to become members was "mischief" enough.[14] White Charlestonians, even after the church had all but abandoned antislavery efforts, believed Methodists were "disorganizers who could not be trusted among the negroes without danger to the public peace."[15] In a climate where the questioning of slavery made southerners a "danger to the public peace," white Methodists may well have been unable to see their own bigotry, dwarfed as it must have seemed by the invidious, overt racism of their critics.

Some white Methodists struggled mightily against their own prejudices. The untiring antislavery advocate James Meacham recorded an incident in his journal that shows a remarkable degree of self-conscious criticism. Meacham was riding to a preaching appointment in 1789, when "I overtook a poor black Bro[ther] on foot I passed on after conversing a little with him. Some time afterward I saw him a Distance before me in a run, my poor heart began to melt while I remember'd his burden. I thought it was my duty to get down and walk and let my black bro[ther] ride. I thought, if it was a white perhaps my heart would submit to give him my seat."[16] Meacham was aware of his prejudice and, despite his sympathy for the slave "Brother," unable to overcome it. Most whites of his era would not have had second thoughts or soul-searching about not surrendering a horse to a slave. But Meacham, who considered all of his fellow Methodists "brothers" and "sisters," was aware of the inequality in his Christian family and even in his own heart.

Ezekiel Cooper's desire to be free of color prejudice caused him to temporarily suspend Methodist rules requiring the condemnation of sin when he visited a wealthy mulatto woman of Maryland. She was a tavern keeper "of property of land and slaves." Cooper took special note of her "high head" (a reference to her hairstyle) and her knowledge of the "things of the world ancient and modern." What is striking about this encounter is Cooper's lack of criticism of either her worldly hairstyle ("high heads" were a favorite target of Methodist preachers) or her ownership of slaves. Instead, he delighted in the fact that she proved "that it is not [color] that disqualifies people" for success. Cooper's pride in her achievements prevailed over both his antislavery sentiment and his asceticism.[17] Cooper was better equipped than most preachers to understand the way racism undergirded slavery. He was the most familiar of the clergy with proslavery arguments and regularly wrote antislavery essays for the secular press. This unusual incident illustrates the difficulty even a highly educated and committed antislavery Methodist had in consistently attacking slavery in such a racist society. Preachers were supposed to denounce sin wherever they found it. The fact that this slaveholder was a genteel black woman should not have made a difference.

Cooper and Meacham were unusually self-conscious about racial prejudice. Many Methodists did not even recognize their own racism and thus were poorly equipped to fight the bigotry of others. Whites who wished to be part of the evangelical movement and yet were unwilling to renounce prejudice may have seen some church practices as tacit endorsement of white supremacy, such as when black members were relegated to balconies or forced to commune after whites had communed. Even after free blacks let clergy know in no uncertain terms that they considered segregated arrangements odious and un-Christian, white church leaders made no effort to adopt a policy against such seating in slave or in free states. Nor did they seem to grasp that segregation in meetinghouses compromised their doctrine of sanctification. If God made no distinction in "colour or seat"[18] in Heaven, why were Methodists, striving to emulate God, making such distinctions?

Entangled in their own prejudices, Methodists did not formulate a doctrinal position on racism and they did not take seriously enough the way racism undergirded slavery. Methodists cited greed, pride, and, above all, irreligion as the primary reasons men and women kept slaves. Ezekiel Cooper, writing as "A Freeman," attacked a proslavery poem in the *Maryland Gazette*. The poet had alleged that freedmen and -women would "be lazy, steal, and court the gallows," but Cooper countered that blacks were in the main an "industrious, civil people" who stole in slavery only to avoid starving. Yet even in this piece, Cooper blamed "avarice" for the southern proslavery position and intimated that the author was concocting racist arguments to hide his true motive, greed. Bishop Asbury likewise called white fears about freedmen a "pretext" for holding slaves, "when the true cause was avarice." Methodist preachers had frequent contact with pious and industrious free blacks and thus could not imagine how any white could believe the horrid predictions of proslavery spokesmen. The Methodists certainly had a point in foregrounding greed, yet their denial that slaveholders' prejudices were authentic clearly limited the breadth of their attack.[19]

The church's antislavery position was first and foremost Wesleyan, and from John Wesley, American missionaries inherited hostility to wealth (and hence greed) as well as a belief that slavery was an evil. Wesley did not come to his views in the abstract; he was first prompted to consider the morality of slavery by his own encounters with slaves and slavery on his early eighteenth-century mission to America. The juxtaposition of masters' brutal treatment of slaves with slaves' receptivity to his message jarred him. For Wesley, as for his American followers, it was personal contact with enslaved Christians that motivated him to oppose slavery.[20] When Wesley wrote the first *Discipline* for English Methodists, he prohibited "the buying or selling" of "the bodies and souls of men, women, and children."[21] This restriction was probably sufficient to keep English Methodists free of slavery, for it barred slave traders from membership and prohibited the purchase of slaves. This rule remained part of the *Discipline* in the colonies, but there it was fatally flawed. Slavery was so widespread in the American colonies by the time Wesley's missionaries arrived that numerous men and women never had to purchase slaves to become slave owners—and the *Discipline* did not prohibit inheriting or owning slaves.

Wesley's *Thoughts Upon Slavery* elaborated his views about the evils of slavery and the slave trade and heavily influenced his antislavery followers in the American South. Published in 1774, the tract borrowed liberally from Anthony Benezet's writings on Africa and the slave trade, and shows how indebted Anglo-American Methodists were to Quaker abolitionists. One major strength of the treatise is Wesley's inimitable style—the tract is written like one of his sermons. (The concluding section, in homiletic fashion, refers to an "application.") The central moral lessons Wesley tried to impart were that slavery violated the Golden Rule and that if slave traders and slave owners did not abandon their ways, they could expect retribution in the afterlife.[22] But Wesley first had to convince his readers that they were morally culpable for distant actions taken by others, for many slaveholders took refuge in the idea that since they themselves had not personally turned free Africans into slaves, they could not be blamed for the slave trade or slavery. Wesley explained how this was far from true: "Now it is *your* money that pays the Merchant, and thro' him the Captain, and the *African* Butchers. *You* therefore are guilty, yea principally guilty, of all these frauds, robberies and murders [of the slave trade]. You are the spring that puts all the rest in motion: they would not stir a step without *you*."[23] Wesley even alluded to a level of national responsibility for slavery and the slave trade, suggesting that merely by being a citizen of a nation that participated in human traffic, Britons were tied to the sins of that commerce.

To expand his readers' "causal horizons," however, Wesley had to get them to empathize with the suffering of people, some of whom they would never meet, and all of whom their culture considered primarily as inferior and as property. Wesley was not the first theologian to argue that slavery violated the Golden Rule, one of the most central tenets of Christ's teachings, but in using such ancient precepts to justify new ways of thinking, he was part of the movement that resulted in a new "humanitarian sensibility."[24] To convince his readers to extend their circle of moral responsibility even to slaves, Wesley appealed, as he so often did in his writings, to sentiment. "Are you *a man?*" he asked. "Then you should have a *human* heart. . . . What is your heart made of? Is there no such principle as Compassion there? Do you never *feel* another's pain? Have you no Sympathy?"[25] He urged them to put themselves in the place of Africans and slaves, to imagine being torn from their homeland and family, to imagine their own children forced into slavery.

The tract ended with two concessions that, considering subsequent American history, were ominous. After all of his condemnations and pleas, Wesley closed with a prayer in which he asked God to "burst thou [slaves'] chains in sunder; more especially the chains of their sins." With this prayer, Wesley introduced a principle that would eventually undermine American Methodist efforts to end slavery. His priority and the priority of his followers was always saving souls. When American clergy abandoned the antislavery position, they could always point as consolation to their black converts. Wesley and his American followers were at heart evangelists and only secondarily abolitionists.[26] Wesley also introduced another concession—he offered slaveholders an intermediate out. If they would not free their slaves, Wesley said, at least they could treat them with more humanity and less cruelty. So he, on the one hand, decried slavery and the slave trade as absolute moral evils, and, on the other hand, suggested ways to make slavery more "moral." It was a pivotal contradiction.

Just as Wesley was first made to ponder the morality of slavery when he encountered slaves receptive to his message, his American followers were profoundly influenced by their personal contact with blacks. These face-to-face encounters made Wesley's views against slavery more urgent. Not once on the boat journey over did either Joseph Pilmore or Francis Asbury refer to an anticipated black audience in America or to slavery, but soon after their arrival each one made comments about black worshipers—and about the equality of all people before God. Seeing blacks as God's people destined for heaven made slavery the more abominable. For Pilmore, it was a black class meeting where many of the members were "very happy" that provoked him to note how they were "witnesses that [God] is no respecter of persons."[27] Black Methodists kept the indignities and cruelties of slavery on white preachers' minds. Pilmore received a letter from a slave that was ostensibly an apology for not attending class meeting. But the letter was also a plea on behalf of slaves. The man wrote: "my *bondage* is such I cannot possibly attend with the rest of the Class. . . . I wanted to come to the Church at the Watch-night, but could not get leave. . . . I beg an interest in your prayers that I may be able to bear up under all my difficulties with patient resignation to the will of God." Slaves repeatedly complained to preachers when their masters would not let them come to services. Some even complained of abuse, maltreatment, and neglect.[28]

Pressured by slave members and their own consciences, in 1780 American Methodist leaders issued a statement declaring that "slavekeeping is contrary to the laws of God, man, and nature" and a violation of the Golden Rule. The governing body, the conference, also wrote that "we pass our disapprobation on all our friends who keep slaves, and advise their freedom." It was not until 1784, however, when they organized as a separate church, that Methodist leaders attempted to rid their society of slaveholders. By this time, some slaveholders had been Methodists over a decade, and the presence of these men and women was one of the biggest obstacles to Methodist opposition to slavery. (Because they had been members for so long, even strong antislavery men like William Ormond would oppose expelling them with an ex post facto ruling.)[29] The 1784 rules gave slave owners twelve months to free their slaves; those who did not were to be denied the sacrament. No additional slaveholders were to be allowed into the church.[30] Two important exemptions were included, one specifically for Virginia members, the other for members in states that did not allow manumission. Virginians were given an extra year to comply.

Members who owned slaves in states where manumission was not allowed were not penalized under the rule. The deference to state law was a critical compromise, although it is not at all clear what alternatives the church had. In North Carolina, for example, manumission by deed or will was never legal, and thus even the man to whom most people erroneously give sole credit for Methodist antislavery efforts, Thomas Coke, refused to preach against slavery in that state. Daniel Grant, prohibited by Georgia law from emancipating his slaves outright, granted a slave named Sampson freedom in the only way he could—by allowing him to work for himself on Grant's plantation. Legally, however, Sampson remained a slave. Preacher Jesse Lee believed that Gabriel Long, a North Carolina Methodist who wanted to free his slaves, had intentionally left no will because of "his being opposed to slavery, and the laws of the state would not allow him to free them, and he was not disposed to will them to any particular person." Long's ineffective gesture and Sampson's quasi freedom illustrate how the options of lawful protest in some states were decidedly limited.[31]

Methodists seemed to have realized that they would have to try and change state laws if they were to end slavery. Although they prided themselves on their apolitical nature, they felt slavery was a moral problem that they as moral leaders had to address. Preachers' willingness to pressure politicians, to go against their deeply held view that they should refrain from meddling with government, shows how strong their anti-slavery commitment was. They tried first in Virginia, perhaps believing the tide was turning against slavery there. In 1782, Virginia had liberalized manumission laws, allowing slave owners to free adult, nonelderly slaves by will or deed. Emboldened by their convictions and the state's action, in 1785 the church circulated petitions calling upon the General Assembly to abolish slavery either immediately or gradually. Over two hundred Virginians registered their support for abolition by signing these petitions, a small but significant start for such an endeavor. Methodist leaders Francis Asbury and Thomas Coke even tried to get the support of the newly elected George Washington. Washington's help would have been invaluable to the church, which at this time contained few statesmen in its ranks. But the president felt that signing the Methodist antislavery petitions was inappropriate, although he seemed to have promised to make his support for abolition known if Virginia considered the measure. Except in Delaware, Methodists would find few southern spokesmen in the political arena.[32]

The fate of the Virginia effort was tragic. Instead of inspiring lawmakers to consider abolition, Methodist petitions provoked such outrage that the Assembly even considered rescinding the recent law allowing manumission. The repeal was defeated by a vote of 52 to 35, but the fact that Virginia had even considered closing the door to freedom so soon after opening it boded ill. More important to subsequent southern history was the response of Virginia's slaveholding citizens who were so aghast at the Methodist effort that they rushed through proslavery petitions of their own. It must have been horrifying to Methodist leaders that their efforts, so idealistic in intent, served to awaken interest in a sustained defense of slavery. The secular side of these documents stressed two important themes of the proslavery position—that slave owning was intrinsically tied to white liberty and that emancipation would cause utter ruin. The claimants passionately described their rights to property as one of the liberties for which they had fought the late war. The Revolution, they intimated, had been fought, among other reasons, to protect their freedom to hold humans as slaves.[33]

Most of these petitions equated antislavery Methodism with Loyalism, resurrecting the wartime charge that Methodists were Tories. During the Revolution, though, officials did not overtly link Methodist opposition to slavery with Toryism. The Virginia petitions of 1785 did. One called Methodists "Enemies of our Country, Tools of the British Administration." The authors of another seemed most alarmed by the fact that some "Men of considerable weight" supported Methodist antislavery and that these pro-Methodist statesmen (who in reality were few in number) had been "prostituting their [views] by uniting them with a proscribed Coke an imperious Asb[ur]y and other contemptible Emissaries and hirelings of Britain." A third petition referred to "Persons We may reasonably suppose disaffected to our State and Government" who were "pretending to be moved by Religious Principles and taking for their motive universal charity." A fourth put all the various charges together and called the antislavery petitioners "the Enemies of our Country, Tools of the British Administration

. . . supported by a Number of deluded Men," and directly referred to the Methodists' antislavery pronouncements as an attempt "to cover their Design, with the Veil of Piety and Liberality of Sentiment."[34]

Coke was likely singled out for special contempt because he alone was closest to being a British "emissary"—Wesley had sent him to ordain Methodist leaders in late 1784—and Coke was indeed an English citizen. Asbury had been labeled a Tory during the war, but the suggestion that he was a "hireling" of the British was undoubtedly hyperbolic. It is nonetheless easy to see how slave owners made the leap from antislavery to British conspiracy. Revolutionaries had argued, as the petitioners did, that evil British ministers had conspired to "dispose of our Property without our Consent." Virginia masters believed another conspiracy to take away their property was afoot and associated it in typical southern Anglophobic fashion with Britain. The charges that Methodists were insincere are not so easily explained. Perhaps the petitioners were being disingenuous, perhaps they could not believe anyone would religiously object to slavery. The most likely explanation is that Virginia's slave owners connected the attack on slavery to Methodists' antigentry values and pronouncements; to masters, both seemed motivated by envy and rebelliousness, not piety. For Methodists who were watching, the references to loyalism were troubling. By linking Toryism, antislavery attitudes, and Methodism, the proslavery signers had raised the specter of a repeat of wartime persecution.[35]

The proslavery petitions also included many of the arguments that would later appear in the antebellum South. Abolition would cause economic, social, and moral ruin, the petitioners charged. Depredations would be committed on whites, especially white women, if slaves were emancipated. The signers even claimed to have the best interests of the "helpless black Infant and superannuated Parent" at heart.[36] The only thing separating these petitions from later proslavery writings is that they do not mention the evils of "free labor" nor do they make any reference to "the North" at all. With this exception, the petitions represent a very early version of what scholars usually describe as the mature secular proslavery argument.

These documents also include a curious component for legislative petitions. They devote as much space (sometimes more) to biblical defenses of slavery as they do to arguments about property rights. Slave owners were primarily being attacked on religious grounds, and they sensed a need to respond in kind. It is almost amusing to contemplate hundreds of alarmed masters rushing to their Bibles to find support for their contention that slavery was ordained of God. Among the verses cited (many of which were quoted in full) were Leviticus 25: 44–46, Ecclesiastes 2: 7, 1 Corinthians 7: 20 and 24, and numerous verses from Genesis. Although such arguments had been used prior to 1785, these petitions, signed by over 900 citizens, certainly represent a more enhanced level of popular interest in a complex political and religious defense of slavery than had been previously exhibited.[37]

As the Methodist circuit riders set out in 1785 from the conference in which their new rules against slavery had been added to the *Discipline*, and as their antislavery petitions were circulating, one wonders whether they expected the hostility they encountered as a result. Certainly they knew that some slave owners would be recalcitrant. They also probably expected some additional harassment. But public disapproval had reached a new level. Thomas Coke was pursued by mobs, and one woman offered a reward to anyone who would assault him. Francis Asbury was confronted by slave-holders who protested Methodist meddling with slavery.[38] Hundreds of Virginians had signed their names to petitions that included lengthy proslavery arguments as well as allegations that Methodist leaders were acting not out of conscience but out of loyalty to resentful Englishmen. In the face of this opposition, Methodist leaders decided to suspend the offensive rule, leaving in the *Discipline* their statement that they continued to "hold in deepest abhorrence, the practice of slavery; and shall not cease to seek its destruction by all wise and prudent means." They likewise maintained the prohibition against buying and selling slaves.[39]

After the failure of the Virginia effort, only a deep loathing for human bondage explains why Methodists dared try again to influence lawmakers. In 1800, likely fearing that they were losing momentum, Methodist leaders urged state legislatures to abolish slavery. They issued a broadside, entitled *The Address of the General Conference of the Methodist Episcopal Church, to all their Brethren and Friends in the United States*, pleading for members, friends, and ministers to support abolition by petitioning state legislatures to that effect. Because of this initiative, Charleston minister George Dougherty, already under suspicion because he taught black children in a Methodist school, was almost killed. Dougherty's colleague there, John Harper, received copies of this 1800 *Address* through the mails and showed the document to a local minister of another sect. When word got out about the *Address*, mobs went looking for Harper, and found Dougherty instead. Dougherty was dragged to a pump, held under it, and "almost drowned." The fear of South Carolinians, especially Charleston residents, was that slaves would be encouraged to revolt if exposed to Methodist antislavery beliefs.[40]

Afraid for his life, John Harper issued a statement to a local paper that he had not and would not show the *Address* to any slaves, and that he did not wish to see "that which the address recommends, carried into effect by any other than lawful, honorable, and innocent means." In a letter to a longtime friend, Harper revealed—with chilling insight into the psychology of South Carolinians—why his language was so indirect: "There is one striking Peculiarity in this Contest. I have done something very bad, yet my Biterest Enemies dares not lay it before the publick, to let them see how bad it is, nor dare I in my defense, so that lookers on know not what we are Fighting about."[41] The conflict over the *Address* even reached the interior of the state, where James Jenkins was riding circuit. Jenkins came to a small town and a mob followed him to church. When he began administering the sacrament to black members, one of the mob commanded Jenkins not to let the blacks commune and ordered the blacks out of the house.[42]

The highest state officials took prompt notice of the *Address*, with one senator, Jacob Read, cautioning the governor that slave insurrections would surely follow. "Quakers and Methodists have long been sapping the existence of the Southern States . . . ," Read warned. "The former are however harmless when compared to the latter." The governor forwarded the *Address* to the state legislature, along with his condemnation of it.[43] Most disturbing to the Methodist clergy was the fact that the South Carolina legislature both "reprobated" the document in session and enacted a law prohibiting ministers "to instruct blacks with the doors shut" and authorizing "a peace officer to break open the door in such cases, and disperse or whip the offenders." The Palmetto legislators knew the tenderest point at which to strike, for blacks were a large percentage of Methodists in many parts of that state. Once again, it seemed to clergy that anti-slavery efforts resulted not in liberalized laws but in proscriptions against their most vulnerable members.[44]

The *Address* was the church's last attempt as a national body to influence southern lawmakers on slavery. Although Methodism retained rules against slaveholding itinerants (the ostensible cause of the split in 1844), action taken against members who held slaves in the early nineteenth century tended to be based on regional decisions, and these decisions were made with fear and circumspection. In 1808, for example, the Western conference debated slavery again. Itinerant Jacob Young recalled the mood of the clergy at this meeting: "We were sitting here in a slave state, and we had to move with a great deal of caution."[45] Some Methodists took their battle against slavery outside the church. Methodists joined humane and abolition societies in Virginia, Maryland, Delaware, and the western states. In Delaware, prominent Methodists pushed for legislation to end slavery. Henry Boehm reported that Methodists in one area of Maryland had closed down the interstate slave markets there.[46]

Methodists worked on another front to end slavery in the South. In sermons, private appeals, and through the clever use of testimony, Methodists tried to convince slave owners to liberate their slaves. Methodist clergy were masters of persuasion, and thus when Francis Asbury resolved to war against slavery with words—"I will try if words can be like drawn swords, to pierce the hearts of the owners," he wrote—he had some cause for hope.[47] This belief, infused with idealism about the capacity of humans for reform, was the touchstone of probably the most successful[48] of the church's antislavery efforts. Many preachers, most of whom were southern born, campaigned from the pulpit and in private for emancipation during the eighteenth and some into the nineteenth century. Joseph Everett "abhorred slavery, and preached against it with all his might."[49] Preacher John Ray, who served mainly in Tennessee and Kentucky, worked both in the church and outside of it against slavery. Once, he prosecuted a man who had kidnapped a free black family. Ray was so zealous about abolition that it was said he would "seldom lodge at the house of a slave-holder" and when invited home by any parishioner, Ray's "prompt interrogatory would be: 'Have you any negroes?' "[50] Freeborn Garrettson, William Ormond, James Meacham, Henry Boehm, and John Kobler were other clergy who both preached against slavery and counseled members privately to emancipate.[51] Lay men and women testified against slavery in services, spoke against slavery in their families, and put pressure on their fellow members to emancipate.

Some slaveholders followed the path taken by Henry Ennalls, who decided to free his slaves immediately after conversion.[52] But Methodists were never widely successful at making manumission a condition or "sign" of conversion. John Kobler called slavery a "reproach," yet there is no evidence that he denied the authenticity of slaveholders' conversions.[53] While men and women were under conviction of their sins, or immediately after conversion, would have been an ideal time to press the need for emancipating their slaves. Methodists described their conversions as seeing the world with new eyes, where all moral notions were inverted. If the authenticity of conversion had been consistently linked to emancipation, perhaps the Methodists would have been more successful at stemming the tide of slave owning among their members. The likeliest reason they did not fully exploit this tactic is that in their first years in the New World, the *Discipline* was brought over from England without modification. And this *Discipline* did not bar the ownership or inheritance of slaves, thus suggesting one could become a "new creature" and a Methodist as a master.

Most men and women who made the decision to free their slaves came to it gradually. They had been reared in a society that allowed little criticism of slavery, especially the kind of criticism that Methodists leveled. The Methodist position required men and women to admit their commission of evil, to admit their ancestors and parents had committed evil, and to imagine themselves as slaves in order to comprehend the enormity of this evil. Slave owners were brought up to believe that their white skin made them superior to the black slaves about them. Many also believed that their human property was more property than human. For some, the most difficult hurdle to overcome was their economic interest. For others, it was their identity as slaveholders. For many the most difficult obstacle would be the way they viewed their obligations to their children. As they had more contact with religious blacks, and as clergy and sometimes family and friends began to entreat them to free their slaves, some began to develop a new sense of moral responsibility.

Antislavery Methodists did not constitute a "movement," but they did, along with their other religious efforts, keep the issue of slavery's evil in public view. Despite important similarities, southern Methodists differ substantially from northern abolitionists in several key respects. Methodists, working for change from within the South, were more economically and socially vulnerable than northern reformers. Antislavery Methodists were not, like northern abolitionists, committed to "free labor" capitalism and thus Methodist arguments were unencumbered by a connection to bourgeois self-interest. Slaveholders could not accuse Methodists of attacking one form of exploitation while ignoring another. Although less self-interested, the Methodist antislavery position was also less comprehensive than later northern abolitionism, in part because Methodists did not devote much time to pondering what would happen after slavery's demise. The closest they came to articulating a vision of the ideal southern economy was to herald the virtues of every man working for himself. The church had no set policy on what compensation a master owed a slave after freedom, nor did white Methodists seem to understand that slavery was only the first of a series of barriers southern blacks confronted.

To many Methodist ministers, the immorality of slavery was so apparent as to need no elaboration. Some of the most zealous antislavery clergy made moral pronouncements that were designed to reprove masters, not to persuade others of their position. Often antislavery preachers defended their views only in response to proslavery arguments. Eventually Methodist leaders developed something close to a moral position on slavery, one that adapted Wesley's views to the South. The keystone of southern Methodist antislavery efforts was the Golden Rule; it made slavery evil in and of itself. Because of the related ideal of Christian brotherhood, some Methodists recoiled at the idea of owning another member of God's family. Slavery, Methodists also warned, encouraged both master and slave to indulge in other sins. Methodists even incorporated a unique reworking of patriarchal obligation into their antislavery position, urging fathers to leave their children a moral rather than an economic inheritance. And finally, antislavery Methodists, drawing on republican ideology, critiqued the association of freedom for whites with the enslavement of blacks.

Just as central as the arguments Methodists used were the techniques they employed to try and persuade slave owners to emancipate. Methodist opposition to slavery was gendered in ways that help explain its successes among some members and its wider failure in the South. Antislavery preachers believed that once a slave owner understood and felt the suffering he or she inflicted on fellow humans, the decision to emancipate would soon follow. While this may seem naive, conversions offered daily evidence of how "heart" changes led to behavioral changes. Antislavery Methodists stressed those values, beliefs, and ideals typically associated with the "feminine"—emotion, empathy, feeling—and largely ignored the masculine values of the marketplace—profit, self-interest.[54] When Methodists did address masculine values, such as when they artfully revised patriarchal obligations or integrated republican appeals into their religious position, they seem to have won wider support among masters. The Ohio emancipators were especially moved by the patriarchal strain of Methodist antislavery: beyond citing it as a reason for their decisions, they repeated it frequently in letters to slaveholding friends.

Methodists were essentially making a feminized appeal to an overwhelmingly masculine audience of slaveholders, and they seem to have convinced precious few non-Methodists with these tactics. Most slaveholders were more committed to profit and honor than to empathy. Antislavery Methodists were doing what they knew best; Methodism was a religion of the heart. But the Wesleyan worldview allowed little room for critical appraisals of method. When preachers failed to persuade their listeners to emancipate, they predictably blamed slave owners' "hardened" hearts.[55] And when Methodists mixed (masculine) market calculations and (feminine) pleas for empathy, as in their rules on buying and selling slaves, the chaotic results riddled Methodist antislavery with internal contradictions. The emotional suffering of slaves—ostensibly the reason for the rules—became secondary to the economic suffering of masters. Methodists' feminized appeal nonetheless advanced an interpretation of slavery radically at odds with prevailing white supremacist notions.

Methodists did not publish learned theological treatises on emancipation, but they agreed that the Bible condemned slavery. Francis Asbury began to elaborate a theological defense of his antislavery position in 1789. "Servitude," he determined, was permitted by God among the Israelites only because it prevented the greater evils of "slavery and oppression, death, and loss of limbs." Christians were not subject to the "ceremonial law" that governed Moses and his people, Asbury concluded, preserving the distinction between the "Mosaic" and "Christian dispensations" that separated Jews from Christians. Under the "Christian dispensation," he believed, slavery was forbidden. In the explanatory notes Asbury and Thomas Coke authored for the 1798 *Discipline*, they reiterated (along with a casual anti-Semitism) the difference between the Old and New Testament. Slavery, they wrote, was "in *some measure*, overlooked in the Jews by reason of the wonderful hardness of their hearts, as was the keeping of concubines and the divorcing of wives at pleasure, but it is totally opposite to the whole spirit of the gospel." The bishops' mention of concubines and divorce at will was undoubtedly included to remind southerners who justified slavery by referring to the Old Testament that it also sanctioned a number of practices southerners abhorred. Ezekiel Cooper likewise reminded his adversary in the secular press that humanity was in no way destined to repeat the evils of the past. The sanction of slavery in the Old

Testament was overturned in the New. For Cooper, as for others, the Golden Rule firmly established that slaveholding was incompatible with Christianity.[56]

The Golden Rule was cited more often than any other biblical argument by antislavery clergy and Methodist emancipators. Several antislavery sermons were based on this text and many manumission deeds refer to it. In antislavery sermons, private appeals, and official church pronouncements, Methodists claimed that slavery violated the foundational maxims Christ laid out in Luke when he told a lawyer that the keys to eternal life were loving God and loving "thy neighbor as thyself." The language of the Golden Rule surfaced time and again. Freeborn Garrettson proudly reported that a Brother Downings of Virginia had in 1787 decided "to do as he would be done by" and liberated his slaves. In a manumission deed, four members of the Maryland Withgott family expressed their views that "slavery is contrary to the Golden Law of God on which hang all the law and prophets." In Delaware, Thomas White's manumission deed also cited the Golden Rule. To keep slaves, he wrote, would be "not doing as I would be willing to be done by."[57] The slight rewording by individual masters indicates how fervently these men and women believed the Golden Rule was personally directing them to free their slaves.

Methodists also emphasized how slavery tainted those connected with it by encouraging other sinful behavior. With humans essentially corruptible, the institution encouraged cruelty and despotism by making "one man . . . arbitrary over a nother." In the *Discipline*, bishops Asbury and Coke claimed slavery had "an immediate tendency to fill the mind with pride and tyranny, and is frequently productive of almost every act of lust and cruelty which can disgrace the human species." The bishops' statement was one of the few that alluded to the sexual abuse slave women suffered, and its inclusion in the one book (after the Bible) every Methodist was encouraged to buy is therefore significant. Slavery also promoted greed and worldliness and encouraged master and chattel to indolence. James Meacham censured slave owners who "rob [slaves] of all their Labour, just to highten our pride and indulge thousands in laziness." Methodists believed that hard work was good for the soul, for when leisure and luxury were abundant, so was sin. Many clergy made remarks similar to those Thomas Morrell made on his first visit to North Carolina: "the people are not so industrious as they might be, and this is owing to the number of blacks they possess." William Colbert directly connected the way irreligious Marylanders were "swelld with pride" to the "horid practice of slave holding."[58] The condemnations of slave owners' pride, idleness, and luxury fit squarely within Methodist opposition to conspicuous consumption and wealth. The censure of lust and cruelty directly related to Methodist ideals of love and harmony within families and communities.

The belief in Christian, specifically Methodist, "brotherhood" is more elusive than other aspects of the antislavery effort to modern readers, but is pivotally important. Despite white prejudices, the practices and ideals of evangelicals like the Methodists promoted an authentic sense of community among all believers—one that could at times transcend race. Methodists expressed this evolving sense of brotherhood in numerous ways. One man who desired to emancipate his slaves wrote that he considered slaves "human creatures indued with Immortal souls capable of everlasting happiness or liable to everlasting misery."[59] A Virginia antislavery preacher publicly denounced as hypocritical a man who could "sell his brother" and turn around and try to pray. It is not coincidental that the uncompromising advocate for emancipation, William Colbert, frequently spoke of black members as "my black friends" and "my good black brethren." Slaves were human property, but Methodism helped some whites value slaves' humanity before their economic value. So declared Mary Layton in her manumission deed: "no person can be a true and faithful follower of our blessed Saviour who retains and keeps any of the human race a slave." When William Colbert urged whites in a class meeting to see the "impropriety of holding their fellow creatures in bondage," he hoped to evoke a sense of common humanity.[60]

The intimacy that sometimes developed between blacks and whites in Methodist services, particularly between preachers and members, reinforced the message of Christian brotherhood. James Meacham routinely met with blacks, and his hatred for slavery deepened with almost every service he had with them. One evening he heard slaves singing in their quarters and went out to join them. Two of the slaves prayed, and "the Lord soon visited them in an uncommon manner." Although Meacham had never met these people before, his "Soul felt as if Heaven was just then at hand." He closed this day's entry in his journal by raving yet again at "bloody oppressors" and the "accursed Sin" of slavery.[61] The daily close contact preachers like Meacham had with black brothers and sisters undoubtedly helped fortify his commitment to freedom when circumstances gave him little cause to hope.

None of these beliefs inexorably led those who held them to free their slaves. There were proslavery men and women who believed in the Golden Rule, in the corrupting nature of slavery, and in slaves' humanity. Methodists who cited these precepts as reasons for emancipating slaves crossed a moral threshold that their cohorts did not, and the task is to understand why they were one of the largest blocs of liberators in the postwar South. While the line between oppressor and liberator was quite sharp, the line between Methodist values and Methodist antislavery values is far more blurred. Methodism created a fertile context for the antislavery message to take root in; the normal practices and foundational values of the church seem to have prepared some men and women to examine anew their involvement with slavery.

One aspect of Methodism that shaped some of its followers' views on slavery was asceticism. The church encouraged its members to rigorously examine their own conduct, motives, desires, and thoughts; some Methodists turned this inner critical eye on their ownership of slaves. A Georgia master began in the 1790s to feel that in owning slaves he was violating God's law. When Daniel Grant looked at slavery from what he believed to be God's standpoint, the only arguments he could make in its favor were selfish ones. Weighing his decision, he cited the reasons for keeping his slaves as "ease & self intrest & the granduer of life & the thoughts that my Postirety may labour hard for a living, and perhaps not be thought so much of in the world as if they had slaves." Yet he also pondered his obligations as a Christian, for "to think that they are considerd in the eye of the law & many times by the owners no more than the dumb beasts it fills my mind with horror & detestation."[62] Like all Methodists, Grant strove for "deadness to the world" in order to emulate Christ who "despised the great & gay things of the world."[63] Grant's frank admissions of self-interest and family interest, so different from the rhetoric we usually identify with defensive slave owners, are less startling if we think of his soul-searching in the context of Methodism. He believed in a God who was able to read human hearts and minds without illusion. He believed that men and women were often seduced from the path of righteousness by the world. He believed that his eternal fate was in his own hands and that God wanted human beings to strive for perfection on earth. To be perfect, he had to examine all parts of his life. This worldview enabled him to question whether as a slaveholder he could be a good Methodist. Not all masters and mistresses turned a critical eye on slave owning, but Methodism encouraged psychological habits that caused some men and women to do so.

Another aspect of Methodism that helped some whites look upon slavery differently was the Wesleyan notion of judgment, without which the specific belief that God would punish slaveholders in the afterlife would have had little bearing. There were very few "accidents" in Methodists' lives. The Methodist God was intimately involved with his people and used various means to chastise them in order to keep them holy. Sometimes he merely removed their peace and joy in communion with him. Occasionally he would throw them off their horses or let them narrowly escape death. He could send a flood or a drought, a plague or a bankruptcy, and he often inflicted illness. Sometimes he even punished men and women by taking from them those whom they cherished most. Such suffering was instructional. God punished them when they strayed because he loved them. But Methodists also knew that these small judgments were more forgiving than their Judgment at death would be. And they also believed in hell. Many had seen the devil's kingdom at some time, often during conversion. Those who had not caught a glimpse of it were able to vividly imagine what hell was like when preachers described it. Hell was a place of endless torment—where, as Methodist sermons reminded them, "the worm dieth not, and the fire is not quenched."[64]

Many preachers felt that slaveholders would either be barred from heaven or have more difficulty being admitted than nonslaveholders. Some masters came to similar conclusions. One man wrote in his manumission deed of 1790 that he believed "if I continued to hold them in bondage I should never be received into that rest that remains for the people of God."[65] Methodist manumitters frequently indicated that they freed their slaves because they feared God's judgment. And the onus of judgment in Methodism was on the individual and his or her heart, his or her actions. Again, Daniel Grant's comments are revealing. He wrote that he expected to be brought before God's "Impartial barr" and held "accountable . . . for what I do in this life." A Methodist emancipator who had moved to Ohio, Frederick Bonner, wrote back to a Virginia friend he was trying to persuade to follow his example and cautioned: "I find you wate [sic] to be driven from that country of oppression by some judgment."[66] When James Meacham debated the morality of slavery with a Presbyterian man named Faris, he stressed that "God required Equity and Justice between Man & Man" and asked Faris if he thought "an oppressor could stand Equitable before God at the Last day." Even a Methodist master who seems never to have contemplated emancipation admitted some doubts on this score and in a letter to a friend noted: "Lord, brother, I wish I never owned, or was master of negroes! They are a hell to us in this world and I fear they will be so in the next."[67]

Another factor that influenced some members' decisions to emancipate their slaves was the way both Methodism and Methodist antislavery conviction appealed to the heart. Sentimentality was not uniquely Methodist. Other southern opponents of slav-

ery as well as northern abolitionists in later years tried to get their audiences to empathize with slaves. Sentimentality did not, in and of itself, move people from emotion to action. Countless eighteenth- and nineteenth-century Americans shed tears for
the misery of fictional characters or distant others without feeling any need to end
suffering they themselves had direct responsibility for.[68] And masters were probably
the least sentimental of all southerners, especially when it came to their slaves. Although Methodists' feminized appeals to the heart failed to influence many outside
their membership, it is nonetheless clear that some members became emancipators
because they emotionally identified with slaves' misery. Preachers stressed emotion
and empathy in every aspect of their antislavery message. The Golden Rule would not
have been as meaningful an antislavery precept had members failed to empathize with
slaves' plight. Most southern masters, of course, could not imagine slaves feeling the
same pain whites did. The proximity of the "suffering others" seems to have made
identification with them nearly impossible. It was far easier to weep for someone
whose suffering was caused by a distant oppressor than to admit personal responsibility for a monstrous evil.

Yet the case of Brother and Sister Cross indicates that *some* Methodists were moved
by empathy. James Meacham stressed suffering—his own and slaves'—when trying to
convince the Crosses to free their slaves. He first spoke of how slavery was "a dead
weight" on his own heart and then "poured out my mixture of grief." Brother Cross's
"tender Christian heart seem'd to Melt," claimed Meacham, and "we simpathized together." The Crosses were swayed by Meacham's emotional plea, and "yielded to God,
and declared to break the yoke, 'and let the oppressed go free.'" Although Meacham
may also have appealed to reason, his stress was upon feelings. He added that he
hoped God would "conquer every bloody oppressors *heart.*"[69] While appeals to empathy were largely ineffective outside of evangelical communities, the fact remains that
some men and women were moved to liberate their slaves because of the "melting" of
their "tender Christian hearts."

Brother Cross likely developed his "tender Christian heart" in the Methodist
church. The culture of honor had little respect for emotional tenderness outside the
white family circle. In historical romances—the closest secular analog to evangelical
sentimentality—a white cavalier's tender affections for his lady were presented in a
context in which patriarchy, white supremacy, and slavery seemed natural and right.
The hero could not, however, seem *too* emotional. His rationality and coolness under
pressure distinguished him from his "inferiors."[70] Methodists, however, prized emotion over reason and made emotions central to human experience. In class meetings,
services, and church literature, Methodists learned a complex rhetoric of emotion
and, just as important, they learned how to label and distinguish between previously
inchoate feelings. The nearer to God a Methodist was, the more he or she was full of
love and happiness; when estranged, the more anguished and miserable. A Methodist's
religious life thus regularly included extremes of emotional experience.

The way these emotions were induced is critically important to understanding
how they functioned in an antislavery context. Methodist preachers aimed at their audience's emotions and often made patent their own grief or joy as they were preaching. The feeling would run from heart to heart—so Methodists described it—until
most of the audience were also in tears or shouting for joy. The pivotal and unique

Methodist ritual of the love feast was designed around the recounting and vicarious experiencing of personal spiritual stories. The very name "love feast" stressed empathic sharing, and for this reason, some lay people used love feast testimony to condemn slavery. Asbury noted how in a 1783 church conference, "We all agreed in the spirit of African liberty, and strong testimonies were borne in its favour in our love feast." In 1791, Sister Whitehead of Virginia poignantly spoke of her "grief" that "was more than she could bear up under" at Methodists who kept slaves "cruelly oppressed, half starved, and nearly naked," and queried slave owners "is this the religion of my adorable master Jesus?" A Maryland man who had freed his slaves told the story of how he came to this decision at a love feast in this same year.[71]

In urging manumission the evocative words Methodists used were compassion, mercy, and pity—words that in a context divorced from slavery described God's feelings toward undeserving humanity. Only mercy, compassion, and pity, as Methodist conversion stories make clear, could motivate God to pardon worthless men and women. In using such rhetoric in antislavery appeals, clergy invited members to recall their own conversions and gave them an opportunity to transcend their human weakness by emulating God. Francis Asbury in 1796 lamented that Methodists in North Carolina were hiring out slaves in public auctions and remarked, "on the side of the oppressors there are law and power, but where are justice and mercy to the poor slaves? what eye will pity, what hand will help, or ear listen to their distresses?" James Meacham, to cite another example, preached an antislavery sermon in which he "drew the line of mercy and love."[72]

Within such a context, it is not surprising that some men and women became capable of empathizing with slaves. Preachers in particular left evidence of such empathy and would have made John Wesley—who had asked "do you never feel another's pain?" in his antislavery treatise—proud. After being told of a mass whipping, Benjamin Lakin recorded in his journal: "I felt sensible pain in heareing of the cruelties exercised on the poor Slaves." Preacher John Kobler witnessed a group of slaves working in a field, having to "bear the burden and the heat of the day, toiling from morning to even." Some of them were, Kobler said, "old enough for my grandfather" with "afflicted bodies half naked, and . . . withered limbs." At such a sight, Kobler reported, "tears runs down my eyes and sorrow fills my soul."[73] Most whites of Kobler's generation were ill-equipped both culturally and psychologically to watch elderly slaves toiling in the sun and liken them to a dear loved one. But Kobler, immersed in a counterculture of weeping, feeling, and emotion, and persuaded by his church that in Christ there was neither "black nor white, bond nor free," had both the vocabulary and mental habits to do so.

Methodists used more than sentiment and religious precepts in their antislavery appeals. Over time, Methodists developed arguments against slavery that took southern secular values into account. A major obstacle to Methodist antislavery efforts was southerners' sense of obligation to their children. Custom and duty required that parents leave their children an inheritance. This became a circular argument at times, with many slaveholders evading responsibility by claiming they had had slavery thrust upon them by their own parents or "English" slave traders. Francis Asbury argued with a Maryland "gentleman" who "acknowledged the wrong done the blacks by taking them from their own country, but defended the right of holding them." William

Ormond exacted a promise from a Methodist woman that she would free her slaves, but only, she said, if she had no children. Ormond privately prayed that she be kept barren.[74] Methodists developed an ingenious solution, albeit one with limited appeal, to this problem—a way members could reconcile their obligations as patriarchs and parents with their obligations as Methodists: they urged parents to free their children from the pollution of slavery. Instead of passively viewing slavery as a burden passed on to innocent children, Methodists urged parents to activism—to exercise their agency and break the baneful cycle for the rising generation. This is best seen in the letters of Methodists who, like Philip Gatch, decided not only to liberate their slaves but also to flee "slave soil" altogether.

Gatch described his decision in precisely these terms. "I felt unwilling," he wrote, "to Lay my Bones [in Virginia], and leave my children whom I tenderly loved in a land of slavery not knowing what the Evils thereof would amount to in there [sic] time." To Frederick Bonner, Ohio seemed like the Methodist Promised Land, for by 1807, when he moved there, "the Legislature of V[irgini]a has determined against liberty and our preachers and people will be purchasing Slaves without a prospect of liberating them." In Ohio, however, "our children are saved from the bane full practice of trading on their fellow creatures in the manner I understand some of our old friends have done in the states where slavery exists."[75] Ohio emigrant Bennet Maxey cautioned his friend Edward Dromgoole not to move west if his only reason was to "make money enuph for your children and grand children." If, however, he had more moral considerations, if "because you live in a land of Slavery, and have you doubts whether it be right in the sight of god for you to die there [in Virginia] and [leave] your children and grandch[ildren] in that land of oppression, when their is a [far] more excellent place provided and that you might be the happy instrument under god to plant them in this good land where that evil is not," he should, Maxey said, "Come in the Name of the Lorde."[76]

This unique reworking of patriarchal obligations was even advanced from the pulpit. On February 26, 1797, Richard Whatcoat delivered an antislavery sermon on a text prima facie unrelated to slavery: "And great shall be the peace of thy children." What he said in this sermon was not preserved (although we are told that this was an antislavery sermon and that it angered local slaveholders) but it is likely he used arguments similar to those of the Ohio emigrants, such as urging mothers and fathers to free their children from the pollution of slavery. Since Methodists connected slavery to related sins of pride, greed, lust, and cruelty, emancipating patriarchs were removing their descendants from a context of perpetual temptation.[77]

Another nod to secular ideals came when Methodists integrated republican rhetoric into their antislavery message. Ezekiel Cooper, especially in his articles for the secular press in Virginia and Maryland, returned to the themes of natural rights and liberty again and again, calling liberty "the grand American shrine" and "freedom the just due of every man." Cooper was the most clever of the Methodists at countering proslavery arguments. When an opponent declared that "Negroes were providentially intended to be slaves" and used biblical justification for this assertion, Cooper quickly used Revolutionary logic to counter him. The fact that "there were slaves of old no more proves the right of slavery now than ancient monarchies and despotic powers prove that we should have a despotic monarchy to rule us." The revolutionaries themselves had trampled on tradition; Cooper would not let them take refuge in it now.[78]

Cooper also used the concept of natural rights in his sermons. He told one audience that freedom was the "rights" and "due" of "every man" from the "crowned head to a poor slave." But when addressing Methodists, he usually played on both the religious and secular conceptions of freedom. Cooper's most poignant evocation of Revolutionary ideals came on July 4, 1790, when he awoke in Annapolis to see the American flag "raised on the state dome." The flag and the anniversary of independence caused Cooper to ponder how "astonishing" it was that "civil slavery" should continue in a "country so much for freedom." Thus inspired, Cooper decided to address "the inconsistency and injustice of slavery among us as a free people" in his sermon that day. His text was well suited for such a disquisition. He preached from "If the son shall make you free you shall be free indeed."[79] Jacob Gruber (who was later indicted for inciting slaves to rebellion because of an antislavery sermon) also used this text for an antislavery Fourth of July sermon. Americans loved to boast of their liberty, freedom, and independence, he told the crowd, but the country was only free "to all that are not slaves." Gruber then inventively played on the religious and secular meaning of freedom to make a claim that surely angered slaveholding listeners. Those who were in bondage to sin were slaves. Slave owning was a sin, slaveholders were thus in bondage to sin, and were, in turn, dependent slaves.[80]

Most official church statements, especially those addressed to legislatures, made some reference to the founding ideals of America. The *Address* of 1800, in which leaders urged their members to petition state legislatures for gradual emancipation, was the most strident of these, calling slavery "repugnant to the unalienable rights of mankind, and to the very essence of civil liberty."[81] One almost senses the desperation in which this document was written, for there was a directness in it that was unmatched in Methodists' other official statements. Things were not moving toward the eradication of slavery in the South and not even in the church; the authors of the *Address* admitted their efforts had heretofore been "insufficient." In order to "give a blow at the root to this enormous evil," the preachers had "therefore determined at last to rouse up all our influence, in order to hasten . . . the universal extirpation of this crying sin." In a passage hardly designed to be conciliatory, they struck at American hypocrisy: "that so large a proportion of the inhabitants of this country, who so truly boast of the liberty they enjoy, and are so justly jealous of that inestimable blessing, should continue to deprive of every trace of liberty so many of their fellow-creatures equally capable with themselves of every social blessing and of eternal happiness—is an inconsistency which is scarcely to be paralleled in the history of mankind!" Here it was—the Golden Rule writ in terms of American ideals.[82]

Antislavery Methodists so melded the vocabulary of republicanism with that of Christian egalitarianism that words like "liberty" and "equality" and their opposite, "oppression," became infused with religious meaning. A Methodist who agreed to manumit his or her slaves was frequently described as "a friend of liberty," the same language, incidentally, used by Ben Woolfolk, one of Gabriel Prosser's followers, to describe why they would spare white Quakers, Frenchmen, and Methodists. Slaveholders were "oppressors," a term with political as well as religious significance. In emancipation deeds, Methodists effortlessly segued from religious to Revolutionary language.

One Maryland emancipator declared "slavery is contrary to the Golden Law of God . . . and to the Glorious Revolution that has lately taken place in America." Freeborn Garrettson on one occasion tellingly spoke of antislavery as "the doctrine of freedom."[83]

Antislavery Methodists were a minority in the South. The church and its members were largely shut out of the corridors of power. One-quarter to one-third of the membership was enslaved, and slaves' advocacy of emancipation was the least likely to sway masters. The extent of the success of Methodist antislavery efforts is difficult to document, but at least some things are clear. Results varied dramatically by region. In Delaware, parts of Maryland, and some counties in Virginia, Methodist antislavery appeals had a tremendous impact. In South Carolina, Kentucky, and Tennessee, individual slaves gained their freedom, but in nothing like the proportions in the Upper South. In Georgia and North Carolina, Methodist manumissions were rarer still, in large part because of state laws. Pockets of strong antislavery Methodists in the upcountry regions of the central South defied the actions of most southern Methodists and continued to prosecute slaveholders and protest slavery long after the rest of the southern conferences had stopped doing so.

From the war's end until the first decade of the nineteenth century, one Methodist rule on slavery did remain in effect in many states—the rule against buying and selling slaves. Clergy found the internal slave trade almost as odious as the international one, for it gave dramatic witness to the legal reality that slaves were property that could be disposed of like chairs, cattle, or land. Perhaps ministers also hoped to somehow stem the spread of slavery with these rules. Since the prohibition on buying and selling slaves had been imported from England, it had the added attraction of not being an ex post facto requirement. The *Discipline* required members who bought slaves in states where emancipation was allowed to write emancipation deeds guaranteeing freedom for the purchased slaves after a number of years. Some optimistic clergy even forced violators in states without emancipation laws to write deeds promising to emancipate purchased slaves if manumission ever became possible.

Most of these deeds calculated the service period of the slave based on the slave's gender, price, and age. Future children of purchased bondwomen were often declared in these deeds free at birth; the *Discipline* at a minimum required that future daughters be free at twenty-one, sons at twenty-five. Members who sold slaves were to be expelled. This rule remained on the books until 1804, when the church recognized state prohibitions by specifically exempting members in North Carolina, South Carolina, Georgia, and Tennessee.[84] Manuscript journals show that while and where the window of emancipation was open, many preachers enforced this rule. Jeremiah Norman, who served in North Carolina, South Carolina, and Georgia, both expelled people who sold slaves and wrote emancipation deeds for those who purchased slaves. Richard Whatcoat likewise calculated manumission dates for a number of slaves in Virginia and North Carolina, requiring at least one Tarheel slave owner to post a hefty bond to the Humane Society as a guarantee. Preachers saw these decisions as being fair to slaves as well as masters. Whatcoat wrote of one ruling that he had "setled the point for Tho[ma]s Duprees three Neagros."[85]

Two 1800 decisions on slavery in the Tar River circuit show how preachers' efforts to enforce the rule on buying slaves entangled them in the very pricing of human "bodies and souls" they abhorred. Mark Cooper was required to free, in ten years, a forty-year-old bondman whom he had purchased for 250 dollars. To come up with the ten-year figure, the circuit elders assessed the value of the slave's labor by considering his age, gender, and physical condition, concluding that the slave would produce a 250-dollar profit for Cooper in a decade. Similarly, James Duns was ordered to free, after twelve years, a slave woman thirty-eight years old for whom he had paid $175. As a woman, her labor was "worth" less than a man's; even though Dun paid less for her than Cooper did for his bondman, she had to serve two years more than he to compensate her master. She was also presented with a Manichean choice. If she had children, the church ordered, "they shall be liberated agreeable to the rules of the Methodist church and the above obligations shall be void." If she had no children, she would become free in twelve years. If she had children, they would eventually be free but she would remain a slave.[86] Moreover, as various states restricted manumission and forced newly freed slaves out of their borders, those slaves who were emancipated because of Methodist actions were often forced to leave friends and family. And as the church compromised further (during the ten and twelve years these two slaves were required to serve) many of these agreements may well have been rescinded or never fulfilled.

One need not doubt the preachers' sincerity to note how they effectively trivialized the church position on slavery with their decisions. Although few other Protestant bodies were still requiring slave owners to manumit slaves after 1800, it is also clear that by 1800, the various compromises Methodists made with slaveholders had left them—by their own standards—in a morally ambiguous position. Elaborate contracts designed to compensate the slave buyer for his investment in human property suggested that slavery was not as absolute an evil as the church said it was. The policy was pragmatic, but in offering incentives for members to do good, the church treated the sin of buying human beings less stringently than other sins. Methodists would have ridiculed and charged with popery any sect that offered absolution of sin for a price. Their decisions about purchased slaves were not far removed from such a practice.

The rules on buying slaves at least had the potential for changing masters' minds about slaveholding; the rules against selling slaves were strictly punitive. It is possible that some Methodist masters refused to sell slaves because they feared expulsion, yet there is no evidence of such an effect. Violators of the rule, however, were numerous. In 1790, a colleague of James Meacham expelled some Virginia members for selling slaves. Meacham himself expelled three men for this reason. William Ormond expelled James Tooley for selling a slave. George Wells expelled a member for selling a slave in 1791.[87] Expulsion was a tool of limited use, however, for if a member was expelled, that ended any leverage the church would have over him or her. Sometimes preachers modified the rules. In 1809, for example, Thomas Shaw was convicted of slave trading. He acknowledged the "iniquity of the practice" and seems to have been readmitted to the church.[88]

Although church rules helped secure the freedom of some slaves—a matter of no small consequence to those freed—these policies were largely ineffective at reducing the number of slaveholders in the church. In states where manumission was never allowed, the emancipation agreements were moot. When a member was expelled for selling a slave, the slave who was sold remained with a master now hostile to the church. The calculations for purchased slaves put manumission dates years into the future—so far that later state laws would make many of those agreements void. True, whites who inherited slaves either by will or through marriage, those who were given slaves as gifts, and those who held slaves were told by the *Discipline* that slavery was an "enormous evil."[89] Yet in this very era, the "necessary evil" defense of slavery reigned; church compromises seem to have allowed slave-owning members to sadly shake their heads, agreeing that slavery was an evil, yet continue to hold slaves.

From the moment Methodist missionaries landed in America, their efforts to end slavery had coincided with another reform measure—to ameliorate the conditions of bondage. Methodists did not turn to amelioration after antislavery efforts failed; all along they attempted to reform slavery even as they worked to end it. When antislavery zeal diminished, this was all that remained. Church leaders believed that they were more successful at making their members improve the conditions of slavery than at persuading them to renounce it.[90] Preachers viewed the move to reform slavery and to end slavery as entirely compatible. Even Daniel Coker, a black Methodist minister, in his antislavery pamphlet encouraged those masters unwilling to free their slaves to at least treat them better. This strategy was pragmatic but compassionate, for it could help alleviate some human suffering while clergy worked to persuade masters to emancipate. Judging by ministers' comments, many slaves in the late eighteenth century were ill-fed, ill-clothed, poorly sheltered, and cruelly treated.[91] James Meacham often made note of "naked bending captives" he saw on his travels. One November he was especially "grieved to see the poor blacks naked in the cold a trudging about as if they was not flesh and blood." Freeborn Garrettson, who also complained about the "cruel usage of slaves" and spoke of "naked slaves," in 1781 was visiting slaves in their quarters and found them "laying on the floors without a spirit" because of ill treatment. John Kobler encountered some slaves "reduced so low it . . . is a scandal to human nature." Even the moderate Jeremiah Norman noted a case of "half naked and starved" slaves.[92]

Preachers condemned neglect of slaves and brutality toward slaves in sermons and private appeals. Perhaps even more important in a region hostile to interference in patriarchal decisions were Methodist efforts to discipline slave owners who abused slaves. William Ormond expelled a man named "J. Lovet" for shooting a slave. A mistress was expelled by William Colbert for "puting so many irons on her negro woman." Freeborn Garrettson repeatedly counseled slave owners both in and outside the church to treat their slaves with more humanity. By default, the church represented one of the only checks on the abuse of slaveholding power.[93] Gradually, more and more preachers began to take note of how some masters, particularly Methodists, were treating their slaves better than they had before. Thomas Morrell, who most of his career worked in the North, on a trip South with Bishop Asbury commented on how in North Carolina, "the few Methodists that have slaves treat them with more humanity" than other owners. Asbury also began to believe some slave owners had become less cruel and abusive. In a letter to a New York antislavery minister, he even justified the church's retreat on slavery by linking access to masters with better treatment of slaves. He told a story of a "tyrannical" master who had treated his slaves "like dogs." But within a year of his conversion, Asbury claimed, "I saw that man much softened, his people admitted into the house of prayer, the whole plantation, 40 or 50 singing and praising God. What now can sweeten the bitter cup like religion?"[94]

Asbury's views well illustrate the ambivalence that characterized the church's policy of denouncing slavery as an absolute evil and yet trying to reform the institution. He and Coke had claimed in the 1798 *Discipline* that slavery was "totally opposite to the whole spirit of the gospel" and "frequently productive of almost every act of lust and cruelty which can disgrace the human species." In the same section, they also commended masters who allowed slaves "full liberty to attend the preaching of the gospel."[95] Early in his career, Asbury had applauded Quaker efforts for abolition, but dourly noted how "some are more intent on promoting the freedom of their bodies, than the freedom of their souls; without which they must be the vassals of Satan in eternal fire." With each bold or hesitant step the church took against slavery, slave owners countered by refusing to allow their bondmen and -women to attend Methodist services, because, as Asbury said, they feared "the influence of our principles." Minister George Dougherty, the Charleston preacher attacked by the mob in 1800, ruefully admitted that the largest impact the antislavery *Address* of 1800 had made was to drastically shrink the number of blacks in attendance.[96]

By the turn of the century many preachers had concluded that their efforts to end slavery had been unsuccessful and more important, bad strategy. Jesse Lee's comments to this effect are perhaps the best known. Lee was opposed to slavery, yet he, like others, also opposed ex post facto rules. By 1810, Lee wrote that the efforts to purge Methodism of slavery and to push for abolition were ill-chosen, for the "language . . . was calculated to irritate the minds of our people, and by no means calculated to convince them of their errors." Asbury, too, pondered whether they had made a mistake in pushing for emancipation and queried, "would not an effort at *amelioration* in the condition and treatment of slaves have produced more practical good to the poor Africans, than any attempt at their *emancipation?*"[97] At this distance, his question is absurd and morally repugnant. But in the context of southern intransigence and Wesleyan values, it was not illogical. His belief that Methodists treated their slaves more humanely than other masters may well have been a rationalization for the church's retreat; his belief that Methodist antislavery efforts had served to harden proslavery positions seems incontestable.

Preachers and white members witnessed the cruelty and callousness of masters firsthand and at times, short of abandoning their opposition to fighting, they felt helpless to stop it. At a resting place in Maryland, Asbury beheld "such cruelty to a Negro that I could not feel free to stay." He called for his horse and "delivered my own soul, and departed."[98] The most fatalistic comment was made by the would-be emancipator Daniel Grant, thwarted by Georgia law from freeing his slaves. On September 8, 1792, he described his thoughts when a young slave boy belonging to a neighbor died. "I cannot grieve much at the death of a poor little black," he noted, "who perhaps were they [sic] to live might have a life of great suffering here but now it is indeed free from its master & I doubt not but happy forever."[99] Methodists had always believed that heaven would be a place of bliss and hell a place of torment. Many antislavery men resigned themselves to the fact that slavery would not end in their lifetimes and came to emphasize instead the need to "sweeten" slaves' "bitter cup" with the blessings of Christianity. John Littlejohn even hinted that God would allow slaves a final say. "O how will those sons and daughters of Africa stand in Jud[gmen]t ag[ain]st the Whites [who] call themselves Christians," he lamented after a service for blacks. "I exhorted them to serve God and be faithfull," he continued, "till they go where the Serv[an]t is free from his Master."[100] Since their beginnings in America, Methodist preachers had stressed that conversion was the most important aspect of their ministry. Even antislavery men had linked the freedom of slaves to the freedom of men and women from sin. In the wake of their retreat on slavery, it was this other-worldly freedom that preachers promoted.[101]

Even before the church had all but abandoned efforts to abolish slavery, many clergy had expressed their fears and some their hopes that God would eventually bring slavery to an end with a single stroke. As antislavery ministers began keeping their hatred of slavery to themselves, they increasingly left the matter to God. In 1796, Asbury pondered why God had sent a devastating flood into Georgia. He confided in his journal that "I suppose they would crucify me if I were to tell them it is the *African flood*; but if they could hear me think, they would discover this to be my senti-ment."[102] After the antislavery effort ended, many left slavery up to God, and concen-trated on evangelizing master and slave. This fatalistic position, along with the comfort clergy took in the number of slaves they had led to spiritual liberty, may have rein-forced the argument that slavery was a "necessary evil." Both positions share a resig-nation to circumstance and a focus on the Christianization of blacks.

Our story would be incomplete if we did not acknowledge the resistance from within the church to the antislavery clerical majority. John Lee (the brother of Jesse Lee) returned to Virginia in 1791 after a long stint in New England. In the Old Do-minion he discovered that "some of the preachers" there "insisted on his preaching against slavery; but [John] did not find freedom to say any thing about that delicate subject in public; as in his judgment it would neither profit the master or the slave." John Lee's silence would not be remarkable but for the fact that he favored emancipa-tion, joined the Virginia Humane Society, and even purchased a bondman in order to liberate him.[103]

Preacher Jeremiah Norman also disagreed with the antislavery majority of his church, terming them "altogether for the negroe" while he viewed himself in favor of "an Equalibrium with Master & servant." He did not believe that all slaveholders would go to hell, and he especially felt that the church position was too strong in North Carolina, where state law prohibited emancipation.[104] Although Norman en-forced church rules against the buying and selling of slaves, other of his actions sent a different message. As a local preacher and schoolmaster in 1796, he helped a Mr. Forbes search for a runaway slave. They were unsuccessful, yet Norman found the pur-suit a "recreation." As an itinerant in 1800, he agreed to return a captured runaway back to his owner. "He was brought to me in wooden handcuffs," Norman reported. "I had him set free from them, & only kept hold of the rope which was round his neck." It is impossible to know whether slave owners' fears about antislavery Method-ism in Norman's circuit were alleviated by this spectacle, nor does Norman discuss his own feelings (much less the slave's) about this event. At best, Norman was sending radically contradictory messages to his white audience by, on the one hand, punishing slave owners and, on the other, helping to enforce the master's authority.[105]

The church was experienced by its members as a local institution, so Methodist rules and pronouncements against slavery were only as strong as the preachers enforcing them. Some, like Norman, were less zealous than others. James Meacham was outraged that a man suspended for buying a slave child had "[crept] into society again" because of a lax itinerant. Meacham was less forgiving than his coworker, and when the man refused to promise to manumit the slave, he "Blacked his name" from the membership roll.[106] We also know very little about the mentality of Methodist masters who never contemplated freeing their slaves. One familiar anecdote, however, is revealing. Colonel Burton of Virginia, it was said, "While the preacher was going on with his sermon . . . would sit and pat his foot, or, as it was phrased, 'keep the spinning-wheel moving;' but if, at any time, the speaker said anything that seemed to bear on slavery, such as 'Let the oppressed go free,' &c., the spinning-wheel would stop until the preacher passed on to some other topic." Burton, it seemed, kept his mind closed on the subject of slavery.[107]

The southerners who entered the church after 1800 found themselves in a far different environment than those who had joined in the 1780s or 1790s. Extant journals of southern-born preachers who began their ministries after 1800 show far less opposition to slavery than those of their forebears. Thomas Mann, for example, never made antislavery comments in his journal. James Jenkins was born into a slaveholding family and worked in his early adult life as a slave overseer. He later spoke of how in this position he had seen his temper rage as he "increased in vice daily." Although he once reproved from the pulpit a "negro speculator" for his "inhuman traffic," he opposed the 1800 *Address* on slavery, for it "almost shut up the door of usefulness" in the South, especially among slaves. Members guided by such clergy were able to be both Methodists and masters or mistresses without much opposition—as long as they were not overly cruel and permitted slaves to come to church.[108]

The failure of Methodist antislavery action was in some sense predictable. Methodism was a despised and ridiculed sect, and most of its members did not own slaves. Few Methodists were in positions of power and influence during the church's greatest antislavery campaigns. Seeing their choice as either abandoning the effort to convert slaves or abandoning opposition to slavery, ministers chose the latter. The individualistic emphasis of their feminized appeals to the heart also undermined their efforts to extirpate slavery. Clergy made impassioned pleas to masters and mistresses hoping to convince them that God wanted them to free their slaves. In placing the emphasis on subjective reality—on individual emotions and individual ideas about God's will, Methodists left the option open to slaveholders that they could keep their slaves until God spoke to them in a clear voice and told them otherwise. Methodists had rejected a formalistic view of religion that tied salvation to works or deeds, and they could not change course now.

Since Methodists allowed slaveholders to join the church, it was possible to become a "new creature" in Christ even as a slaveholder. To emancipate one's slaves became, like sanctification, something members were urged to strive for, but not a prerequisite for eternal life. An incident in Freeborn Garrettson's ministry is revealing. In 1781 he was asked to write a man's will. But when he "came to a division among the negroes, at first I thought I could not pen it: I used my influence in showing him the injustice of slave keeping, he went aside to consult his wife and continued near an hour, I was exceeding happy whilst praying to the Lord to open his eyes to strip him of self: he returned (self was too strong) and told me he did not see it his duty."[109] By placing the onus on the individual heart and hoping that this heart would be moved (with the help of ministerial entreaties) to see slavery as wrong, Methodist preachers even of the strongest antislavery principles had allowed for the inverse to happen.[110]

By 1800, the church contained people with totally divergent views on slavery. Besides the obvious difference between members in northern states where slavery was gradually abolished and in southern states where slavery was thriving, there was also the split between southern-born white members, and between masters and slaves. Methodists like Freeborn Garrettson and Philip Gatch became convinced that slaveholding was an abomination and along with numerous others left the South altogether, regionalizing the church in the process. These emigrants might be viewed as the vanguard of the "come-outer" abolitionism historians associate with the 1830s and 1840s. It is surely not coincidence that many of these former southerners began to speak of the South as a tainted region whose soil was stained with blood. Slave owning members in states where manumission was illegal had never been forced to choose between their church and their slaves, and these men and women began to associate their church's early antislavery stand with England, Ohio, and the North. Clergy, by shifting their emphasis to slave conversion and improved slave treatment, offered slaveholding members a way to be a "moral master," an intermediate position that can be traced back to Wesley himself. Edward Dromgoole, a local preacher in the church, was the frequent correspondent of Ohio emigrants. Despite their numerous appeals to his conscience and to his obligations as a father, he remained in Virginia and increased his slaveholdings.[111]

Early Methodist efforts to end slavery were not in vain. Some of the men and women freed by white members went on to become leaders in the African American community, and some who went North worked for abolition. Many white Methodists in the West and North—some of them exiled southerners—joined abolitionist ranks. Methodism was so associated with antislavery sentiment in the Upper South that some societies there chose not to join the southern wing of the church when it seceded.[112] More important than these surviving antislavery pockets was the challenge earlier Methodists made to slaveholder hegemony. As short-lived and ineffectual as the Methodist effort to end slavery was, it still represents an important episode in southern history. This small group of southerners did not accept the notion that white liberty depended on the enslavement of blacks. They harangued slaveholders about the evils of slavery from the pulpit. Those who freed their slaves bore witness to the sincerity of their views and forced their neighbors to ask questions about the morality of an institution they had taken for granted. Antislavery Methodists did not realize their vision; at times they compromised it, and eventually the church leadership abandoned it. But for a few brief decades, they held out an ideal of a more humane, more just, and more united South and they did so despite the power, wealth, and influence arrayed against them.

Early antislavery Methodists remind us that slavery's perpetuation and expansion were the result of conscious choices made by self-interested southerners between clear alternatives. To men like James Meacham, the "hateful bloody name of oppression, I say the spirit of blood, kills the life of love and liberty." Although few southerners chose "mercy" and "love" over "blood" and "oppression," those few nonetheless tried to expose to light the naked power their contemporaries masked with rhetoric of independence and liberty. Sometimes the influence of the early antislavery legacy was profound. Recall John M'Lean, who took time out of his busy schedule as a Supreme Court Justice to write the biography of the early antislavery preacher, Philip Gatch. In 1857 M'Lean, prominent Methodist and longtime foe of slavery, authored one of the two dissenting opinions in the momentous Dred Scott decision.[113]

Turning the World Upside Down

The Stakes of the Conflict

IN 1807, JESSE LEE preached a sermon in New Bern, North Carolina, on Acts 17: 6, "These that have turned the world upside down are come hither." The men referred to in the Bible verse were Christian leaders who had been forcibly brought by a mob of "lewd fellows" before city officials and charged with attempting to invert the world. Lee proudly identified himself and his fellow Methodist preachers as having a similar mission, a mission justified by Lee's claim that the world was currently "wrong side up" because of sin and that "it was . . . the business of the ministry to restore it to its original position." The following morning, people in New Bern awoke to a "ridiculous" sight: "Wagons, boats, signs, gates, almost everything was bottom side upward." According to Henry Boehm, "the authors of the mischief . . . laid it to the preacher, who they said had come to turn the town over that it might be right side up."[1]

These mischief makers apparently agreed with many of the church's critics that their world was just fine as it was. Charlestonians had accused the Methodists of "attempting to subvert the established order of things," and many southerners sympathized with some Virginians who accused them of "'turning the world upside down.'" As Lee did in New Bern, Methodist leaders often pointedly announced their belief that the world was backwards, assertions that were cold comfort to their critics.[2] The New Bern incident was relatively harmless, but other actions by the opponents of Methodism took a hostile turn. From frequent harassment to occasional violence, opposition was a fact of life for the early church. But anti-Methodist views and actions were not random. By analyzing the sources, complaints, and types of opposition, we can better appreciate what the participants themselves believed to be the issues at stake in the contested ascendancy of southern evangelicalism.[3] Methodists were not passive victims in these dramas. They saw themselves as soldiers for Christ who wanted to defeat the enemy. Sally Eastland, for example, spoke of having "waged war against Hell" and "going into an ingagement, with the powers [of] darkness," adding, "I feel as if Id die rather than yeald."[4] Although very few seem to have sought out violence, opposition served an affirming role for early Methodists. In their worldview, persecution was one way of judging whether Christians were doing their jobs. Believers who were formal, cold, or "settled on their lees" could coexist peacefully with the "world," while those who were active and vibrant in their faith could expect the world's resistance. Persecution confirmed their faith.

In the late eighteenth and early nineteenth centuries, Methodists encountered a steady stream of resistance.[5] The debates between Methodists and their critics over morality, family authority, gender roles, racial conventions, and social order took place all across the South; the ubiquity of these conflicts provides ample evidence that early Methodists were perceived as a threat by their opponents.[6] Most of these opponents share one characteristic, regardless of their criticisms or mode of expressing them. Whether the response was violence, harsh accusations, or the many interruptions of Methodist services, most of those involved were white men. In the sources consulted for this study, including the few extant memoirs of African American Methodists from this era, black opposition even to other blacks was extremely rare. White women's opposition was more frequent than that of blacks, but it was still the exception to the rule. A major task, then, is to uncover and analyze the many reasons that white men were the most persistent and violent of Methodists' detractors.

Sectarian differences account for some of the hostility Methodists faced.[7] High churchmen and conservative Protestants were disturbed by Methodism's apparent disrespect for order and hierarchy. These critics tended to make sweeping denunciations of Methodists, including accusations that they were under satanic influence. Conservative clergy agreed on certain key parts of their critique. Both Presbyterians and Episcopalians harangued the Methodists for their way of choosing ministers. Methodists, they complained, brought disrepute and dishonor on the ministry by licensing uneducated and sometimes even illiterate men to preach (a charge that was true). Because the status of clergy after disestablishment was uncertain, Presbyterian and Episcopalian leaders believed it particularly important to maintain rigorous standards of education and training for the clergy. As other denominations moved toward professionalizing the ministry, early Methodists both resisted the trend and denounced it. In conservative Protestants' minds, Methodists added insult to injury by allowing any and every lay person to teach, exhort, and testify in services. How could good order and sound doctrine prevail under such conditions?[8] Episcopalian and Presbyterian congregants were on average wealthier than Methodists, and class differences played a major role in the way these Protestants saw the Methodists. Class also helps explain why Baptist-Methodist disputes did not reach the same level of rancorous name-calling, for members of the two sects were more similar in status, and sometimes were denounced in the same breath and the same terms by their wealthier detractors. One Virginian accused both groups of licensing illiterate men and dismissed both for appealing largely to slaves and lower-class whites.[9]

Anglican cleric Devereux Jarratt's criticism was even more pointedly elitist. Jarratt was most troubled by Methodists' opposition to slavery, a stand that he attacked both on religious and class grounds. Jarratt complained that Methodists completely misread the Bible, which in his view gave ample support to slave owning. Methodists made matters worse by equating slave owning with more "common" sins. Slave owners, he wrote, "ought not to be put upon a levil [sic], (as they are now) with *horsethieves*, and *hogstealers, knaves* etc." Methodists, he strongly implied, did not know their place in southern society, for these "insults" came "from men, who are as incapable of discerning or judging in these matters as a schoolboy almost."[10] Jarratt's language emphatically shows the different moral universes of elite Episcopalians and plain folk Methodists. In Methodists' minds, they were not "insulting" their betters, but denouncing sin. The fact that slaveholders were often elites, in the Wesleyan worldview, made their sin at least as bad as that of the poor man who stole a hog. And finally, Methodists did not believe they needed education (or even the experience that came with age) in order to discern moral truths.

An Episcopal minister of Baltimore emphasized Methodists' ill breeding, denouncing Methodist preachers for their "ranting, noise and other follies, which disgrace their profession." Why, he wondered, could not Methodists be "rational and dignified" like "the clergy of almost all other churches." A New Jerusalem minister agreed and called Methodist preachers "ignorant understrappers, who know of nothing but jumping, hallowing, and squeezing." A North Carolina gentleman felt that Methodist converts were as ill-bred as their clergy, "the heights of whose ambition seems to be, to deal out fanaticism [and] ignorance to their society [and] the rabble."[11] Other conservatives were more worried about the secular impact of Methodist fanaticism on the social order, especially on southerners deemed subordinate. Religion, they argued, should not interfere with other responsibilities, or as Presbyterian critics worded it in an antirevival tract, should not "render them unfit for the duties of their several stations." Methodists, "by the protracting of their publick exercises of religion," might anger God, if by this means they "neglect the duties of the closet or family, or those of their secular callings."[12]

Attacks by ministers of other denominations stressed both the incompetence of Methodist clergy and the effect of Methodism on the "rabble," specifically on the poor, women, blacks, and to a lesser extent, children. The critics who worried about people neglecting their secular duties also condemned Methodists' "high pretensions to extraordinary divine illuminations and impulses," which they claimed led to "spiritual pride and self-conceit." The fact that the pretentious and proud included people "of all ages from eight years and upwards, male and female, rich and poor, the blacks" was especially troubling. When children, women, and slaves were neglecting their work, judging for themselves about morality, and claiming to speak directly to God, both the secular world and the ministry were in danger.[13] When inferiors were thus empowered, they became proud and pretentious, attributes unbefitting their station in life. Conservative Protestants also feared that religious empowerment might lead to broader problems of social discipline, such as those Jarratt identified in unlearned Methodists' attacks on slaveholders. In a properly ordered world, they suggested, the "rabble" would be guided and supervised by their betters, and not, as Methodists allowed, by lay and clerical leaders who themselves were from the suspect classes.

Methodist women in particular were singled out for scorn by conservative Protestants. One vocal critic of Methodist practices was the Reverend Adam Rankin, a Presbyterian. Rankin's first argument was that only educated clergymen should be entrusted to preach, teach, and guide the flock. That Rankin was not merely critiquing Methodist ministers for their lack of formal training became evident when he turned to the issue of women's roles in these services. At camp meetings, he wrote, "a lady lays aside all her modesty, the principal ornament of her sex, and in open defiance of the divine interdiction . . . will in one hour after she falls into one of these dead fits, be harangueing an assembly, ten times too large for her voice to reach, where there will be ten or twenty professed clergymen." Revealing perhaps a little jealousy, he noted with even more horror that these immodest women were seen as authorities by the camp meeting crowds: "The astonished multitude are pressing round the orators, with all ardent attention, eating every word, as if their eternal all depended upon their information, instead of conducting the Bedlamites to close confinement."[14]

The five Presbyterian authors of the pointedly entitled *Evils of the Work Now Prevailing in the United States of America, Under the Name of a Revival of Religion* also claimed that the revivals discredited the ministry. If every convert was "called to be a publick teacher," these divines protested, there would be no need for the clergy. Exhorting, counseling, and teaching were the work of ministers. But most dangerous, to the authors, was women's usurpation of ministerial authority: "if it be disorderly for any persons whatsoever to take it upon themselves, without a regular call, to teach and exhort publickly; the disorder is still more flagrant, when women do so; their speaking in the publick assemblies being so expressly forbidden." Perhaps making a sly reference to Methodists' penchant for honoring pious female leaders with the title of "Mother in Israel," the critics handily discounted Deborah as a proper exemplar: "that women, who are no prophetesses, should take upon them[selves] to teach and exhort publickly, is forbidden by the apostle, as inconsistent with the due subordination and modesty of their sex."[15] The authors did not reveal how a true "prophetess" was to recognize her call.

The authors of both tracts referred to Paul's command for women to "keep silence" (from 1 Timothy and 1 Corinthians), verses also cited by other critics of Methodism. When a Presbyterian minister of Prince Edward County complained to Methodist preacher William Spencer that Methodists were violating Paul's order, Spencer retorted that Paul had not meant to prevent women from praying, praising, and testifying in churches, nor to bar them from actively recruiting new converts. In Spencer's view, Paul had meant only that women should not "meddle with church business."[16] Spencer's retort appears to have been one of the few times Methodists sought to justify women's public speaking; apparently most Methodist preachers and members considered women's participation normal and consistent with Scripture. Although both anti-Methodist tracts refer to "modesty," the claim that modesty was women's "principal ornament" was not Saint Paul's but Adam Rankin's. For conservative Protestants, southern secular ideals of female modesty, subordination, and silent deferral to educated white men were indistinguishable from Christian edicts.

Lay opponents focused on Methodist values rather than their practices. One of the most intriguing kinds of opposition centered around objections to Methodist asceticism and took two basic forms: the first, making allegations that Methodists were hypocrites, and the second, attempting to force Methodists into hypocritical acts. Several preachers were offered grog by hostile onlookers, and at least one narrowly escaped having liquor poured down his throat at a tavern. Rumors were circulated that Ezekiel Cooper had secretly requested a private view of a horse race, that William Ormond was jailed, and that John Kobler was a horse thief. Stith Mead was alleged to have been both a horse thief and a murderer. Opponents of the church once took Francis Asbury's horse and raced it on a horse track. Philip Gatch was the victim of a rumor that he was a highwayman who disguised himself by wearing blackface, perhaps an attempt to link him to his black parishioners in ways other whites would find abhorrent.[17] A few itinerants, of course, committed violations of the Discipline and were expelled by the church. But the charges of hypocrisy, which in these cases appear unsubstantiated, served other purposes and were motivated by more than moral concerns. Itinerants begged for money, owned little property, and seemed to have no honor. People who disliked the sect hoped to stifle Methodism's popularity by discrediting its ministers. Because of the church's controversial policies, these unknown travelers were viewed as troublemakers. Neither is it coincidental that itinerants were accused of hypocritically engaging in traditionally male vices. Perhaps southern men needed to believe that preachers could not live up to the feminized ascetic ethic of the church.

A related source of opposition came in response to the policies of the church that infringed on white male independence. White men who were expelled or excluded from services often responded with disbelief and rage. One man was able to vent his anger at both the rules and the clergy by throwing a copy of the book of Discipline at the preacher who expelled him. Several preachers reported being harassed by members they had disciplined or expelled. A Kentucky man, shut out of a love feast in the morning, returned to the church in the afternoon to disrupt the service. As the presiding minister tellingly described it, he "raged like a bullock unaccustomed to the yoke." Some young Alexandria men were so angry at being locked out of a love feast that they tried to break into the barn where Methodists were meeting; one knocked a hole in the wall. Some white southerners, as these and other cases show, found it difficult to submit (a charged word in a slave society) to church authorities. The church's close scrutiny of members, especially of white men, significantly threatened their independence. Their exclusion from the public sphere was also a relative novelty, and probably contributed to their rage.[18]

Another type of encounter that precipitated opposition occurred when Methodists violated unspoken southern rules about privacy or personal space, rules closely related to the code of honor. It is easy to see how intrusive Methodists might have appeared to others, especially when they physically touched strangers or asked nonmembers the same kinds of soul-searching questions they routinely asked one another in class meetings. John Littlejohn's query about whether a man had religion brought the angry response: "When I turn Papist and you are Fath[e]r confessor I will ans[we]r you." When a group of onlookers rushed in after Methodists began to cry aloud, John Kobler took one, a "tall stalking" Kentucky man, by the hand and "asked him if he had no desire to save his soul." The man "jirked back in the most violent manner and declared vengeance" if Kobler said any more. Kobler pursued him further, warning him: "God will bring you to judgment." The man later followed Kobler to his lodging, verbally "abused" him, and told him, "I will let you know what it is to talk to me."[19]

Methodists were often quite specific about the sins other men were committing.

Francis Asbury, after telling his host that he "feared the face of no man," outraged the Tennessee distiller by praying loudly in his house and "speaking against distilling and slave holding." On another occasion, the bishop unwisely lectured a man he had hired to be his guide, but "when I began to show him his folly and the dangerous state of his soul," Asbury recalled, the guide abandoned him to find his own way through the swamps. Methodists' close talk and their penchant for exposing what they saw as others' sins was often unwelcome. Preachers' intrusiveness was especially despised in the South because white men zealously guarded their independence. And when an outsider interfered in a man's private moral decisions, he dishonored the man involved. Amis, the Tennessee distiller, was not safe from such interference even in his own home.[20]

The most common form that opposition took between 1770 and 1810 was for critics to interrupt Methodist worship services. No setting was off-limits, whether the services were in private homes, groves, courthouses, or church buildings. The frequent interruptions that litter the record make patently clear that in the views of many of early Methodists' contemporaries, the church was at least a nuisance and at worst a danger to southern white mores. It is easy to imagine why, when Methodism first entered an area, such scenes might have occurred. By word of mouth and reports in the press, the reputation of Methodist services for strange goings-on was well established. Many skeptical attendees probably agreed with the arguments Rebecca Ridgely's friends used to encourage her to go listen to a Methodist preacher. "Doe [sic] go," they told her. "[I]t is as good as a play to hear him."[21] Yet white men, long after Methodists had been established in a locale, continued to attend services merely to harass the worshipers and ministers.

The intent of many who interrupted services was ostensibly just to disturb those present. These scenes, however, follow the contours of shaming rituals, with their ultimate object being the collective dishonor of Methodists. One man loudly cracked nuts throughout a service; another came in the middle of a sermon smoking a cigar. Ezekiel Cooper and his flock were subject to the ringing of bells, Henry Boehm to a false fire alarm. A Virginia man mocked Methodist enthusiasm by singing, jumping around, and dancing in services, "pretending that he was influenced by the spirit."[22] Several opponents brought animals into Methodist churches, perhaps thinking that Methodists acted more like animals than "rational men." In Sussex County, Virginia, shopkeepers "alarmed" at the reports of their neighbors falling down and "crying for mercy" in Methodist services, came to a meeting and "brought a monkey, and turned it loose." Stith Mead's society was harassed first by guns fired around the meeting-house and second by a screech-owl "thrown through the window" among the women. The choice of a "screech-owl" to respond to people who shrieked and moaned was likely intended to shame and insult them for their unruly behavior.[23] Shaming rituals had little effect on committed members because Methodists interpreted these dramas as evidence of their own righteousness and their opponents' sinfulness. Each outrageous interruption only further marked those in the church as separate from those in the world. Men who attempted to shame the unruly Wesleyans thus ironically fostered Methodists' identity as a persecuted, faithful minority. Preachers had told their members that unconverted southerners were "mockers" of the Lord. What further evidence did members need than these incidents in which the godless tried to mock the people of God?

A number of the "mockers" who interrupted Methodist services were identified as "gentlemen"—a word most preachers used derisively. Ezekiel Cooper was repeatedly disturbed by gentlemen. On one occasion he even appealed to the very refinement the church scorned and told some elite men that "it was beneath the character of a gentleman to misbehave." Cooper's invocation of gentility was a bit like rude opponents' calls for order and it had no effect. In 1790, Cooper's worship service was again invaded by some young men "who think themselves gentlemen," as he put it, who brought eggs, sand, and brickbats and "played on the congregation." His confused listeners believed the gallery was falling and "jumped on one another to escape," but the house was too crowded. This intensified their fear, many screamed, and Cooper "feared some women would go into fitts [*sic*]."[24] Evidently, gentlemen lost no status among their peers for such conduct in this era. Methodists were outside the circle of honor; as such, they were fair game for whatever gentlemen could think to do to them.

Elite men seem to have considered Methodists beneath them but too numerous to ignore, especially when their slaves, children, and wives were joining the church. "Gentlemen" showed their contempt in grandiose ways, making noisy and belated entrances into services, leaving gruffly in the middle of worship, or challenging ministers verbally. Some of these men made a scene because they felt they were being attacked for their wealth or status. A wealthy man in Mississippi interrupted a sermon against pride to claim he was being singled out for insult by the preacher, an incident that shows the touchiness of elite men of honor. Francis Asbury preached in Delaware on one of Methodists' favorite antigentry scriptures: "Ye cannot serve both God and mammon." A gentleman "much in pursuit of the world," and who had previously been "condemned" by local Methodists, stood up following Asbury's sermon, "and said, he was the man pointed at, and desired another hearing."[25]

The gentry were right to see Methodists as a threat, for Methodists' strictures against ostentation, their views about the corrupting nature of wealth, and their refusal to offer deference challenged the hegemony of elites. Asbury, in effect, claimed that his rich auditors were ungodly. While elite southern men were not collectively known for their excessive piety, Methodists tried to strip them of any claim to moral authority by suggesting they behaved counter to God's will. God can be used by any side in any argument, but in an era when most southerners believed themselves to be Christians, being stigmatized as ungodly was enough of a challenge that some gentlemen felt they had to respond. To publicly attack an elite man in front of people who were considered inferiors was to contest his claim to status and superiority. Methodists may have denied that they were anarchic levelers, but many of their pronouncements looked suspiciously like leveling. John Early, for example, said of a Virginia lawyer "that if he would come down low enough to be a Methodist he would get right into the life of religion."[26] Early's creative use of "low enough" is telling. The gentry had hierarchically ranked and ordered their worlds, and they knew who was high, who was low, who was honorable, and who was not. Because most Methodists were men and women of little status and position, their celebration of being "down low" effectively turned worldly rankings on their head.

Methodists challenged the white male code of honor in a number of ways, most obviously by transforming some men of honor into evangelicals. Jacob Young was one of the many young men who converted against their fathers' wishes. Jacob described himself as a "sportsman" who loved the "ball-room" and "card-table," gambled on the Sabbath, and fought with other men. But on his first visit to a Methodist service, Jacob "lost the power of speech—my tears flowed freely, my knees became feeble, and I trembled . . . my strength failed and I fell upon the floor—the great deep of my heart appeared to be broken up."[27] William Gassaway was another typical young man of the South: "In his youth he was wild and reckless, full of fun and frolic, and withal somewhat given to those pugilistic encounters which were deemed among the young men of that day strong evidence of manliness."[28] James Finley was an archetypal "backwoods boy" reared within the assertive and combative culture of honor. Before becoming a Methodist, he would dance, "swear when angry; and fight, when insulted, at the drop of a hat."[29] Although John Young, Sr., never blasphemed in his youth, he remembered he was "wicked enough in other respects [—] reveling gambling raceing cockfighting."[30] Fighting when insulted, gambling, racing, and cockfighting were all amusements men of honor enjoyed. When men converted, they voluntarily gave up these pursuits and united with a church that prized meekness, ascetic self-control, and humility.

Perhaps no aspect of southern honor was as democratic as drink. Whether rich or poor, white men could enjoy conviviality and demonstrate their manhood by downing ale, brandy, or hard liquor. As might be expected, men said to have been "drunk" comprised a large number of those who argued or yelled in Methodist services, but these interruptions involved more than male anger at the church's opposition to drink. Men who drank believed that the world of the tavern was under assault by the church.[31] A number of men contrasted (masculine) taverns with (feminine) church meetings in their conversion accounts. An Iredell County, North Carolina, man began to feel convicted at a camp meeting and left for the familiar safety of a tavern, but the stirrings of religion changed his perception entirely: "while one of the [tavern] company was blaspheming, he was struck with such dread and horror" that he returned to the camp meeting to be prayed for. Tavern-goers in Rockingham, Virginia, were so curious about what was going on at a nearby Methodist service that they appointed a man named Mackey to go and see and report back to them, "as he was not afraid." Mackey began to count the number of people who had fallen when he, too, fell and said goodbye to the tavern indefinitely.[32] Men's fears become clearer when we look at the conversion process itself.

James Finley's story is particularly instructive. Finley decided to attend a Kentucky camp meeting out of curiosity and boasted to his friends that he would not fall as others had: "as I prided myself upon my manhood and courage, I had no fear of being overcome by any nervous excitability." But once at the service, Finley began to feel strange. "My heart beat tumultuously, my knees trembled, my lip quivered, and I felt as though I must fall to the ground," he recalled. "I became so weak and powerless that I found it necessary to sit down." He retreated to the woods, "to rally and man up my courage," but when he returned to the meeting, he again was overcome. Finley then resolved to go to a nearby tavern and "get some brandy, and see if it would not strengthen my nerves." But having been touched by religion, he was "disgusted with the sight" of "men engaged in drunken revelry, playing cards, trading horses, quarreling, and fighting," activities Finley had previously enjoyed. By the week's end Finley, who had feared that falling down would "put a final quietus on my boasted manhood and courage," was prostrate and crying for mercy.[33]

Finley was not unique. Men's conversion accounts resound with the language of passivity, of being "overpowered," "trembling," "yielding," "helpless," or "feeble."[34] A South Carolinian, Major Guerry, literally became feminine before his brother-in-law's eyes as he converted. Guerry ("a very large man") had a "peculiarly imposing" appearance and a "rather austere" look that "would inspire reverence more than love." Once Guerry began his transformation, his "countenance [became] as soft as love itself," his "bearing," "the very expression of meekness." His brother-in-law "saw a tear in the eye which I had not thought capable of a tear, and a suffusion on the cheek which might not have been suspected of anything so tender."[35]

Powerless. Meek. Helpless. A man of honor was not supposed to acknowledge such feelings, much less proudly record them for posterity. Only "negroes and weak-minded women" were overcome by evangelical religion in such demonstrative ways. The copious weeping of male converts was equally forbidden in the secular world. Only "shallow men, ignorant women, and silly children" wept emotionally in public.[36] These emotions and behaviors were "feminine" and "slavish" to those outside the evangelical fold. Male converts not only "unmanned" themselves; they did so in full view of their scoffing peers and, by secular standards, their inferiors—children, white women, and slaves. The code of honor demanded that white men keep their weaker emotions hidden from public view, that they wear masks of power and strength. To ritualize and memorialize these moments of men's utter helplessness was to laud the qualities an honorable, independent man was supposed to repress.

The many reports of men fleeing for taverns make perfect sense in the gendered context of these scenes. Drinking, especially public drinking at taverns and grogshops, was primarily a male activity. Over a dram, men tested their honor and solidified their standing among other men. The tavern was masculine both in its importance within male culture and in its exclusion of women. As evangelicalism expanded in the South, church services offered an analogous public outlet for self-expression, exuberance, and camaraderie, but one in which all were welcome and where people had fellowship without the aid of drink. Some men were hostile to the largely feminine world of the church because they, like Finley, feared that if they came under its influence, they too would become "powerless," and they, too, would have to forsake the male world symbolized by the tavern. Powerlessness had gendered and racial implications in the South. To become "powerless" was to become like women, children, and slaves; to be "powerless" was to be unmanned. Once converted, southern white men abandoned many of the male-only public domains for the bigendered and biracial public world of evangelicalism.[37]

Another common reason that Methodists, especially clergymen, were harassed indicates even more clearly the challenge the church made to southern notions of masculinity. These scenes followed a typical course: a preacher would reprove a man in the audience for his disruptive behavior, and that man would in turn threaten the preacher with violence. William Colbert accused a man named Lecher of ungentlemanly conduct during a service. Lecher became enraged, demanded his house keys from his wife, who was also present, and returned later wielding a club. Methodist women protected Colbert from assault, although Lecher continued to rant and rave for awhile. Ezekiel Cooper was threatened with a beating from a "young gentleman" he had called down in a service. At a Kentucky revival, Jacob Young's reproof was met by a similar threat. James Meacham and Francis Asbury were both threatened several times by men they had criticized from the pulpit.[38]

To understand why such incidents occurred, we must briefly review how verbal insults were handled in the secular code of honor. Honor was defensive; perceived insults and humiliations required assertive, sometimes violent, responses. James Finley described his preconversion mind-set, the worldview of plain folk and middling yeomen, in these terms: "No man was permitted to insult another without resentment; and if an insult was permitted to pass unrevenged, the insulted party lost his standing and caste in society." Elites developed an elaborate ritual designed to preserve the honor of both the man insulted and the man who had given insult. The term for the balance of honor ideally achieved was "satisfaction." Once "satisfaction" had been granted to the offended party without causing offense to the offending party, the conflict was considered resolved. The exchange of letters and visits between the two principals and their representatives ideally solved the problem without violence, but if not, the ritualized violence of the duel existed as a last resort. If a man was insulted by someone he considered to be of lesser social standing, he sometimes ignored the incident, but could also seize a cane or stick and beat the offending party.[39]

Methodist preachers (and male members) represented an anomaly in the white male world, however, because they would neither apologize for the insults they rendered, nor would they, with rare exception, fight even in self-defense with the offended party. Perhaps itinerants could have been ignored as being outside the circle of honor and thus unworthy of any response had they not delivered these insults in public. The typical Methodist audience, moreover, included women and slaves, and insults delivered in front of (and at times by) these subordinate groups especially rankled. It is probably not coincidental that Methodist preachers were often threatened by mobs, in ambushes, or with sticks, rocks, or clubs, for as they would not have been perceived as equals, they would not have been worthy of a "fair" fight. Several opponents of the church suggested that Methodists should be publicly whipped, a punishment reserved only for those outside the circle of honor, especially for slaves. After an enthusiastic service, John Kobler was told that "they that made such a noise ought to be tyed up and have 70 lashes"—extreme even by contemporary standards.[40]

Sometimes the insulted men even used the language of honor to describe these conflicts. In Blacksburg, Virginia, "father" Carson was delivering a sermon when a young man "arose, put on his hat and took a stand just in front" of the pulpit. Carson asked him to be seated and the young man reportedly "uttered some insulting and blasphemous language" and left the service. He returned soon after and blocked Carson's exit from the chapel, claiming, "You insulted me, sir, and I'll have the satisfaction." Resolution was not forthcoming, however, for Carson, after being hit, tried to push past the man. Because Carson refused to fight, the young man swore a complaint against the preacher.[41] Perhaps encounters like these convinced some men to seek satisfaction in other ways. When an opponent would not fight or was deemed unworthy of a fight, men could seek revenge on their insulter's nose. In the culture of honor, men sensitively guarded their noses from such assaults.[42] A Norfolk man believed that "special reference had been made to him in a very severe part" of a sermon in 1806.

When the preacher was walking out of the meetinghouse, "the man approached, charged [the preacher] with insulting him, and seizing his nose wrung it violently."[43]

Methodists were aware that they were deviating from southern customs and took great pleasure in the way they challenged secular masculinity. Francis Asbury reported the conversion of a man who had been an "opposer, proud and self-righteous, but [is] now brought low, penitent, and submits to prayer, and Methodist conversation; thus does God bring down." Lovick Pierce remembered the conversion of his father, who despite "all his stern manhood, commenced shaking like a leaf in the wind, and down he fell upon the floor." Recall the story of Mary Hinde's reproof of her neighbor, Major Martin, a "confirmed deist" and "a man of standing in society at large." Martin, a man who "would have conceived it a disgrace to take an insult, or to bear even a rebuke from any man" was "assailed by an elderly woman" and converted after her rebuke. For many Methodist men, the initiating rite of passage into the church involved a similar rejection of southern masculine norms. For Martin, the act was suffering a rebuke from a woman; for others it was being physically overcome or converting under a slave's leadership.[44]

Methodism assaulted southern mores on many levels, and thus the reasons for opposition were often complex. Nowhere can this be seen more clearly than in opposition to Methodist enthusiasm. The shouting, weeping, and falling that Methodists so frequently exhibited during services elicited a multifaceted and strident response from critics. Among the many criticisms leveled at Methodist enthusiasm was that it was disorderly. High churchmen claimed that noise and physical displays were unnecessary and even repugnant in the house of God. The screaming and yelling in the pulpit, in their opinion, caused the chaos in the pews. As a man once said to preacher John Young, "the more the People hollered the more I encourged [sic] them." Methodists' enthusiastic style of worship was offensive to some, sacrilegious to others. Perhaps certain critics would have objected even if elite white men were the only enthusiasts. Yet the evidence indicates that many critics went beyond distaste and theological disapproval. As Methodists liked to point out, southerners critiqued them for noise while loud, rambunctious, physically exuberant tavern-goers, for example, were not accused of being mad or bewitched.[45]

Critics were divided as to whether enthusiasm fell under the rubric of delusion, insanity, or the supernatural. Clergy of other denominations occasionally faulted Satan, but were more likely to claim that Methodists were irrational. Competing ministers were especially troubled that enthusiastic practices emphasized the passions and the body instead of reason and the mind, where they believed religion properly belonged. Anyone could fall down, they argued, while a work of grace was more durable and deep. One Episcopalian believed Methodism to be an "insult" on the "reason" of his parish and warned preacher William Colbert not to "confuse the minds of the weak."[46] A hostile Virginia lawyer felt Methodism appealed to those of "weak minds" and worked on their "heated imaginations." Presbyterian critics—the same who opposed women's teaching and exhorting—lectured that the Holy Spirit worked "upon the soul in its higher faculties [of] the understanding and the will" and not on the lower ones "of the imagination, of the affections, and of the body itself." Adam Rankin distinguished "delusion" from "religion" on similar grounds, with the deluded basing their faith "upon their passions" and the religious basing theirs on Christ.[47]

A related and common charge was that Methodist enthusiasm incited believers to madness. All across the South, ministers were accused of "driving people mad" or of making them "deranged." These accusations reached a fever pitch in the camp meeting era, when scores of fallen participants littered the grounds and newer and stranger behaviors, such as jerking, dancing, and barking, accompanied conversions. But even in Methodism's first decades in the South, enthusiasm was synonymous with madness in the eyes of many outside the church.[48] Those who interpreted events in a more traditional religious framework preferred to link enthusiasm with devil worship or witchcraft. Crying, falling, jerking, and weeping were repeatedly referred to as "the work of the devil," "the magic art," or as the result of a preacher's having "bewitched the people." When preacher Thomas Darley elicited an enthusiastic reaction from a crowd in South Carolina's Barnwell district, local residents called it "magical, or wizardly," and some even said Darley possessed "strange powders, which he had wrapped up in his handkerchief, and that during the exercises he gave it a flirt, and these powders fell on the men and women present."[49]

Some southerners were earnestly convinced that enthusiasm was satanic or pagan; a common reaction by non-Methodists to enthusiasm was to run away in fright. No doubt the sight of weeping, falling, and shouting crowds was terrible to those unfamiliar with Methodist ways and seemed to conjure up collective folk memories of times when witches and devils walked the earth creating havoc among mortals—or, for elites, fears of revolution. John Early once tersely described a scene familiar to many Methodists: "Some cried and some shouted and some ran away." When Methodists fell to the floor in a service George Wells conducted, "others took to their heels and sum [some] jumpt out of the windows." Benjamin Abbott and John Kobler both reported many services where some people fled when the Methodists became enthusiastic.[50]

Although critics rarely stated it so baldly, it is obvious that their concerns focused as much on *who* was exhibiting enthusiasm as on the enthusiasm itself. By looking carefully at these many incidents, we can see that verbal and physical displays by two groups of converts in particular elicited the most adverse reactions—white women and blacks. Class was sometimes interwoven with these complaints. Thomas Haughton, who viewed Methodist worshipers as "rabble," described a Methodist conference in which "confusion, shouting, praying, singing, laughing, talking, amorous engagements, falling down, kicking, squealing, and a thousand other ludicrous things prevailed." Another critic of enthusiasm complained that "Methodists bawl out their tenets with the greatest success amongst the lower orders of people." John Kobler described a service where "many of the poor" were crying while "some of the rich stood up and looked on with astonishment."[51]

White Methodist women were often ridiculed and censured for their enthusiastic behavior, and many critics believed women (who were "naturally" frail) were especially susceptible to preachers' harangues. Women were considered the more emotional and passionate of the two sexes; men were believed more logical and reasonable. While the body was said to explain much of women's behavior, the mind was determined to explain men's actions. The mind, rationality, and logic were valued by Methodists' critics as of a "higher" order than the body, emotions, and passions.[52] But Methodists seemed to celebrate as strengths what high churchmen and secularists viewed as women's weaknesses; in the church, emotion and passion were prized as evidence of heart religion. Judging by preachers' accounts, white women were far more physically and emotionally demonstrative than white men and women's enthusiasm was more pronounced than men's. To Methodist preachers, of course, these reactions were evidence of divine inspiration and not of mania or indecency.

The ecstatic displays of women's spiritual power frightened people outside the church. Typical was the reaction of an audience in western Virginia in 1776. During Freeborn Garrettson's sermon, "the word took such effect on the heart of a woman, that she cried so loud as to make the church ring: the people being unacquainted with such things, strove to get out; but the ailes, and every place were so crouded that they could not." A similar scene transpired years later during Henry Smith's ministry. During his sermon, a woman "trembled, and fell off her seat, and cried to God for mercy." The audience "was much alarmed; some pushed for the door, others stood trembling, and those that were out of doors looked frightened."[53] When a South Carolina woman "began to praise God aloud" at a camp meeting, a group of "rowdies" that were looking on from the forest "came thundering into the camp . . . producing a scene of the utmost tumult and confusion." In Lincoln County, North Carolina, a widow Morris shouted loudly and "the congregation were panick-stricken: the old German ladies pressed their way to Nancy L. Morris, the widow's daughter, and exclaimed in the utmost fright, 'Your mother has had a fit, indeed she has; and she is going to die.'"[54] Clearly, these onlookers were not merely protesting the Methodists' approach to worship; they were frightened or worried at the specific reactions of Methodist women.

Some people, typically men, who objected to their female relations exhibiting such behavior came to services to remove them by force, attempting to publicly reassert their authority. Hannah Arrington of Iredell County, North Carolina, "fell from her seat and begged for mercy" during an 1802 service. Her brother Joel "rushed to her caught her arm, snatched her from the house and literally dragged her home!" At an enthusiastic meeting Thomas Mann attended, he witnessed "one sinner tak[e] his sister out." Jeremiah Norman described another enthusiastic service where some in attendance "ran off" during the prayer. Many returned shortly after, when "the men came to take away their wives. Some went, others would not." The next day, Norman and his colleague were lectured about "the last nights meeting" by a husband who was "much exasperated and said several illnatured things." A man's three sisters fell to the floor in Sussex County, Virginia, and he picked one up to "carry her out, swearing she should not expose herself there."[55] As the phrase "expose herself" suggests, in the minds of some opponents, there was a link between Methodism and sexual license. A European traveler's comparison of men's and women's enthusiasm at camp meetings is revealing: "I have seen women jumping, striking, and kicking, like raving maniacs; while the surrounding believers could not keep them in postures of decency."[56]

Charges that Methodist women were being seduced, violated, and encouraged to sexual sin abounded even outside the context of enthusiasm. One common allegation was that Methodist ministers were taking sexual advantage of their female converts. A man told preacher William Colbert that he had heard of the "slippery tricks" of itinerants, such as trapping young women in corn houses. Freeborn Garrettson had to publicly deny a rumor that a Methodist preacher "had attempted to ravish" a woman.

James Jenkins was the victim of a similar slander, although he was vindicated when an Irish shoemaker admitted that he had been the one who had "frightened" the women involved.[57] Historically, religions that have empowered women or allowed for personal interaction with God in possession rituals have been accused of sexual license and promiscuity. Critics of Methodism normally blamed preachers and not the women themselves. Preachers were accused of casting spells, working magic, or just exploiting the "minds of the weak."[58] Perhaps to accuse Methodist women of sexual immorality in an era increasingly defining "woman" as "moral guardian" seemed out of place. Perhaps it was easier to believe that ministers were unscrupulous manipulators than to admit that women had voluntarily chosen to join the despised sect.

Critics' allegations were not, however, without a certain logic. Ministers' prolonged and often unsupervised contact with adult women certainly gave them opportunities for sexual relationships. The intimacy that developed between female members and itinerants may also have caused outside observers to believe, or to opportunistically charge, that the passion Methodist women displayed was somehow sexual. Sarah Jones was extremely close to one of her ministers. The two had contracted to be convenant partners—to pray at a set time every day—and although miles usually separated them, in prayer she often felt his presence. She termed their partnership "our union, in Jesus." Once, after he had left for his next appointment, Sarah went to the room he had stayed in and "fell on my knees upon the carpet, believing there you had lifted your hands and heart to my adorable Jesus." Such relationships, filled with the emotion and zeal that infused all of Methodism, were easily misinterpreted by the uninformed and hostile. Yet one suspects there is more to these charges of sexual impropriety than a misunderstanding. Methodist itinerants formed long-lasting and close-knit relationships with many women outside of their families. They respected women for their intellect, piety, and wisdom. When opponents sexualized these friendships, they revealed more about the secular view of women than about potential Methodist abuses. Some men outside the church, it seems, could not imagine such intimacy without sex.[59]

Women's religious passion was nonetheless highly eroticized. The closest religious relationship for Methodist women was the one they had with Christ, and the language they used to describe this "union" presumed a link between the spiritual and physical. Sally Eastland spoke of her private prayer sessions in such terms: "He's left me as it [were] help less on the ground, ah sweet momentes, how fain would I faint away in his arms." Sarah Jones, while in religious ecstasy, claimed to be "so overwhelmed that I was like to faint for real possession." "Jesus's hands, his soft and lilly hands! I as sensibly, through faith, handled the sacred touch," she wrote on one occasion. On another, she made no reference to her language being metaphorical: "Boundless, matchless, adorable Jesus! Sometimes I feel like my breath would cease in his embraces." Jones had "longings" for Christ's love that were infused with romantic and sensual imagery: "I sink, I burn, I die, I glow to be fully possessed of all thy killing charms, thy soul-transporting smiles." It is reasonable to assume that non-Methodists did not approve of viewing Christ as a lover any more than they did of women fainting and shouting. With Methodist women blurring religious and sensual passion, critics' perceptions of sexual license become easier to understand.[60]

Enthusiastic worship displayed women's passions before the public in a era when passion was ideally confined to encounters between husbands and wives in private. One extremely harsh critic, a New Jerusalem clergyman, claimed that at Methodist services "more prostitutes of both sexes meet under the mask of a sanctified face and plain bonnet" and that camp meetings especially attracted female prostitutes because they worked at night. Another man critiqued the way preachers attempted to move women's "passions" at camp meetings and was disgusted that in the throes of enthusiasm "young maids" would faint with "All their charms and their zeal to display." This author particularly objected to the interracial mingling at camp meetings, where "a negro [man] so strong" might walk off "lovingly" with a white woman.[61] Presbyterian Adam Rankin felt it inevitable that sexual promiscuity would result at camp meetings, for he felt the temptation was strong when men and women were lying around together. He ingeniously linked (Arminian?) doctrinal "errors" to his charge, claiming that "spiritual adultery is almost inseparably connected with natural." A French traveler likened enthusiastic Methodist women to "priestesses" in the East Indies who, after having visions of God, took off all their clothes.[62]

Methodists were not the only sect to be criticized for enthusiasm and for exploiting women's alleged weaknesses. As a group, they were more united in their approval of revivalism than other Protestants, but Cumberland Presbyterians and some Baptists joined wholeheartedly in the camp meeting movement. Paul Henkel, a Lutheran pastor in the North Carolina piedmont, left a fascinating account of the revivals there at the turn of the century. Instead of singling out Methodists, Henkel criticized certain practices common to the camp meetings. Henkel agreed with other critics that women were the victims of fanatical preachers. "Women were driven into fear," he wrote of one meeting, and "aroused in their emotions. . . . The preachers took advantage of the opportunity." At another, he was astonished that "Anybody who wished could preach: men, women, young men, young women."[63] Observing a Methodist camp meeting in 1802, Henkel was even more disdainful: "three or four preachers harangued at the same time with the most fearful expressions they could invent until finally two young women rushed to the platform among the preachers, began to sink to the floor, and to cry out with much agony and agitation." The crowd took its cue, and all were soon crying and falling. Henkel observed "a weak woman with a child in her arms, who was so deeply agitated that . . . she began to tremble and become quite pale." Afraid she would fall and harm the child, Henkel tried to persuade her that physical displays were not the "true" way to God. Her husband was extremely grateful to Henkel for his warnings; a Methodist "openly rebuked" Henkel for interfering with the woman.[64] Henkel's account was less hyperbolic and less denunciatory than most, but even he seemed to feel that preachers were seducing women, if not into sexual misbehavior, into religious error.

Black enthusiasm was also met with hostility by those outside the church, who often emphasized the "disorder" of it. Many critics of Methodism believed blacks to be persons of "weak minds" and therefore, like women, susceptible to Methodist harangues. Charles Janson repeated the complaints of many when he wrote that Methodists "do great mischief among the slaves." As other critics did with women, Janson expressed concern for the "uninformed negroes," because he believed white Methodists "aggravate the hardships of their situations, by disordering their minds." Frenchman Moreau de St. Mery agreed in principle, claiming that Methodist sermons "fill

Negroes' superstitious souls with terror" and that blacks "believe in sorcerers, and their superstitious weakness of mind makes them ready prey to the Methodists."[65] Presbyterian William Hill, considered by his fellow members to be too "much like a Methodist," also decried black enthusiasm. He preached to a Methodist audience in Sussex County, Virginia, and "had very little satisfaction, for the congregation exhibited a sense of wild disorder and confusion for nothing could be heard from the preacher on account of the shouts and exclamations which were raised, especially by the negroes and fanaticism and vociferation seemed to be the order of the day."[66]

If black enthusiasm was "wild disorder" to a "methodistic" Presbyterian, it is not hard to imagine how it must have appeared to less sympathetic whites. Seeing blacks, especially slaves, congregate in large groups and shout, fall, and weep must have been frightening for whites already fearful about slave insurrections. Although it was rare, some criticism of black enthusiasm came from whites within the Methodist church. William Colbert reported that a white brother named Riggin was upset when "the black people began to shout and jump about"; Riggin "said the devil was among them, and told the people to go out from among them." Freeborn Garrettson, who normally approved of black enthusiasm, feared that "Satan got an advantage" of one Virginia bondwoman in 1781, when she "fell down, thumped her breast and puked all over the floor."[67]

On more than one occasion, non-Methodist whites laughed at or mocked black enthusiasm, but they sometimes reacted more harshly. In 1808, a "gentleman" who objected to the "noise" of black Methodists had the Charleston city guard, armed with muskets, surround the church and jail the black members. One Virginia mistress hosted a service for blacks and whites in her home, where some fell "prostrate on the floor and others wept out loud." The next morning, the preacher noted, the woman showed "a great deal of resentment," said "she could not bear such hollering," and "gave one of her servants a lecture for her conduct the night past."[68] Jeremiah Norman noted how at one service, "one of the Blacks cryed out aloud, which gave great offense." John Littlejohn was preaching in the Richmond courthouse to a large audience with "many Blacks" when "towards the close the poor Africans could forbear no longer but with strong cryes and tears called for mercy; most of the whites frighten[e]d, left the house, in confusion and dismay as if the great deep was going to overwhelm them." Littlejohn paused until the whites had all left, and "continued to point the Bl[ac]ks to Jesus as their only ark of safety from the storm."[69]

As is usual with these incidents, there is more to this scene than meets the eye, and to avoid reductionism, it is perhaps appropriate to consider the other factors. First, the physical context was a courthouse, normally a source of white power and authority. Before the sermon had begun, Littlejohn had reproved a "lady" for laughing, and told her "this is now Gods house," a statement that perhaps was a small critique of Virginia's justice system, and that in any event sought to draw a line between secular and sacred assemblies. Second, Littlejohn's sermon text that day was Jonah 1: 6, wherein Jonah, who was sleeping while everyone else prayed for mercy, was awakened by sailors during a fierce storm at sea and told to pray; indeed all the mariners were praying "every man unto his God." Jonah was at sea because he was fleeing from God's commandment, and when the other sailors learned this, they blamed Jonah for the storm. They threw him overboard, while they themselves, who were "innocent," were spared and the waters calmed. The implication in Littlejohn's comments was that white Virginians feared the "great deep" because of their own unfaithfulness, and conversely that the faithful blacks would be spared because they cried to their God.[70]

William Colbert also encountered whites who objected to black enthusiasm. Preaching to a mixed race audience in 1790, Colbert "wanted to see a move among them . . . and sure enough, there was a move for the blacks behind began to shout aloud jump and fall the whites to look wild and go off." He attributed white attitudes to "prejudice," which was definitely an understatement. One white woman who fled declared that she would never hear another Methodist and told Colbert "that she believed I should kill myself."[71] Strong words indeed, and they would seem grossly out of proportion to the actual events were it not for the fact that whites believed Methodism challenged the southern racial hierarchy. Because of the church's early stance against slavery, Asbury noted as late as 1809 that some slaves were not allowed to attend Methodist services because "their masters are afraid of the influence of our principles." The mere fact that white Methodists encouraged slaves to congregate was seen as threatening by those outside the church. Furthermore, once assembled, blacks regularly engaged in behavior that seemed to threaten racial hierarchy.[72]

The communal shouts that preceded white flight or provoked white anger (and as we will see, white violence) symbolized black unity and defiance. In communal shouts, blacks—slave and free—seemed to be transported en masse to a psychic place where whites could not frighten or worry them. In the throes of religious possession, African American Methodists did not even seem cognizant of white authority. The fact that so many whites linked black Methodism with imminent revolution was undoubtedly related to white fears of collective black enthusiasm. Blacks' transcendence in this context was a threat to white racial control, and whites outside the church responded by attacking black enthusiasm, or by attacking black Methodists themselves.

Thus far, we have seen many of the points of contention as centering on Methodist belief and practice. Yet as the reactions to Methodist enthusiasm show, opponents of the church often did not divorce Methodist ways and values from the Methodists themselves. Many of the controversies surrounding Methodism centered on the converts themselves and the *effects* of church values and practices on them. Critics believed that Methodism challenged racial, class, and gender conventions and that the church was a danger to cherished southern ways. The threats Methodism posed become clearer after examining some of the more violent encounters Methodists faced.

Many southerners perceived Methodists as a threat to patriarchal authority. Conflicts between children and parents, primarily fathers, were routine. Once again, we must consider the southern context for these incidents. Southern patriarchs cherished their ability to govern their affairs and family as they saw fit; any intervention checked manly independence, tied as it was to control over others. Patriarchs' mastery over households muted class conflict by conferring status, power, and superiority to all white men.[73] Although only a minority owned slaves, a majority had wives and children. When Methodists challenged a father's power, they thereby undermined his standing in the larger white male community. Methodist clergy, it should be noted, would have denied that they challenged parental authority. John Wesley firmly believed in children's absolute and total obedience to godly parents, and he urged mothers and fathers to make, by any means necessary, the child's will the mirror of the parents' will in order to prepare the child for obedience to God in later life. Wesley's thoughts on child rearing were published in American Methodist periodicals, and there is little reason to believe that American ministers differed with his views. Yet we miss one of the main thrusts of Wesley's beliefs if we substitute "all parents" for "godly parents." In practice, Methodist ministers tended to support such absolute obedience only when the parents themselves were Methodists; if they were not, all bets were off.[74]

Southern parents had good reason to believe Methodist clergy were encouraging their children to disobey. Some preachers rebuked parents who opposed their Methodist children. Benjamin Abbott told a tale of a young male convert whose Quaker parents opposed him and with "their violence and displeasure" kept him from the church. According to Abbott, the young man became not a good Quaker but a profligate, which Abbott saw as "a warning to parents who oppose their children in religious sentiments." Perhaps in response to such views, an exasperated German Reformed minister who was losing many of his congregants to the Wesleyans told one mother that according to the Bible, children had to follow their parents in religious matters, even if their parents were heathens. Methodists obviously disagreed.[75]

James Finley published a story of infidel parents who scorned religion that, to outsiders, probably seemed to justify children's disobedience. These parents were outraged to learn that their daughter Eliza went to a Methodist meeting and became convicted for her sins. Warning her to stay away from "those ignorant fanatics," her father threatened to banish her if she disobeyed. Eliza was in a quandary, for she had never disobeyed parental injunctions, but she wanted to attend services. In this state, she remembered a Methodist preacher's discussion of the words of Christ that "whosoever loveth father or mother more than me is not worthy of me; and whosoever will not forsake father and mother for my sake and the Gospel's shall not enter heaven." She determined to "forsake all for Christ," became a member, and refused to submit even after her father whipped her and banished her from his home.[76] Brother West told a similarly didactic tale to a Methodist audience in South Carolina: "A little girl, who had embraced religion, was greatly opposed by her parents, but all to no effect. At last her father threatened to whip her if she did not quit praying; so she made up her mind to take the whipping, and bringing a switch to him, she fell on her knees, saying, 'Pa, whip me, but let me serve God.'" To the audience, this story was invigorating, "like fire to stubble." To people outside the church, anecdotes like these must have confirmed their suspicions that Methodists were subverting parental authority. While the church did not encourage children to rebel without cause, Methodism offered children and other subordinates a rationale for disobedience of ungodly superiors and supported them in domestic rebellions for the sake of religion.[77]

Non-Methodist parents, we should note, had some perfectly reasonable fears that help explain why they opposed their children's joining the church. The church in its early decades was a fringe movement, despised by some and ridiculed by many. Parents may well have feared that their children would have more difficulty finding mates if they joined the church or that their financial futures could be affected. Elite parents, for example, knew how difficult it would be for their daughters to court if they refused to dress as others did. Parents of all classes seem to have worried when sons chose a career in the Methodist itinerancy, probably fearing that these young men would have trouble marrying and that they would be living on the edge of poverty. Sometimes it is clear that parents were worried about their children's mental and physical health. A young man of twenty-three, after becoming convicted for his sins but before becoming converted, went through a period of depression and "was much tempted to make away with myself." His mother sought help and was "advised to keep [him] from hearing the Methodists preach." [78]

Other parents, however, opposed their children's defection from the family's church to a suspect sect because they believed their children's conversion would adversely affect the family's reputation. Jacob Young's father, for example, "was sorry that his son . . . should disgrace him and his family" by converting to Methodism. John McGee's mother was a Presbyterian, and when she heard that her son had converted to Methodism and had begun itinerant preaching, she "thought seriously of disowning him." Peter Moriarty was raised in a Maryland Catholic home, and at age sixteen began to attend Methodist services despite being "forbidden by my parents." During his conversion, his parents feared he was mad, for he could not "eat, drink, nor sleep." His father claimed that his "weeping and wailing" would "bring a disgrace on the family" and threatened to banish him from the home.[79]

A common thread among Methodists' biographies was the explicit rejection of the father's religion, which Methodist youth seemed to take pleasure in. Moriarty showed how intolerant new converts could be to other faiths—he referred to his Catholic upbringing as "this blind way" and Catholic beliefs as "delusions of Satan." One can imagine how his parents must have felt. Normally, the man or woman who had most influenced the convert became their surrogate "father or mother in the gospel," rhetoric that only highlights the break many Methodist converts made with their parents. And when young people converted their parents, Methodists often reflected on the irony of the son or daughter becoming the mother or father to the parents, a spiritual if not a material inversion.[80]

On occasion, Methodist youth condemned their parents in services or reported their "sins," practices that probably contributed to parental opposition. John Kobler told of a young man who "exclaimed against his parents for bringing him up in such great ignorance" to religion. Nelson Reed met a young woman who wanted to "serve God but could not read." He blamed her illiteracy on her parents, noting that they "would have to give an account of their conduct" to God. A little girl told Ezekiel Cooper that she loved to pray, but her "Papa and Mama went to balls and that [wasn't] so good as prayers." John Jacob visited a sick woman who blamed her father for not teaching her about prayer or religion.[81] It is possible that young people's conversion to Methodism against parental wishes was a form of adolescent or early adulthood rebellion directed more against their parents than toward Methodism, but if so, this form of rebellion was rather drastic. There were, first, all the rules a convert had to obey. And for many young southerners, the consequences of disobedience were severe. The father of "Miss R. B." would not let her come home until she left the Methodists.[82] She was not the only daughter to be banished from her father's home because of Methodism. Thomas Hinde, when he banished his daughter Susanna, set similar conditions for her return.

A southern father who could not control his offspring's behavior may have chosen banishment or disinheritance in order to preserve the illusion that he was the master of his household. There are many cases in which the pivotal issue for parents, especially fathers, was one of authority. Philip Gatch's father ordered him to stay away from the Methodists because his house would not hold two religions. When Philip disobeyed, his father became one of many to conclude that Methodists "created divisions in families." Other sons were not as lucky as Gatch. In such a violent culture, it is not surprising that fathers resorted to force. John Cooper's father forbade his son even to pray. When John disobeyed and was caught, his father tossed hot embers on him. Robert Wright first forbade his son Thomas from joining the church, next threatened Thomas with disinheritance, and finally turned to violence and whipped his son. A Virginia man who refused to hear the Methodists himself also refused to let his daughters hear them, and catching them at a church, "drove his two daughters home before him." Louis Fechtig was beaten by both his father and the master he was apprenticed to, for they hoped to "'whip Methodism out of him."[83]

In the Methodist worldview, violent persecution was interpreted as evidence of righteousness, and thus sons and daughters were armed both with a rationale for religious disobedience and with an expectation that they would be opposed. Face-to-face encounters between Methodists and their opponents sometimes resulted in truces; abusive fathers little expected that their violence would sustain their children's faith. David Richardson, enraged to learn that his sons attended Methodist services "contrary to his express orders," seized one of them and began "dealing out his blows with his staff in a most unmerciful manner." Instead of beating Methodism out of his son, Richardson actually pushed his son into conversion during the beating. Richardson felt remorseful and outfitted a building on his property for the Methodists to use.[84] Violence and other harsh measures, even if accepted in the secular culture as appropriate under these circumstances, do not seem to have been a very useful tool for reasserting parental will. Methodist children appear to have absorbed the sect's views on persecution and suffering and usually met violence with forgiveness or prayer. They were told by Methodist ministers about the persecution of the Israelites, the early Christians, and of Jesus, and heard sermons and sang hymns that extolled suffering as a purifying force. Those parents whose minds were changed seem to have been influenced by the placid, praying, and brave demeanor of their children, a demeanor made possible in part by the support of other Methodists.

If some observers detected in Methodism a level of hostility to parental authority, many believed the church directly threatened the authority of husbands over wives. Preachers did not encourage wifely disobedience per se, for they believed that a godly husband was the proper head of a family. But here, as elsewhere, clergymen's notions of who was and was not godly were rather narrow. At their most tolerant, Methodists considered men who were converted or who wanted to be converted as godly; at their most intolerant, the godly were only those who were members of the Methodist church. And preachers would all have agreed that any husband who would stand in the way of a Methodist wife was not godly.

Methodist preachers supported in numerous ways women who were opposed by their husbands. George Wells's level of aid to one wife was unusual. When a Maryland woman "got reacht" in a service, her husband "wanted to drag hir of[f]," but Wells "got him round the neck and prevailed upon him to stay and let his wife stay." More common were rebukes of those considered "persecutors" from the pulpit. Preachers also gave these women emotional support and sympathy, and by recording their stories and sharing them with other members, preachers assured women persecuted by their husbands that they were not suffering alone.[85] As a result, preachers were often threatened and sometimes attacked because of the women they served. A Mrs. Fisher converted during a revival in Camden, South Carolina, while her husband was out of town. Mr. Fisher returned home, heard of his wife's conversion, and "became furious." He "ordered his wife to take her name off the Church-book, and swore he would cowhide the preacher on sight." The preacher, William Gassaway, was lucky. Although Fisher brought his cowhide and sat in the front row, he was reached by the sermon and "cried for mercy." A man whose wife was converted by one of Philip Gatch's colleagues decided to "revenge himself" on Gatch and assembled a mob who seized and tarred the preacher. In western Virginia, a man "got into a dreadful rage" when he found out his wife had converted, and came the next day to the service to "flog the preacher for converting his wife."[86]

Some husbands used every means at their disposal to try and keep their wives from the church. Thomas Hinde denied Mary the use of a horse; Tignal Jones threatened to shoot Sarah. All over the South, women faced similar opposition. Not all of these encounters involved force or threats of force. Robert Carnan tried to laugh and jest his wife out of Methodism. Many men tried (usually unsuccessfully) to prevent their wives from attending Methodist services. Often we do not know what method husbands used. Francis Asbury told of one Delaware man who "persecuted and kept back his wife," and another who was known for "persecuting his wife and children for coming to hear" the Methodists. Some husbands allowed their wives to attend services but tried to keep them from joining the church. Once when William Ormond asked potential members to come forward, he noted that "one woman wanted to join and her husband got angry and prevented." Her son also got in on the act, and "abused" Ormond as well.[87]

Other husbands opposed their wives' least showing of religious sensibility. One man "got angry w[i]th his wife . . . for telling him w[ha]t God had done for her soul." Although the details surrounding this incident were not given, other cases give us some clues. A husband who was an "avowed enemy to the Methodists" was away when Ezekiel Cooper called to visit his Methodist wife. The husband returned home, however, while Cooper was praying with her. According to Cooper, the husband "opened the door and called his wife by name to come to him—She did not rise from her knees nor [did] I stop praying. . . . [A]t length he came in violently and stood over me. . . . [H]e swished his handkerchief once or twice just by my head." When the prayer was finished and the husband had stopped pacing, Cooper asked why praying made the man so angry: "He did not like his wife should be led astray he said, and the methodists he did not like."[88]

This contest of wills between Cooper and the Methodist wife, on the one hand, and the opposing husband, on the other, helps explain why Methodism was seen by some critics as a threat to patriarchal power. The threat Cooper and the wife presented here may seem small to us, but in its temporal and cultural context, it was serious enough. Against the patriarch's wishes, Cooper had come to his home and engaged in prayer with his wife. When the husband attempted to reassert his authority by calling his wife, Cooper had continued to pray. The woman had a choice—to rise from her knees and offend her God and her preacher or to disobey her husband. She chose to disobey. If we knew the content of the prayer or the nature of the man's objection to the Methodists, we could better understand whether the husband disagreed with church doctrine or merely with the fact that his wife was pursuing her own course in religion. It is nonetheless clear that Cooper did not respect the husband's prerogative here, and neither did the wife.

Some husbands used violence against their Methodist wives, although here again, it often had little effect. In 1801, a woman "blessed God for what she had been able to suffer for the sake of religion" in a North Carolina love feast. Her preacher later learned that she had been "opposed, even to stripes," by her husband. In a western Virginia service, a "poor woman got powerfully converted, and praised the Lord aloud; but her husband was much offended. . . . He forced his wife away, swearing what he would do when he got her home, she continuing to shout 'Glory to God!' Before they got out of hearing, she fell upon her knees, and begged him, with many tears, to let her go back. He got more enraged, and fell upon her, and beat her unmercifully" with a stick.[89] Wife beating was not unusual in the South, and it is possible that this Virginian was beaten even before this incident at the church. For women who were regularly abused, Methodist values may have offered a way to reinterpret and psychologically withstand a situation they could not control.

White husbands had many reasons to oppose their Methodist wives, but one reason such opposition was pervasive was that some men believed their wives were criticizing them in public, a charge that seems to have some validity. A Virginia man disrupted a service of John Kobler's to claim in a loud voice that the Methodists had "ruined his wife. She was not only a lyar, but also a tatler." Despite the faulty logic of this man's claim, his frustration at his wife's public discussions of him is clear. James Jenkins's sister, like many women, was "opposed by her husband." After Jenkins's brother-in-law heard his first Methodist sermon, in which he saw his sins laid before him, "he accused his wife of telling the preacher all about him." Some women used class meetings and love feasts to describe the opposition they faced from husbands. From other Methodists, wives received comfort and support for their continued rebellion. And by telling their stories to other Methodists, wives won recognition for their persecutions and enhanced status as martyrs for the faith.[90]

The converts who were most at risk from violence were blacks, especially slaves. They were the least powerful Methodists economically, socially, and legally, and thus they were the most vulnerable to action by all sorts of different groups. Legislatures, city and county officials, and local slave patrollers could limit the hours that slaves and free blacks met in worship, and could bar night meetings altogether. Masters as well had authority to keep their slaves from Methodist services or to limit slave worship by place and time. Blacks also faced violence and threats from white mobs for the most seemingly innocuous of behaviors. Opposition to black Methodists began in the North in the late 1760s and early 1770s and spread southward with Methodism. Wesley's first missionaries to America, Richard Boardman and Joseph Pilmore, encountered slaves whose masters tried to keep them from Methodist services. Pilmore met a New York bondwoman whose "Mistress has persecuted her very much" because she attended services, but who thought it better to be "'beaten for hearing the word of God here; than to burn in Hell to all eternity.'"[91]

These patterns continued and escalated in the South. Several slaves approached Nelson Reed one evening, asking him to "advise how to serve God and save their souls, telling me that their masters never suffered them to go to hear preaching." Sometimes a group of masters appears to have worked in concert to keep their slaves from the church. It took several months after George Dougherty was almost drowned by a proslavery mob in Charleston before he was "again cheered with the sight of some black faces in the galleries at night."[92] Slave worshipers attended evening services at Luke Branson's house in April and May of 1794, but in June they were "warned to attend no more meetings" there. David Smith converted to Methodism while a slave to a Catholic master. "All the family became my bitter oppressors and persecutors," he later recalled, and his master, John Burnibue, was "so enraged" about Smith's religion that he tried to sell Smith into Georgia. In Hopewell, South Carolina, wealthy whites tried a different method. Upset that James Jenkins had raised a large society of blacks in the area, they hired a Presbyterian minister in the hopes that Jenkins would leave the area, "but in this," he said, "they were mistaken."[93]

Masters had various reasons for opposing Methodist slaves. It is possible that in cases like that of David Smith, slave owners of different faiths earnestly believed that Methodism was a religion of error and that slaves would not obtain salvation as Methodists. But taking Smith's case as an example, there are strong hints that the conflict was not about doctrine but about control. In the Burnibue family, slaves were required to attend Catholic services and the way Mrs. Burnibue normally punished her slaves, according to Smith, was to "shut us up in the closet and tell us how the Saviour was displeased with our bad conduct."[94] One wonders how well such a shaming punishment would work with a slave who espoused a different religious creed than his or her owner, especially considering the Methodist focus on the inner voice of conscience. By Methodist standards, the Burnibues were not "saved" because they had not experienced conversion, and also by Methodist standards, Smith, who was "saved," was able to interpret God's will for himself. Let us also recall a story with a different ending, the story of the slave Cuff who was repeatedly beaten by his irreligious owner merely for praying. Cuff, in this contest of wills, responded like many of his fellow Methodists under persecution; he told his owner that "you may kill me, but while I live I must pray." Outraged, the slave owner "cursed God" for creating "the negro and all his race." His curse brought on a torrent of guilt, and the master began to fear God would damn him. He asked his wife to send for someone to pray for him, and the only religious leader on the plantation was Cuff. With Cuff's guidance and prayers, the master converted, and immediately decided to free his "brother in Christ."[95]

Masters with religiously defiant slaves were facing a formidable challenge. Methodism did not make slaves suicidal nor did it cause them to throw caution to the wind, but it did provide them a religious justification for resisting their owners. Slave owners could bar their slaves from services, whip them for praying, threaten them with sale, but they could not control their minds. Slaves who claimed to be obeying a higher authority than that of their masters challenged the very core of slave owner identity. In the Methodist worldview, the pious expected to be persecuted, like Christ had been, for their holiness. Some slaves, working within these expectations, could turn power relations on their head. Whipping was a blatant demonstration of the master's power to enforce his will upon a slave. When a religious slave like Cuff manfully withstood a beating for his heavenly Master's sake, denying and transcending bodily pain, he stripped pain of its connection to his owner's power and will. And in doing so, he turned the tragically routine brutality of slavery into a dramatic contest of evil against good, one where good would win as long as Cuff held fast to his faith. A master's options in such cases were limited. To kill a defiant slave would mean a capital loss. For the most pious slaves death would mean a spiritual gain; even nonbelieving masters had to be aware of the martyrology in the New Testament. There is little wonder, then, that a few, like Cuff's owner, simply surrendered.

Although black Methodists seem to have been opposed most often by their own masters, other whites tried to interfere with and harass them as well. In Richmond, Virginia, a Methodist society composed primarily of blacks (and four or five whites) was targeted by local officials and by white residents. Much of white Richmond joined in the persecution: preacher Alexander M'Caine said the opponents included the "great," the "middle," and "the lower classes" of whites. The mayor of Richmond tried to frighten Methodist leaders by calling their worship "abominable enthusiasm," but when they were resolute, he decided to pass an ordinance to "stop the blacks" from coming. This city law prohibited five or more "people of colour" from assembling at night. The penalty for defiance was a fine of three dollars per person present at the meetings or, alternately, for M'Caine to receive thirty lashes on the bare back. With the society too poor to pay fines, M'Caine, unwilling to be lashed, chose to cancel his night meetings.[96]

Night meetings of slaves and free blacks were especially targeted by whites, who passed numerous local ordinances and state laws to restrict or prohibit them. Yet some white Methodists fought harder than others to keep these services open. In King William County, Virginia, local Methodists braved disdain and the law to hold their services. In 1789 a county sheriff wrote the governor cataloguing a list of complaints against "a sett of disorderly People who call themselves Methodists" (joined by "some" "who call themselves Baptists"). Two or three times each week, the lawman explained, these religionists called in "all the Negroes they can gather and a few whites and free mulatoes who pretend under the [cloak] of Religion to meet at School house . . . and there they pretend to preach and pray with a sett of the greatest Roges of Negroes in this County." These meetings, the sheriff declared, lasted until two or three in the morning. By statute, he was authorized to break up such "unlawful" gatherings, which King William's masters wholeheartedly wished him to do.[97]

In the sheriff's opinion, if the Methodists were not stopped, "we shall not have a negroe to Command & I am afraid with a little encorigement they themselves [the slaves] will drive away the Patterolers & there will be an end to all such Power." His fears were not altogether unfounded, for Methodists had communicated their resolve to protect black worshippers by force if necessary. And local church leaders had already used force. On one occasion a Methodist had thrown patrollers out of a church meeting, warning them they would not seize any slaves that night. Outnumbered by the worshipers, the patrollers left, and, the sheriff reported, they refused to return "without some protection." Almost in passing, the county sheriff revealed that a white woman was behind this massive conspiracy, for he described the man who had physically thrown out the patrollers as "Mr. Charles Neale who's mother is the head of this Crim[e]." The sheriff concluded by asking for the governor's advice, adding that "I hope your Excellency will order me to treat Mr. Charles Neale and his party as they deserve."[98]

The fears and biases running through this appeal illustrate the many reasons non-Methodist whites objected to black and biracial Methodist gatherings. For one thing, slave owners were concerned about productivity. A tired slave was an unproductive slave, and these meetings lasted until a few hours before dawn. Moreover, as the local sheriff complained, "our Negroes are not to be found when we are in want of them, but at some such meetings."[99] A second reason that some whites opposed meetings was that they seem to have believed religion was wasted on slaves. Much like the slave owners advertising for the return of Methodist fugitives, the King William County sheriff disdainfully reported that the slaves and free blacks "call themselves" Methodists and "pretend" to meet, preach, and pray. Their "real" purpose in meeting he was not sure of, but he reported that black participants, on their way home from services, "goes through the neighborhood & steele everything that they can lay there hands on." Some whites outside the evangelical churches seem to have agreed with conventional racist views that blacks were inherently immoral; thus they treated black religious expression with ridicule and scorn and believed slave religious meetings were pretenses for illegal behavior. Methodist beliefs about the assurance of salvation and the possibility of perfection probably exacerbated the contempt of white supremacists, who obviously did not think that blacks merited salvation or were capable of holiness.[100]

A third reason that night assemblies provoked reaction was that whites outside the church feared that at these meetings slaves were being encouraged to resist their enslavement. Some even feared these meetings would lay the groundwork for slave rebellion. The King William sheriff implied as much. If masters could not prevent slaves from attending services, he claimed, slaves would next "disobey the orders of there Masters under the pretence of religion." Since there were a number of southern slaves who did disobey their masters on religious grounds, the sheriff was not necessarily paranoid. From disobedience, he imagined a total collapse of power and order, until "we shall not have a negroe to Command." The combination of darkness, slave assembly, and evangelical religion seemed a potently dangerous mix to many whites.[101]

The fact that whites were abetting slave disobedience merely made the situation more urgent. It is clear from the sheriff's complaint that "the masters of the Negroes" were arrayed not only against their slaves, but also against "these people who are determined to encorige our Negroes to Wrong"—nonslaveholding evangelical whites. Local Methodist leaders, if the sheriff may be believed, needled the sheriff and his patrollers by sending word of an upcoming meeting along with a warning that if the patrollers came, Methodists "wood pretect the Negroes." Described as "disorderly" people with "no person of credit" among them, the white Methodists involved were likely poor or struggling and as such, were seemingly, to elite whites, the most natural allies of slave rebels. By trying to prevent these biracial gatherings, King William masters may have unwittingly created ideological divisions among whites that would not have otherwise existed. Most white Methodists had no desire to see slaves revolt; few would have wanted to use Methodist services as a fomenting ground for insurrection. But when King William masters and the law decided that there would be no night services for blacks, they turned Charles Neale and his mother into the allies of black brothers and sisters in the gospel and into enemies of the state and local elites. It is easier to understand the many insurrection scares blamed on the Methodists when we factor in local conflicts like that in King William. In the era when the church was regionally campaigning against slavery, there were local protests being lodged as well.[102]

The church and its black members challenged the racial hierarchy in other ways. Some blacks complained to ministers about the actions of slave owners. Some also reported on whites who had violated church rules. While at the home of a white man named Reaves, Thomas Mann made the following entry in his journal: "I was told today by a Black person that Reaves gits Drunk and Swars tho has been a perfeser along tim." Slave owners unsympathetic to the church were justifiably concerned that their authority was on some level challenged when Methodists allowed slaves to be moral guardians for whites. It probably did not help matters that white itinerants ministering to slaves sometimes spoke as if slave owners had no legitimate claims to authority. James Meacham once derisively noted of a slave owner that he was a "Master so called (but I do not know why so)."[103] White fears about the collapse of racial hierarchy sometimes spurred them to violence. In Charleston, a black Methodist employed to "snuff the candles" in the church was beaten "unmercifully with a stick" by a white visitor from North Carolina who was not a member, "because the poor black only desired [the North Carolinian] not to talk whilst the minister was preaching." His ostensibly mild request, when made across the color line and across the sectarian divide, was not, as it turned out, mild at all. White Methodist leaders sided with their sexton and had the assailant arrested.[104]

On at least two occasions, white mobs brutally attacked black Methodists. Through analyzing each of these violent public incidents, we can better see the complexity of white fears and the extent of black Methodist resistance. The first occurred in a well-attended quarterly meeting in Virginia in 1780. The sermon preached by brother Adams that day emphasized how the faithful would triumph over the sinful: "This is the victory that overcometh the world"(1 John 5: 4). After the sermon, Philip Gatch exhorted, and "the power of God came down more and more," which translated from Methodist parlance meant that the crowd was beginning to become enthusiastic. Angry onlookers "ston[e]d the house and whipt some of the black people that was there." Despite this violence—and considering Methodist beliefs about suffering and persecution, perhaps in response to this violence—"there was a great blessing pour[e]d forth upon the people," and Nelson Reed, who recorded these events, optimistically believed that God's "work will take a start from this meeting and prosper more abundantly."[105]

Working within what we have previously discovered, we can see several ways that this day's events elicited such an angry reaction. First, the sermon's message centered on the division between the "world" and the people of God and on how God would grant "victory" to his people. In the midst of the Revolutionary war, it is likely that the term "victory" had martial connotations, but whether or not it did, the implication was that there would be a victory of the (black) faithful over the sinful (white) world. Second, the enthusiastic reaction of the society, which Methodists termed "power," probably contributed to white anxiety. As we have seen, black enthusiasm, especially when it was communal, was a repeated target for criticism by those outside the church and seemed to provoke white fears on a primal racist level.

The second case of white mob violence against black Methodists occurred on James Meacham's circuit in 1789. Meacham's detailed description of this incident is worth quoting from at length, for it illuminates how the various points of contention between Methodists and their opponents could, in any given situation, overlap. Meacham had finished his sermon when

> the dear black people was filled with the power & spirit of God and began with a great Shout to give Glory to God—this vexed the Devil. He entered into the cruel white men with violence (who) eagerly ran into the Church with sticks clubs and caines—abeating and abusing the poor Slaves them outcast of Men for praising of God. . . . Remark—a Magestrate, that has take the oath, was the Instagator of it. . . . [W]ith bitter oaths and gnashing of teeth he put up a prayer that we the preachers was all in Some Miserable Infernal Place. . . . I think if I ever saw happy people it was today under persecution—O the tears, screams, crys and groans for the wicked it was awful. . . . [A] poor black bro[ther] [looked] me in the face, with bursting grief tears of blood, roling down his bruised face, and cryed, ["]this is what I have got for praising of my dear Jesus.["]

Throughout his description, Meacham interposed numerous comments against slavery and "blood" and "oppression."[106]

Considering the subsequent attack, Meacham's sermon on this autumn day of August 30 was almost prescient, which should alert us once again to the way that Methodists sometimes courted opposition. His text was from Jude's short epistle, in which Jude reminds his fellow Christians first, that they must fight for the faith, second, that God's historical way of dealing with the ungodly was destroying them, and third, that the day of judgment was coming. Meacham chose to speak on the final of the three themes, Jude's warning that "there should be mockers in the last time" who were ungodly and "sensual, having not the Spirit." Meacham also reiterated Jude's comfort to the righteous, God's "beloved," who would receive "eternal life." Meacham inverted secular rankings, for the slaves—"them outcast of Men"—were seen by him as God's "beloved," while the powerful magistrate and his band, in charge by non-Methodist standards, were seen by Meacham as "mockers" and children of Satan.

Meacham had preached on these same verses ten days prior to this attack, and his journal entry for that day helps explain his interpretation of this text. On August 20, he faced a largely non-Methodist crowd and described his task in preaching as "to face my enemy. To whome I cryed these be they who separate themselves, sensual, having not the Spirit." Many, as we might expect, "behaved badly." On August 20, too, Meacham witnessed white hostility to black enthusiasm. When a black man got "happy" and shouted, a white "backslider began to laugh at him." Meacham "sharply reproved" the white man, who as he left the scene "gnashed his Teeth," something he also claimed that the abusive magistrate did. In both cases, Meacham seems to have used this text when black Methodists were being observed, or as on the day of the attack, surrounded, by hostile whites.[107]

The more immediate "cause" of the August 30 attack was a black shout, which Meacham interpreted to mean that his black audience was "filled with the power and spirit of God." Black enthusiasm was generally opposed, of course, but there may have been special circumstances here. James Meacham, one of the most dedicated antislavery preachers in the church, had condemned slavery and slaveholders to both members and nonmembers throughout this circuit. If whites in this area, like others elsewhere, suspected that ministers were preaching incendiary sermons to slaves, Meacham would have been a likely target of such suspicions. The magistrate's condemnation of white preachers during the attack suggests this may indeed have been the case. The combination of an antislavery minister and an exuberant black audience would have been viewed as a danger.

Analysis of this scene would not be complete without considering how Methodists interpreted this attack. The slaves were reportedly "happy" while being persecuted, and actually groaned and cried on behalf of their persecutors. Although they certainly did not enjoy being beaten, their religious values did help them to be brave in the face of danger. Following a host of biblical precedents, they (who could not fight back without risking their lives) showed mercy to the merciless, a posture that in Methodist views conferred moral superiority in several ways—in using suffering to advantage, in meeting evil with good, and in caring about the eternal fate of people who by human logic would not have merited such concern.[108] Meacham placed the events into a framework of absolute good and absolute evil, with whites representing Satan and blacks representing Christ, and the slaves surely agreed. The bloodied slave whose words so touched Meacham chose to speak of the attack as motivated by his own righteousness; he was beaten because he was "praising . . . my dear Jesus." By putting the events of the day in such terms, the slave made the response of the whites seem even more unjust, even more unprovoked, and even more heinous than it already was. And by sacralizing his victimization, the bondman could place the attack in a broader historical context, linking himself to all the heroes and martyrs who had suffered for religion. If this Brother remained a Methodist, he likely repeated many times the story of how he had persevered in the faith despite being bruised and bloodied by the sons of Satan. Within the considerable constraints of slavery, slaves found in religion the means to assert themselves heroically, identifying themselves with Christ.

Black Methodists were of all members the most vulnerable to official and unofficial proscription and attack. Their masters could use their power to limit slaves' movements and actions. Whites in general who were opposed to them could pass laws restricting their access to services, institute patrols to harass them at worship, or engage in mob actions against them or their meetinghouses with impunity. In the long term, of course, the campaign against black Methodists failed to achieve its objectives; blacks continued to join the church. The campaign had greater effect on white Methodist leaders. The clergy analyzed the attacks on black Methodists as having two major sources. First, they believed—and not without cause—that blacks were denied their rights to religion because of the church's stand against slavery. Second, they believed blacks were being attacked for religion's sake, because the Bible told them that the righteous would always be persecuted by the ungodly. This reasoning had profound consequences. If the struggle was between the godly and the ungodly, the solution was to convert the ungodly, something Methodists were quite skilled at. And it is into evangelism that they put their energy, and not into formulating a religious stand against prejudice.

The numerous conflicts that arose between Methodists and their opponents over values, authority, gender roles, and racial conventions sometimes ended with Methodists winning over their opponents. Cuff converted his master, Mary Hinde converted the husband who believed she was mad, children converted their irreligious parents, poor workmen converted rich lawyers. In many of these cases, the persecutor seemed genuinely impressed with the resolute perseverance of Methodists, and ashamed at his or her own behavior in the face of such determined, albeit nonviolent, resistance. But there was a tendency in Methodism to celebrate the conversions of people who had flagrantly rejected religion more than those who had not. Ministers became openly gleeful when they converted a man who had been "a proud opposer of religion"—it was as if they believed that the world would become right side up if enough of these people turned to God. Opponents who converted did have to forsake many of their old ways, and in adopting Methodist values, changed some behaviors that directly benefited people they had previously persecuted. The victories won by Methodists, however, were more personal than social. The economic, gender, racial, legal, and social inequalities that had precipitated many of the conflicts between Methodists and their opponents remained largely untouched.

Still, these numerous battles have shown that the opponents of the church believed Methodists were "turning the world upside down" because so many of their values and ways were under assault by the Methodists. From "drunks" who feared Methodists would outlaw manly "amusement," husbands who believed the church was encouraging their wives' defiance, and slave owners who felt their authority was undermined when their slaves became Methodists, opponents perceived the church as at least a nuisance and at worst a threat to order and "established ways." All of these fears were in some part justified by Methodists' behavior. One of the enduring legacies of Methodism to both black and white southerners was the notion that people in the right could expect to be opposed. The church offered its members a way to interpret persecution that enabled them to stand firm in the face of it. For Methodists who suffered from harassment, criticism, and violence, this worldview sustained them in their dark hours, bringing hope, spiritual comfort, and a way to preserve their own values in a hostile world.

The opposition that early Methodists so often faced from other southerners is one of the primary indications that the southern church in the late eighteenth century was different from the church in the late antebellum years. To be a Methodist in the 1850s was to be a member of a respected denomination; to be a Methodist in the 1780s was to accept a certain level of opposition as inevitable. This is not to say that southern Methodists lost their relish for martyrdom, but over time they played the martyr to different opponents. As the nineteenth century progressed, white southern Methodists began to believe that their northern counterparts were unjustly persecuting them. It was a small step from the early Methodist principle—those who were in the right would inevitably face persecution, to the form it took for whites later in antebellum years—those who were "persecuted" must be in the right. Even after the Civil War, we see continuity between early southern Methodism and postwar views. There is a great deal of resonance, for example, between the Lost Cause mentality and the early Methodist worldview. Lost Cause proponents turned a military defeat into an ideological and spiritual victory by viewing suffering as salutary, defeat as purification, and opposition to godliness as inevitable, all premises any early Methodist would have assented to. The circumstances had changed, but the fundamental ideas had not.[109]

Over the course of the nineteenth century Methodism would become more "respectable," but vestiges of its earlier reputation remained. In 1818, when the Methodist society of Morganton, North Carolina, composed of ten white and fifteen black members, built their first chapel, they encountered opposition, and their preachers were "insulted whil[e] preaching." As late as 1845, Methodism was still associated with antislavery sentiment in some areas. One minister stopped over in Charleston in that year and noted that his church had "had hard toiling in Charleston. Their enemies have been many and vigilent." He faulted "the old slang of our being abolitionists and seeking the down-fall of the slave and Southern institutions."[110] Black Methodists in particular would continue to be targeted by irate whites. For white Methodists the outcome was different. As church leaders began to depict their northern brethren as the source of persecution, and as church historians began to revise and distort the southern Methodist past, expunging many references to antislavery activity and women's prominent, vocal roles in the early church, white southern Methodists lost much of their ability first, to sympathize with their black brethren, and second, to envision their role as that of cultural critics.

In their first decades, Methodists vigorously challenged a number of southern ways and values. Their challenges were so fierce, their successes so steady, their converts so changed, and their members so resolute that those who opposed them feared their world was at stake. Methodists were "turning the world upside down," but to the extent that they did so, they did it one convert at a time. Their attack was no less real to those living through it. Consider the following description of the western revivals written by the Reverend Thomas S. Hinde, son of the indefatigable Mary and her erstwhile deist husband: "To see a *bold* and courageous *Kentuckian* (undaunted by the horrors of war) turn pale and tremble at the reproof of a weak woman, a little boy, or a poor African; to see him sink down in deep remorse, roll, and toss, and gnash his teeth, till black in the face, entreat the prayers of those he came to devour; and through their fervent intercessions and kind instructions, obtain deliverance, and return in the possession of a meek and gentle spirit, which he set out to oppose;—who would say the change was not supernatural?"[111] No wonder critics accused the Methodists of turning the world upside down! Here all the southern hierarchies of race and gender are inverted—women over men, children over male adults, blacks over whites—and the Kentuckian is reduced to a supplicant and pupil before people that secular society placed him above by reason of birth. The transformation of the bold Kentucky veteran is complete when he rhetorically becomes a black woman.

Epilogue

> Methodists are becoming great on this shore: Ah! let them
> take heed. *The respectable society of people called Methodists.* "Woe unto
> you when all men shall speak well of you." Save us from this!
> Never in any past period have we had so much cause to hope
> or to fear as a society.
>
> —Francis Asbury, Maryland, 1811[1]

A S THE SECOND DECADE of the nineteenth century dawned, there were unmistak-
able signs that southern Methodism was moving out of its despised and marginalized position and into the Protestant mainstream. Two events, both of 1810,
alarmed Francis Asbury, for they clearly indicated the church's transformation. The
first was the election of a Methodist minister as chaplain to the United States House
of Representatives, which caused Asbury to lament: "So; we begin to partake of the
honour that cometh from man: now is the time of danger. O Lord, keep us pure, keep us
correct, keep us holy!" This same year, the North Carolina legislature volunteered to
let the Methodists use the Raleigh State House for their next church conference. Asbury's primary worry was that using the elegant Raleigh building would "corrupt
our preachers."[2] By 1811, when the bishop bemoaned the fact that Maryland Methodists were "becoming great," it was obvious that the outcast sect had become a
"respectable" denomination.

By 1810, Methodists and Methodism had changed in a number of ways. Although
plain folk continued to dominate the church, some white Methodists moved up in
class position and more wealthy men and women became members. With the growth
in membership, the church became difficult to govern as a national body, and regional
conferences were given increased responsibilities and authority. As Methodists built
more meetinghouses, the position of white women and blacks in local societies was
altered. The institutionalization of camp meetings wrought subtle change in where
and how southerners converted to Methodism. Church leadership began to shift as
well. More ministers left the itineracy to marry and become local preachers and more
preachers began to serve their entire careers in slaveholding states. Lay leadership
changed, too, with fewer women appointed as class leaders and fewer black men assigned to lead biracial classes.

Just as important were the shifts in the way Methodists were perceiving themselves and the way they were perceived by others. The reputation of the Methodists for disorder, leveling, and for social disruption gradually abated as Methodists became more numerous and as church leaders abandoned efforts to rid their membership of slaveholders. During the nineteenth century, southern Methodists manipulated the historical record and gradually obscured the slow movement to conservatism in the southern church. Opposition to the Methodists for all reasons declined in the nineteenth century, in part because Methodism became less unique. Schisms among Baptists and Presbyterians produced Arminian wings of both churches while nineteenth-century revivalism grew increasingly Arminian in general. As other Protestants embraced free will, Methodists appeared less peculiar and were less often criticized for their doctrines. Methodist leaders, too, contributed to this change, for they began to decrease their emphasis on sanctification, one of the doctrines that had set them apart.[3] But another reason opposition decreased was that Methodists in the South became less critical and more accepting of southern secular norms.[4]

One sign of Methodism's growing respectability and, in ministers' views, decline, was that opposition by the wealthy was decreasing. Asbury remarked on an 1810 trip to Maryland that the "rich, too, thirty years ago, would not let me approach them; now I must visit them and preach to them." Other clergy also noted the growing interest in the sect among the wealthy and the growing success of Methodist members.[5] The church's abandonment of its antislavery stand in the South coincided with the expansion of the cotton kingdom; white Methodist men who dreamed of success could, in the nineteenth century, purchase slaves without being urged by their preachers to free them. There is anecdotal evidence, moreover, that some plain folk turned away from Methodism in communities where members were prosperous. Freeborn Garrettson, who since 1788 had been stationed in the North, visited his former Maryland circuit in 1809. He, too, sensed the growing prosperity of the membership. "The extravagance," he noted, "of some of our people has had a greater tendency to fill other churches than [our] own."[6] Although Methodism continued to attract more common people than elite converts, preachers certainly believed they were witnessing a new era in which they were no longer despised by the rich and when the association of Methodism with the "rabble" would be increasingly rare.

Organizational change also played a role in the church's transformation. As the church grew, it became increasingly regionalized, due both to the outmigration of antislavery Methodists and to the way sheer numbers dictated new modes of church governance. In the 1770s and 1780s, national conferences had set church policy and procedure. But as both the amount of territory Methodism covered and the number of itinerants increased, the national conference began to turn matters over to the regional conferences, including the important matter of enforcing (or not, as the conferences decided) church rules on slavery. The sheer size of the membership also meant that conferences had more administrative matters to attend to with each passing year. While eighteenth-century Methodist conferences were largely special seasons of worship, conferences in the nineteenth century were devoted to church business. An appalled Freeborn Garrettson attended the 1824 Methodist Conference where the clergy spent four days simply "fixing rules by which the session was to be governed." Sectional strife contributed to the focus on procedure, for at this conference southern clergy denounced New England clergy for pew rentals and "Eastern" preachers denounced southern preachers for slavery.[7]

Three years later Garrettson sounded a carefully worded note of warning in his sermon celebrating the fiftieth anniversary of American Methodism: "we have in connection six or seven thousand ministers and preachers, local and itinerant, and nearly four hundred thousand in membership. To preserve such a body in union and spiritual prosperity, will require all the graces and gifts which we can possibly attain, and we need more than human wisdom. . . . We have been gathered into church fellowship from associations of various descriptions of people, who all possessed their own modes, sentiments, and prejudices; but these should be tested by the sacred truths of God's word, to which they should implicitly yield."[8] Garrettson's subtle references to sectional tensions and to a single set of "sacred truths" against which sectional claims should be measured show both his realization that the church had changed and his desire to return to the days when church leaders had tried to maintain the same standards throughout the continent. Garrettson did not live to see the great schism, when southern preachers explicitly declared they would never yield on slavery.

Some of the most important changes in the church involved the ministry. In the late eighteenth century, most itinerants had been single, and the men who left the itineracy to become "local preachers" normally did so because of infirmity or old age. But as the church gained respectability, more women were willing to marry itinerants and as more ministers became married, more of them "located" to a permanent duty station. By 1810, at least 400 of the 700 preachers in the church were married and that same year, when 99 new itinerants were licensed, 51 former itinerants became local preachers.[9] Methodist leaders had long believed that the rotation of ministers inhibited alliances between local interests and the clergy, and they had long feared that local interests would corrupt ministers. Asbury repeatedly condemned the trend toward what he called "the growing evil of locality" in his church. But Methodism was expanding too fast for church leaders to refuse talented men who were willing to preach, even if this meant abandoning to some extent their rotation system.[10] Local preachers, to support their families, usually had a second career; many became farmers and some became slave owners. Meanwhile, urban membership continued to grow, and societies in cities and towns usually received a stationed minister, further adding to the number of preachers tied to a locale. In 1813, for example, out of 700 itinerants, 100 were assigned to towns, cities, or "small rich circuits." Local societies, especially ones that received "stationed" preachers, began actively trying to influence the selection of their ministers.[11]

The slow move away from the itinerant system to a balance of traveling and stationed preachers had tremendous repercussions for the southern church. Itinerants depended on plain folk, especially women, for food, shelter, and companionship. In the eighteenth century, preachers' first footholds were often in women's homes and their first converts were women. The intimacy that developed from these ties bound preachers to the plain folk and to women in ways more mutual than hierarchical. Stationed preachers, however, were less dependent on local women's leadership, less dependent on their financial support and labor, and did not, in settled areas, need women to defy gender conventions and neighbors just to keep the church alive. The increase in stationed ministers also meant a concomitant increase in the number of men who were confined to locales where slavery could not be questioned. And ministers settling in plantation belts were more likely to be men who did not find slavery's presence an abomination.[12]

The increase in stationed preachers was only one of the ways the ministry was changing. Another was the growing call for ministerial education. In 1827, Freeborn Garrettson warned against the tendency to look upon the ministry as a "learned profession." In the early years, he recalled, a potential candidate was never asked "how many languages he understands, or whether he can solve the problems of Euclid." Instead, he was asked if he was converted, had evidence of a call, and was successful at bringing people to God. Garrettson especially rued the fact that more and more ministers were trying to "display" skill at "oratory" rather than bringing sinners "to the foot of the cross, stripped of self and of all self dependence."[13] Henry Smith, who had entered the itinerancy in the late eighteenth century, noted many of these same trends. Comparing preachers of the 1840s with those from the 1790s, Smith conceded that "preachers in those [earlier] days were inferior to the present race of preachers in literary attainments; but in disinterestedness, in enterprise, in zeal, in self-denial, in holy living, and success, they were inferior to no set of men that any church ever produced."[14]

The clearest sign that his church was becoming corrupted, Smith believed, was that ministers were being evaluated by their "popularity." In the eighteenth century it was common to say of a successful minister that "he is gifted," but by 1840, Smith noted, "we have a much shorter way now, by saying, 'He is popular;' or 'very popular;' or 'he is unpopular,' &c. And sometimes, 'He is a gentleman, a Christian gentleman, a perfect gentleman.'" Smith scorned these measures of preachers' abilities: "Popular is a word that could not have been used with any degree of propriety in a Methodist conference fifty years ago; for the first Methodist preachers that I knew were the most unpopular men in the land. They were despised and hated almost everywhere, and all manner of evil was said of them." Even worse, in Smith's view, was the fact that Methodists were losing their earlier simplicity, a trend he detected in the growing ornamentation in Methodist church buildings. By 1840, Smith wrote, his fellow Methodists were saying, "We must have a grand church, cost what it will. Rich men are necessary, for they have the cash—and money we must have."[15]

Smith put his finger on several important changes, including the growing popularity of the church and the tendency of antebellum Methodists to cultivate the wealthy. Yet it is his terminology that is most revealing. Early Methodists had used the word "gentleman" most often in a derogatory fashion, for men who were considered "gentlemen" by secular standards had been their fiercest opponents. The first American *Discipline* of 1784 had warned preachers against "affecting" the gentleman. By 1840, however, the word was being used by some Methodists in a positive sense. The "Christian gentleman" was not a carbon copy of a worldly gentleman, but he was also different from the weeping prophets and bold reprovers of sin who had occupied earlier pulpits. Smith did not analyze the changes in his church in terms of race, slavery, or gender, but his comments have implications for all three. To be "popular" in the South of the 1830s and 1840s meant of necessity to accept slavery as an institution and white supremacy as an ideology. To be "popular" in the South in the 1830s and

1840s meant to be opposed to the "isms" prominent in the North, among them northern feminism and abolitionism.

The positions of white women and blacks in the southern church were in flux in the nineteenth century. The very construction of meetinghouses had a negative impact on both groups of believers. Through hosting services or by volunteering their labor and goods to clothe, feed, and shelter the ministry, women had assured themselves a special place in terms of geography and of influence in the early church. As Methodists constructed church buildings and parsonages, the geographic and effective centers of Methodism became those new buildings. Moreover, in those new buildings, which often included a balcony specifically for slave members, black Methodists were far more likely to be physically separated from whites than they had been in private homes. In older societies, when the whites built new meetinghouses, they would relegate blacks to the older building. African Americans, moreover, were not trusted to worship entirely on their own as the nineteenth century progressed. Antebellum whites were often uneasy about allowing blacks autonomy and periodically monitored or otherwise interfered with black members.

Official leadership roles for white women and blacks were also in transition. While black men continued to lead other blacks in classes and as preachers, fewer seem to have led biracial groups. Black preachers continued to play vital roles in the slave and free black communities, yet these men were increasingly suspected of fomenting insurrection in the antebellum era. Earlier black preachers had represented Methodists, not just black Methodists, but state and local restrictions as well as the white Methodist hierarchy's growing paternalism severely limited antebellum opportunities for black men to be official church spokesmen. White Methodists' growing emphasis on an educated ministry also subtly contributed to the ways whites came to believe that a black preacher's place was in a ministry to African Americans, while a white preacher's place was wherever the church sent him. Women's opportunities for leading other adults also seem to have declined in the nineteenth century. Extant sources show that women class leaders became increasingly rare by the nineteenth century. In the church as a whole, class meetings gradually were replaced by other types of gatherings, such as Sunday schools and women's missionary societies. Women were often the teachers of children in Sunday schools and some had authority over women's groups, but opportunities for women to lead adult men in official capacities were extremely limited.[16]

The changes in women's leadership roles occurred at the same time the church began promoting a women's piety centered in the home. In Methodist periodicals of the later nineteenth century, the rhetoric of domesticity became a prominent feature and separate columns were written for "females," "mothers," or "ladies." Bold and assertive women who exercised moral authority outside the home still appeared in nineteenth-century church publications—but usually in the obituary sections.[17] Early Methodism had supported, under certain conditions, women's rebellions against patriarchal authority and had stressed love and harmony as the basis of familial relationships. Yet as the church became more acceptable to southerners, fewer white men objected to their female relations joining. And with the church more successful, ministers no longer needed to urge their listeners to defy husband and father for the sake of religion. Southern women's growing concentration on training children in the faith and converting the rising generation gave a more conventional meaning to their roles as Mothers in Israel. The age when a southern Methodist woman could publicly denounce slavery or the actions of her husband was fast waning.

Camp meetings remained one of the areas where black preachers had authority and where Mothers in Israel still had influence over "seekers" and "mourners." But camp meetings were not as exclusive and insular as love feasts and class meetings had been. The small ritualized communal gatherings exemplified in love feasts and class meetings gradually declined in importance, thereby decreasing the distance between Methodists and the world that early Methodists had worked so hard to maintain. As camp meetings became institutionalized, special areas were set apart for "mourners" who would then be guided through to conversion by preachers and trusted members as the meeting went on. Camp meetings and revivals were times when societies *expected* conversions. Although women's family evangelism continued to be important, women's roles as evangelists subtly shifted. In early Methodism, white men's conversions were often initiated by a woman's reproof or counsel, and took place while a preacher was away on his rounds. Every time such converts told the story of how they came to be saved, women's leadership and zeal was publicly credited. The responsibility for revival conversions, however, was more diffuse and women's roles as evangelists were thus more hidden.[18]

The shift in how Methodists were perceived by others and by themselves was equally important to the transformation of the church. Although the antislavery legacy of the early years did not fade entirely from collective southern memory, the men and women who became Methodists after 1808 in the plantation regions of the South were joining a church that maintained it was possible to be a "moral master." Some earlier southern Methodists had critically examined their social relationships, a number even their ownership of slaves, but those most persuaded that slaveholding was evil and corrupting left the South altogether. Antebellum church historians minimized early southern antislavery radicalism, obscured the dominant, vocal roles women played in the early church, and overemphasized the conversions of elite men. These revisions, although they are inaccurate, tell us what antebellum Methodists wanted their church to look like—respectable, conservative, and more masculine.

Two very different episodes from the mid-nineteenth century will illustrate the changes southern Methodism underwent in the decades after 1810; one early Methodist's struggle to live in a world she could not conquer will illustrate how some converts used their religion to form a separate peace. The distance between antebellum Methodists and their predecessors is most apparent in the arguments southern church leaders used in the great schism—the division of the church in 1844 into northern and southern wings. A vestige of the earlier Methodist antislavery position had survived in the *Discipline*—the rule requiring church officials to be nonslaveholders. As a consequence, more and more southern clergy were disqualified from higher offices because they owned slaves. At the same time, Methodist abolitionists in the American North and in Britain began to pressure the American church to take a firmer stand against slavery. A number of clergy sided neither with proslavery spokesmen or abolitionists, but instead supported colonization, continued compromise, or neutrality, but by the 1840s the loudest voices were those of the proslavery and abolitionist camps.

In 1844, a little-noted marriage provided both proslavery and antislavery men with the issue they needed to force the church into either a more unified stand on slavery or a sectional split. James Osgood Andrew had been appointed bishop in 1832 and owned two slaves before his controversial marriage. The first was a girl whose former mistress had left her to Andrew with the stipulation that when she turned nineteen she would be sent to Liberia. Andrew claimed that she refused to go to Liberia and instead remained his slave because he could not free her by law. The second was a young boy whom Andrew promised to liberate when he came of age. In 1844 Andrew married a slave-owning widow, and, by Georgia law, his wife's human property became his. Fearing that his marriage would cause trouble in the church, Andrew secured the slaves to his wife in a deed of trust.[19] Both antislavery and proslavery clergy saw Andrew's case as an opportunity to revise the church's position on slavery, although they had opposite goals. Abolitionist clergy wanted the church to take a firm stand against slavery by removing Andrew from the bishopric. Proslavery southerners felt increasingly marginalized because of antislavery agitation and believed their honor and privileges in the church as well as in the South were at stake. They came to the debates ready to secede from the church if the leaders did not explicitly declare they had no power to regulate the ownership of slaves by clergy. The dispute over Andrew's case led to the division of the church.

The debates and positions taken were complex and multifaceted but two in particular illustrate how far preachers in most of the South had drifted from their predecessors. One telling aspect of the Andrew case was the way early Methodist history was used differently by proslavery southerners and by southern-born clergy who had left the region. James Finley, born a Kentucky backwoodsman, was an Ohioan by 1844. He, like other antislavery men who wished to dissolve connections between church officials and slavery, claimed they were the true heirs of the Wesleyan heritage. "I stand on the ground that my fathers in Methodism took, the great Wesley, Coke, Asbury, M'Kendree, and the venerable men of the old western conferences," Finley solemnly declared. "[I]f I would compromit these great principles . . . I would deserve to be branded with the name of Judas on my forehead." William Capers, speaking for the proslavery South, chose to emphasize the persecution early ministers suffered because of their ill-advised antislavery pronouncements, and he argued that if Andrew was dismissed, Methodist clergy would lose access to slaves once again. "Throw us back, if you will," he proclaimed, "to those evil times."[20] While Finley may have more accurately portrayed early Methodist history, Capers's version of the past was not idiosyncratic. Southern preachers writing memoirs or histories in the antebellum era had perfected the myth that antislavery was an "English" import, that it had been "misguided," and that its only effects had been to harm slaves by keeping them from Methodism.

The second aspect of the Andrew debates that merits attention here is the way proslavery preachers in the 1844 schism mirrored southern secular values—the same values church leaders of the eighteenth century had contested so vehemently. Southern proslavery preachers in the great debate argued that there was a northern conspiracy "to deprive southern ministers of their rights, and to disfranchise the whole southern Church" and described southerners as "ruthlessly trodden under foot by a majority." Others spoke of antislavery pronouncements as "insulting to the feelings of members and citizens of the South" or as the "disgrace and insult heaped upon us."[21]

Kentucky ministers claimed they were willing to bend if an "honorable compromise" could be reached, but, they said, the majority had instead acted as an "aristocracy, at whose feet the episcopacy must bow in submissive, not to say abject, dependence."[22] Bishop Andrew repeatedly described himself as "an honest and independent man" who could not be "bound by any opinions or views" he disagreed with and referred to the antislavery men as his "avowed persecutors."[23] After the schism, a southern conference applauded Bishop Andrew for his "manly, dignified, and decided course in the protection of his own rights and the rights of the Church he represented" and his "manly and dignified conduct . . . by refusing to prostrate himself before the 'Juggernaut of perdition.'" Many southern clergy agreed and were unwilling to entertain any measures short of the church's withdrawal of any position on slavery whatsoever. To do less, they stated, would be "submission."[24]

For Methodists in the eighteenth century, "submission" had had positive and not negative connotations, duties had been invoked much more often than rights, and southerners' sensitivity to "insult" had rarely stopped clergy or members from speaking their minds. But by 1844, the southern church was so thoroughly enmeshed in the preservation of slavery and in southern mores that its spokesmen were more concerned with being slighted or insulted than with the impending division of the church. Their persistent references to Andrew's uncompromising conduct as "manly" are also revealing, for in the eighteenth century, clerical "manliness" had been associated with humility, meekness, and selflessness and not with prideful assertions of "rights." The newly formed Methodist Episcopal Church, South, even recognized its divergence from Wesleyan principles on this matter. Arguing that to "submit" to the majority would have placed southern clergy in "a most humiliating recognition of the inferiority of caste" within the church, they wrote: "It may be no virtue to avow it, but we confess we have no humility courting the grace of such a baptism."[25]

Early Methodists, because of their experiences first in the Revolution and second with antislavery petitions, had become convinced that they must stay out of political matters. Southern Methodists in 1844 sought refuge in the apolitical posture of their predecessors but seemed to have conveniently overlooked the fact that it was precisely on the issue of slavery that their predecessors had repeatedly taken a political position. Antebellum southern Methodists were blind to the fact that their defense of slavery was a political stance. As if to complete the irony, South Carolina officials—who had earlier plagued southern Methodists with proscriptions—had not surprisingly by 1844 changed their minds. The governor was grateful that "With becoming spirit, the patriotic Methodists of the south dissolved all connection with their brethren of the north; and for this they are entitled to lasting honor and gratitude from us."[26]

The debates of the 1844 schism illustrate how much the attitudes of southern ministers had changed in a half century. Another incident that shows the transformation of southern Methodism can be found in a series of letters written in 1852 by an escaped slave, Henry Bibb, to his former master, Albert G. Sibley. Bibb joined the abolitionist cause after his escape and published his letters in a newspaper for Canadian refugees, *Voice of the Fugitive*. Bibb strongly denounced the southern wing of the Methodist church for its support of slavery and condemned Sibley as a tyrant and hypocrite. Bibb's scriptural arguments against slavery and his appeal to sentiment and emotion have much in common with the early antislavery views of many southern clergy and almost nothing in common with the views of southern clergy in the 1850s.

The interesting thing about Bibb's letters for our purposes is that he repeatedly appealed to Sibley *as a Methodist* and to southern members *as Methodists*. His first scathing attack stressed that Sibley had been a Methodist class leader and exhorter for "more than twenty years" and that his "church sanctions the buying and selling of men, women, and children." In his next letter, Bibb again condemned Sibley's hypocrisy: "You profess to be a christian—a leader in the M. E. Church, and the representative of the Lord Jesus Christ, and yet you sold my mother from her little children . . . you sold my brother George from his wife and dear little ones while he was a worthy member, and Clergyman, of the same church, to which *you belong*." "Oh! what hypocrisy is this," Bibb continued, "A Methodist class leader, separating husbands and wives. . . . Vain is your religion—base is your hypocrisy."[27]

In each subsequent letter, Bibb repeatedly emphasized that Sibley was "a Methodist class leader" and as such was especially guilty before God for selling one of his own ministers and brethren away from his family. In November, Bibb warned Sibley not to be "deceived by the long practice of your church"; God would damn him if he did not change his ways. In December, Bibb further warned Sibley that as a man who had "[allowed] your name to be enrolled on the class books of the M. E. Church" he was guiltier even than others for slaveholding, for "the religion which you profess forbids it."[28] Although Bibb's arguments were undoubtedly lost on his former master, the fact that he believed that Methodism and slavery were inherently contradictory while southern clergy were claiming the two were providentially interconnected indicates that the early antislavery activity of southern ministers was not in vain. Bibb was neither the first nor the last abolitionist to claim that southern Methodists had perverted the Bible. But his numerous references to Sibley's position as a class leader would make little sense without that earlier antislavery legacy.

For a few decades, Methodism challenged southern mores on many levels and introduced a genuinely alternative worldview. When most white southerners believed that their freedom and independence rested on their actual or potential ownership of slaves, Methodists claimed that freedom was possible only if southerners liberated themselves from the sin of slavery. Methodists might have been more successful had slavery been an institution that depended solely on individual conviction, but slavery spread its poison throughout southern society. Methodists aimed to cure the disease by treating the symptoms, and with their Wesleyan worldview, it is unlikely they could have done otherwise. By the time of the church schism, many southern Methodists were baffled and embarrassed by their predecessors' diagnoses. Yet even though the Methodists were unsuccessful, their efforts were important. When the church was institutionally at its weakest, Methodist critics of slavery were at their boldest. Methodists, who were outnumbered and largely excluded from the corridors of power, found the courage to dissent. The assertions of resignation to slavery by southern elites who were their contemporaries seem shallow and cowardly in comparison.

One of the enduring aspects of early Methodism was its expansion of human agency. Converts from all walks of life found in the church a sense of power and control over their own destiny. Through religion, white women, slaves, free blacks, and the poor carved out a realm of experience in which they were the masters of their fate, over which they had ultimate control. Methodist ideals taught that before class, race, gender, or status came the believer's relationship with God, who judged not as southern elites did, but by the purity and devotion of the human heart. A number of Methodists, from slaves who defied their masters' orders, wives who converted against their husbands' wishes, and plain folk who cheered their preachers when they attacked southern elites, found in religion the strength to fight for themselves as they fought for their faith. Through loyalty to their church and its values, Methodists protected and nurtured a worldview in which they were the most worthy, in which they were morally superior. The eloquence and influence of white women, slaves, and poor men in the public arena of the church dramatized that worthiness and superiority to others. Methodists created a public sphere in which the most powerless southerners developed their talents, spoke for themselves, and transcended worldly rankings.

In its first decades, Methodism was a religion of the dispossessed and as such challenged elite male hegemony. Methodists espoused an inner-directed morality, opposed the exclusive white male world of the tavern, and held up a masculine ideal of meekness, love, humility, and piety. Methodists eschewed the code of honor's violence and its focus on the opinions of others and, moreover, were thankful for being despised and reviled. For white Methodist men, to join the church meant to largely abandon the rituals of the male world, including drinking, fighting, gambling, and dueling, and to enter a public space where being white and male did not automatically confer status and privilege. Methodism established a masculine ideal that was worlds apart from the secular South, and although the church incorporated aspects of the code of honor into its defense of slavery, Methodists remained opposed to drinking, gambling, fighting, and dueling throughout the antebellum era. The distance between the secular male world and the world of the church was still vast as the nineteenth century ended.

The position of Methodism in the post-Revolutionary South mirrored the position of many of its converts. This book began with the drastic transformation of Thomas Hinde from a genteel man of honor to a Methodist who envied the dog his humility. Let us end with an equally famous convert, for her struggles in many ways parallel those of the early church. Sarah Jones battled Satan, rich merchants, and a violent husband and was victorious over all of them, but this powerful woman was unable to follow her conscience in two matters. As a good Methodist, she disapproved of her children's worldly attire. "I have openly talked it over with Mr. Jones and brother S-l," Jones wrote a friend, "and Mr. Jones is my head, my dear, and he positively commands my children to dress as others do." Jones understood her subordination, but also rued it. "I abhor dress and fashion," she lamented. "O my dear, it is my grief, I can witness it by my class and neighbours—I cannot help it." Whether Sarah's class members were blaming her for what was beyond her control is unclear; her sense, however, was that other Methodists somehow faulted her for her husband's sin.[29]

A much larger source of grief to Jones was her husband's refusal to emancipate his many slaves. "How can Christians be saved that are clouded in Ethiopes blood?" she wondered. In her mind, God's command was clear: "blood, blood, I will avenge, mine arm shall get victory—bend O nations, bow O Virginia, loose the captives . . . or my sword shall wreak your bowels." Although she was respected, admired, and deferred to in her church, Jones, as a legally dependent wife, had limited power in her home. "God knowing my inmost mind would say amen, to loose the poor negroes," she wrote a friend, "but I am bound and must go on beneath it." She was not content with her subordination, nor with her husband's intransigence. Two years later, she was still anguished: "I will beg in dust for humanity, I will cry for charity. Although the oppressed stare me through, I will try to be clear of their blood. My witness is in Heaven, my record is on high." Desperately clinging to the belief that God, who knew she was adamantly opposed to slavery, would not blame her for her husband's sins, Jones nonetheless believed that her husband's slaves blamed her for not living up to her convictions. Against the intractable power of a slaveholding patriarch and amid the prodding looks of the slaves, she found a separate peace with her God. Others might fault her, her conscience and the family's slaves might wound her, but her "witness" was in heaven. Her resignation parallels that of Methodist leaders after their abortive attempts to influence public officials to abolish slavery. When the world proved intractable, Methodists like Jones could fall back on their hope for eventual judgment.[30]

Southern patriarchal power extended beyond the grave; in wills, men could punish and reward as they saw fit, affecting generations of their descendants to come. Through Methodism, Sarah Jones, too, had a final say. Like a number of southern women, she chose the text for her funeral sermon before she died. Bishop Asbury, who preached the sermon, memorialized her in his journal: "She has had a painful journey through life; but her persecutions and troubles are now at an end. . . . She was doubtless a woman of sense, vivacity, and grace. . . . She would pray in any place, and before any people; she reproved with pointed severity, and sung with great sweetness." Jones chose Job 3:17 as her message to the living: "There the wicked cease from troubling; there the weary be at rest."[31] With this text, Jones reproved her husband for "troubling" her and steadfastly proclaimed that her piety would be rewarded in heaven. Her pointed and severe last word reminds us that, in a South where they had little power and authority, even the most remarkable Methodists fell short of their ideals. Religion gave their struggle meaning, comforting and sustaining them in a hostile world.

Appendix

White and Black Membership, 1786–1810

Year	White Members	Black Members
1786	18,791	1,890
1787	21,949	3,893
1788	30,809	6,545
1789	35,019	8,243
1790	45,949	11,682
1791	63,269	12,884
1792	52,109	13,871
1793	51,416	16,227
1794	52,794	13,814
1795	48,121	12,170
1796	45,384	11,280
1797	46,445	12,218
1798	47,867	12,302
1799	49,115	12,236
1800	51,442	13,542
1801	57,186	15,688
1802	68,075	18,659
1803	81,617	22,453
1804	89,603	23,531
1805	95,629	24,316
1806	103,313	27,257
1807	114,727	29,863
1808	121,687	30,308
1809	131,154	31,884
1810	139,336	34,724

Source: Minutes of the Annual Conferences of the Methodist Episcopal Church for the Years 1773–1828 (New York: T. Mason & G. Lane, 1840).

Notes

AHR	American Historical Review
AmQ	American Quarterly
AM	The Arminian Magazine
ChurchH	Church History
DelH	Delaware History
FemStud	Feminist Studies
JAH	The Journal of American History
JNH	The Journal of Negro History
JSH	The Journal of Southern History
MHM	Maryland Historical Magazine
MassR	The Massachusetts Review
MethH	Methodist History
MMag	The Methodist Magazine
MMQR	The Methodist Magazine and Quarterly Review
TCHP	[Trinity College] Historical Papers
VMHB	The Virginia Magazine of History and Biography
WMQ	William and Mary Quarterly

Introduction

1. MMQR 12:2 (April 1830), 122–23.

2. For Hinde's life, see MMQR 12:2 (April 1830) and A. H. Redford, *The History of Methodism in Kentucky*, volume 1 (Nashville: Southern Methodist Publishing House, 1868), 373–81; quotations from MMag 10:6 (June 1827), 263.

3. MMag 10:7 (July 1827), 310–12.

4. See J. B. Wakeley, *The Patriarch of One Hundred Years: Being Reminiscences, Historical and Biographical, of Rev. Henry Boehm* (New York: Nelson & Phillips, 1875), 406.

5. MMQR 12:2 (April 1830), 123 and 125.

6. Redford, *Methodism in Kentucky*, 380–81.

7. MMQR 12:2 (April 1830), 124.

8. For scholars who argue that there was "a South" by this era, see William J. Cooper, Jr., and Thomas E. Terrill, *The American South: A History* (New York: McGraw-Hill, 1996), 97; John Richard Alden, *The South in the Revolution, 1763–1789* (Baton Rouge: Louisiana State University Press, 1957) and *The First South* (Baton Rouge: Louisiana State University Press, 1961). For the classic account of how slavery and white supremacy became entrenched in the colonial era, see Edmund Morgan, *American Slavery, American Freedom: The Ordeal of Colonial Virginia* (New York: Norton, 1975).

9. James Meacham Papers, Special Collections, Duke University, Durham, North Carolina. Hereafter cited as Meacham Papers.

10. The Diary of Jeremiah Norman, Stephen B. Weeks Papers, Southern Historical Collection, the University of North Carolina at Chapel Hill, Chapel Hill, North Carolina. Hereafter cited as Jeremiah Norman Diary.

11. June 1, 1799, the Original Journals of Richard Whatcoat, microfilm courtesy of the University of Chicago Divinity School Library, Chicago, Illinois; originals at the Library of Congress and Garrett-Evangelical Theological Seminary, Evanston, Illinois. Hereafter cited as Whatcoat Journals.

12. Elmer T. Clark et al., eds., *The Journal and Letters of Francis Asbury* (London: Epworth Press, 1958), 3: 141, hereafter cited as JLFA.

13. Robert Drew Simpson annotated Freeborn Garrettson's published journal and transcribed and annotated his unpublished journal. They are both published in Simpson, ed., *American Methodist Pioneer: The Life and Journals of the Rev. Freeborn Garrettson, 1752–1827* (Rutland: Academy Books, 1984). Rev. Edwin Schell compared Francis Asbury's 1792, 1802, and 1821 editions of his journal. The results are published in "Discovery," ed. Frederick E. Maser, MethH 9 (1971), 34–43.

14. William W. Bennett, *Memorials of Methodism in Virginia* (Richmond: by the author, 1871), 129.

15. Samuel W. Williams, *Pictures of Early Methodism in Ohio* (Cincinnati: Jennings and Graham, 1909), 98. For contradictions, see his descriptions on 109, 111–12, 121.

16. See debates in Charles Elliott, *History of Great Secession from the Methodist Episcopal Church in the Year 1845, Eventuating in the Organization of the New Church, Entitled the "Methodist Episcopal Church, South"* (Cincinnati: Swormstedt & Poe, 1855), 266.

17. For a small sample of the works that offer comparisons, see Donald G. Mathews, *Religion in the Old South* (Chicago: University of Chicago Press, 1977); Jan Lewis, *The Pursuit of Happiness: Family and Values in Jefferson's Virginia* (Cambridge: Cambridge University Press, 1983); Terry D. Bilhartz, *Urban Religion and the Second Great Awakening: Church and Society in Early National Baltimore* (Rutherford: Fairleigh Dickinson University Press, 1986); John B. Boles, *The Great Revival, 1787–1805: The Origins of the Southern Evangelical Mind* (Lexington: University Press of Kentucky, 1972); Jon Butler, *Awash in a Sea of Faith: Christianizing the American People* (Cambridge: Harvard University Press, 1990); James D. Essig, *The Bonds of Wickedness: American Evangelicals Against Slavery, 1770–1808* (Philadelphia: Temple University Press, 1982); Albert J. Raboteau, *Slave Religion: The "Invisible Institution" in the Antebellum South* (New York: Oxford University Press, 1978).

18. For Delaware, see John A. Munroe, "Reflection on Delaware and the American Revolution," DelH 17:1 (Spring/Summer 1976), 1–11; William H. Williams, "Delaware and the Methodist Revolution," DelH 22:4 (Fall/Winter 1987), 219–40.

19. T. H. Breen, *Tobacco Culture: The Mentality of the Great Tidewater Planters on the Eve of Revolution* (Princeton: Princeton University Press, 1985); Morgan, *American Slavery, American Freedom*; Lacy K. Ford, Jr., *Origins of Southern Radicalism: The South Carolina Upcountry, 1800–1860* (New York: Oxford University Press, 1988); Kenneth S. Greenberg, *Masters and Statesmen: The Political Culture of American Slavery* (Baltimore: Johns Hopkins University Press, 1985); Stephanie McCurry, "The Two Faces of Republicanism: Gender and Proslavery Politics in Antebellum South Carolina," *JAH* 78:4 (March 1992), 1245–64, and "The Politics of Yeoman Households in Antebellum South Carolina," in *Divided Houses: Gender and the Civil War*, ed. Catherine Clinton and Nina Silber (New York: Oxford University Press, 1992); J. William Harris, *Plain Folk and Gentry in a Slave Society: White Liberty and Black Slavery in Augusta's Hinterlands* (Middletown, Conn.: Wesleyan University Press, 1985).

20. Bertram Wyatt-Brown, *Southern Honor: Ethics and Behavior in the Old South* (New York: Oxford University Press, 1982); Edward L. Ayers, *Vengeance and Justice: Crime and Punishments in the 19th Century American South* (New York: Oxford University Press, 1984). Evangelicals, as Ayers argued and as this work argues, dissented from the code of honor.

21. Rhys Isaac, *The Transformation of Virginia, 1740–1790* (New York: Norton, 1988); Mathews, *Religion in the Old South*.

22. Jean E. Friedman, *The Enclosed Garden: Women and Community in the Evangelical South, 1830–1900* (Chapel Hill: University of North Carolina Press, 1985); Richard Rankin, *Ambivalent Churchmen and Evangelical Churchwomen: The Religion of the Episcopal Elite in North Carolina, 1800–1860* (Columbia: University of South Carolina Press, 1993). For gender and Methodism in the Ohio Valley, see A. Gregory Schneider, *The Way of the Cross Leads Home: The Domestication of American Methodism* (Bloomington: Indiana University Press, 1993). Christine Leigh Heyrman's *Southern Cross: The Beginnings of the Bible Belt* (New York: Alfred A. Knopf, 1997) came out while this book was in press. Heyrman's study is an engaging, comprehensive, and insightful analysis of southern religion that foregrounds gender as well as race and class and that explores the region's religiosity from a multidenominational viewpoint.

1: Revolutions Civil and Religious

1. Rev. W. H. Daniels, *The Illustrated History of Methodism in Great Britain and America, From the Days of the Wesleys to the Present Time* (New York: Methodist Book Concern, 1880), 375–78. For the debate over origins, see Russell Richey, *Early American Methodism* (Bloomington: Indiana University Press, 1991).

2. Daniels, *Illustrated History*, 384, 379, 390.

3. For myth, see Mircea Eliade, *Myth and Reality* (New York: Harper and Row, 1963); Henry Nash Smith, *Virgin Land: The American West as Symbol and Myth* (Cambridge: Harvard University Press, 1950); Catherine L. Albanese, *Sons of the Fathers: The Civil Religion of the American Revolution* (Philadelphia: Temple University Press, 1976); Charles Reagan Wilson, *Baptized in Blood: The Religion of the Lost Cause* (Athens: University of Georgia Press, 1980).

4. For a somewhat different emphasis, see Russell E. Richey, "The Four Languages of Early American Methodism," *MethH* 28:3 (April 1990), 165, and Richey, *Early American Methodism*. Methodists did not flee religious oppression and thus do not fit the republican paradigm discussed by Albanese in *Sons of the Fathers*, 21–23.

5. *JLFA*, 1:4–5.

6. *AM* (November 1790 and December 1790), 555–63; 601–09. Rhys Isaac, "Preachers and Patriots: Popular Culture and the Revolution in Virginia," in Alfred F. Young, ed., *The American Revolution: Explorations in the History of American Radicalism* (Dekalb: Northern Illinois University Press, 1976), especially 145–46; Bernard Bailyn, *The Ideological Origins of the American Revolution* (Cambridge: Harvard University Press, 1967); Breen, *Tobacco Culture*; Gordon Wood, *The Creation of the American Republic, 1776–1787* (Chapel Hill: University of North Carolina Press, 1969); and Ruth

Bloch, "The Gendered Meanings of Virtue in Revolutionary America," *Signs* 13:1 (Autumn 1987), 37–58.

7. See also R. Laurence Moore, *Religious Outsiders and the Making of Americans* (New York: Oxford University Press, 1986), xi. As Moore suggests, groups like Methodists were a "sect" before they were a "denomination." I also use the somewhat anachronistic word "church" to describe what is, until 1784, properly a movement.

8. The literature on Wesley and English Methodism is vast. See, for example, Frank Baker, *From Welsey to Asbury: Studies in Early American Methodism* (Durham: Duke University Press, 1976); Bernard Semmel, *The Methodist Revolution* (New York: Basic Books, 1973); Robert G. Tuttle, Jr., *John Wesley: His Life and Theology* (Grand Rapids: Zondervan, 1978); Robert F. Wearmouth, *Methodism and the Common People of the Eighteenth Century* (London: Epworth Press, 1945); E. P. Thompson, *The Making of the English Working Class* (New York: Vintage Books, 1966); and F. Ernest Stoeffler, "Pietism, the Wesleys, and Methodist Beginnings in America," in F. Ernest Stoeffler, ed., *Continental Pietism and Early American Christianity* (Grand Rapids: William B. Eerdmans, 1976).

9. Thompson, *Making of the English Working Class*; Deborah Valenze, *Prophetic Sons and Daughters: Female Preaching and Popular Religion in Industrial England* (Princeton: Princeton University Press, 1985); Linda Kerber, "Women and Individualism in American History," *MassR* 30 (Winter 1989), 589–609. American Methodists printed and sold works by Hester Ann Rogers and Eliza Bennis. One preacher noted that the two books people on his circuit wanted to buy were the hymn-book and "Mrs. Rowe's Devout Exercises," July 21, 1800, Jeremiah Norman Diary.

10. Daniels, *Illustrated History*, 393–96. This pattern was repeated in America. See, for example, *JLFA*, 3:129–30, and Jesse Lee, *A Short History of the Methodists in the United States of America* (1810; reprint, Rutland: Academy Books, 1974), 84–85.

11. Daniels, *Illustrated History*, 377.

12. Pamphlet, "An Invitation to Tour the Robert Strawbridge Country, Birthplace of American Methodism," from Lovely Lane Museum, Baltimore, Maryland.

13. *JLFA*, 1:9, n. 19; John Lednum, *A History of the Rise of Methodism in America* (Philadelphia: n.p., 1859), 426–27. Peter Williams was later purchased and freed by New York Methodists. The editors of Asbury's journal call Betty a "servant" but because of the way these terms were used, it is unclear whether she was indentured or enslaved.

14. Daniels, *Illustrated History*, 394.

15. Frederick Norwood, ed., *The Methodist Discipline of 1798* (Rutland: Academy Books, 1979), 146–49.

16. I would argue that we should not see the church solely as individualistic or as communitarian. It was both, and John Boles and Donald Mathews both have cogent points on this matter. See also Anne C. Loveland, *Southern Evangelicals and the Social Order, 1800–1860* (Baton Rouge: Louisiana State University Press, 1980).

17. Peter Pelham to Edward Dromgoole, 1809, Edward Dromgoole Papers, Southern Historical Collection, University of North Carolina at Chapel Hill. Hereafter cited as Dromgoole Papers.

18. July 29, 1791, September 2, 1791, October 7, 1781, December 16, 1791, William Ormond Papers, Special Collections, Duke University. Hereafter cited as Ormond Papers.

19. In 1784 Wesley sent ordained men to America to in turn ordain Asbury and others, conferring legitimacy on the American church.

20. Local preachers could not vote in General Conferences and were licensed for a specific place or area. They could be ordained as "deacons" after four years of service. Novice itinerants were not immediately ordained, but placed on trial and given licenses.

21. The phrase and concept are Benedict R. Anderson's. See *Imagined Communities: Reflections on the Origin and Spread of Nationalism* (London: Verso, 1983).

22. In 1784, the Americans became the Methodist Episcopal Church and published their

own version of the doctrines and discipline. Until the slavery compromises, there was little difference between the American discipline and the British.

23. Norwood, ed., *The Methodist Discipline of 1798*, 133–35.

24. For "purging," see, for example, July 1, 1798, Ormond Papers; March 9, 1790, Ezekiel Cooper Journals, originals at Garrett-Evangelical Theological Seminary, Evanston, Illinois, photocopy loaned by Baltimore-Washington United Methodist Historical Society, Lovely Lane Museum, Baltimore, Maryland; Thomas Sheredine Chew to Edward Dromgoole, August 20, 1784, Dromgoole Papers. For "sifting," see February 18, 1792, Journal of George Wells, Baltimore-Washington United Methodist Historical Society, hereafter cited as George Wells Journal. The Methodists were much less democratic than the Baptists and judging by clergymen's comments, Methodist itinerants alone decided in most instances whether a violation had occurred and what punishment was in order. The procedures for disciplining members did change over the years under study here, with increasing provisions made for the input of members.

25. Isaac, *Transformation of Virginia*.

26. Ibid. For the contrast between oral (evangelical) culture and written (planter) culture, see Isaac, "Preachers and Patriots."

27. See Charles Pettigrew letters in the Pettigrew Family Papers, Southern Historical Collection, University of North Carolina at Chapel Hill; the Devereux Jarratt letters in *A Brief Narrative of the Revival of Religion in Virginia* (London: n.p., 1786) and *Thoughts on Some Important Subjects in Divinity: In a Series of Letters to A Friend* (Baltimore: n.p., 1806), 75–84; and Jarratt's letters to Edward Dromgoole of May 31, 1785, and March 22, 1788, in the Dromgoole Papers.

28. *JLFA*, 3:24. Jarratt concurred with his friend, although he expressed his hope that some Methodists were still loyal (*JLFA*, 3:25).

29. Freeborn Garrettson, William Watters, and Jesse Lee all supported the principles of the Revolution. Lee and Garrettson were also pacifists. See also Richey, "Four Languages," 155–70; Theodore C. Linn, "Religion and Nationalism: American Methodism and the New Nation in the Early National Period, 1766–1844," Ph.D. diss., Drew University, 1971. Doris Elisabett Andrews persuasively links Methodist views about women's roles and duties to republicanism as well as revivalism in general with republicanism, an argument my research supports. See Andrews, "Popular Religion and the Revolution in the Middle Atlantic Ports: The Rise of the Methodists, 1770–1800," Ph.D. diss., University of Pennsylvania, 1986, especially 201 and 317. For the early republic, see Robert M. Calhoon, *Evangelicals and Conservatives in the Early South, 1740–1861* (Columbia: University of South Carolina Press, 1988), part 2.

30. Isaac, "Preachers and Patriots," 144–46.

31. William R. Phinney, Kenneth E. Rowe, and Robert B. Steelman, eds., *Thomas Ware, a Spectator at the Christmas Conference: A Miscellany on Thomas Ware and the Methodist Christmas Conference* (Rutland: Academy Books, 1984), 25, 27, 29. Ware's war fever waned during his service.

32. Ibid., 30, 46. The distinction between "soul" and "civil" liberty was used most notoriously in dealing with slavery. See *JLFA*, 1:273–74; 2:591.

33. Bloch, "The Gendered Meanings of Virtue"; Linda Kerber, "The Republican Mother: Women and the Enlightenment—An American Perspective," *AmQ* 27 (Summer 1976), 187–205, and Jan Lewis, "The Republican Wife: Virtue and Seduction in the Early Republic," *WMQ*, 3rd ser., 44 (October 1987), 689–721.

34. March 13, 1777, Journal of John Littlejohn, original as Louisville Conference Historical Society, typescript loaned by Baltimore-Washington United Methodist Historical Society. Hereafter cited as Littlejohn Journal.

35. *JLFA*, 1:184.

36. See, for example, Diary of Nelson Reed, Baltimore-Washington United Methodist Historical Society, hereafter cited as Nelson Reed Diary. In Reed's journal the war rarely intrudes.

37. There are a few scant references to elections, but not to the candidates and issues. Simi-

larly, preachers' geography was that of the circuit, so that preaching stations referred to in any given journal could well encompass several states.

38. June 14, 1790, Whatcoat Journals.

39. John Ffirth, *The Experiences and Gospel Labours, of the Rev. Benjamin Abbott* (New York: Daniel Hitt and Thomas Ware, 1813), 30.

40. John Wesley, *A Calm Address to Our American Colonies* (London: 1775); Lednum, *Rise of Methodism*, 193. For Webb, see Daniels, *Illustrated History*, 386–89. For Clowe, see Lednum, *Rise of Methodism*, 214; Simpson, ed., *American Methodist Pioneer*, 68, 74; Keith Mason, "Localism, Evangelicalism, and Loyalism: The Sources of Discontent in the Revolutionary Chesapeake," *JSH* 56:1 (February 1990), 40–41; and Thomas O'Brien Hanley, *The American Revolution and Religion: Maryland, 1770–1800* (Washington: Catholic University of America Press, 1971), 31.

41. Simpson, ed., *American Methodist Pioneer*, 50.

42. Douglas R. Chandler, "Prelude to a Church, 1774–1784," in Gordon Pratt Baker, ed., *Those Incredible Methodists: A History of the Baltimore Conference of the United Methodist Church* (Baltimore: Commission on Archives and History, Baltimore Conference, 1972), 47–49.

43. Wyatt-Brown, *Southern Honor*, 55–59.

44. Baker, ed., *Those Incredible Methodists*, 49; Lee, *Short History*, 65, 77; *JLFA*, 1:265; Lednum, *Rise of Methodism*, 264, 273; September 20, 1780, Nelson Reed Diary. For Delaware, see James W. May, "Francis Asbury and Thomas White: A Refugee Preacher and His Tory Patron," *MethH* 14 (1976), 141–64.

45. See Simpson's introductory essay in *American Methodist Pioneer*.

46. Isaac, *Transformation of Virginia*.

47. Lee, *Short History*, 74–75; Mason, "Localism, Evangelicalism, and Loyalism."

48. *JLFA*, 1:313.

49. Simpson, ed., *American Methodist Pioneer*, 391.

50. William Watters, *A Short Account of the Christian Experience, and Ministereal Labours, of William Watters* (Alexandria, Virginia: n.p., 1806), 49–50.

51. Isaac, "Preachers and Patriots," 149. See also Wyatt-Brown, *Southern Honor*, and Bloch, "The Gendered Meanings of Virtue."

52. Minton Thrift, *Memoir of the Rev. Jesse Lee. With Extracts from His Journals* (1823; reprint, New York: Arno Press & New York Times, 1969), 32.

53. Simpson, ed., *American Methodist Pioneer*, 71.

54. Lednum, *Rise of Methodism*, 147.

55. Ibid., 148.

56. Simpson, ed., *American Methodist Pioneer*, 48, 74, 95, 391, 404–05.

57. This comparison is made possible because of the efforts of Robert Drew Simpson in Simpson, ed., *American Methodist Pioneer*. Edwin Schell made a similar comparison of two versions of part of Asbury's journal and likewise found that negative comments about slavery and slave owners were omitted from the later published edition. See Frederick E. Maser, ed., "Discovery," *MethH* 9 (1971), 34–43.

58. Simpson, ed., *American Methodist Pioneer*, 49.

59. Ibid., 147.

60. Ibid., 50.

61. Ibid., 147.

62. Ibid., 158.

63. Hanley, *American Revolution and Religion*, 239.

64. Sylvia Frey, *Water from the Rock: Black Resistance in a Revolutionary Age* (Princeton: Princeton University Press, 1991).

65. Ronald Hoffman, "The Disaffected in the Revolutionary South," in Young, ed., *The American Revolution*, 273–316.

66. Lathan A. Windley, compiler, *Runaway Slave Advertisements: A Documentary History from the 1730s to 1790*, volume 2, *Maryland* (Westport, Conn.: Greenwood Press, 1983), 210, 215, 270; see also Gerald Mullin, *Flight and Rebellion: Slave Resistance in Eighteenth-Century Virginia* (New York: Oxford University Press, 1972), 128–30.

67. Lednum, *Rise of Methodism*, 213.

68. Lee, *Short History*, 60.

69. Frederick A. Norwood, ed., *Sourcebook of American Methodism* (Nashville: Abingdon Press, 1982), 48. Wesley did not link chattel slavery with colonists' rhetoric of slavery, as Rankin did.

70. Norwood, ed., *Sourcebook*, 49. Given the regional composition of this body and Rankin's wording, it is likely that many he addressed were southern.

71. Morgan, *American Slavery, American Freedom*.

72. Hoffman, "The Disaffected," 286; Isaac, *Transformation of Virginia*.

73. Chandler, "Prelude to a Church, 1774–1784," 49. Some Methodists joined patriot societies, as Chandler shows (50).

74. David Brion Davis, *The Problem of Slavery in the Age of Revolution, 1770–1823* (Ithaca: Cornell University Press, 1975); Winthrop Jordan, *White Over Black: American Attitudes Toward the Negro, 1550–1812* (Chapel Hill: University of North Carolina Press, 1968), chapter 7; James Oakes, *The Ruling Race: A History of American Slaveholders* (New York: Vintage Books, 1983), chapter 1.

75. See, for example, Simpson, ed., *American Methodist Pioneer*, 98–100.

76. Bennett, *Methodism in Virginia*, 138.

77. Gary E. Peluso, "Francis Asbury on American Public Life," *MethH* 30:4 (July 1992), 206–16, and Richey, *Early American Methodism*, chapter 3.

78. See Lee's *Short History*, 60, 62, 72. Lee shifted the focus of the Methodist story away from lay people and to ministers once Wesley's missionaries arrived. Lee rarely mentioned women by name in his *Short History*. Blacks, when mentioned, appear as a nonindividuated mass.

79. Bennett, *Methodism in Virginia*, 129, 132–33, 137–38.

2: The Marrow of the Methodist Self

1. Sarah Jones, *Devout Letters: Or, Letters Spiritual and Friendly. Written by Mrs. Sarah Jones.*, ed. Jeremiah Minter (Alexandria: Jeremiah Minter, 1804), 132–33.

2. Jones, *Devout Letters*, 39–40.

3. For religious identity see Curtis D. Johnson, *Islands of Holiness: Rural Religion in Upstate New York, 1790–1860* (Ithaca: Cornell University Press, 1989), especially 6–8.

4. Jacob Young, *Autobiography of a Pioneer: Or, the Nativity, Experience, Travels, and Ministerial Labors of Rev. Jacob Young* (Cincinnati: L. Swormstedt & A. Poe, 1857), 40.

5. Ffirth, *Abbott*, 33.

6. The works most central to my discussion include Boles, *Great Revival* and "Revivalism, Renewal, and Social Mediation in the Old South," in Randall Balmer and Edith L. Blumhofer, eds., *Modern Christian Revivals* (Urbana: University of Illinois Press, 1993), 60–83; Dickson G. Bruce, *And They All Sang Hallelujah: Plain-Folk Camp Meeting Religion, 1800–1845* (Knoxville: University of Tennessee Press, 1974); Robert E. Cushman, *John Wesley's Experimental Divinity: Studies in Methodist Doctrinal Standards* (Nashville: Kingswood Books, 1989); Essig, *Bonds of Wickedness*; Frey, *Water from the Rock*; Lewis, *Pursuit of Happiness*; Loveland, *Southern Evangelicals*; Mathews, *Religion in the Old South*; Raboteau, *Slave Religion*; Rankin, *Ambivalent Churchmen*; Richey, *Early American Methodism*; Schneider, *Way of the Cross* and "The Ritual of Happy Dying Among Early American Methodists," *ChurchH* 56:3 (September 1987), 348–63; Mechal Sobel, *Trabelin' On: The Slave Journey to an Afro-Baptist Faith* (Princeton: Princeton University Press, 1988) and *The World They Made Together: Black and White Values in Eighteenth-Century Virginia* (Princeton: Princeton University Press, 1987); William H. Williams, *The Garden of Methodism: The Delmarva Peninsula, 1769–1820* (Wilmington, Del.: Scholarly Resources, 1984); Wyatt-Brown, *Southern Honor*.

7. John Higham, *From Boundlessness to Consolidation: The Transformation of American Culture, 1848–1860* (Ann Arbor: William L. Clements Library, 1969); Lewis, *Pursuit of Happiness.*

8. Indeed, to Methodists, Satan functioned much like we believe the unconscious or subconscious functions.

9. For a few doctrinal disputes, see March 28 and August 7, 1791, Ezekiel Cooper Journals; September 27 and 29, 1799, Nelson Reed Diary; December 17, 1790, and August 21, 1791, Rev. John Kobler's Journal, Baltimore-Washington United Methodist Historical Society, hereafter cited as Kobler Journal; and Simpson, ed., *American Methodist Pioneer,* 199 and 279.

10. For Arminianism and agency, see Raymond P. Cowan, "The Arminian Alternative: The Rise of the Methodist Episcopal Church, 1765–1850," Ph.D. diss., Georgia State University, 1991; Nancy Cott, "Young Women in the Second Great Awakening in New England," *Feminist Studies* 3:1/2 (Fall 1975), 15–29; Paul E. Johnson, *A Shopkeeper's Millennium: Society and Revivals in Rochester, New York, 1815–1837* (New York: Hill and Wang, 1978); Nancy Hardesty, *Your Daughters Shall Prophesy: Revivalism and Feminism in the Age of Finney* (Brooklyn: Carlson, 1991); Kerber, "Women and Individualism"; Boles, *The Great Revival;* and Mathews, *Religion in the Old South.*

11. Mathews, *Religion in the Old South,* 31–34, emphasizes the similarities between evangelicals.

12. Phinney et al., eds., *Thomas Ware,* 21.

13. December 17, 1790, Kobler Journal.

14. Maj. John Overstreet to Rev. John Baldwin, September 10, 1810, copy in the Journal of William Spencer, microfilm, Baltimore-Washington United Methodist Historical Society. For Rankin, see *A Review of the Noted Revival in Kentucky, Commenced in the Year of Our Lord, 1801* (Lexington, Kentucky: n.p., 1802), 54.

15. *AM* (December 1789) and *MMag* (February 1797).

16. Jones, *Devout Letters,* 34. Viewing God as Mother instead of as Father has interesting implications for gender ideology, especially in such a patriarchal society as the early national South. The image of God as stern patriarch surfaces most often in Methodist writings when Wesleyans were discussing the way God would handle the unconverted.

17. Simpson, ed., *American Methodist Pioneer,* 286; Robert Paine, *Life and Times of William M'Kendree, Bishop of the Methodist Episcopal Church,* volume 1 (Nashville: Southern Methodist Publishing House, 1869), 92.

18. Phinney et al., eds., *Thomas Ware,* 103–04; Betsy Goodwin to William Spencer, n.d., copy, William Spencer Journal. Few predestinarians spoke in such absolute terms of their salvation in this era.

19. Calvinists did believe that they could blaspheme against the Holy Spirit. See Julius H. Rubin, *Religious Melancholy and Protestant Experience in America* (New York: Oxford University Press, 1994), especially 169–76. For a sample of the disputes over falling from grace, see Thrift, *Jesse Lee,* 141–42; September 27, 1779, September 29, 1779, Nelson Reed Diary; December 8, 1799, Jeremiah Norman Diary; November 18, 1790, Ezekiel Cooper Journals; James Jenkins, *Experience, Labours, and Sufferings of Rev. James Jenkins, of the South Carolina Conference* (n.p.: for the author, 1842), 39; *JLFA,* 1:437; 1:585.

20. April 10, 1777, Littlejohn Journal; Rankin, *A Review of the Noted Revival,* 54–55.

21. Thrift, *Jesse Lee,* 141–42.

22. William Hill, *Autobiographical Sketches of Dr. William Hill.* Historical Transcripts No. 4 (Richmond: Union Theological Seminary in Virginia, 1968), 55.

23. *JLFA,* 1:756; Simpson, ed., *American Methodist Pioneer,* 210; *Extracts of Letters,* 23. For sanctification, see Simpson, ed., *American Methodist Pioneer,* 178; Jenkins, *Experience, Labours, and Sufferings,* 135; May 4, 1777, June 11, 1777, June 12, 1777, August 3, 1778, August 11, 1778, Littlejohn Journal; *JLFA,* 1:388, 1:482, 1:526; 1:756; Paine, *M'Kendree,* 50, 63, 106–07, 110, 112. This is a small sample.

24. Jones, *Devout Letters,* 134. For Wesley on sanctification, see Baker, *From Wesley to Asbury,*

163–76. See Timothy L. Smith, *Revivalism and Social Reform in Mid-Nineteenth-Century America* (New York: Abingdon Press, 1957), 115–16, and John Leland Peters, *Christian Perfection and American Methodism* (New York: Abingdon Press, 1956), for differing views of the centrality of sanctification.

25. *AM* (January 1790), 20.

26. Jones, *Devout Letters*, 66, 74; Elizabeth Anderson to John Owen, October 21, 1810, Campbell Family Papers, Special Collections, Duke University; Jones, *Devout Letters*, 81; Daniel Grant to John Owen, June 14, 1792, and October 4, 1788, Campbell Family Papers; August 4, 1777, Littlejohn Journal.

27. Joanna Bowen Gillespie, "1795: Martha Laurens Ramsay's 'Dark Night of the Soul,'" *WMQ* 48:1 (January 1991), 68–92; Rubin, *Religious Melancholy*.

28. Sarah Jones to Edward Dromgoole, n.d., copy, Dromgoole Papers.

29. "The Journal of Benjamin Lakin," in William Warren Sweet, *Religion on the American Frontier, 1783–1840*, volume 4: *The Methodists* (Chicago: University of Chicago Press, 1946), 223; Ezekiel Cooper to R. Roy, December 10, 1795, Ezekiel Cooper Collection, Garrett-Evangelical Theological Seminary, Evanston, Illinois. Francis Asbury even used the term "heart religion." *JLFA*, 1:776. My analysis is somewhat at odds with that of Albert J. Raboteau's *Slave Religion* on this point, for I believe that at least in this earlier period, both black and white Methodists sought "heart religion."

30. January 12, 1779, Nelson Reed Diary; May 20, 1793, Meacham Papers. See also Paine, *M'Kendree*, 94; "The Journal of Benjamin Lakin," 235; February 14, 1792, Ormond Papers.

31. July 5, 1777, Littlejohn Journal. See also *JLFA*, 1:658. For Wesley, see E. Brooks Holifield, *Health and Medicine in the Methodist Tradition: Journey Toward Wholeness* (New York: Crossroad, 1986), 67.

32. March 6, 1792, Ormond Papers; June 30, 1806, November 18, 1805, Thomas Mann Papers, Special Collections, Duke University, hereafter cited as Mann Papers; September 24, 1795, Ormond Papers; Sarah Jones to Edward Dromgoole, n.d., copy, Dromgoole Papers.

33. Wesley quoted in *AM* (November 1789), 527; Joseph Pinnell to Daniel Shine, March 16, 1805, Daniel Shine Papers, Special Collections, Duke University; Sally Eastland to Edward Dromgoole, February 21, 1790, Dromgoole Papers. As is clear from my "transcription" of Sally Eastland's letter, it is often very difficult to properly render Methodists' handwritten letters into typescript. They frequently wrote the words "Jesus" or "God" or "love" in large, bold, capital letters that cannot be adequately depicted here.

34. May 9, 1777, Littlejohn Journal; February 11, 1794, Kobler Journal; "The Journal of Benjamin Lakin," 209.

35. David Smith, *Biography of Rev. David Smith, of the A.M.E. Church. Being a Complete History, Embracing Over Sixty Years' Labor in the Advancement of the Redeemer's Kingdom on Earth* (Xenia: n.p., 1881), 15, 24.

36. See journal in William Hill, *Autobiographical Sketches*.

37. *AM* (April 1790), 171.

38. *MMag* (January 1797), 10.

39. See also Butler, *Awash in a Sea of Faith*, 238–39.

40. [1774], Littlejohn Journal, typescript, 9–10, 12.

41. "The Journal of Benjamin Lakin," 218–19; *JLFA*, 1:441. Birds were a common motif in dreams and visions.

42. April 5, 1777, Littlejohn Journal.

43. Ibid.

44. Richey, *Early American Methodism*, 82–83. It is difficult to document the extent of enthusiastic behavior. Not every church service produced noise or demonstrative behavior. But clergy judged themselves successful when they provoked some reaction, demonstrative behavior was normal, and Methodists were known for it.

45. August 11, 1778, Littlejohn Journal. There is evidence to suggest that southern Methodists were more enthusiastic than their northern counterparts. See *Extracts of Letters*, 8–9.

46. January 18, 1792, George Wells Journal.

47. July 2, 1791, Kobler Journal.

48. "Diary of John Early, Bishop of the Methodist Episcopal Church, South," *VMHB* 34:4 (October 1926), 311; July 3, 1779, Nelson Reed Diary; Sarah Jones to Edward Dromgoole, n.d., copy, Dromgoole Papers.

49. Sarah Harrison to Daniel Shine, August 28, 1809, Daniel Shine Papers.

50. Jones, *Devout Letters*, 30. See also Laurel Thatcher Ulrich, *Good Wives: Image and Reality in the Lives of Women in Northern New England, 1650–1750* (New York: Vintage, 1991), 223–26.

51. Isaac, *Transformation of Virginia*; Mathews, *Religion in the Old South*; Williams, *Garden of Methodism*.

52. Simpson, ed., *American Methodist Pioneer*, 219; Lednum, *Rise of Methodism*, 283.

53. July 4, 1780, Nelson Reed Diary.

54. For trifling, see April 27, 1778, Littlejohn Journal and "The Diary of Elizabeth M'Kean," *MMag* (May 1797), 228. For Grant, see Grant to John Owen, August 20, 1789, and November 4, 1792, Campbell Family Papers. For others listed, see "The Journal of Benjamin Lakin," 206, 209, 211; August 5, 1791, Kobler Journal; July 7 and 11, 1797, Meacham Papers; Thomas Sheredine Chew to Edward Dromgoole, August 20, 1784, Dromgoole Papers.

55. See also Schneider in *Way of the Cross*.

56. May 17, 1796, May 20, 1796, July 29, 1796, March 30, 1798, July 17, 1800, January 14, 1801, Ormond Papers, quote on April 25, 1796; Simpson, ed., *American Methodist Pioneer*, 219; Jeremiah Minter, *A Brief Account of the Religious Experience, Travels, Preaching, Persecutions from Evil Men, and God's Special Helps in the Faith and Life, etc. of Jerem. Minter* (Washington, D.C.: for the author, 1817), 13–15.

57. Simpson, ed., *American Methodist Pioneer*, 111, 86; Ffirth, *Abbott*, 41; for suicide, see, for example, *JLFA*, 1:421. See also fasting to excess in *JLFA*, 1:358.

58. Minter, *A Brief Account*, 16. Asbury pitied Minter but also recognized the scandal his castration brought on Methodism. See *JLFA*, 1:671.

59. December 22, 1789, Ezekiel Cooper Journals.

60. Simpson, ed., *American Methodist Pioneer*, 182, 304.

61. December 24, 1791, Ezekiel Cooper Journals; Daniel Grant to John Owen, ca. 1791, Campbell Family Papers. See also July 14, 1796, July 4, 1798, and July 8, 1798, Jeremiah Norman Diary. See also Holifield, *Health and Medicine*, 63–95.

62. July 16, 1795, Whatcoat Journals; Rebecca Ridgely to Prisey, October 1, 1790, Ridgely-Pue Papers, MS. 693, Maryland Historical Society, Baltimore, Maryland.

63. *AM* (August 1790), 413–15; Wakeley, *Patriarch*, 156; See also "The Benefit of Afflication," *AM* (April 1790), 206. Such stoicism must be placed in the context of the very real, intense, and often protracted suffering that disease and illness could cause in the late eighteenth and early nineteenth centuries.

64. Norwood, ed., *The Methodist Discipline of 1798*, 134–35. James Essig argues that whites identified their own religious persecution with the persecution of slaves in *Bonds of Wickedness*, 43–52.

65. *MMag* (December 1797), 570.

66. Schneider, "The Ritual of Happy Dying," 348–63. See also Schneider, *Way of the Cross*; Lewis, *Pursuit of Happiness*; Holifield, *Health and Medicine*.

67. Maddox and Pamela Andrew to Ezekiel Cooper, April 23, 1798, Ezekiel Cooper Collection.

68. *AM* (March 1790), 147.

69. December 10, 1794, Whatcoat Journals; *AM* (March 1789), 137; see also Schneider, *Way of the Cross*.

70. The exceptions were sermons for George Washington, which were eulogies. See Thomas Morrell, *A Sermon on the Death of General George Washington* (Baltimore: Warren & Hanna, 1800).

71. For sermons on 1 Corinthians 15:55–57 see February 25, 1792, Meacham Papers; JLFA, 2:317. On 1 Corinthians 15:26, see August 29, 1791, Kobler Journal; Simpson, ed., *American Methodist Pioneer*, 161; JLFA, 1:249. For 2 Timothy 4:7–8, see Simpson, ed., *American Methodist Pioneer*, 231; JLFA, 2:534. See also the funerals on the text "Blessed are the dead which die in the Lord," August 22, 1788, September 14, 1788, October 2, 1788, Meacham Papers; January 24, 1796, February 3, 1796, Ormond Papers; October 17, 1791, William Colbert Journals, original at Garrett-Evangelical Theological Seminary, photocopy courtesy of Baltimore-Washington United Methodist Historical Society, hereafter cited as Colbert Journals; Simpson, ed., *American Methodist Pioneer*, 77. For people shouting these verses on their deathbeds, see MMag (October 1797), 462; Simpson, ed., *American Methodist Pioneer*, 190; William Coulter to Editor [Ezekiel Cooper], March 29, 1800, Ezekiel Cooper Collection.

72. MMag (May 1798), 240; Ezekiel Cooper to Rebecca Ridgely, June 16, 1790, Ridgely-Pue Papers. See also AM (August 1789), 403.

73. Dromgoole's meditation can be found following the entry for July 27, 1784, in his journal, Dromgoole Papers.

74. Lewis, *Pursuit of Happiness*, 105.

75. Elizabeth Anderson to John Owen, October 21, 1810, Campbell Family Papers.

76. For funeral sermons on Hebrews 9:27, see November 21, 1794, and December 6, 1794, Colbert Journals; JLFA, 1:318. For funeral sermons on Matthew 18:3, see December 7, 1794, Jeremiah Norman Diary; July 15, 1791, Kobler Journal; August 17, 1803, Ormond Papers. For John 5:28–29, see July 25, 1784, Edward Dromgoole Journal, Dromgoole Papers; April 16, 1796, September 19, 1791, Ormond Papers; May 18, 1790, August 7, 1791, August 31, 1794, Colbert Journals.

77. Ffirth, *Abbott*, 100–101.

3: Slaves and Free Blacks in the Church

1. The use of the terms "race" and "racism" is anachronistic to a degree but late eighteenth-century words like "color" inadequately convey what early Methodists and their contemporaries meant. White Methodists spoke and wrote in terms of "color," but it is clear from their descriptions that they were talking about more than complexion.

2. Methodist slaves and Methodist slave owners shared some, but not all, values. When Richard Allen and others seceded from the Methodist Episcopal Church, they named their new church "African Methodist Episcopal," and kept most of the *Discipline* and doctrine from their old church. They did bar slaveholders, limit admission to African Americans, and give black members and clergy full rights and privileges. African Methodist Episcopal founders were loyal to Methodism and had a distinct consciousness about the injustice of slavery and discrimination. Their dual identity informs my discussion of Methodist slaves and free blacks, the vast majority of whom did not leave their own records. See Daniel A. Payne, *History of the African Methodist Episcopal Church* (1891; reprint, New York: Johnson Reprint Corporation, 1968), Allen quoted on 73.

3. Mathews, *Religion in the Old South*; Genovese, *Roll, Jordan, Roll*; Drew Gilpin Faust, "A Southern Stewardship: The Intellectual and the Proslavery Argument," AmQ 31 (1979), 63–80 and "The Proslavery Argument in History," in Faust, ed., *The Ideology of Slavery: Proslavery Thought in the Antebellum South, 1830–1860* (Baton Rouge: Louisiana State University Press, 1981), 1–20; Klein, *Unification of a Slave State*; Larry E. Tise, *Proslavery: A History of the Defense of Slavery in America, 1701–1840* (Athens: University of Georgia Press, 1987). For eighteenth-century slavery see Willie Lee Rose, "The Domestication of Domestic Slavery," in *Slavery and Freedom*, ed. William W. Freehling (New York: Oxford University Press, 1982).

4. The term "biracial" may connote more equality and integration than churches practiced, but the alternative—"white"—is less satisfactory. Methodism was white controlled, but it was

only a "white" church in a few areas. See the racial breakdowns in *Minutes of the Annual Conferences of the Methodist Episcopal Church, for the Years 1773–1828*, volume 1 (New York: T. Mason and G. Lane, for the Methodist Episcopal Church, 1840).

5. Wightman, *Capers*, 124–29; Jenkins, *Experiences, Labours, and Sufferings*, 120–21; Rev. Charles F. Deems, *Annals of Southern Methodism for 1855* (New York: n.p., 1856), 260; and Rev. Jesse Armon Baldwin, "History of Methodism in North Carolina," Senior thesis, Trinity College, 1893, 11–12, in Methodist Church Papers, Special Collections, Duke University.

6. For other interpretations of Capers's remarks see Klein, *Unification of a Slave State*, 288–89 and Rankin, *Ambivalent Churchmen*, especially 29.

7. Wightman, *Capers*, 126–28.

8. Ibid., 128.

9. Jenkins, *Experience, Labours, and Sufferings*, 120, 136; Baldwin, "History of Methodism in North Carolina," 11.

10. Raboteau, *Slave Religion*, 238–39. Deferential behavior by a slave or free black did not signal approval of white authority, but instead was often a survival mechanism or dissemblance.

11. Frederick Douglass, *Narrative of the Life of Frederick Douglass, an American Slave* (1854, reprint, New York: Penguin, 1968), 84–85. A final point that could be made about the temperance discussion is that many Methodist whites gave up drinking alcohol, too, and they did so for religious reasons.

12. For late eighteenth-century slave religion, see Sobel, *World They Made Together*; Frey, *Water from the Rock*, chapter 9; Raboteau, *Slave Religion*, especially chapter 3; Margaret Washington Creel, *A Peculiar People: Slave Religion and Community-Culture Among the Gullahs* (New York: New York University Press, 1988). For antebellum slave religion, see Mathews, *Religion in the Old South*; Elizabeth Fox-Genovese, *Within the Plantation Household: Black and White Women of the Old South* (Chapel Hill: University of North Carolina Press, 1988), chapter 6; Lawrence Levine, *Black Culture and Black Consciousness: Afro-American Folk Thought from Slavery to Freedom* (New York: Oxford University Press, 1977), chapter 1; Friedman, *Enclosed Garden*; Sobel, *Trabelin' On*; Genovese, *Roll, Jordan, Roll*; John B. Boles, *Black Southerners, 1619–1869* (Lexington: University Press of Kentucky, 1984), 166–67, and *Religion in Antebellum Kentucky* (Lexington: University Press of Kentucky, 1976); Sterling Stuckey, *Slave Culture: Nationalist Theory and the Foundations of Black America* (New York: Oxford University Press, 1987).

13. The memoirs of James Jenkins and William Capers were published in the post–Nat Turner era. Jenkins, *Experience, Labours, and Sufferings*, was published in 1842. Capers's autobiography was published (Wightman, *Capers*) in 1859.

14. March 16, 1799, September 23, 1799, October 9, 1799, March 15, 1800, and February 25, 1800, Jeremiah Norman Diary. Norman's gradualist views on slavery and his racism will be discussed in more detail in a later chapter.

15. September 23, 1799, June 8, 1779, Jeremiah Norman Diary.

16. See chapter 6.

17. Ffirth, *Abbott*, 98. Abbott does not give the women's race but it is implied they are white. Moreau de St. Mery claimed that there were separate pew areas for slaves and free blacks in a Richmond church. See Kenneth and Anna M. Roberts, eds., *Moreau de St. Mery's American Journal* [1793–1798] (New York: Doubleday, 1947), 48.

18. Richey, *Early American Methodism*.

19. June 12, 1791, Kobler Journal; Jesse Lee, *Short History*, 131, 134.

20. Ffirth, *Abbott*, 102–03; July 7, 1791, Kobler Journal.

21. See, for example, May 10, 1789, Meacham Papers. Meacham opposed this segregated arrangement.

22. October 4, 1801, Henry Boehm Journals, original at Drew University Library, Madison, New Jersey, typescript loaned by Rev. Edwin Schell, Lovely Lane Museum, hereafter cited as Boehm Journals.

23. For temporal segregation, see Boehm Journals and Whatcoat Journals; for night meetings, see Colbert Journals.

24. August 5, 1790, Meacham Papers. The communion service is found in *The Doctrines and Discipline of the Methodist Episcopal Church in America* (Philadelphia: for John Dickins, 1792), 231–32.

25. July 30, 1797, Ormond Papers.

26. For sermons, see January 8, 1797, Ormond Papers; Simpson, ed., *American Methodist Pioneer*, 190; October 11, 1791, "A Journal and Travel of James Meacham, Part 2," TCHP Series 10 (1914), 91; Smith, *David Smith*, 15. See also Levine, *Black Culture*; Raboteau, *Slave Religion*; Genovese, *Roll, Jordan, Roll*; Sobel, *Trabelin' On*.

27. September 14, 1792, Meacham Papers.

28. August 31, 1794, Colbert Journals; June 3, 1792, Meacham Papers, emphasis added.

29. JLFA, 2:128. Other antislavery sermons will be addressed in subsequent chapters.

30. July 4, 1790, Ezekiel Cooper Journals.

31. Ibid., July 4 and July 7, 1790.

32. July 15, 1791, and November 15, 1797, Kobler Journal.

33. Littlejohn Journal, typescript, 4.

34. June 5, 1792, Meacham Papers; October 30, 1793, Jeremiah Norman Diary.

35. Quoted in Jordan, *White Over Black*, 394. See also Mullin, *Flight and Rebellion*, 149–54. For a differeing interpretation, see Douglas R. Egerton, *Gabriel's Rebellion: The Virginia Slave Conspiracies of 1800 and 1802* (Chapel Hill: University of North Carolina Press, 1993).

36. Quoted in Jordan, *White Over Black*, 395, 396, 399.

37. Norwood, ed., *The Methodist Discipline of 1798*, 102, 169, 171.

38. Robert Armour, "The Virginia Reaction to the Antislavery Position of the Methodists During the Eighteenth Century," *Virginia United Methodist Heritage* 2 (Fall 1974), 12–17, quotation on 14.

39. June 29, 1800, Jeremiah Norman Diary; JLFA, 2:530. Brother I. West "lectured" on Ephesians 6; the verse was not specified and thus may have been any (or all) of the verses in this chapter. Meacham's words that "some of the blacks were much effected" indicate a positive reception to a sermon. Ezekiel Cooper spoke "pointedly" to blacks on their "duty," not specifying his text or theme. October 4, 1792, Meacham Papers; December 11, 1791, Ezekiel Cooper Papers. For Gruber's trial see John B. Boles, "Tension in a Slave Society: The Trial of the Reverend Jacob Gruber," *Southern Studies* 18 (1979), 179–97.

40. AM (February 1790), 94. See also June 15, 1781, Nelson Reed Diary; June 6, 1794, Colbert Journals.

41. Statistics from 1790 are found in *Minutes of the Annual Conferences*. For New Bern see Virginia Conference Minutes, Methodist Church Papers. For the western piedmont society see July 21, 1805, Mann Papers.

42. Lednum, *Rise of Methodism*, 154; JLFA, 1:57 and 2:622. For a black woman's withdrawal from the church, despite ministerial entreaties for her to stay, see January 19, 1798, Jeremiah Norman Diary.

43. Raboteau, *Slave Religion*; April 13, 1800, Jeremiah Norman Diary.

44. JLFA, 2:325. Richard Allen was evidently, in 1799, the first black to be ordained a deacon. See Carol V. R. George, *Segregated Sabbaths: Richard Allen and the Emergence of Independent Black Churches, 1760–1840* (New York: Oxford University Press, 1973), and Reginald F. Hildebrand, "Methodist Episcopal Policy on the Ordination of Black Ministers, 1784–1864," MethH 20:3 (April 1982), 124–42.

45. For contemporary accounts of Hosier see JLFA, 1:403; Simpson, ed., *American Methodist Pioneer*, 237–38, 266ff. For a nineteenth-century biography, see Lednum, *Rise of Methodism*, 282–83, and Wakeley, *Patriarch*, 90–92.

46. Redford, *Methodism in Kentucky*, 106–08.

47. For Jeremiah, see 1806 and 1807 in Mann Papers

48. *JLFA*, 2:524.

49. December 6, 1795, and July 21, 1800, Ormond Papers.

50. June 1, 1799, Whatcoat Journals. See also Andrews, "Popular Religion," 255; Bennett, *Methodism in Virginia*, 534.

51. *Memoir of Old Elizabeth, A Coloured Woman* (1863), reprinted in *Six Women's Slave Narratives* (New York: Oxford University Press, 1988). Black women did preach in Methodist churches in later years. See William L. Andrews, ed., *Sisters of the Spirit: Three Black Women's Autobiographies of the Nineteenth Century* (Bloomington: Indiana University Press, 1986).

52. Payne, *History of the African Methodist Episcopal Church*, 71–83. See also George, *Segregated Sabbaths*.

53. Jordan, *White Over Black*; Davis, *The Problem of Slavery in the Age of Revolution*; Duncan MacLeod, *Slavery, Race, and the American Revolution* (London: Cambridge University Press, 1974); Ira Berlin, *Slaves Without Masters: The Free Negro in the Antebellum South* (New York: Pantheon Books, 1974).

54. James P. Finley, *Sketches of Western Methodism: Biographical, Historical, and Miscellaneous* (Cincinnati: for the author, 1855), 380.

55. Genovese, *Roll, Jordan, Roll*, 255–79.

56. *JLFA*, 1:413, Jenkins, *Experience, Labours, and Sufferings*, 110. Manuscript accounts from 1770–1810 that were consulted for this study contain few statements as sweeping as Jenkins's. Henry Boehm wrote about Hosier's "fall" with no mention of his white audiences: "poor Harry was so petted and made so much of that he became lifted up." In Wakeley, *Patriarch*, 92.

57. For class leaders see Wightman, *Capers*, 138–39; Andrews, "Popular Religion," 255, 267; Smith, *David Smith*, 17, 25. Bilhartz, in *Urban Religion*, describes a Baltimore society with "8 black class leaders, 10 black exhorters, and 9 black local preachers" on 176, n. 19.

58. Archie Vernon Huff, Jr., *Tried by Fire: Washington Street United Methodist Church, Columbia, South Carolina* (Columbia: R. L. Bryan, 1975), 15.

59. December 8, 1805, January 19, January 26, February 2, February 6, February 11, April 27, 1806, September 5, 1810, Mann Papers; March 10, 1800, Jeremiah Norman Diary; October 12, 1794, Colbert Journals; September 1809, Rocky River and Montgomery Circuit Quarterly Meeting Minutes, Methodist Church Papers; Simpson, ed., *American Methodist Pioneer*, 62; and Luther P. Jackson, "Religious Development of the Negro in Virginia from 1760 to 1860," *JNH* 16:1 (April 1931), 168–239.

60. January 23, 1794, Colbert Journals. Black members also built a "large fine brick house" for Methodist worship in Lynchburg, Virginia. "Diary of John Early," *VMHB* 34:3 (1926), 249.

61. Young, *Autobiography of a Pioneer*, 90–91.

62. July 21, 1805, Mann Papers.

63. See, for example, Allan Gallay, "Planters and Slaves in the Great Awakening," in John B. Boles, ed., *Masters and Slaves in the House of the Lord: Race and Religion in the American South, 1740–1870* (Lexington: University Press of Kentucky, 1988), 35.

64. Herbert G. Gutman, *The Black Family in Slavery and Freedom, 1750–1925* (New York: Vintage Books, 1976), 216–27.

65. September 4, 1794, and October 11, 1794, Colbert Journals; Smith, *David Smith*, 24; Lednum, *Rise of Methodism*, 275; Payne, *History of the African Methodist Episcopal Church*, 74–75; October 18, 1790, Myles Greene Journal, Special Collections, Duke University.

66. Raboteau, *Slave Religion*, especially chapter 6. The black member who reported on the white member is in June 30, 1805, Mann Papers.

67. *JLFA*, 2:46; March 7, 1790, Meacham Papers. Itinerants were not allowed to own slaves in this era, but there was no such prohibition on local preachers.

68. Redford, *Methodism in Kentucky*, 370.

69. September 6, 1789, Whatcoat Journals; Finley, *Western Methodism*, 384–85; Payne, *History*

of the *African Methodist Episcopal Church*, 72–73. For the Goughs, see Lednum, *Rise of Methodism*, 154, and *JLFA*, 3:218.

70. Windley, compiler, *Runaway Slave Advertisements, Maryland*, 186–87.

71. Payne, *History of the African Methodist Episcopal Church*, 71–73.

72. Ibid., 73.

73. Ronald W. Long, "Religious Revivalism in the Carolinas and Georgia, 1740–1805," Ph.D. diss., University of Georgia, 1968, 202.

74. About slaves in Baltimore, he wrote: "[R]eligious reformation made this class of men and women better servants, and by their good behavior many of them became free." In *David Smith*, 20, 23.

75. For churches and slavery, see Donald G. Mathews, *Slavery and Methodism: A Chapter in American Morality, 1780–1845* (Princeton: Princeton University Press, 1965); Davis, *Problem of Slavery in the Age of Revolution;* H. Shelton Smith, *In His Image, But . . . : Racism in Southern Religion, 1780–1910* (Durham: Duke University Press, 1972); James Brewer Stewart, *Holy Warriors: The Abolitionists and American Slavery* (New York: Hill and Wang, 1976); Kenneth L. Carroll, "Religious Influences on the Manumission of Slaves in Carolina, Dorchester, and Talbot Counties," MHM 56:2 (June 1961), 176–97.

76. March 4, 1790, Meacham Papers.

77. Ibid. It is possible that this woman was formerly a slave of "bro. S." The fact that the adult male slave spoken of was enrolled for freedom indicates this owner may have been following the Methodist recommendations for manumission, in which slaves' ages (or for newly purchased slaves, their purchase price) was used to calculate their dates of manumission. As this incident also shows, Methodists were not opposed to corporal punishment for children.

78. *Memoir of Old Elizabeth*, 7.

79. Ibid., 4 and 6.

80. July 12, 1791, Kobler Journal.

81. Smith, *David Smith*, 12, 14; January 13, 1797, Meacham Papers.

82. Orlando Patterson's insights in *Freedom in the Making of Western Culture* (New York: Basic Books, 1991) are especially appropriate here.

83. *JLFA*, 1:403; Windley, compiler, *Runaway Slave Advertisements, Maryland*, 386, 401.

84. Quoted in Marjorie Moran Holmes, "The Life and Diary of the Reverend John Jeremiah Jacob (1757–1839)," Master's thesis, Duke University, 1941, 153; August 4, 1792, George Wells Journal.

85. Rose, "The Domestication of Domestic Slavery"; Peter Kolchin, "Re-Evaluating the Antebellum Slave Community: A Comparative Perspective," *JAH* 70 (1983), 582–88; Eugene Genovese, *The Political Economy of Slavery: Studies in the Economy and Society of the Slave South* (New York: Vintage Books, 1967).

86. Simpson, ed., *American Methodist Pioneer*, 227.

87. *Memoir of Old Elizabeth*, 10.

88. See, for example, the ads in Windley, compiler, *Runaway Slave Advertisements, Maryland;* Jordan, *White Over Black*, 150–51.

89. *Memoir of Old Elizabeth*, 7; Payne, *History of the African Methodist Episcopal Church*, 74.

90. *Memoir of Old Elizabeth*, 4 and 8.

91. Finley, *Western Methodism*, 382–84.

92. Ibid., 383.

93. September 9, 1790, and May 27, 1791, Meacham Papers.

94. September 2, 1790, February 23, 1792, Meacham Papers, and March 23, 1800, Jeremiah Norman Diary.

95. August 29, 1790, Colbert Journals; August 26, 1781, Nelson Reed Diary; May 10, 1795, Whatcoat Journals; June 16, 1801, the Journal of Noah Fidler, typescript loaned by Balti-

more-Washington United Methodist Historical Society, original at Upper Room Devotional Library and Museum, Nashville, Tennessee.

96. October 4, 1792, Meacham Papers; June 14, 1789, Myles Greene Journal; January 3, 1802, Boehm Journals; December 3, 1791, George Wells Journal; June 8, 1794, Whatcoat Journals.

97. May 11, 1794, Colbert Journals; May 26, 1777, August 7, 1777, Littlejohn Journal; November 7, 1789, October 9, 1792, Meacham Papers.

98. Levine, *Black Culture*; Raboteau, *Slave Religion*; Genovese, *Roll, Jordan, Roll*; Sobel, *Trabelin' On*.

99. July 19, 1800, Boehm Journals.

100. Few theologians were, by this time, claiming that blacks were a separate creation. Still, as Winthrop Jordan, in *White Over Black*, reminds us, there was a persistent tension between the idea that blacks were inferior to whites (as in constructs such as the "Great Chain of Being") and the idea that humans essentially differed from beasts in that they alone could attain salvation.

101. August 21, 1792, Meacham Papers.

102. Genovese, *Roll, Jordan, Roll*, 162–68, and John Jentz, "A Note on Genovese's Account of the Slaves' Religion," in Paul Finkelman, ed., *Religion and Slavery* (New York: Garland, 1989), 307–15. Quote from *JLFA*, 1:656.

103. M. H. Moore, *Sketches of the Pioneers of Methodism in North Carolina and Virginia* (Nashville: Southern Methodist Publishing House, 1884), 288; The Autobiography of John Young Sr., John Young, Sr., Papers, Special Collections, Duke University, 22.

104. *Memoir of Old Elizabeth*, 11–12.

105. *Memoir of Old Elizabeth*, 17; George, *Segregated Sabbaths*; Daniel Coker, *A Dialogue Between a Virginian and an African Minister* (Baltimore: Joseph James, 1810).

106. Windley, compiler, *Runaway Slave Advertisements, Maryland*, 183, 210, 270, 402.

107. January 29, 1800, Ormond Papers.

108. Coker, *Dialogue*, 16.

109. Coker was a member and clergyman in the Methodist Episcopal Church when he wrote this work. Coker used the term "Africans," denoting pride in origins, rather than the one used in the *Minutes*, "colored." See *Minutes of the Methodist Conferences Annually Held in America From 1773 to 1813, Inclusive*, volume 1 (New York: Hitt and Ware, for the Methodist Connexion in the United States, 1813). Coker also had to know that when he wrote, the vast majority of itinerant ministers in the church, especially in the nonurban areas, were white. The fact that former slaves like Coker and Allen left the Methodist Episcopal Church to form a body in which blacks would have more rights and privileges not only indicates the limits of white Methodist egalitarianism but also suggests that Methodism did not teach these men to be content with second-rate status. This is yet another example of the different ways blacks and whites interpreted the Methodist message.

110. Coker, *Dialogue*, 34.

111. January 12, 1789, Meacham Papers.

4: The Poverty of Riches

1. December 24, 1789, and July 12, 1793, Whatcoat Journals.

2. Schneider, "Ritual of Happy Dying," 351.

3. Johnson, *Shopkeeper's Millennium*. The masculine "he" is essential to this paradigm, for although Johnson acknowledges the female majority in revivals, he does not explicitly address women's role in promoting "bourgeois" values. The notion that evangelical women's interests mirrored those of bourgeois men is at the least unproved. Since women outnumbered men as members, we cannot infer that the majority of evangelical women came from middle-class

households simply by examining the class position of male members. See also Max Weber, *The Protestant Ethic and the Spirit of Capitalism*, trans. Talcott Parsons (London: Unwin Hyman, 1930), and Thompson, *Making of the English Working Class*, especially chapter 11.

4. Klein, *Unification of a Slave State*, chapter 9; Allan Kulikoff, *Tobacco and Slaves: The Development of Southern Culture in the Chesapeake, 1680–1800* (Chapel Hill: University of North Carolina Press, 1986); Isaac, *Transformation of Virginia*. See also Mathews, *Religion in the Old South*; Lewis, *Pursuit of Happiness*; Andrews, "Popular Religion"; Bilhartz, *Urban Religion*; Bruce, Jr., *Hallelujah*; Boles, "Revivalism, Renewal, and Social Mediation in the Old South," 60–83; Mary P. Ryan, *Cradle of the Middle Class: The Family in Oneida County, New York, 1790–1865* (Cambridge: Cambridge University Press, 1981); Loveland, *Southern Evangelicals*, especially chapter 6; T. Scott Miyakawa, *Protestants and Pioneers: Individualism and Conformity on the American Frontier* (Chicago: University of Chicago Press, 1964); Schneider, *Way of the Cross*; Williams, *Garden of Methodism*.

5. In this paradigm, there would be a peculiar form of "false consciousness" at work, one where neither exploiting masters (who opposed the church) nor exploited slaves (a number of whom joined the church) recognized their own self-interests.

6. Rhys Isaac, in *Transformation of Virginia*, portrays the Baptists as fashioning their ideology in reaction to the southern gentry. The Methodists do not fit with Isaac's paradigm because their views on wealth and ostentation were already formed in Britain.

7. *AM* (January 1789), 28–29.

8. Ibid., 32–33.

9. *The Methodist Discipline of 1798*, 134, 159.

10. *AM* (February 1790), 62.

11. Ibid., 63.

12. *AM* (January 1789), 29.

13. *AM* (April 1790), 174.

14. *The Methodist Discipline of 1798*, 134.

15. James Smith, "Tours into Kentucky and the Northwest Territory," *Ohio Archaeological and Historical Publications*, volume 16 (1907), 395. See also Michael J. McKay, ed., *The Journals of the Rev. Thomas Morrell* (Madison, New Jersey: Historical Society Northern New Jersey Conference, United Methodist Church, 1984), 16; "Observations on the N.W. Territory" (following the entries for April 1799), Kobler Journal.

16. For the "other-directed" nature of honor, see Wyatt-Brown, *Southern Honor*, 155. See Breen, *Tobacco Culture*, for planters' debts in this era. See also Kenneth S. Greenberg, *Honor and Slavery: Lies, Duels, Noses, Masks, Dressing as a Woman, Gifts, Strangers, Humanitarianism, Death, Slave Rebellions, the Proslavery Argument, Baseball, Hunting, and Gambling in the Old South* (Princeton: Princeton University Press, 1996); Steven M. Stowe, *Intimacy and Power in the Old South: Ritual in the Lives of the Planters* (Baltimore: Johns Hopkins University Press, 1987); Boles, "The Discovery of Southern Religious History," in John B. Boles and Evelyn Thomas Nolen, eds., *Interpreting Southern History: Historiographical Essays in Honor of Sanford W. Higginbotham* (Baton Rouge: Louisiana State University Press, 1987), 528.

17. This composite description is based on numerous anti-Methodist writings, explored at length in chapter 7. For the Revolution, see Bailyn, *Ideological Origins*, 272–300.

18. Simpson, ed., *American Methodist Pioneer*, 196; Jenkins, *Experience, Labours, and Sufferings*, 11–12.

19. The story of Lazarus is found in Luke 16:20ff. For sermons on this text, see Simpson, ed., *American Methodist Pioneer*, 182; "The Journal of Benjamin Lakin," 204; August 24, 1791, and September 3, 1791, Ormond Papers; *JLFA*, 1:179, 1:238.

20. This query is found in two places: Matthew 16:26 and Mark 8:36. For sermons on this query see November 5, 1807, July 5, July 7, July 9, July 13, July 17, July 20, 1810, Mann Papers; November 7, 1791, Ormond Papers; August 10, 1794, and August 12, 1794, Colbert Journals; Thrift, *Jesse Lee*, 94; McKay, ed., *The Journals of the Rev. Thomas Morrell*, 14, 19, 35, 36; *JLFA*, 1:69, 1:264, 1:379, 1:457.

21. Thrift, *Jesse Lee*, 94–95.

22. "Mrs. R. R. Experience," Ridgely-Pue Papers, MS. 693.

23. Simpson, ed., *American Methodist Pioneer*, 203 (emphasis added) and 256; October 7, 1789, November 22, 1789, Kobler Journal.

24. Wakeley, *Patriarch*, 132; January 2, 1789, Ezekiel Cooper Journals.

25. April 3, 1790, Ezekiel Cooper Journals.

26. Eleanor Dorsey to Harry Dorsey Gough, September 17, 1802, Gough-Carroll Papers, MS. 2560, Maryland Historical Society.

27. Ibid.

28. Ibid.

29. Thomas Lyell, Unnumbered Autobiographical Manuscript, Aldert Smedes Papers, Southern Historical Collection, University of North Carolina at Chapel Hill.

30. It is not clear whether Whatcoat is referring to Wilmington, Delaware, or Wilmington, North Carolina. Methodists in the coastal North Carolina city were poorer, and largely slaves and free blacks, and thus it is probably North Carolina to which he refers. December 27–28, 1792, January 14, 1793, June 5–7, 1793, Whatcoat Journals; Jenkins, *Experience, Labours, and Sufferings*, 70.

31. Jesse Lee, *Practical Piety, The Substance of a Sermond, Preached at a Watch-night Held in Johns-town, Delaware State. On November 18, 1783* (Baltimore: John Hagerty, 1814), 4–6.

32. *Extracts of Letters*, 95.

33. June 4, 1797, Kobler Journal.

34. Ibid., March 1 and September 25, 1795.

35. Bailyn, *Ideological Origins*; Gordon S. Wood, *The Radicalism of the American Revolution* (New York: Knopf, 1992); Isaac, *Transformation of Virginia*.

36. Isaac, *Transformation of Virginia*, 61–65. George Wells described a parson whose wig and gown "did not set well" with the audience. July 6, 1792, George Wells Journal.

37. See also Schneider, "Ritual of Happy Dying," 351; Miyakawa, *Protestants and Pioneers*, 49. Methodist preachers occasionally ascended into elevated pulpits to preach—when they "borrowed" the use of a meetinghouse from another sect.

38. Young, *Autobiography of a Pioneer*, 242–45.

39. Ibid.

40. Ibid., 86–87.

41. Henry Smith, *Recollections and Reflections of an Old Itinerant* (New York: Lane and Tippett, 1848), 13.

42. February 25, 1794, Kobler Journal.

43. Lee, *Short History*, 99.

44. Some preachers, especially those who entered in the nineteenth century, began to "affect the gentleman." See epilogue. William Capers, son of a wealthy slaveholder, is representative of the "gentleman-preacher" and his attitudes toward the poor were often patronizing and condescending. He does not, even in antebellum years, seem to have been typical. Wightman, *Capers*.

45. October, 1795 (page 106), Jeremiah Norman Diary; October 4, 1795, Ormond Papers.

46. *JLFA*, 2:523 and 1:608.

47. Lee, *Short History*, 131.

48. December 27–28, 1792, January 14, 1793, March 16, 1793, April 22, 1793, Whatcoat Journals.

49. Wakeley, *Patriarch*, 454; Simpson, ed., *American Methodist Pioneer*, 108; Redford, *Methodism in Kentucky*, 380. For the antebellum era, see Loveland, *Southern Evangelicals*, chapter 6. For Methodists' formal charity to the poor, see Andrews, "Popular Religion," 186, 193–94.

50. *JLFA*, 2:120; October 11, 1791, "A Journal and Travel of James Meacham, Part II, 1789–1797," TCHP Series 10 (1914), 91; June 11, 1796, Ormond Papers.

51. Undated sermon in George A. Reed Papers, Special Collections, Duke University; *JLFA*, 1:601 and 2:424.

52. James B. Finley, *Autobiography of Rev. James B. Finley; or, Pioneer Life in the West*, W. P. Strickland, ed. (Cincinnati: n.p. 1854), 260.

53. October 8, 1789, Kobler Journal.

54. Thomas Lyell, "Unnumbered Autobiographical Manuscript."

55. Kulikoff, *Tobacco and Slaves*, 424.

56. William Weems to Ezekiel Cooper, March 15, 1791, Ezekiel Cooper Collection.

57. Lee, *Short History*, 31; *JLFA*, 2:592; Redford, *Methodism in Kentucky*, 369. See also the subsequent discussion of manumission.

58. Breen, *Tobacco Culture*; Wyatt-Brown, *Southern Honor*; Mullin, *Flight and Rebellion*, chapter 1; Joan E. Cashin, *A Family Venture: Men and Women on the Southern Frontier* (New York: Oxford University Press, 1991); quotation from *JLFA*, 1:78.

59. See, for example, Joseph Travis, *Autobiography of the Rev. Joseph Travis, A.M., A Member of the Memphis Annual Conference.* (Nashville: E. Stevenson and F. A. Owen, for the Methodist Episcopal Church, South, 1856), 56.

60. Wakeley, *Patriarch*, 429. For Bassett, see Williams, "Delaware and the Methodist Revolution," 264–98; John Munroe, "Delaware and the Constitution: An Overview of Events Leading to Ratification," *DelH* 22:4 (Fall–Winter 1987), 219–41.

61. Wakeley, *Patriarch*, 427–29; *Extracts of Letters*, 19, 25–27; Williams, "Delaware and the Methodist Revolution," 296–97.

62. *Extracts of Letters*, 19, 25–27.

63. James H. Keys to Edward Dromgoole, August 3, 1810, Dromgoole Papers.

64. Simpson, ed., *American Methodist Pioneer*, 256; *JLFA*, 1:561; early Methodist minister quoted in *North Carolina Christian Advocate* (January 19, 1933), 13.

65. August 25, 1794, Colbert Journals.

66. Young, *Autobiography of a Pioneer*, 116.

67. For "rabble," see Don Higginbotham, "Methodism Moves East: Annual Conference, New Bern, North Carolina, 1807," *The Wesleyan Quarterly Review* 1 (1964), 41; for "enthusiasts" see Elizabeth Connor, *Methodist Trail Blazer: Philip Gatch, 1751–1834* (Rutland: Academy Books, 1970), 3; for "Negro church" see Huff, Jr., *Tried by Fire*, 14. See also Williams, "Delaware and the Methodist Revolution," 290. Richard Rankin in *Ambivalent Churchmen* argues that elite women were more receptive to Methodism than elite men.

68. February 15, 1792, Ormond Papers. For mobs led by the wealthy, see, for example, John Harper to Ezekiel Cooper, [1800], Ezekiel Cooper Collection.

69. Williams, "Delaware and the Methodist Revolution," 289.

70. Mathews, *Religion in the Old South*, 36.

71. Lee, *Short History*, 71, 98–99.

72. *AM* (April 1790), 170–75, quotation on 170.

73. James Smith, "Tours into Kentucky and the Northwest Territory," 377. Miyakawa describes the success of many Ohio Methodists in *Protestants and Pioneers.*

74. A point previously made by Williams, "Delaware and the Methodist Revolution." See also Ford, Jr., *Southern Radicalism*.

75. Lee, *Short History*, 31–32.

76. For the development of long-range moral responsibility. Thomas L. Haskell, "Capitalism and the Origins of the Humanitarian Sensibility, Part 1," *AHR* 90:2 (April 1985), 339–61, and "Capitalism and the Origins of the Humanitarian Sensibility, Part 2," *AHR* 90:3 (June 1985), 547–66.

77. November 21, 1810, Mann Papers.

78. Lee, *Short History*, 32.

79. This perceptive and eloquent phrasing is that of Boles in "Discovery of Southern Regional History," 528.

80. February 16, 1790, Meacham Papers.

81. July 6, 1791, Colbert Journals.

5: "Mothers in Israel"

1. July 28–29, 1798, Kobler Journal.

2. Mary Hinde's son wrote under the pseudonym "Theophilus Arminius" in MMag 10:8 (August 1827), 369.

3. For the "feminization" of American religion, see Barbara Welter, "The Feminization of American Religion: 1800–1860," in Mary S. Hartman and Lois Banner, eds., *Clio's Consciousness Raised* (New York: Haper Torchbooks, 1973); Harry S. Stout and Catherine A. Brekus, "Declension, Gender, and the 'New Religious History,'" and Terry D. Bilhartz, "Sex and the Second Great Awakening: The Feminization of American Religion Reconsidered," both in Philip R. Vandemeer and Robert P. Swierenga, eds., *Belief and Behavior: Essays in the New Religious History* (New Brunswick: Rutgers University Press, 1991). For southern women's religion, see Friedman, *Enclosed Garden*; Gillespie, "1795: Martha Laurens Ramsay's 'Dark Night of the Soul'"; Joan R. Gundersen, "The Non-Institutional Church: The Religious Role of Women in Eighteenth-Century Virginia," *Historical Magazine of the Protestant Episcopal Church* 51 (December 1982), 347–57; Cynthia Kierner, "Woman's Piety Within Patriarchy: The Religious Life of Martha Hancock Wheat of Bedford County," *VMHB* (January 1992), 79–98; Lewis, *Pursuit of Happiness*; William L. Lumpkin, "The Role of Women in 18th Century Virginia Baptist Life," *Baptist History and Heritage* 8 (July 1973), 158–67; Rankin, *Ambivalent Churchmen*; Schneider, *Way of the Cross*; John H. Wigger, "Taking Heaven by Storm: Enthusiasm and Early American Methodism, 1770–1820," *Journal of the Early Republic* 14:2 (Summer 1994), 167–94; Andrews, "Popular Religion." Donald G. Mathews, in *Religion in the Old South*, includes a brief yet brilliant discussion of southern women and religion. Many conclusions reached here owe an immense debt to those informed pages in Mathews.

4. What women's involvement in evangelical churches meant for women, men, families, and gender relations has not been a matter of historiographical consensus. Historians studying northern evangelicals argue that churches offered opportunities for women's self-expression and moral leadership and enhanced their pride and self-esteem. See Cott, "Young Women in the Second Great Awakening in New England" and *The Bonds of Womanhood: "Woman's Sphere" in New England, 1780–1835* (New Haven: Yale University Press, 1977); Hardesty, *Your Daughters Shall Prophesy*. Susan Juster, in *Disorderly Women: Sexual Politics and Evangelicalism in Revolutionary New England* (Ithaca: Cornell University Press, 1994), argues that New England Baptists became more patriarchal and discriminatory toward female members after the Revolution.

Donald Mathews, in *Religion in the Old South*, sees southern evangelical churches as performing many of the same functions Cott found in the North (104). By contrast, Jean Friedman, in *Enclosed Garden*, maintains that evangelical churches in the years 1830 to 1900 isolated white women from nonkin, restricted their activities to those approved by men, offered white women very few leadership opportunities, and used disciplinary procedures to punish women for violating gender conventions. Rachel Klein's *Unification of a Slave State* (chapter 9) compellingly portrays early South Carolina evangelicals, especially the Baptists, largely as defenders of patriarchy and white male authority.

5. Wyatt-Brown, *Southern Honor*; Breen, *Tobacco Culture*; Cashin, *A Family Venture*; Mullin, *Flight and Rebellion*, chapter 1; and McCurry, "The Two Faces of Republicanism."

6. Schneider, *Way of the Cross*; Mathews, *Religion in the Old South*, 111. Early Methodists assumed that there were fundamental differences between the sexes but did not attempt, as later Meth-

odists did, to confine women's piety to the home, or to bifurcate male and female spheres of influence.

7. See John Wesley, Sermon V, in MMag (June 1797), 241–55. Wesley gave special attention to mothers but does not describe motherhood as women's only or highest duty. A short piece, "A Pattern for Christian Wives," used St. Augustine's mother to suggest how women with impious husbands could win them over to the faith. AM (September 1790), 464. For bold women in the "Letters" section, see AM (June 1790), 303, and MMag (April 1797), 188.

8. AM (July 1789), 336–37. Italics in original. Unlike previous interpreters, Methodists did not believe that women became "male" in Heaven.

9. John 1:47. For Israelites without guile, see, for example, JLFA, 1:55, 1:419, 2:81, 2:93, 2:517. For Wesley's sermon, see AM (September 1790), 425–34.

10. Judges 5:7. For Ridgely, see Francis Asbury to Rebecca Ridgely, May 24, 1804, and May 7, 1810, Ridgely-Pue Papers. For "barrenness," see Wyatt-Brown, Southern Honor, 236–38. For the others, see, in order, November 27, 1789, Ezekiel Cooper Journals; Phinney et al., eds., Thomas Ware, 80; Simpson, ed., American Methodist Pioneer, 65; December 20, 1799, Jeremiah Norman Diary; April 18, 1797, Meacham Papers. For a differing interpretation of "mothers in Israel," see Schneider in Way of the Cross, 194.

11. JLFA, 2:599, 2:628. See also Wakeley, Patriarch, 198, 230, 442; March 16, 1803, May 29, 1803, Ormond Papers.

12. Charles F. Deems, ed., Annals of Southern Methodism for 1856 (Nashville, Tennessee: Stevenson & Owen, 1857), 242–43.

13. August 7, 1790, Meacham Papers; JLFA, 1:518; July 7, 1779, Nelson Reed Diary; Sarah Hagerty to Edward Dromgoole, February [25], 1775, Dromgoole Papers. For Sarah Jones, see her letters to Edward Dromgoole in Dromgoole Papers; August 14, 1789, "A Journal and Travel of James Meacham," TCHP Series 9 (1912), 87; Jones, Devout Letters.

14. Historical Sketch of Wilkes County, North Carolina, Methodist Church Papers; Young, Autobiography of a Pioneer, 123–24.

15. Over time, disciplinary proceedings became more formalized. Jeremiah Norman recorded several "trials," including one "bundling" case in which six men and six women were "jurors." See, for example, June 11, July 1, 1799, and October 3, 1800, Jeremiah Norman Diary. Rates of discipline and dispositions of cases varied from preacher to preacher. The gender differences here do not mirror those found in New England Baptist churches. Quarreling was, in southern Methodism, a male and female offense. Nor do Methodists accuse women of usurping preachers' authority in discipline. See Juster, Disorderly Women.

16. The count was taken from James Meacham's journals in Meacham Papers. Disciplinary cases against preachers were not counted. The disposition, where given, of Meacham's cases were Expulsions—7 men, 8 women, 17 unknown gender; Suspensions—2 men, 3 women. The offenses were Disputes between members—2 men, 2 women, 2 unknown; Marrying an unbeliever—2 women, 1 unknown; Slave trading—3 men, 3 unknown; Nonattendance—2 women; Immorality—2 men; Drunkenness and fighting—1 man; Sexual immorality—1 man, 1 woman; Violating the Sabbath—i man; Attending a ball—1 woman, 1 unknown. The specific offenses were not listed in the cases of 3 women, 1 man, and 12 of unknown gender.

17. This count is taken from Whatcoat's original journals owned by Garrett-Evangelical Theological Seminary and the Library of Congress, microfilm of both at University of Chicago Divinity Library. Preachers such as Whatcoat and Meacham were not stationed in a single society, but were on circuits. The rate of expulsion is for the entire circuit and not a single society.

18. Figures are from the Edenton Methodist Church Record Book, microfilm, Southern Historical Collection. I did not include black members in my count of discipline, and they account for very few disciplinary cases.

19. Doris Andrew's intriguingly argues that this rule increased young Methodist women's authority over their choice of marriage partners. See "Popular Religion," 178.

20. Rankin, in *Ambivalent Churchmen*, argues that for elite women, dress was a form of self-expression analogous to the avenues in churches (33–34). The primary purposes of dress for single women was to aid in courtship, and for married, to reflect their family's status. Dress was thus intimately connected with women's relationships to others. The major difference between the two forms of self-expression is that dress is mute, and as such was acceptable to elite men in a way that women's public speaking was not.

21. Cooper to Thomas Coke, August 28, 1789, Ezekiel Cooper Collection.

22. Pregnancies: November 20, 1810, Mann Papers and May 14, 1792, Colbert Journals; adultery: McKay, ed., *The Journals of the Rev. Thomas Morrell*, 10; couple, November 5, 1807, Mann Papers; young man and woman, July 25–26, 1794, Meacham Papers. There was another woman who already had been expelled when Littlejohn noted her pregnancy. October 22, 1777, Littlejohn Journal. If the second party to a sexual offense was not a member (and men were far less likely to be members than women), then the church would have no jurisdiction over him or her. Thus, the fact that pregnant women were expelled does not in and of itself prove a double standard. For a different interpretation, see Friedman, *Enclosed Garden*.

23. July 30, 1772, *Virginia Gazette*.

24. Thomas Lyell Autobiography, Aldert Smedes Papers, Southern Historical Collection. For audiences dominated by women, see, for example, JLFA, 2:31, 2:41, 2:285.

25. Phinney et al., eds., *Thomas Ware*, 92–93. White women, it seems safe to say, outnumbered men by at least three to two. See also the Edenton Methodist Church Book, M-3075, Southern Historical Collection. Only two Edenton women shared a surname with the male members. See also Andrews, "Popular Religion," 171.

26. Huff, Jr., *Tried by Fire*, 14; 1776, Littlejohn Journal, typescript, 13; Lednum, *Rise of Methodism*, 249. Another way to discover who within families first joined the church is ministers' journals. Clergy referred to members normally as "Brother" and "Sister" and nonmembers as "Mister," "Miss," and "Mrs." (and occasionally by military rank or "Esquire"). Tracing the order in which people in families converted is often possible. Later church histories tend to blur the fact that women preceded men into the church by making claims for couples that should be made only for the wives. For northern women evangelists, see Paul Johnson, *A Shopkeeper's Millennium*.

27. Wilkes County, Historical Sketches, Methodist Church Papers; for Triplett, see December 4, 1791, Ezekiel Cooper Journals; JLFA, 1:89 and 1:697.

28. June 1778–February 1779, Nelson Reed Diary. See also 1797, Meacham Papers; June 28, 1789, Myles Greene Journal.

29. Letters from Francis Asbury to Rebecca Ridgely in Ridgely-Pue Papers, MS. 693; "Diary of John Early," *VMHB* 34:2 (April 1926), 133; July 18, 1805, December 28, 1805, Mann Papers; JLFA, 1:758; Young, *Autobiography of a Pioneer*, 104. See also Cartwright, *Autobiography of Peter Cartwright* (Nashville: Abingdon Press, 1856), 74.

30. JLFA, 1:106, 1:532.

31. February 27, 1793, Meacham Papers; June 14, 1794, Kobler Journal; June 5, 1796, Ormond Papers.

32. Jones, *Devout Letters*, 28–29, 47; Stith Mead, *A Short Account of the Experience and Labors of the Rev. Stith Mead* (Lynchburg: n.p., 1829), 9.

33. See Albert M. Shipp, *The History of Methodism in South Carolina* (Nashville: Southern Methodist Publishing House, 1884), 276; *Extracts of Letters*, 50; discussion in chapter 7 herein.

34. Ibid., 69.

35. Mary Avery Browder to Edward Dromgoole, November 1777, copy, Dromgoole Papers.

36. For a discussion of the gendered nature of individualism, see Kerber, "Women and Individualism."

37. Shipp, *Methodism in South Carolina*, 175–76; December 19, 1791, George Wells Journal.

38. Redford, *Methodism in Kentucky*, 308; *MMag* (November 1826), 408; *MMag* (November 1820), 446; see also *MMag* (December 1822), 446.

39. Young, *Autobiography of a Pioneer*, 42–43; *MMag* (July 1818), 275; Redford, *Methodism in Kentucky*, volume 2, 87.

40. John A. Munroe, ed., "James Hemphill's Account of a Visit to Maryland in 1802," *DelH* 3:2 (September 1948), 67; *JLFA*, 2:34.

41. Ulrich, *Good Wives*, 239.

42. *JLFA*, 1:524; April 4, 1794, Colbert Journals; January 11, 1795, Whatcoat Journals. See also April 6, 1794, Kobler Journal.

43. Phinney et al., eds., *Thomas Ware*, 90.

44. "A Journal and Travel of James Meacham," *TCHP* Series 10 (1914), 92–93.

45. November 27, 1810, Mann Papers; Travis, *Autobiography of the Rev. Joseph Travis*, 62; William E. Smith, ed., *Memoirs of a Methodist Circuit Rider—Francis Wilson* (Austin, Texas: for the editor, 1983), 11; *MMag* (November 1826), 408; Thrift, *Jesse Lee*, 97. Prudence Hudson's dying admonition to her husband was to warn him against keeping slaves. See Lednum, *Rise of Methodism*, 345. See also woman in Smith, *Recollections*, 109.

46. "The Diary of John Early," *VMHB* 34:2 (April 1926), 133; *JLFA*, 2:360; June 14, 1796, April 23, 1797, Jeremiah Norman Diary.

47. For class leaders, see Lednum, *Rise of Methodism*, 89–90, 187, 270; *JLFA*, 2:136; and November 27, 1792, January 16, 1793, June 11, 1793, July 9, 1793, July 23, 1793, August 13, 1793, Whatcoat Journals; Simpson, ed., *American Methodist Pioneer*, 237; Andrews, "Popular Religion," 200 and 216, n. 68. For Smith, see *Recollections*, 252. The careful reader suspects that there were more female class leaders who were not explicitly identified as such. Nelson Reed met "a class all of the female sex" at Sister Woodward's in 1779. It may well be that this class had a female at its head. See March 17, 1779, Nelson Reed Diary. There are other female class leaders mentioned but not by name. Compare also *JLFA*, 1:66 and Lednum, *Rise of Methodism*, 90.

48. *JLFA*, 2:428, 1:697; January 8, 1811, Boehm Journals.

49. *JLFA*, 1:735, 1:748; March 21, 1791, Ezekiel Cooper Journals; Bennett, *Methodism in Virginia*, 483. Black women, as we saw in a previous chapter, also led prayer meetings.

50. Lednum, *Rise of Methodism*, 115; Wakeley, *Patriarch*, 43; *JLFA*, 3:431; Charles F. Deems, ed., *Annals of Methodism for 1856* (Nashville: Stevenson & Owen, 1857), 243.

51. Finley, *Western Methodism*, 533–36.

52. August 3, 1777, September 21, 1777, Littlejohn Journal.

53. We cannot conclude that there was official prohibition against women's preaching merely because of the use in the *Discipline* of the terms "man," "men," "brethren," or other masculine pronouns. Methodists used masculine nouns and pronouns as collective references throughout the *Discipline*. Modern evidence shows that such practices have discriminatory impact, but in this, as in many other matters, early male Methodists were products of their time.

54. Mead, *A Short Account*, note on 16; Lednum, *Rise of Methodism*, 270. For women's prayer in the antebellum era, see Kierner, "Women's Piety Within Patriarchy."

55. Dorothy Ripley, *The Extraordinary Conversion and Religious Experience of Dorothy Ripley, With Her First Voyage and Travels in America* (New York: for the author, 1810), 113–18, 152.

56. *JLFA*, 2:31.

57. Terry Bilhartz, in *Urban Religion*, writes that in Baltimore, stewards, class leaders, and trustees tended to be more prominent and wealthier than the average member. He analyzes the wealth of white males and thus his conclusions about class leaders (although not stewards and trustees) would need to be modified if black class leaders and women class leaders were taken into account. Bilhartz suggests that Maryland law restricted trustees to white males (31).

58. Friedman, *Enclosed Garden*, 9, 18–19; Williams, "Delaware and the Methodist Revolution,"

280–81. As Williams indicates in n. 20, it was Delaware state law that prohibited women from voting in churches.

59. In one important sense these three women were unrepresentative: their families all had some wealth. Jones's husband owned over 70 slaves. Russell's husband owned a saltworks. Hinde's husband was a physician. Methodist lay sources favor the literate and the upper class. Numerous common women named and unnamed who were equal to these three in their zeal, defiance, and self-assertion do appear in ministers' journals and church periodicals, although we know less of their circumstances.

60. Phinney et al., eds., *Thomas Ware*, 167–69.

61. See Minter's introduction to Jones, *Devout Letters; JLFA*, 2:34; April [6], 1806, Mann Papers; May 21, 1790, and August 4, 1790, Meacham Papers.

62. *Devout Letters*, 23, 36, 143.

63. Phinney et al., eds., *Thomas Ware*, 167; April 24–25, 1790, Meacham Papers; *JLFA*, 1:510–11, 2:34. Jeremiah Norman even noted of Tignal Jones that "it is said his wife is the greatest woman [in the dominion?]." December 28, 1793, Jeremiah Norman Diary.

64. Jones, *Devout Letters*, 109.

65. Ibid., 99, 124–25, 130–31.

66. Redford, *Methodism in Kentucky*, 326, 373–76.

67. Ibid., 326, 374–75.

68. Ibid., 368–69; Wakeley, *Patriarch*, 406.

69. Young, *Autobiography of a Pioneer*, 128; Thomas L. Preston, *A Sketch of Mrs. Elizabeth Russell. Wife of General William Campbell, and Sister of Patrick Henry* (Nashville: Publishing House of the M. E. Church, South, 1888), 42. See also Phinney et al., eds., *Thomas Ware*, 152–53; Elva Runyon, "Madame Russell, Methodist Saint," Master's thesis, University of Virginia, 1941.

70. Preston, *Mrs. Elizabeth Russell*, 29.

71. Young, *Autobiography of a Pioneer*, 129; Preston, *Mrs. Elizabeth Russell*, 37–38; and Runyon, "Madame Russell," 57–58.

72. See also Mathews, *Religion in the Old South*, 104.

73. March 30, 1792, Meacham Papers; Lednum, *Rise of Methodism*, 164.

74. May 19, 1792, July 4, 1792, Ormond Papers; September 5, 1792, Meacham Papers.

75. Isaac, *Transformation of Virginia*; Wyatt-Brown, *Southern Honor*; Cashin, *A Family Venture*; Morgan, *American Slavery, American Freedom*; Breen, *Tobacco Culture*.

76. Philip J. Greven, *The Protestant Temperament: Patterns of Child-Rearing, Religious Experience, and the Self in Early America* (New York: Knopf, 1977). For southern men and religion, see Rankin, *Ambivalent Churchmen*, and Christopher Waldrep, "The Making of a Border State Society: James McGready, the Great Revival, and the Prosecution of Profanity in Kentucky," *AHR* 99:3 (June 1994), 767–84. See Smith, *Recollections*, 293. Several aspects of Methodist theology may well have made them seem more of a threat than other dissenting groups. Unlike the Quakers, who were the most progressive sect when it came to women, Methodists aggressively and successfully proselytized. The Baptists posed a gendered threat, yet they did not initially promote free will and thus did not place as much emphasis on the individual's agency.

77. Simpson, ed., *American Methodist Pioneer*, 71.

78. Joanna Bowen Gillespie, "'The Sun in Their Domestic System': The Mother in Early Nineteenth Century Methodist Sunday School Lore," in Rosemary Skinner Keller, Louise L. Queen, and Hilah F. Thomas, eds., *Women in New Worlds*, volume 2, *Historical Perspectives on the Wesleyan Tradition* (Nashville: Abingdon Press, 1982).

79. *MMag* (May 1797), 198. The biographer of Jacob Gruber told a grim story that illustrates that the rules were well known and also that not every clergyman was as enlightened as Wesley. A Methodist, persecuted and verbally abused by his wife, left the church because he could not beat her while he was a member. According to Strickland, the woman, after being

beaten, converted. The attitude taken by the narrator is not typical. Precious few preachers would have approved of a member withdrawing in order to be able to break church rules. W. P. Strickland, *The Life of Jacob Gruber* (New York: Carlton and Porter, 1860), 71.

80. John Young Autobiography, 24, John Young, Sr., Papers; July 19, 1797, Meacham Papers; Shipp, *Methodism in South Carolina*, 185. See also Andrews, "Popular Religion," 179–81.

81. JLFA, 2:457.

82. MMag (August 1822), 306–10.

83. Quoted in Rankin, *Ambivalent Churchmen*, 36.

84. "The Diary of John Early," VMHB 34:4 (October 1926), 306.

85. For Wesley on childrearing, see Greven, *Protestant Temperament*. Children were counseled, for example, to "Do every thing which your father or mother bids, be it great or small, provided it not be contrary to any command of God." He repeated this caveat three times. In MMag (September 1797), 388–89.

86. Lednum, *Rise of Methodism*, 344.

87. Lewis, *Pursuit of Happiness*.

88. Sarah Miller to Daniel Shine, July 9, 1809, Daniel Shine Papers.

89. July 22, 1778, July 27, 1778, Nelson Reed Diary.

90. "Mrs. R. R. Experience," in Ridgely-Pue Papers, MS. 693.

91. Fredrika Teute Schmidt and Barbara Ripel Wilhelm, "Early Proslavery Petitions in Virginia," WMQ 30:1 (1973), 133–46, especially 143; Jenkins, *Experiences, Labours, and Sufferings*, 136; July 21, 1805, Mann Papers; April 20, 1790, Meacham Papers; Young, *Autobiography of a Pioneer*, 91. For women who hosted meetings for blacks in their homes, see, for example, April 1, 1801, Boehm Journals; February 17, April 7, May 11, September 30, and October 5, 1794, Colbert Journals; October 14, 1794, Meacham Papers; April 22, 1795, Whatcoat Journals.

92. John M'Lean, *Sketch of Rev. Philip Gatch* (Cincinnati: Swormstedt & Poe, 1854), 46; May 8–9, 1778; Littlejohn Journal. For the war era, see Simpson, ed., *American Methodist Pioneer*, 82–83. Because of Methodism's association during the war with Toryism, pacifism, and slave insurrection, women's defense of their preachers takes on added political and cultural significance.

93. JLFA, 2:41; for Kugley, see Deems, ed., *Annals of Southern Methodism for 1856*, 228; Deems, ed., *Annals of Southern Methodism for 1855*, 250.

94. For antebellum individualism in the white South, see Fox-Genovese, *Within the Plantation Household*, 63.

95. Jones, *Devout Letters*, 120, italics in original. This chapter has benefited from the rich literature on white southern women, including Fox-Genovese, *Within the Plantation Household*; Cashin, *A Family Venture*; Suzanne Lebsock, *The Free Women of Petersburg: Status and Culture in a Southern Town, 1784–1860* (New York: Norton, 1984); Anne Firor Scott, *The Southern Lady: From Pedestal to Politics, 1830–1930* (Chicago: University of Chicago Press, 1970); Victoria E. Bynum, *Unruly Women: The Politics of Social and Sexual Control in the Old South* (Chapel Hill: University of North Carolina Press, 1992).

6: Slavery, Racism, and the Master-Slave Relationship

1. M'Lean, *Philip Gatch*, 102. The use of "empathy" in this chapter (a term from a later era) is somewhat anachronistic but "sympathy" inadequately conveys what early Methodists and their contemporaries meant. When Methodists urged whites to "feel another's pain" (see below) they had in mind more than sympathy.

2. Connor, *Methodist Trail Blazer*.

3. For slavery and early antislavery efforts, see, for example, Mathews, *Slavery and Methodism*; Davis, *Problem of Slavery in the Age of Revolution*; Baker, *From Wesley to Asbury*; Calhoon, *Evangelicals and Conservatives*; Essig, *Bonds of Wickedness*; Smith, *In His Image, But . . .*; Frey, *Water from the Rock*; Klein, *Unification of a Slave State*, chapter 9.

4. See Haskell, "Capitalism and the Origins of the Humanitarian Sensibility," Parts 1 and 2.

5. See *JLFA*, 1:10; *Extracts of Letters*, 25; Glen A. McAninch, "We'll Pray for You: Methodist Ethnocentrism in the Origins of the African Methodist Episcopal Church in Baltimore," Master's thesis, University of North Carolina at Chapel Hill, 1973.

6. Methodists did not write tracts about the origins of racial difference—we find these references only incidentally in clergymen's journals. For Ham, see March 24, 1790, Colbert Journals.

7. McKay, ed., *Journals of the Rev. Thomas Morrell*, 14; June 1, 1799, Whatcoat Journals.

8. Strickland, *Gruber*, 52.

9. For scholars who emphasize the inequalities in churches, see Klein, *Unification of a Slave State*; Frey, *Water from the Rock*; Raboteau, *Slave Religion*; McAninch, "We'll Pray for You."

10. Methodists did not use the Ham myth to justify racially based bondage. For Ham, see Jordan, *White Over Black*; Thomas Virgil Peterson, *Ham and Japheth: The Mythic World of Whites in the Antebellum South* (Metuchen, N.J.: Scarecrow Press, 1978); Tise, *Proslavery*. The few extant references to slavery's origins, discussed below, suggest that Methodists traced slavery's origins to the era of Moses.

11. January 8, 1789, Meacham Papers; Simpson, ed., *American Methodist Pioneer*, 65; Wakeley, *Patriarch*, 214. McAninch, in "We'll Pray for You," argues that such language was also condescending, yet the numerous references to whites as "poor" suggests that the term was used for many different groups.

12. Paine, *M'Kendree*, 125.

13. "A Journal and Travel of James Meacham," *TCHP* Series 9 (1912), 88.

14. Charles William Janson, *The Stranger in America, 1793–1806* (New York: Press of the Pioneers, 1935), 101. It is possible that Janson attended an unsegregated service, but the date suggests this is highly unlikely.

15. Wightman, *Capers*, 137.

16. November 14, 1789, Meacham Papers.

17. December 23, 1790, Ezekiel Cooper Journals.

18. January 18, 1794, Kobler Journal.

19. *Calendar of the Ezekiel Cooper Collection of Early American Methodist Manuscripts, 1785–1839* (Chicago: Illinois Historical Records Survey project, 1941), 11. For Asbury, see Norwood, ed., *Soucebook*, 39.

20. Frank Baker, "The Origins, Character, and Influence of John Wesley's *Thoughts upon Slavery*," *MethH* 22:2 (January 1984), 75–86.

21. Quoted in Mathews, *Slavery and Methodism*, 5.

22. John Wesley, *Thoughts Upon Slavery* (London: n.p., 1774).

23. Ibid., 50.

24. Haskell, "Capitalism and the Origins of the Humanitarian Sensibility," Parts 1 and 2.

25. Wesley, *Thoughts Upon Slavery*, 46.

26. Ibid., 53.

27. Frederick E. Maser and Howard T. Maag, eds., *The Journal of Joseph Pilmore: Methodist Itinerant* (Philadelphia: Historical Society of the Philadelphia Annual Conference of the United Methodist Church, 1969), 74.

28. Maser and Maag, eds., *Joseph Pilmore*, 107. See also *JLFA*, 1:190; June 6, 1794, Colbert Journals; *AM* (February 1790), 94; Norwood, ed., *Sourcebook*, 41; March 4, 1790, Meacham Papers.

29. *Minutes of the Annual Conferences, 1773–1828*; September 29–31, 1796, Ormond Papers.

30. *Minutes of the Annual Conferences*.

31. "The Journal of Thomas Coke," *AM* (July 1789), 345; Daniel Grant to John Owen, Jr., [1792], Campbell Family Papers; Thrift, *Jesse Lee*, 244.

32. Merton L. Dillon, *Slavery Attacked: Southern Slaves and Their Allies, 1619–1865* (Baton Rouge:

Louisiana State University Press, 1990), especially chapter 5; Armour, "The Virginia Reaction," 12–17; Robert K. MacMaster, "Liberty or Property? The Methodists Petition for Emancipation in Virginia, 1785," *MethH* 10 (October 1971), 43–55; *JLFA*, 1:489.

33. Schmidt and Wilhelm, "Early Proslavery Petitions," 136.

34. Ibid., 139, 141–45.

35. Ibid., 138. For Anglophobia, see Greenberg, *Masters and Statesmen*. For more on these proslavery petitions, see Calhoon, *Evangelicals and Conservatives*, 125–28.

36. Schmidt and Wilhelm, "Early Proslavery Petitions," 139.

37. Ibid., 138–46. The count is only for the petitions written in response to the Methodist actions.

38. "The Journal of Thomas Coke," 344–45; *JLFA*, 1:488, 1:498.

39. *Minutes of the Annual Conferences.*

40. For Charleston, see Deems, ed., *Annals of Southern Methodism for 1855*, 249–50; Deems, ed., *Annals of Southern Methodism for 1856*, 228; [1800], John Harper to Ezekiel Cooper, Ezekiel Cooper Collection.

41. [1800], John Harper to Ezekiel Cooper, Ezekiel Cooper Collection. Harper sent Cooper clippings of his newspaper statement.

42. Jenkins, *Experience, Labours, and Sufferings*, 97.

43. Quoted in Dillon, *Slavery Attacked*, 107.

44. *JLFA*, 2:272.

45. Young, *Autobiography of a Pioneer*, 249–50.

46. For abolition societies, see April 16, 1790, August 27, 1792, and November 27, 1794, Meacham Papers; Mathews, *Slavery and Methodism*, 14. Methodist names can also be found in Constitution of the Maryland Society, *For Promoting the Abolition of Slavery, and the Relief of Free Negroes, and Others, Unlawfully Held in Bondage* (Baltimore: Goddard & Angell, 1789), 8. For Delaware, see Williams, *Garden of American Methodism*, 164–65. For Boehm, see Wakeley, *Patriarch*, 69.

47. *JLFA*, 2:109.

48. It is impossible to quantify which effort actually caused which master or mistress to liberate slaves. The evidence suggests that the timing of manumission decisions was directly related to personal pressure from other Methodists. The sources are predisposed to credit clerical appeals, however, which is why the cause and effect cannot clearly be measured.

49. Wakeley, *Patriarch*, 26; *JLFA*, 1:582.

50. Redford, *Methodism in Kentucky*, 127–30.

51. Simpson, ed., *American Methodist Pioneer*; Ormond Papers; Meacham Papers; Wakeley, *Patriarch*; Kobler Journal.

52. *JLFA*, 1:656.

53. November 15, 1797, and April 1799, Kobler Journal; Mathews, *Religion in the Old South*, 74.

54. For one of the few references to honor in Methodist antislavery, see November 26, 1794, Kobler Journal. Even here, the honor Kobler speaks of is qualitatively different from the culture of southern honor.

55. "A Journal and Travel of James Meacham," *TCHP* Series 9 (1912), 79.

56. *JLFA*, 2:149; Norwood, ed., *The Methodist Discipline of 1798*, 138–39; April 18, 1791, Ezekiel Cooper Collection.

57. See, for example, September 15, 1791, Daniel Grant to John Owen, Jr., Campbell Family Papers; Simpson, ed., *American Methodist Pioneer*, 234; August 22, 1790, Meacham Papers; Carroll, "Religious Influences," 192; Henry C. Conrad, *Samuel White and His Father Judge Thomas White: Papers of the Historical Society of Delaware 40* (Wilmington: Historical Society of Delaware, 1903), 13; *JLFA*, 3:260, n. 100; *Minutes of the Annual Conferences*; Simpson, ed., *American Methodist Pioneer*, 257.

58. August 1, 1790, December 29, 1795, Meacham Papers; McKay, ed., *Journals of the Rev. Thomas Morrell*, 16; September 1, 1790, Colbert Journals.

59. Methodists used "brethren" to refer to both genders, but in this case, the masculinized language may have been effective with male masters, and thus I have not attempted to use a gender-neutral term in its place. Daniel Grant to John Owen, Jr., September 3, 1790, Campbell Family Papers.

60. Strickland, *Gruber*, 53; Carroll, "Religious Influences," 192; July 26, 1791, Colbert Journals.

61. "A Journal and Travel of James Meacham," TCHP Series 9 (1912), 79.

62. Daniel Grant to John Owen, Jr., September 3, 1790, Campbell Family Papers.

63. Ibid., October 25, 1791.

64. See the Wesley sermon on Mark 11:48 in *AM* (December 1789).

65. Carroll, "Religious Influences," 192.

66. Daniel Grant to John Owen, Jr., September 15, 1791, Campbell Family Papers; Frederick Bonner to Edward Dromgoole, July 19, 1807, Dromgoole Papers.

67. August 1, 1790, Meacham Papers; James A. Keys to Daniel Dromgoole, October 22, 1805, Dromgoole Papers.

68. Essig, *Bonds of Wickedness*, 42, analyzes the ambiguities of sentimentality in the South.

69. November 30, 1788, Meacham Papers, emphasis added.

70. See William R. Taylor, *Cavalier and Yankee: The Old South and American National Character* (New York: G. Braziller, 1961); John Mayfield, "'The Soul of a Man!': William Gilmore Simms and the Myths of Southern Manhood," *Journal of the Early Republic* (Fall 1995), 477–500. I am also indebted to a graduate student, R. Todd Romero, for his analysis of the work of William Gilmore Simms.

71. JLFA, 1:441; "A Journal and Travel of James Meacham," TCHP Series 10 (1914), 92–93; September 18, 1791, Ezekiel Cooper Journals.

72. JLFA, 2:109; February 27, 1790, Meacham Papers.

73. November 22, 1790, Kobler Journal; "Journal of Benjamin Lakin," 248.

74. JLFA, 1:442; August 26, 1796, Ormond Papers.

75. Philip Gatch to Edward Dromgoole, February 11, 1802, Frederick Bonner to Edward Dromgoole, July 19, 1807, Dromgoole Papers.

76. Bennet Maxey to Edward Dromgoole, July 27, 1807, Dromgoole Papers.

77. February 26, 1797, Meacham Papers. The text is Isiah 54:13.

78. November 8, 1790, Ezekiel Cooper Collection.

79. November 28 and July 4, 1790, Ezekiel Cooper Journals.

80. Strickland, *Life of Jacob Gruber*, 99–109.

81. *The Address of the General Conference of the Methodist Episcopal Church, to All Their Brethren and Friends in the United States* ([Baltimore?]: n.p., 1800).

82. Ibid.

83. Isaiah 58:6 also uses "oppressed." For "friend to liberty," see May 26, 1790, July 16, 1790, and May 23, 1791, Meacham Papers; for "oppressors," etc., see March 24, 1790, Colbert Journals; April 26, 1796, Whatcoat Journals; JLFA, 2:109; [January] 19, 1802, Boehm Journals. For manumission deed, see Carroll, "Religious Influences," 192. For Garrettson, see Simpson, ed., *American Methodist Pioneer*, 65.

84. *Minutes of the Annual Conferences*. The 1796 conference specified how manumission dates were to be calculated; before this buying and selling slaves was an offense punishable by automatic expulsion.

85. February 22, 1800, Whatcoat Journals; see also Carroll, "Religious Influences," 193–95. For North Carolinian, see August 25, 1798, Whatcoat Journals.

86. Tar River Circuit Minutes, Methodist Church Papers.

87. February 19, 1790, August 5, 1790, March 22, 1792, January 24, 1797, Meacham Papers; August 19, 1796, Ormond Papers; November 9, 1791, George Wells Journal. Masters who sold slaves in order to keep families together were not expelled.

88. 1809, Rocky River and Montgomery Circuit Quarterly Meeting Minutes, Methodist Church Papers.

89. Norwood, ed., *The Methodist Discipline of 1798*, 171.

90. One reform that had limited success (because of non-Methodist opposition) was the effort to educate blacks. See *Extracts of Letters*, 18–19; JLFA, 1:625, 2:128; Luther P. Jackson, "Religious Development," 186.

91. For the importance of shelter, food, and clothes, see Rose, "Domestication of Domestic Slavery," 30.

92. November 7, 1789, and November 18, 1789, Meacham Papers; Simpson, ed., *American Methodist Pioneer*, 198, 65, 188; November 22, 1789, Kobler Journal; March 6, 1800, Jeremiah Norman Diary; see also "A Freeman" to *Maryland Gazette*, [1791?], Ezekiel Cooper Collection. Since these preachers often ate what they could scrounge, their comments about "starving" slaves should be taken seriously. So too should their comments about slave dress in winter. Methodist standards of modesty may have made clergy more sensitive to clothes that showed more flesh, but they did not speak of "immodest" or "scandalous" slave dress, and they placed the responsibility for slave clothing on the owners.

93. January 28, 1796, Ormond Papers; May 17, 1790, Colbert Journals; Simpson, ed., *American Methodist Pioneer*, 65, 188, 198.

94. McKay, ed., *Journals of the Rev. Thomas Morrell*, 16; JLFA, 3:160.

95. Norwood, ed., *The Methodist Discipline of 1798*, 138–39.

96. JLFA, 1:273–74; 2:591; *Extracts of Letters*, 18–19.

97. Armour, "The Virginia Reaction," sees Jesse Lee as a more reluctant foe of slavery than I do. Lee's name was on the explosive *Address* of 1800, he claimed to be opposed to slavery, and he urged his own father to emancipate his slaves in his will. Lee's difference with leaders like Coke was primarily over tactics. Thrift, *Jesse Lee*, 235; Jesse Lee, *Short History*, 72; JLFA, 2:591.

98. JLFA, 1:442.

99. Daniel Grant to John Owen, Jr., September 8, 1792, Campbell Family Papers.

100. April 23, 1777, Littlejohn Journal.

101. [May] 7, 1802, Boehm Journals.

102. JLFA, 2:80.

103. Jesse Lee, *A Short Account of the Life and Death of the Rev. John Lee, a Methodist Minister in the United States of America* (Baltimore: n.p., 1805), 125–26.

104. June 8, 1799, November 1, 1795, Jeremiah Norman Diary.

105. March 16, 1796, August 8–9, 1800, Jeremiah Norman Diary. It is more difficult to tell what effect this action had on Norman's black audience. The next day he reported a large number of blacks at worship, and several requested to be baptized. It is reasonable to assume that a runaway slave would rather have been returned by a preacher with some hostility to slavery than by a slave catcher. Perhaps Norman's conversation with the runaway was responsible for the large crowd.

106. August 5, 1790, Meacham Papers.

107. Lednum, *Rise of Methodism*, 341. This anecdote implies that antislavery sermons were quite common.

108. Thomas Mann Journals; Jenkins, *Experience, Labours, and Sufferings*, 13, 32, 95, 102, 137.

109. Simpson, ed., *American Methodist Pioneer*, 199.

110. Had Garrettson railed at this man, it is doubtful he would have even considered the matter. The strategy of conversion-style appeals was flawed, but it is not at all clear whether a different strategy would have had greater success.

111. See tax records in Dromgoole Papers.

112. See Carroll, "Religious Influences."

113. "A Journal and Travel of James Meacham," *TCHP* Series 9 (1912), 67. M'Lean's dissent

included wording reminiscent of the early Methodist antislavery language. He declared that a slave "bears the impress of his Maker, and is amenable to the laws of God and man, and he is destined to an endless existence." For Dred Scott, see Vincent C. Hopkins, *Dred Scott's Case* (New York: Fordham University Press, 1951), quote on 81. For M'Lean's earlier rulings in Ohio, see Paul Finkelman, *An Imperfect Union: Slavery, Federalism, and Comity* (Chapel Hill: University of North Carolina Press, 1981).

7: Turning the World Upside Down

1. The story of Jesse Lee's sermon is from two sources. Wakeley, *Patriarch*, 412, and Bennett, *Methodism in Virginia*, 208.

2. Shipp, *Methodism in South Carolina*, 202; Paine, *M'Kendree*, 39.

3. For works on Methodism's challenges to southern values, see Robert Alexander Armour, "The Opposition to the Methodist Church in Eighteenth-Century Virginia," Ph.D. diss., University of Georgia, 1968; Mathews, *Religion in the Old South*; Rankin, *Ambivalent Churchmen*; Schneider, *Way of the Cross*; Williams, *Garden of American Methodism*; Huff, Jr., *Tried by Fire*; Ayers, *Vengeance and Justice*, especially 27–31, 118–24; Bilhartz, *Urban Religion*; Boles, *Great Revival*; Isaac, *Transformation of Virginia*; Klein, *Unification of a Slave State*; Lewis, *Pursuit of Happiness*; Long, "Religious Revivalism"; Loveland, *Southern Evangelicals*; and Waldrep, "Making of a Border State Society." See also the works cited in previous chapters.

4. Sally Eastland to Edward Dromgoole, February 21, 1790, Dromgoole Papers.

5. Sometimes the sources do not give clear indicators of what precipitated the incidents, such as the incident in Simpson, ed., *American Methodist Pioneer*, 85, 153.

6. For some of the many instances of arson and vandalism against Methodist churches, see Lednum, *Rise of Methodism*, 126; October 29, 1789, Kobler Journal; Huff, Jr., *Tried by Fire*, 11; Jenkins, *Experience, Labours, and Sufferings*, 86 and 138.

7. Methodists, of course, criticized other sects and other clergy, and sometimes in denunciatory language. John Littlejohn called satanic a Presbyterian's view that "a person could be converted and not know it." March 29, 1777, Littlejohn Journal. For Methodist-Baptist conflict, see Shipp, *Methodism in South Carolina*, 262–63.

8. For an illiterate minister, see Phinney et al., eds., *Thomas Ware*, 94. In the West, cooperation between Methodists and Presbyterians was largely the rule. The conflict over "Methodistical" ways and doctrines helped precipate the split in the Presbyterian church between the prorevival, Arminian leaning side (the Cumberland Presbyterians) and the antirevival adherents to the Westminster Confession. It is the latter group that I refer to as "conservative Presbyterians."

9. Young, *Autobiography of a Pioneer*, 138; for the Virginian, see Armour, "Opposition to the Methodist Church," 31.

10. Jarratt to Edward Dromgoole, March 22, 1788, Dromgoole Papers, underlining in original. See also Jarratt's letter of May 31, 1785, Dromgoole Papers.

11. Francis F. Beirne, *Saint Paul's Parish Baltimore: A Chronicle of the Mother Church* (Baltimore: Horn-Shafer, 1967), 54–55; [A Layman of the New Jerusalem Church], *A Short Reply, to Burk and Guy*, 14; Higginbotham, "Methodism Moves East," 41; see also John Cree et al., *The Evils of the Work Now Prevailing in the United States of America* (n.p., 1804), 14.

12. Cree et al., *Evils*, 8–9. Some Methodists were so affected that they (temporarily) could not work. See Sarah Jones to Edward Dromgoole, September 4, 1788, copy, Dromgoole Papers.

13. Cree et al., *Evils*, 6, 14, 24. The authors quoted a prorevival witness but used his words to show the "evils" of letting these underlings teach and exhort.

14. Rankin, *Review of the Noted Revival*, 83–85. Rankin's reference to the London asylum for the

insane was part of the anti-Methodist's stock-in-trade. John Wesley had attracted a large crowd to a famous British revival very near that institution, and ever since then his critics had associated Wesley and his followers with Bedlam.

15. Cree et al., *Evils,* 27, 39–40.

16. Matthew Lyle to William Spencer, December 31, 1808, William Spencer Journal, microfilm. In 1816, in the Old Northwest, James Finley cited Paul's injunction for women's silence after he was interrupted in the middle of a sermon by a woman prophesying. Finley also offered her the opportunity to exhort when he was finished, which suggests he objected to her interruption and not to women speaking. Finley, *Autobiography,* 286–87.

17. Paine, *M'Kendree,* 88; Bennett, *Methodism in Virginia,* 365, 472–73; October 14, 1789, Ezekiel Cooper Journals; September 26, 1792, Ormond Papers; October 20, 1798, Kobler Journal; *JLFA,* 1:399; Lednum, *Rise of Methodism,* 148–49.

18. December 25, 1810, Mann Papers; April 22, 1790, Meacham Papers; April 22, 1792, George Wells Journal; quote from July 15, 1798, Kobler Journal; February 13, 1791, Ezekiel Cooper Journals. See also *JLFA,* 1:473; May 26, 1803, Ormond Papers. There were secular restraints on the actions of whites, by law and custom, but these were not nearly as detailed, intrusive, and trivial as Methodist rules were. Some men threatened preachers with violence for reproving or expelling their family members. See March 5–6, 1797, Meacham Papers; September 18, 1799, Ormond Papers. Few women acted with rage at expulsion.

19. April 28, 1777, Littlejohn Journal; July 22–23, 1797, Kobler Journal. See also May 27, 1792, Ormond Papers. One man even objected to the (probably pointed) way Nelson Reed looked at him during a service. June 10, 1781, Nelson Reed Diary.

20. *JLFA* 1:633, 1:747. His guide boasted of killing a slave and racing a horse to death, which helps explain Asbury's harsh language here.

21. "Mrs. R[ebecca] R[idgely's] Experience," Ridgely-Pue Papers, MS. 693.

22. "The Journal of Benjamin Lakin," 225; March 28, 1796, Whatcoat Journals; September 8, 1791, Ezekiel Cooper Journals; November 22, 1800, Boehm Journals; October 11, 1793, Kobler Journal.

23. *AM* (February 1790), 91–92; Bennett, *Methodism in Virginia,* 366.

24. November 9, 1788, and May 8–9, 1790, and see also November 22, 1789, March 9, 1791, Ezekiel Cooper Journals.

25. Young, *Autobiography of a Pioneer,* 243; *JLFA,* 1:337.

26. "Diary of John Early," *VMHB* 34:4 (October 1926), 302.

27. Young, *Autobiography of a Pioneer,* 41.

28. Shipp, *Methodism in South Carolina,* 191. His friends knew exactly what would happen. They were said to have remarked: "He is gone! The Methodists have got him; he will never play the fiddle, or drink, or fight, anymore."

29. Finley, *Autobiography,* 164–66.

30. Autobiography, John Young, Sr., Papers.

31. For "drunks" interrupting services, see, for example, October 14, 1790, May 15, 1791, Ezekiel Cooper Journals; January 14, 1778, Littlejohn Journal; September 3, 1790, Meacham Papers; February 19, 1799, Jeremiah Norman Diary; November 16, 1801, Boehm Journals; September 10, 1791, George Wells Journal; Simpson, ed., *American Methodist Pioneer,* 211. My analysis here is indebted to Barbara Leslie Epstein, *The Politics of Domesticity: Women, Evangelism, and Temperance in Nineteenth-Century America* (Middletown: Wesleyan University Press, 1981), 109–10; Wyatt-Brown, *Southern Honor,* 278–83; Isaac, *Transformation of Virginia,* 95, 114. For the postbellum era, see Ted Ownby, *Subduing Satan: Religion, Recreation, and Manhood in the Rural South, 1865–1920* (Chapel Hill: University of North Carolina Press, 1990).

32. *Extracts of Letters,* 38; Bennett, *Methodism in Virginia,* 398.

33. Finley, *Autobiography*, 164, 168–69. See also *Way of the Cross*, 37–38.

34. Shipp, *Methodism in South Carolina*, 197, 276; *Extracts of Letters*, 50; Young, *Autobiography of a Pioneer*, 41.

35. Wightman, *Capers*, 72.

36. Jenkins, *Experience, Labours, and Sufferings*, 184; Strickland, *Jacob Gruber*, 63.

37. For drinking and southern manhood, see Wyatt-Brown, *Southern Honor*, 278–83; Cashin, *A Family Venture*, 103. Distillers and grogshop owners had financial reasons to oppose the Methodists, but they cannot account for all of the opposition. It is interesting to note that Methodist preachers were prone to fears of their own "effeminancy." See JLFA, 3:409, 2:132; "The Journal of Benjamin Lakin," 240.

38. July 4, 1790, Colbert Journals; March 6, 1789, Ezekiel Cooper Journals; Young, *Autobiography of a Pioneer*, 123; August 29, 1790, May 29, 1791, Meacham Papers; JLFA, 2:40; see also Simpson, ed., *American Methodist Pioneer*, 66.

39. For honor and the resolution of conflicts see Wyatt-Brown, *Southern Honor*; 350–61; Greenberg, *Masters and Statesmen*, 23–41; Stowe, *Intimacy and Power*; Dickson D. Bruce, Jr., *Violence and Culture in the Antebellum South* (Austin: University of Texas Press, 1979), 1–43. Finley, *Autobiography*, 154. Methodists were opposed to both fighting and dueling. See, for example, May 17 and May 19, 1794, Colbert Journals.

40. May 22, 1791, Kobler Journal. For shaming rituals, see Wyatt-Brown, *Southern Honor*, 452.

41. Bennett, *Methodism in Virginia*, 537–38.

42. For nose pulling, see Greenberg, *Honor and Slavery*, chapter 1.

43. Bennett, *Methodism in Virginia*, 495.

44. JLFA, 1:308; Shipp, *Methodism in South Carolina*, 585; for the Hinde-Martin story, see MMag (July 1827), 312, and MMag (August 1827), 369. For a similar analysis, see Waldrep, "The Making of a Border State Society," 769–71.

45. *Autobiography*, 23–24, John Young, Sr., Papers. Methodists sometimes disturbed the peace with their services. See Bennett, *Methodism in Virginia*, 373. But, as Methodists perceptively noted, few objected to the noise of secular events. See *Memoir of Old Elizabeth*, 10–12, and AM (November 1790): 559. For Britain, see Michael MacDonald, "Insanity and the Realities of History in Early Modern England," *Psychological Medicine* 11 (1981), 11–25; Albert M. Lyles, *Methodism Mocked: The Satiric Reaction to Methodism in the Eighteenth Century* (London: Epworth Press, 1960); Cynthia Cupples, "Pious Ladies and Methodist Madams: Sex and Gender in Anti-Methodist Writings of Eighteenth Century England," *Critical Matrix* 5 (Spring/Summer 1990), 30–60. For Methodists in New York accused of subverting parental authority, see *Cradle of the Middle Class*, 67–68. Criticism of southern Methodists was therefore not unique. The southern context was.

46. September 21, 1794, Colbert Journals.

47. Armour, "Opposition to the Methodist Church," 18; Cree et al., *Evils*, 13–14; Rankin, *Review of the Noted Revival*, 102.

48. Armour, "Opposition to the Methodist Church," 21; Lednum, *Rise of Methodism*, 94, 357, 402; 1770s (page 4), October 10, 1776, Littlejohn Journal; Ffirth, *Abbott*, 91; Simpson, ed., *American Methodist Pioneer*, 184.

49. Young, *Autobiography of a Pioneer*, 136; June 1, 1793, Meacham Papers; October 9, 1792, Kobler Journal; Shipp, *Methodism in South Carolina*, 585. See also JLFA, 1:315.

50. "Diary of John Early," VMHB 34:2 (April 1926), 131; July 15, 1792, George Wells Journal. For Abbott, see Ffirth, *Abbott*, 105, 109, 188, 197, 209, 210. For Kobler, see February 14, 1790, May 2, 1790, October 5, 1793, October 24–25, 1795, Kobler Journal. Other preachers made similar reports.

51. Higginbotham, "Methodism Moves East," 41; Janson, *Stranger in America*, 101; July 7, 1794, Kobler Journal.

52. See also Carroll Smith-Rosenberg and Charles Rosenberg, "The Female Animal: Medical

and Biological Views of Woman and Her Role in Nineteenth-Century America," *JAH* 60:2 (September 1973), 332–56.

53. Simpson, ed., *American Methodist Pioneer*, 58–59; Smith, *Recollections*, 101. Women's enthusiasm was "womanly power," I would argue, in two ways. First, displays of passions and emotions (regardless of the gender of the enthusiast) elevated characteristics viewed by males as weaknesses to the level of divinely inspired virtues. Second, women's enthusiasm more often provoked fear or condemnation than the enthusiasm of men.

54. Moore, *Sketches of the Pioneers*, 276; Shipp, *Methodism in South Carolina*, 261; see also May 7, 1792, Ormond Papers; Ffirth, *Abbott*, 106; July 2, 1791, Kobler Journal.

55. Methodism in Iredell County, Historical Sketches, Methodist Church Papers; *AM* (February 1790), 93; November 18, 1805, Mann Papers; April 28–29, 1800, Jeremiah Norman Diary.

56. Janson, *Stranger in America*, 107–08.

57. January 24, 1794, Colbert Journals; Simpson, ed., *American Methodist Pioneer*, 227; Jenkins, *Experience, Labours, and Sufferings*, 80. See also [A Layman], *A Short Reply*, 14.

58. For quotation, see September 21, 1794, Colbert Journals. For charges that ministers cast spells or worked magic, see October 9, 1792, Kobler Journal; June 1, 1793, Meacham Papers. See also Clarke Garrett, *Spirit Possession and Popular Religion: From the Camisards to the Shakers* (Baltimore: Johns Hopkins University Press, 1987); David D. Hall, ed., *The Antinomian Controversy, 1636–1638: A Documentary History* (Durham: Duke University Press, 1990); Clement Hawes, *Mania and Literary Style: The Rhetoric of Enthusiasm from the Ranters to Christophe Smart* (Cambridge: Cambridge University Press, 1996).

59. Jones, *Devout Letters*, 44 and 5. Jones and Minter were accused of having more than a spiritual relationship, which they both denied, but it is possible that Minter's decision to have a surgeon castrate him was somehow related to feelings he had for Jones.

60. Sally Eastland to Edward Dromgoole, February 21, 1790, Sarah Jones to Edward Dromgoole, n.d., copy, Dromgoole Papers; Jones, *Devout Letters*, 22, 58, 61, and 85.

61. *A Short Reply*, 8, 14; [Druid of the Lakes], *The Camp Meeting* (n.p.: 1810), 7–8.

62. Rankin, *Review of the Noted Revival*, 86; Bayard quoted in Armour, "Opposition to the Methodist Church," 26.

63. Homer M. Keever, "A Lutheran Preacher's Account of the 1801–02 Revival in North Carolina," *MethH* (October 1968), 42.

64. Ibid., 45.

65. Janson, *Stranger in America*, 101; Kenneth Roberts and Anna M. Roberts, trans. and eds., *Moreau de St. Mary's American Journey* [1793–1798] (Garden City, New York: Doubleday, 1947), 48, 60. One Methodist preacher made a similar racist comment; see Strickland, *Gruber*, 120.

66. *Autobiographical Sketches of Dr. William Hill*, 56. 81.

67. July 4, 1790, Colbert Journals; Simpson, ed., *American Methodist Pioneer*, 187, and see also 319.

68. December 14, 1777, Littlejohn Journal; "A Journal and Travel of James Meacham," *TCHP* Series 9 (1912), 90; Jenkins, *Experience, Labours, and Sufferings*, 155; July 7, 1791, Kobler Journal; Deems, *Annals of Southern Methodism for 1855*, 253.

69. April 8, 1800, Jeremiah Norman Diary; March 16, 1777, Littlejohn Journal.

70. March 16, 1777, Littlejohn Journal.

71. April 5, 1790, Colbert Journals.

72. *JLFA*, 2:591.

73. Ford, Jr., *Southern Radicalism*, 50. See also the discussion of proslavery religionists in Peterson, *Ham and Japheth*, and McCurry, "Two Faces of Republicanism," and "The Politics of Yeoman Households."

74. Greven, *Protestant Temperament*, 35–37; see also Wesley's sermon in *MMag* (September 1797), 385–96. In later decades, American Methodists would join in producing the vast

amounts of child-rearing literature directed toward mothers. See Gillespie, "The Sun in Their Domestic System," especially 53–54.

75. Ffirth, *Abbott*, 43–44; Strickland, *Gruber*, 13.

76. Finley, *Western Methodism*, 365–66.

77. Jenkins, *Experience, Labours, and Sufferings*, 133. See also Rankin, *Ambivalent Churchmen*, 59–60.

78. M. P. to Edward Dromgoole, January 19, 1778, Dromgoole Papers; see also Ffirth, *Abbott*, 208; September 19, 1792, Meacham Papers.

79. Young, *Autobiography of a Pioneer*, 44; Moore, *Sketches of the Pioneers*, 240; J. W. Hedges, comp., *Crowned Victors: The Memoirs of Over Four Hundred Methodist Preachers, Including the First Two Hundred and Fifty Who Died on This Continent* (Baltimore: Methodist Episcopal Book Depository, 1878), 92–93.

80. Schneider, *Way of the Cross*, 35–40; for spiritual fathers, see Maddox Andrew to Ezekiel Cooper, April 23, 1798, Ezekiel Cooper Collection; Hedges, comp., *Crowned Victors*, 92–93.

81. March 3, 1792, Kobler Journal; August 3, 1779, Nelson Reed Diary; February 7, 1789, Ezekiel Cooper Journals; Marjorie Moran Holmes, "The Life and Diary of the Reverend John Jeremiah Jacob (1757–1830)," Master's thesis, Duke University, 1941, 137.

82. December 18, 1790, Ezekiel Cooper Papers.

83. M'Lean, *Philip Gatch*, 10–11; Connor, *Methodist Trail Blazer*, 3; Lednum, *Rise of Methodism*, 146, 350; July 29, 1794, Meacham Papers; Bennett, *Methodism in Virginia*, 493.

84. MMag (June 1827), 263; see also Redford, *Methodism in Kentucky*, 373.

85. November 11, 1792, George Wells Journal.

86. Shipp, *Methodism in South Carolina*, 196–97; M'Lean, *Philip Gatch*, 44; Smith, *Recollections*, 32.

87. Lednum, *Rise of Methodism*, 348; for examples of husbands forbidding their wives, see Wakeley, *Patriarch*, 189; JLFA, 1:310, 1:402; May 19, 1792, Ormond Papers.

88. January 7, 1777, Littlejohn Journal; February 5, 1790, Ezekiel Cooper Papers.

89. Jenkins, *Experience, Labours, and Sufferings*, 107; Smith, *Recollections*, 107. We simply do not know how many women were successfully kept from the church by their husbands' violence. The cases discussed in the sources usually involve women who prevailed, although some did not prevail until their husbands died.

90. June 9, 1792, Kobler Journal; Jenkins, *Experience, Labours, and Sufferings*, 40.

91. Norwood, ed., *Sourcebook*, 41; Sandford, *Wesley's Missionaries*, 19.

92. June 15, 1781, Nelson Reed Diary; AM (February 1790), 94; *Extracts of Letters*, 19.

93. June 6, 1794, Colbert Journals; Smith, *David Smith*, 11; Jenkins, *Experience, Labours, and Sufferings*, 154.

94. Smith, *David Smith*, 10.

95. Finley, *Western Methodism*, 383, 385.

96. Alexander M'Caine to Robert Roberts, September 29, 1802, Ezekiel Cooper Collection.

97. Quoted in James Hugo Johnston, "The Participation of White Men in Virginia Negro Insurrections," JNH 16:1 (January 1931), 158–60.

98. Ibid.

99. Ibid.

100. Ibid. Whether there were actual thefts reported is not clear. Antebellum slaves often believed stealing from slave owners was no sin, while stealing from other slaves was. It is distinctly possible that the author was merely making the charge so many made against Methodists of all kinds: hypocrisy.

101. Ibid. We might recall the law South Carolinians passed restricting slave worship to daylight hours. It is possible as well that the historical folk association of nighttime with the devil was also at work.

102. Ibid. See also Jackson, "Religious Development," 172–73.

103. June 30, 1805, Mann Papers; Wightman, *Capers*, 137; July 8, 1790, Meacham Papers.

104. Thomas Coke, *A Journal of the Rev. Dr. Coke's Fourth Tour on the Continent of America* (London: G. Paramore, 1792), 8. James Jenkins was administering communion to slaves when white ruffians demanded that he stop. Jenkins, *Experience, Labours, and Sufferings*, 97.

105. August 6, 1780, Nelson Reed Diary.

106. "A Journal and Travel of James Meacham," *TCHP*, Series 9 (1912), 94.

107. Ibid., 90 (Jude 19–21).

108. Another Methodist belief that may have come into play here was that of heavenly justice, and of death as a victory. Cuff, after being beaten, sang a hymn about these ideas. In Finley, *Western Methodism*, 384.

109. Wilson, *Baptized in Blood*. It is possible, of course, that northern Methodists saw their southern counterparts as fulfilling a similar function.

110. Historical Sketch of Grace Church, Morganton, North Carolina, Methodist Church Papers; Smith, ed., *Memoirs of a Methodist Circuit Rider*, 127; see also Jenkins, *Experience, Labours, and Sufferings*, 184.

111. *MMag* (August 1819), 305. The quotation is from a description of the western revivals at the turn of the century.

Epilogue

1. *JLFA*, 2:668.

2. *JLFA*, 2:687 and 3:446. See also Thrift, *Memoir of the Rev. Jesse Lee*, 331. Dating this transformation with precision is impossible. The year 1810 does not mark an absolute divide as much as a confluence of events and trends that show a clear change from earlier years.

3. For the growing Arminianism of Protestants, see Mathews, *Religion in the Old South*; Boles, *Great Revival*; Johnson, *Shopkeeper's Millennium*. For the decline in emphasis on sanctification, see Peters, *Christian Perfection*, 98ff, and Smith, *Revivalism and Social Reform*, 115–16, although Smith dates this decline earlier than I do.

4. The change was not uniform throughout the region. Historian Kenneth L. Carroll found that on Maryland's Eastern Shore, between 1810 and 1819, there were 77 manumission deeds registered in Caroline County, 144 in Talbot County, and 210 in Dorchester County—most of them by Methodists. The rate of manumission fell precipitously after 1833. Carroll, "Religious Influences," 195–97. Not all southern conferences were equally committed to schism in 1844, either. Holston Methodists sought compromise. See *History of the Organization of the Methodist Episcopal Church, South, With the Journal of Its First General Conference* (Nashville: Publishing House of the Methodist Episcopal Church, South, 1925), 179–81.

5. *JLFA*, 2:635, and see 3:429; "Diary of John Early," *VMHB* 34:2 (April 1926), 137.

6. Simpson, ed., *American Methodist Pioneer*, 312. See also *JLFA*, 3:429. For the spread of both cotton and evangelicalism, see Ford, Jr., *Origins of Southern Radicalism*, chapter 1.

7. Simpson, ed., *American Methodist Pioneer*, 350–51.

8. Richey, *Early American Methodism*, chapter 5. See also Schneider, *Way of the Cross*, chapter 13. For Garrettson, see Simpson, ed., *American Methodist Pioneer*, 395.

9. *JLFA*, 3:429, 3:432.

10. Ibid., 3:475; see also 3:446, 3:463, 3:523.

11. Ibid., 3:502, 3:465, 3:475; for local societies' pleas, see 3:554 and 3:519. See also Schneider, *Way of the Cross*, 200.

12. Mathews, *Slavery and Methodism*, 24–25.

13. Simpson, ed., *American Methodist Pioneer*, 398–99.

14. Smith, *Recollections*, 31.

15. Ibid., 142–43, 159.

16. Andrews, "Popular Religion," 197–200; Schneider, *Way of the Cross*, 200–207.

17. Schneider, *Way of the Cross*, especially chapter 12; Gillespie, "'The Sun in Their Domestic System.'"

18. Schneider, *Way of the Cross*, 200–207. For one minister's views on the decline of class meetings, see Travis, *Autobiography of the Rev. Joseph Travis*, 224–25. For post–Civil War revivalism and gender, see Ownby, *Subduing Satan*.

19. Most of the arguments in the case, addresses, speeches, and resolutions can be found in Elliott, *History of the Great Secession*.

20. Elliott, *Great Secession*, 989, 1005–07.

21. Ibid., 302, 371, 304, 1044.

22. *History of the Organization of the Methodist Episcopal Church, South* (Nashville: Publishing House of the Methodist Episcopal Church, South, 1925), 167, 154.

23. Elliott, *Great Secession*, 1049, 1053.

24. Ibid., 1043–44, 304.

25. *Organization of the Methodist Episcopal Church, South*, 315.

26. Elliott, *Great Secession*, 1054. See also *Organization of the Methodist Episcopal Church, South*, 201, 212, 308, 182.

27. Bibb's letters are reprinted in John W. Blassingame, ed., *Slave Testimony: Two Centuries of Letters, Speeches, Interviews, and Autobiographies*, 48–57, quotations on 50–51, 53.

28. Ibid., 55–56.

29. Jones, *Devout Letters*, 88. For more on Jones, see Cynthia Lyerly, "Passion, Desire, and Ecstasy: The Experiential Religion of Southern Methodist Women, 1770–1810," in Catherine Clinton and Michele Gillespie, eds., *The Devil's Lane: Sex and Race in the Early South* (New York: Oxford University Press, 1997).

30. *Devout Letters*, 1–2, 7. Jones knew that Methodist preachers usually commented on the surrounding verses of a sermon text and knew her Bible as well as any preacher. She thus had to have been aware that the two verses following Job 3:17 described how in heaven, the "servant is free from his master."

31. JLFA, 2:34.

Selected Bibliography

Manuscript Sources

Baltimore-Washington United Methodist Historical Society, Lovely Lane Museum, Baltimore, Maryland:
  The Letters of Francis Asbury, microfilm
  Lewis R. Fechtig Manuscript Book
  The Journal of Noah Fidler, typescript
  Rev. John Kobler's Journal
  The Journal of John Littlejohn, typescript
  Diary of Nelson Reed, typescript
  Writings of William Spencer, microfilm
  James Watts Journal, photocopy
  The Journal of George Wells

The University of Chicago Divinity School Library, Chicago, Illinois:
  The Journals of Richard Whatcoat, microfilm, originals at the Library of Congress and
    Garrett-Evangelical Theological Seminary

Manuscripts Division, Drew University Library, Madison, New Jersey:
  Henry Boehm's Journal (typescript loaned by Baltimore-Washington United Methodist His-
    torical Society)

Special Collections, Duke University, Durham, North Carolina:
  Campbell Family Papers (includes Daniel Grant Letters)
  Lillie Moore Everett Papers
  Myles Greene Journal
  William and Benjamin Hammet Papers
  Eugene Russell Hendrix Papers

Rev. James Hill's Book, 1804, Methodist Church Papers
Thomas Mann Papers
James Meacham Papers
Methodist Church Papers
John O'Neale Papers
William Ormond Papers
George A. Reed Papers
Daniel Shine Papers
Virginia Conference Minutes, 1806 and 1807, Methodist Church Papers
John Young, Sr., Papers

Manuscripts Library, Garrett-Evangelical Theological Seminary, Evanston, Illinois:
William Colbert Journals (photocopy loaned by Baltimore-Washington United Methodist Historical Society)
William Colbert Letters
Ezekiel Cooper Journal (photocopy loaned by Baltimore-Washington United Methodist Historical Society)
Ezekiel Cooper Letters, Ezekiel Cooper Collection

Maryland Historical Society, Baltimore, Maryland:
Bond Family Papers, # 1207
Gough-Carroll Papers, # 2560
Harford Circuit Register, # 427
William Matthews Letterbook, # 579
Redwood Collection, # 1530
Ridgely-Pue Papers, # 693

Southern Historical Collection, The University of North Carolina at Chapel Hill, Chapel Hill, North Carolina:
Drake Family Letters, Mary Jones Arrington Collection
Edward Droomgoole Papers
Edenton Methodist Church Record Books, M-3075
Green Hill Papers
Hill and Davis Family Papers
Thomas Lyell Autobiography, Aldert Smedes Papers
The Diary of Jeremiah Normon, Stephen B. Weeks Papers
Pettigrew Family Papers
William Thornton Whitsett Papers

Printed Primary Sources

The Address of the General Conference of the Methodist Episcopal Church, to All Their Brethren and Friends in the United States. [Baltimore]: n.p., May 20, 1800.

Capers, William. "Autobiography." In William M. Wightman, *Life of William Capers, D.D.* Nashville: Southern Methodist Publishing House, 1859.

Cartwright, Peter. *Autobiography of Peter Cartwright.* Nashville: Abingdon Press, 1956.

Clark, Elmer T., J. Manning Potts, and Jacob S. Payton, eds. *The Journal and Letters of Francis Asbury.* London: Epworth Press, 1958.

Coke, Thomas. *A Journal of the Rev. Dr. Thomas Coke's Fourth Tour on the Continent of America.* London: G. Parramore, 1792.

Coker, Daniel. *A Dialogue Between a Virginian and an African Minister.* Baltimore: Joseph James, 1810.

Cooper, Ezekiel. *A Funeral Discourse, on the Death of that Eminent Man the Late Reverend John Dickins*. Philadelphia: H. Maxwell, 1799.

Cree, John, and John Anderson, William Wilson, Thomas Alison, and E. Henderson. *Evils of the Work Now Prevailing in the United States of America, Under the Name of a Revival of Religion*. N.p., 1804.

Deems, Charles F., ed., *The Annals of Southern Methodism for 1857*. Nashville: J. B. M'Ferrin, for the Methodist Episcopal Church, South, 1858.

———, ed. *Annals of Southern Methodism for 1856*. Nashville: Stevenson & Owen, 1857.

———, ed. *The Annals of Southern Methodism for the Year 1855*. New York: J. A. Gray's Fire-Proof Printing Office, 1856.

Dow, Lorenzo. *History of Cosmopolite: or, The Writings of Rev. Lorenzo Dow, Containing His Experience and Travels, in Europe and America, Up to His Fiftieth Year, Also His Polemic Writings, to Which Is Added the "Journey of Life," by Peggy Dow*. Cincinnati: A. S. Robertson, 1850.

"Druid of the Lakes." *The Camp Meeting*. N.p., 1810.

Early, John. "The Diary of John Early." *Virginia Magazine of History and Biography*, 1925–1930.

Extracts of Letters, Containing Some Account of the Work of God Since the Year 1800. New York: Totten, for Cooper and Wilson, 1805.

Ffirth, John. *The Experiences and Gospel Labours, of the Rev. Benjamin Abbott*. New York: Daniel Hitt and Thomas Ware, 1813.

Finley, James B. *Autobiography of Rev. James B. Finley; or, Pioneer Life in the West*. Edited by W. P. Strickland. Cincinnati: Methodist Book Concern, 1854.

———. *Sketches of Western Methodism: Biographical, Historical, and Miscellaneous. Illustrative of Pioneer Life*. Cincinnati: Methodist Book Concern, 1855.

A Funeral Sermon, Preached by the Rev. Mr. Prior, Minister of the Methodist Church at Baltimore, on the Death of Miss Christiana Lane, Who Departed This Life, Friday, October 5, 1792. Baltimore: Samuel and John Adams, 1792.

Gannaway, Robertson. "Autobiography of Rev. Robertson Gannaway." *Virginia Magazine of History and Biography* 37:4 (October 1929): 316–22.

Garrettson, Freeborn. *A Dialogue Between Do-Justice and Professing Christian*. Wilmington, Del.: Peter Brynburg, [1805].

Hedges, J. W., compiler. *Crowned Victors: The Memoirs of Over Four Hundred Methodist Preachers, Including the First Two Hundred and Fifty Who Died on This Continent*. Baltimore: Methodist Episcopal Book Concern, 1878.

Hill, William. *Autobiographical Sketches of Dr. William Hill*. Historical Transcripts No. 4. Richmond: Union Theological Seminary in Virginia, 1968.

Hough, Samuel S., ed. *Christian Newcomer: His Life, Journal, and Achievements*. Dayton: Board of Administration, Church of the United Brethren in Christ, 1941.

Janson, Charles William. *The Stranger in America, 1793–1806*. 1807. Reprint, New York: Press of the Pioneers, 1935.

[Jarratt, Devereux]. *A Brief Narrative of the Revival of Religion in Virginia. In a Letter to a Friend*. 3rd ed. London: Paramore, 1786.

Jarratt, Devereux. *Thoughts on Some Important Subjects in Divinity; In a Series of Letters to a Friend*. Baltimore: Warner & Hanna, 1806.

Jenkins, James. *Experiences, Labours, and Sufferings of Rev. James Jenkins, of the South Carolina Conference*. N.p.: for the author, 1842.

Jones, Sarah. *Devout Letters: Or, Letters Spiritual and Friendly. Written by Mrs. Sarah Jones*. Edited by Jeremiah Minter. Alexandria: Jeremiah Minter, 1804.

Lakin, Benjamin. "The Journal of Benjamin Lakin." In William Warren Sweet, ed., *Religion on the American Frontier, 1783–1840*. Volume 4. *The Methodists*. Chicago: University of Chicago Press, 1946.

"A Layman of the New Jerusalem Church." *A Short Reply, to Burk and Guy, With Some Ripe Fruit for a Friend to Truth.* Baltimore: for the author, [1804].

Lednum, John. *A History of the Rise of Methodism in America.* Philadelphia: for the author, 1859.

Lee, Jesse. *Practical Piety: The Substance of a Sermon, Preached at a Watch-night Held in Johns-Town, Delaware State. On Nov. 18th, 1783.* Baltimore: John Hagerty, 1814.

———. *Short Account of the Life and Death of the Rev. John Lee, a Methodist Minister in the United States of America.* Baltimore: John West Butler, 1805.

———. *A Short History of the Methodists in the United States of America.* 1810. Reprint Rutland: Academy Books, 1974.

McKay, Michael J., ed. *The Journals of the Rev. Thomas Morrell.* Madison: Historical Society Northern New Jersey Conference, the United Methodist Church, 1984.

M'Lean, John. *Sketch of Rev. Philip Gatch.* Cincinnati: Swormstedt & Poe, for the Methodist Episcopal Church, Western Book Concern, 1854.

Maser, Frederick E., and Howard T, Maag, eds. *The Journal of Joseph Pilmore, Methodist Itinerant for the Years August 1, 1769 to January 2, 1774.* Philadelphia: Message Publishing House, 1969.

Meacham, James. "A Journal and Travel of James Meacham." [Trinity College] *Historical Papers,* 1912, 1914.

Mead, Stith. *A Short Account of the Experience and Labors of the Rev. Stith Mead, Preacher of the Gospel, and an Elder in the Methodist Episcopal Church; Written by Himself, In a Plain Style.* Lynchburg: by the author, 1829.

Minter, Jeremiah. *A Brief Account of the Religious Experience, Travels, Preaching, Persecutions from Evil Men, and God's Special Helps in the Faith and Life, etc. of Jerem. Minter, Minister of the Gospel of Christ, Written by Himself, in His 51st Year of Age.* Washington, D.C.: for the author, 1817.

Minutes of the Annual Conferences of the Methodist Episcopal Church for the Years 1773–1828. New York: T. Mason & G. Lane, 1840.

Morrell, Thomas. *A Sermon on the Death of General Geo. Washington.* Baltimore: Warren & Hanna, 1800.

Munroe, John A., ed. "James Hemphill's Account of a Visit to Maryland in 1802." *Delaware History* 3:2 (September 1948): 61–78.

Norwood, Frederick, ed. *The Methodist Discipline of 1798.* 1798. facsimile edition, Rutland: Academy Books, 1979.

"Old Elizabeth." *Memoir of Old Elizabeth, A Coloured Women.* 1863. Reprinted in *Six Women's Slave Narratives.* New York: Oxford University Press, 1988.

Paine, Robert. *The Life and Times of William M'Kendree, Bishop of the Methodist Episcopal Church.* Nashville: Southern Methodist Publishing House, 1869.

Phillips, John Wesley, ed. *Teacher, Preacher, and Circuit Rider: The Biography of Reuben Phillips.* N.p., Biography Press, August 1975.

Phinney, William R., Kenneth E. Rowe, and Robert E. Steelman, eds. *Thomas Ware, A Spectator at the Christmas Conference: A Miscellany on Thomas Ware and the Methodist Christmas Conference.* Rutland: Academy Books, 1984.

A Pocket Hymn Book, Designed as a Constant Companion for the Pious. Philadelphia: Prichard and Hall, 1790.

Rankin, Adam. *A Review of the Noted Revival in Kentucky, Commenced in the Year of Our Lord, 1801.* Lexington, Ky.: for the author, 1802.

Ripley, Dorothy. *The Extraordinary Conversion, and Religious Experience of Dorothy Ripley, With Her First Voyage and Travels in America.* New York: for the author, 1810.

Roberts, Kenneth, and Anna M. Roberts, trans. and eds. *Moreau de St. Mery's American Journey* [1793–1798]. Garden City: Doubleday, 1947.

Sandford, P. P. *Memoirs of Mr. Wesley's Missionaries to America.* New York: G. Lane & P. P. Sandford, 1843.

Simpson, Robert Drew, ed. *American Methodist Pioneer: The Life and Journals of the Rev. Freeborn Garrettson, 1752–1827.* Rutland: Academy Books, 1984.

Smith, David. *Biography of Rev. David Smith, of the A. M. E. Church, Being a Complete History, Embracing Over Sixty Years' Labor in the Advancement of the Redeemer's Kingdom on Earth.* Xenia: n.p., 1881.

Smith, Henry. *Recollections and Reflections of an Old Itinerant.* New York, 1848.

Smith, James. "Tours into Kentucky and the Northwest Territory. Three Journals by the Rev. James Smith of Powhatan County, Va., 1783, 1795, 1797." *Ohio Archaeological and Historical Publications* 16 (1907): 348–401.

Smith, William E., ed. *Memoirs of a Methodist Circuit Rider—Francis Wilson.* Austin: for the author, 1983.

"Some Letters of Richard Allen and Absalom Jones to Dorothy Ripley." *Journal of Negro History* 1:1 (January 1916): 436–43.

Strickland, W. P. *The Life of Jacob Gruber.* New York: Carlton & Porter, 1860.

Sweet, William Warren, ed. *The Rise of Methodism in the West, Being the Journal of the Western Conference, 1800–1811.* New York: Methodist Book Concern, 1920.

Thrift, Minton. *Memoir of the Rev. Jesse Lee With Extracts from His Journals.* 1823. Reprint, New York: Arno Press & New York Times, 1969.

Travis, Joseph. *Autobiography of the Rev. Joseph Travis, A. M., A Member of the Memphis Annual Conference. Embracing a Succinct History of the Methodist Episcopal Church, South; Particularly in Part of Western Virginia, the Carolinas, Georgia, Alabama, and Mississippi. With Short Memoirs of Several Local Preachers, and an Address to His Friends.* Edited by Thomas O. Summers. Nashville: E. Stevenson & F. A. Owen, for the Methodist Episcopal Church, South, 1856.

Wakeley, J. B. *The Patriarch of One Hundred Years; Being Reminiscences, Historical and Biographical, of Rev. Henry Boehm.* New York: Nelson & Phillips, 1875.

Watters, William. *A Short Account of the Christian Experience, and Ministereal Labours, of William Watters.* Alexandria: S. Snowden, 1806.

Wesley, John. *A Calm Address to the Inhabitants of England, &c.* London: n.p., 1777.

———. *A Calm Address to Our American Colonies.* London: n.p., 1775.

———. *Thoughts Upon Slavery.* London: R. Hawes, 1774.

Wesley, John, and Charles Wesley. *A Collection of Psalms and Hymns.* Philadelphia: Melchoir Steiner, 1781.

Windley, Lathan A., compiler. *Runaway Slave Advertisements: A Documentary History from the 1730s to 1790.* Volume 2. Maryland. Westport: Greenwood Press, 1983.

Young, Jacob. *Autobiography of a Pioneer: Or, the Nativity, Experience, Travels, and Ministerial Labors of Rev. Jacob Young, with Incidents, Observations, and Reflections.* Cincinnati: L. Swormstedt & A. Poe, 1857.

Periodicals

The Arminian Magazine (Philadelphia) 1789–1790
The Methodist Magazine (Philadelphia) 1797–1798

Secondary Sources

Ahlstrom, Sydney E. *A Religious History of the American People.* New Haven: Yale University Press, 1972.

Albanese, Catherine L. *Sons of the Fathers: The Civil Religion of the American Revolution.* Philadelphia: Temple University Press, 1976.

Andrews, Doris Elisabett. "Popular Religion and the Revolution in the Middle Atlantic Ports: The Rise of the Methodists, 1770–1800." Ph.D. diss., University of Pennsylvania, 1986.

Armour, Robert Alexander. "The Opposition to the Methodists in Eighteenth-Century Virginia." Ph.D. diss., University of Georgia, 1968.

Ayers, Edward. *Vengeance and Justice: Crime and Punishment in the 19th-Century American South.* New York: Oxford University Press, 1984.

Babcock, Theodore Stoddard. "Manumission in Virginia, 1782–1806." Master's thesis, University of Virginia, 1974.

Bailey, David T. *Shadow on the Church: Southwestern Evangelical Religion and the Issue of Slavery, 1783–1860.* Ithaca: Cornell University Press, 1985.

Bailyn, Bernard. *The Ideological Origins of the American Revolution.* Cambridge: Harvard University Press, 1967.

Baker, Frank. "The Origins, Character, and Influences of John Wesley's *Thoughts Upon Slavery*." *Methodist History* 22:2 (January 1984): 75–86.

———. *From Wesley to Asbury: Studies in Early American Methodism.* Durham: Duke University Press, 1976.

Baker, Gordon Pratt, ed. *Those Incredible Methodists: A History of the Baltimore Conference of the United Methodist Church.* Baltimore: Commission on Archives and History, the Baltimore Conference, 1972.

Beeman, Richard R. *The Evolution of the Southern Backcountry: A Case Study of Lunenburg County, Virginia, 1746–1832.* Philadelphia: University of Pennsylvania Press, 1984.

Beirne, Francis F. *St. Paul's Parish Baltimore: A Chronicle of the Mother Church.* Baltimore: Horn-Shafer, 1967.

Bennett, William W. *Memorials of Methodism in Virginia.* 2d ed. Richmond: by the author, 1871.

Bercovitch, Sacvan. *The American Jeremiad.* Madison: University of Wisconsin Press, 1978.

Berlin, Ira. *Slaves Without Masters: The Free Negro in the Antebellum South.* New York: Pantheon Books, 1974.

Bilhartz, Terry D. *Urban Religion and the Second Great Awakening: Church and Society in Early National Baltimore.* Rutherford: Fairleigh Dickinson University Press, 1986.

Bloch, Ruth. "The Gendered Meanings of Virtue in Revolutionary America." *Signs* 13:1 (Autumn 1987): 37–58.

Boles, John B. *The Great Revival, 1787–1805: The Origins of the Southern Evangelical Mind.* Lexington: University Press of Kentucky, 1972.

———. "John Hersey: Dissenting Theologian of Abolitionism, Perfectionism, Millennialism." *Methodist History* 14 (1976): 215–34.

———. "Revivalism, Renewal, and Social Mediation in the Old South." In *Modern Christian Revivals*, edited by Randall Balmer and Edith L. Blumhofer. Urbana: University of Illinois Press, 1993.

———. "Tension in a Slave Society: The Trial of the Reverend Jacob Gruber." *Southern Studies* 18 (1979): 179–97.

Boles, John B., ed. *Masters and Slaves in the House of the Lord: Race and Religion in the American South, 1740–1870.* Lexington: University Press of Kentucky, 1988.

Boles, John B., and Evelyn Thomas Nolen, eds. *Interpreting Southern History: Historiographical Essays in Honor of Sanford Higginbotham.* Baton Rouge: Louisiana State University Press, 1987.

Bowden, Haygood S. *History of Savannah Methodism: From John Wesley to Silas Johnson.* Macon, Georgia: J. W. Burke, 1929.

Bradley, David H. "Francis Asbury and the Development of African Churches in America." *Methodist History* 10 (October 1971): 3–29.

Breen, T. H. *Tobacco Culture: The Mentality of the Great Tidewater Planters on the Eve of Revolution.* Princeton: Princeton University Press, 1985.

Brereton, Virginia Lieson. *From Sin to Salvation: Stories of Women's Conversions, 1800 to the Present.* Bloomington: Indiana University Press, 1991.

Brown, Douglas Summers. "Elizabeth Henry Campbell Russell: Patroness of Early Methodism in the Highlands of Virginia." *Virginia Cavalcade* 30:3 (Winter 1981): 110–17.

Bruce, Jr., Dickson D. *And They All Sang Hallelujah: Plain Folk Camp Meeting Religion, 1800–1845.* Knoxville: University of Tennessee Press, 1974.

————. *Violence and Culture in the Antebellum South.* Austin: University of Texas Press, 1979.

Bull, Robert J. "Lewis Myers' Reminiscences of Francis Asbury." *Methodist History* 7:1 (October 1968): 5–10.

Butler, Jon. *Awash in a Sea of Faith: Christianizing the American People.* Cambridge: Harvard University Press, 1990.

Bynum, Victoria E. *Unruly Women: The Politics of Social and Sexual Control in the Old South.* Chapel Hill: University of North Carolina Press, 1992.

Calhoon, Robert M. *Evangelicals and Conservatives in the Early South, 1740–1861.* Columbia: University of South Carolina Press, 1988.

Carroll, Kenneth L. "Religious Influences on the Manumission of Slaves in Carolina, Dorchester, and Talbot Counties." *Maryland Historical Magazine* 56:2 (1961): 176–97.

Cashin, Joan E. *A Family Venture: Men and Women on the Southern Frontier.* New York: Oxford University Press, 1991.

Censer, Jane Turner. *North Carolina Planters and Their Children.* Baton Rouge: Louisiana State University Press, 1984.

Clark, Elmer T. *Methodism in Western North Carolina.* Nashville: Western North Carolina Conference, Methodist Church, 1966.

Cobb, Jimmy G. "A Study of White Protestants' Attitudes Towards Negroes in Charleston, South Carolina, 1790–1845." Ph.D. diss., Baylor University, 1976.

Connor, Elizabeth. *Methodist Trail Blazer: Philip Gatch, 1751–1834.* Rutland: Academy Books, 1970.

Conrad, Henry C. *Samuel White and His Father, Judge Thomas White.* Papers of the Historical Society of Delaware, No. 29. Wilmington: Historical Society of Delaware, 1903.

Cott, Nancy. *The Bonds of Womanhood: "Woman's Sphere" in New England, 1780–1835.* New Haven: Yale University Press, 1977.

————. "Young Women in the Second Great Awakening." *Feminist Studies* 3 (Fall 1975): 15–29.

Cowan, Raymond P. "The Arminian Alternative: The Rise of the Methodist Episcopal Church, 1765–1850." Ph.D. diss., Georgia State University, 1991.

Cross, Whitney R. *The Burned-Over District: The Social and Intellectual History of Enthusiastic Religion in Western New York.* Ithaca: Cornell University Press, 1950.

Crowther, Edward R. "Holy Honor: Sacred and Secular in the Old South." *Journal of Southern History* 58:4 (November 1992): 619–36.

Cupples, Cynthia J. "Pious Ladies and Methodist Madams: Sex and Gender in Anti-Methodist Writings of Eighteenth Century England." *Critical Matrix* (Spring/Summer 1990): 30–60.

Daniel, W. Harrison. "The Methodist Episcopal Church and the Negro in the Early National Period." *Methodist History* 2 (January 1973): 40–53.

Daniels, W. H. *The Illustrated History of Methodism in Great Britain and America, from the Days of the Wesleys to the Present Time.* New York: Methodist Book Concern, 1880.

Davis, David Brion. *The Problem of Slavery in the Age of Revolution, 1770–1823.* Ithaca: Cornell University Press, 1975.

Dillon, Merton L. *Slavery Attacked: Southern Slaves and Their Allies, 1619–1865.* Baton Rouge: Louisiana State University Press, 1990.

Douglas, Ann. *The Feminization of American Culture.* New York: Alfred A. Knopf, 1977.

Egerton, Douglas R. *Gabriel's Rebellion: The Virginia Slave Conspiracies of 1800 and 1802.* Chapel Hill: University of North Carolina Press, 1993.

Eighmy, John Lee. *Churches in Cultural Captivity: A History of the Social Attitudes of the Southern Baptists.* Knoxville: University of Tennessee Press, 1972.

Epstein, Barbara Leslie. *The Politics of Domesticity: Women, Evangelism, and Temperance in Nineteenth-Century America.* Middletown, Conn.: Wesleyan University Press, 1981.

Essig, James D. *The Bonds of Wickedness: American Evangelicals Against Slavery, 1770–1808.* Philadelphia: Temple University Press, 1982.

Faust, Drew Gilpin. *The Creation of Confederate Nationalism: Ideology and Identity in the Civil War South.* Baton Rouge: Louisiana State University Press, 1988.

————. "A Southern Stewardship: The Intellectual and the Proslavery Argument." *American Quarterly* 31 (1979): 63–80.

Faust, Drew Gilpin, ed. *The Ideology of Slavery: Proslavery Thought in the Antebellum South, 1830–1860.* Baton Rouge: Louisiana State University Press, 1981.

Ford, Jr., Lacy K. *Origins of Southern Radicalism: The South Carolina Upcountry, 1800–1860.* New York: Oxford University Press, 1988.

Fox-Genovese, Elizabeth. *Within the Plantation Household: Black and White Women of the Old South.* Chapel Hill: University of North Carolina Press, 1988.

Frey, Sylvia. *Water from the Rock: Black Resistance in a Revolutionary Age.* Princeton: Princeton University Press, 1991.

Friedman, Jean E. *The Enclosed Garden: Women and Community in the Evangelical South, 1830–1900.* Chapel Hill: University of North Carolina Press, 1985.

Garrett, Clarke. *Spirit Possession and Popular Religion from the Camisards to the Shakers.* Baltimore: Johns Hopkins University Press, 1987.

Genovese, Eugene. *Roll, Jordan, Roll: The World the Slaves Made.* New York: Vintage Books, 1976.

George, Carol V. R. *Segregated Sabbaths: Richard Allen and the Emergence of Independent Black Churches, 1760–1840.* New York: Oxford University Press, 1973.

Gewehr, Wesley M. *The Great Awakening in Virginia, 1740–1790.* Durham: Duke University Press, 1930.

Gillespie, Joanna Bowen. "1795: Martha Laurens Ramsay's 'Dark Night of the Soul.'" *William and Mary Quarterly* 48:1 (January 1991): 68–92.

————. "'The Sun in Their Domestic System': The Mother in Early Nineteenth-Century Methodist Sunday School Lore." In *Women in New Worlds.* Volume 2. *Historical Perspectives on the Wesleyan Tradition,* edited by Rosemary Skinner Keller, Louise L. Queen, and Hilah F. Thomas. Nashville: Abingdon Press, 1982.

Gravely, William B. "A Preacher's Covenant Against Slavery, 1795." *South Carolina United Methodist Advocate* (March 18, 1791): 8–9, 14.

Greenberg, Kenneth S. *Masters and Statesmen: The Political Culture of American Slavery.* Baltimore: Johns Hopkins University Press, 1987.

Greven, Philip. *The Protestant Temperament: Patterns of Child-Rearing, Religious Experience, and the Self in Early America.* New York: Alfred A. Knopf, 1977.

Gunderson, Joan R. "The Local Parish as a Female Institution: The Experience of All Saints Episcopal Church in Frontier Minnesota." *Church History* 55:3 (September 1986): 307–22.

————. "The Non-Institutional Church: The Religious Role of Women in Eighteenth-Century Virginia." *Historical Magazine of the Protestant Episcopal Church* 51 (December 1982): 347–57.

Gutman, Herbert G. *The Black Family in Slavery and Freedom, 1750–1925.* New York: Vintage Books, 1976.

Hall, David D. *Worlds of Wonder, Days of Judgment: Popular Religious Beliefs in Early New England.* New York: Alfred A. Knopf, 1989.

Handy, James A. *Scraps of African Methodist Episcopal History.* Philadelphia: A.M.E. Book Concern, n.d.

Hanley, Thomas O'Brien. *The American Revolution and Religion: Maryland 1770–1800.* Washington: Catholic University of America Press, 1971.

Hardesty, Nancy. *Your Daughters Shall Prophesy: Revivalism and Feminism in the Age of Finney.* Brooklyn: Carlson, Inc., 1991.

Harrell, David E., ed. *Varieties of Southern Evangelicalism.* Macon, Georgia: Mercer University Press, 1981.

Haskell, Thomas L. "Capitalism and the Origins of the Humanitarian Sensibility, Part 1." *The American Historical Review* 90:2 (April 1985): 339–61.

————. "Capitalism and the Origins of the Humanitarian Sensibility, Part 2." *The American Historical Review* 90:3 (June 1985): 547–66.

Higginbotham, Don. "Methodism Moves East: Annual Conference, New Bern, North Carolina, 1807." *The Wesleyan Quarterly Review* 1 (1964): 38–42.

Higham, John. *From Boundlessness to Consolidation: The Transformation of American Culture, 1848–1860.* Ann Arbor: William L. Clements Library, 1969.

Hildebrand, Reginald F. "Methodist Episcopal Policy on the Ordination of Black Ministers, 1784–1864." *Methodist History* 20:3 (April 1982): 124–42.

Hoffman, Ronald. "The Disaffected in the Revolutionary South." In *The American Revolution: Explorations in the History of American Radicalism,* edited by Alfred F. Young. Dekalb: Northern Illinois University Press, 1976.

Holifield, E. Brooks. *The Gentlemen Theologians: American Theology in Southern Culture, 1795–1860.* Durham: Duke University Press, 1978.

————. *Health and Medicine in the Methodist Tradition: Journey Toward Wholeness.* New York: Crossroad, 1986.

Holmes, Marjorie Moran. "The Life and Diary of the Reverend John Jeremiah Jacob (1757–1839)." Master's thesis, Duke University, 1941.

Huff, Jr., Archie Vernon. *Tried by Fire: Washington Street United Methodist Church, Columbia, South Carolina.* Columbia: R. L. Bryan, 1975.

Isaac, Rhys. "Preachers and Patriots: Popular Culture and the Revolution in Virginia." In *The American Revolution: Explorations in the History of American Radicalism,* edited by Alfred F. Young. Dekalb: Northern Illinois University Press, 1976.

————. *The Transformation of Virginia, 1740–1790.* New York: W. W. Norton, 1988.

Jackson, Luther P. "Religious Development of the Negro in Virginia from 1760 to 1860." *The Journal of Negro History* 16:2 (April 1931): 168–239.

Johnson, Curtis D. *Islands of Holiness: Rural Religion in Upstate New York, 1790–1860.* Ithaca: Cornell University Press, 1989.

Johnson, Paul E. *A Shopkeeper's Millennium: Society and Revivals in Rochester, New York, 1815–1837.* New York: Hill and Wang, 1978.

Johnston, James Hugo. "The Participation of White Men in Virginia Negro Insurrections." *Journal of Negro History* 16:2 (April 1931): 158–67.

Jordan, Winthrop. *White Over Black: American Attitudes Toward the Negro, 1550–1812.* New York: W. W. Norton, 1968.

Juster, Susan. "'In a Different Voice': Male and Female Narratives of Religious Conversion in Post-Revolutionary America." *American Quarterly* 41 (March 1989): 34–62.

Karlsen, Carol F. *The Devil in the Shape of a Woman: Witchcraft in Colonial New England.* New York: W. W. Norton, 1987.

Keever, Homer M. "A Lutheran Preacher's Account of the 1801–02 Revival in North Carolina." *Methodist History* 7 (October 1968): 38–55.

Kerber, Linda. "The Republican Mother: Women and the Enlightenment—An American Perspective." *American Quarterly* 37 (Summer 1976): 187–205.

————. "Women and Individualism in American History." *Massachusetts Review* (Winter 1989): 589–609.

Kierner, Cynthia. "Women's Piety Within Patriarchy: The Religious Life of Martha Hancock Wheat of Bedford County." *Virginia Magazine of History and Biography* (January 1992): 79–98.

Kincheloe, Jr., Joe L. "Transcending Role Restrictions: Women at Camp Meetings and Political Rallies." *Tennessee Historical Quarterly* 40:2 (Summer 1981): 158–69.

Klein, Rachel. *Unification of a Slave State: The Rise of the Planter Class in the South Carolina Backcountry, 1760–1808.* Chapel Hill: University of North Carolina Press, 1990.

Kulikoff, Allan. *Tobacco and Slaves: The Development of Southern Cultures in the Chesapeake, 1680–1800.* Chapel

Hill: University of North Carolina Press for the Institute of Early American History and Culture, 1986.

Kurtz, Stephen G., and James H. Hutson, eds. *Essays on the American Revolution.* Chapel Hill: University of North Carolina Press, 1973.

Lebsock, Suzanne. *The Free Women of Petersburg: Status and Culture in a Southern Town, 1784–1860.* New York: W. W. Norton, 1984.

Levine, Lawrence. *Black Culture and Black Consciousness: Afro-American Folk Thought from Slavery to Freedom.* New York: Oxford University Press, 1977.

Lewis, Jan. *The Pursuit of Happiness: Family and Values in Jefferson's Virginia.* Cambridge: Cambridge University Press, 1983.

———. "The Republican Wife: Virtue and Seduction in the Early Republic." *William and Mary Quarterly* 44 (October 1987): 689–721.

Linn, Theodore C. "Religion and Nationalism: American Methodism and the New Nation in the Early National Period, 1766–1844." Ph.D. diss., Drew University, 1971.

Long, Ronald W. "Religious Revivalism in the Carolinas and Georgia, 1740–1805." Ph.D. diss., University of Georgia, 1968.

Loveland, Anne C. *Southern Evangelicals and the Social Order, 1800–1860.* Baton Rouge: Louisiana State University Press, 1980.

Lubach, James L., and Thomas L. Shanklin. "Arbitrations and Trials of Members in the Methodist Episcopal Church, 1776–1860." *Methodist History* 10 (July 1971): 30–49.

Lumpkin, William L. "The Role of Women in 18th Century Virginia Baptist Life." *Baptist History and Heritage* 8 (July 1973): 158–67.

Lupold, Dorothy M. "Methodism in Virginia From 1772–1784." Master's thesis, University of Virginia, 1949.

Lyles, Albert M. *Methodism Mocked: The Satiric Reaction to Methodism in the Eighteenth Century.* London: Epworth Press, 1960.

McAninch, Glen A. "We'll Pray for You: Methodist Ethnocentrism in the Origins of the African Methodist Episcopal Church in Baltimore." Master's thesis, University of North Carolina at Chapel Hill, 1973.

McCurry, Stephanie. "The Politics of Yeoman Households in Antebellum South Carolina." In *Divided Houses: Gender and the Civil War,* edited by Catherine Clinton and Nina Silber. New York: Oxford University Press, 1992.

———. "The Two Faces of Republicanism: Gender and Proslavery Politics in Antebellum South Carolina." *Journal of American History* 78:4 (March 1992): 1245–64.

MacDonald, Michael. "Insanity and the Realities of History in Early Modern England." *Psychological Medicine* 11 (1981): 11–25.

MacLeod, Duncan. *Slavery, Race, and the American Revolution.* Cambridge: Cambridge University Press, 1974.

MacMaster, Richard K. "Liberty or Property? The Methodists Petition for Emancipation in Virginia, 1785." *Methodist History* 10 (October 1971): 43–55.

Maddex, Jr., Jack P. "'The Southern Apostasy' Revisited: The Significance of Proslavery Christianity." In *Religion and Slavery,* edited by Paul Finkelman. New York: Garland, 1989.

Mason, Keith. "Localism, Evangelicalism, and Loyalism: The Sources of Discontent in the Revolutionary Chesapeake." *Journal of Southern History* 56:1 (February 1990): 23–54.

Mathews, Donald G. *Religion in the Old South.* Chicago: University of Chicago Press, 1977.

———. *Slavery and Methodism: A Chapter in American Morality.* Princeton: Princeton University Press, 1965.

May, James William. "From Revival Movement to Denomination: A Re-Examination of the Beginnings of American Methodism (1765–1808)." Ph.D. diss., Columbia University, 1962.

May, James W. "Francis Asbury and Thomas White: A Refugee Preacher and His Tory Patron." *Methodist History* 14 (1976): 141–64.

Miller, Perry. *The New England Mind: The Seventeenth Century.* Boston: Beacon Press, 1939.

Miyakawa, T. Scott. *Protestants and Pioneers: Individualism and Conformity on the American Frontier.* Chicago: University of Chicago Press, 1964.

Moore, M. H. *Sketches of the Pioneers of Methodism in North Carolina and Virginia.* Nashville: Southern Methodist Publishing House, 1884.

Moore, R. Laurence. *Religious Outsiders and the Making of Americans.* New York: Oxford University Press, 1986.

Morgan, Edmund. *American Slavery, American Freedom: The Ordeal of Colonial Virginia.* New York: W. W. Norton, 1975.

Mullin, Gerald W. *Flight and Rebellion: Slave Resistance in Eighteenth-Century Virginia.* New York: Oxford University Press, 1972.

Munroe, John A. "Reflections on Delaware and the American Revolution." *Delaware History* 17:1 (Summer 1976): 1–11.

Norton, Mary Beth. *Liberty's Daughters: The Revolutionary Experience of American Women, 1750–1800.* Boston: Little, Brown, 1980.

Norwood, Frederick A. *Sourcebook of American Methodism.* Nashville: Abingdon Press, 1982.

Oakes, James. *The Ruling Race: A History of American Slaveholders.* New York: Vintage Books, 1983.

Okuye, F. Nwabueze. "Chattel Slavery as the Nightmare of the American Revolutionaries." *William and Mary Quarterly* 37 (January 1980): 3–28.

Payne, Daniel A. *History of the African Methodist Episcopal Church.* 1891. Reprint, New York: Johnson Reprint Corporation, 1968.

Peluso, Gary E. "Francis Asbury on American Public Life." *Methodist History* 30:4 (July 1992): 206–16.

Peters, John Leland. *Christian Perfection and American Methodism.* New York: Abingdon Press, 1956.

Peterson, Thomas Virgil. *Ham and Japheth: The Mythic World of Whites in the Antebellum South.* Metuchen, N.J.: Scarecrow Press, 1978.

Pool, Frank Kenneth. "The Southern Negro in the Methodist Episcopal Church." Ph.D. diss., Duke University, 1939.

Porter, Roy. *Mind Forg'd Manacles: A History of Madness in England from the Restoration to the Regency.* London: Athlone Press, 1987.

Preston, Thomas L. *A Sketch of Mrs. Elizabeth Russell, Wife of General William Campbell, and Sister of Patrick Henry.* Nashville: Publishing House of the M. E. Church, South, 1888.

Purifoy, Lewis M. "The Southern Methodist Church and the Proslavery Argument." *Journal of Southern History* 32 (1966): 325–41.

Rabinowitz, Richard. *The Spiritual Self in Everyday Life: The Transformation of Personal Religious Experience in Nineteenth-Century New England.* Boston: Northeastern University Press, 1989.

Raboteau, Albert J. *Slave Religion: The "Invisible Institution" in the Antebellum South.* New York: Oxford University Press, 1978.

Rankin, Richard. *Ambivalent Churchmen and Evangelical Churchwomen: The Religion of the Episcopal Elite in North Carolina, 1800–1860.* Columbia: University of South Carolina Press, 1993.

Redford, A. H. *The History of Methodism in Kentucky.* Volume 1. Nashville: Southern Methodist Publishing House, 1868.

———. *The History of Methodism in Kentucky.* Volume 2. Nashville: Southern Methodist Publishing House, 1870.

Richey, Russell E. "The Four Languages of Early American Methodism." *Methodist History* 28:3 (1990): 155–70.

———. *Early American Methodism.* Bloomington: Indiana University Press, 1991.

Richey, Russell E., and Kenneth E. Rowe, eds. *Rethinking Methodist History.* Nashville: United Methodist Publishing House, 1985.

Rose, Willie Lee. "The Domestication of Domestic Slavery." In *Slavery and Freedom*, edited by William W. Freehling. New York: Oxford University Press, 1982.

Rubin, Julius H. *Religious Melancholy and Protestant Experience in America.* New York: Oxford University Press, 1994.

Runyon, Elva. "Madame Russell, Methodist Saint." Master's thesis, University of Virginia, 1941.

Ryan, Mary P. *Cradle of the Middle Class: The Family in Oneida County, New York, 1790–1865.* Cambridge: Cambridge University Press, 1981.

Schmidt, Fredericka Teute, and Barbara Ripel Wilhelm. "Early Proslavery Petitions in Virginia." *William and Mary Quarterly* 30:1 (January 1973): 133–46.

Schneider, A. Gregory. "The Ritual of Happy Dying Among Early American Methodists." *Church History* 56:3 (September 1987): 348–63.

———. *The Way of the Cross Leads Home: The Domestication of American Methodism.* Bloomington: Indiana University Press, 1993.

Scott, Anne Firor. *The Southern Lady: From Pedestal to Politics, 1830–1930.* Chicago: University of Chicago Press, 1970.

Semmel, Bernard. *The Methodist Revolution.* New York: Basic Books, 1973.

Shipp, Albert M. *The History of Methodism in South Carolina.* Nashville: Southern Methodist Publishing House, 1884.

Simpson, Matthew. *Cyclopaedia of Methodism, Embracing Sketches of Its Rise, Progress, and Present Condition.* Philadelphia: Louis H. Everts, 1880.

———. *A Hundred Years of Methodism.* New York: Phillips & Hunt, 1876.

Smith, H. Shelton. *In His Image, But . . . : Racism and Southern Religion, 1780–1910.* Durham: Duke University Press, 1972.

Smith, John Q. "Occupational Groups Among the Early Methodists of the Keighley Circuit." *Church History* 57:2 (June 1988):187–96.

Smith, Timothy L. *Revivalism and Social Reform in Mid-Nineteenth-Century America.* New York: Abingdon Press, 1957.

Smith, William C. *Pillars in the Temple; or Sketches of Deceased Laymen of the Methodist Episcopal Church.* New York: Carlton & Lanaham, 1872.

Sobel, Mechal. *Trabelin' On: The Slave Journey to an Afro-Baptist Faith.* Princeton: Princeton University Press, 1988.

———. *The World They Made Together: Black and White Values in Eighteenth-Century Virginia.* Princeton: Princeton University Press, 1987.

Sprague, William B. *Annals of the American Pulpit: or Commemorative Notices of Distinguished American Clergymen of Various Denominations.* Volume 7. *The Methodists.* 1863. Reprint, New York: Arno Press and New York Times, 1969.

Stannard, David E. *The Puritan Way of Death: A Study in Religion, Culture, and Social Change.* Oxford: Oxford University Press, 1977.

Steadman, Jr., Melvin Lee. "Thomas Crenshaw and the 'First Sunday School.'" *Virginia United Methodist Heritage* 1 (Autumn 1973): 10–12.

Stoeffler, F. Ernest, ed. *Continental Pietism and Early American Christianity.* Grand Rapids: William B. Eerdmans, 1976.

Stowe, Steven M. *Intimacy and Power in the Old South: Ritual in the Lives of Planters.* Baltimore: Johns Hopkins University Press, 1987.

Strickland, John Scott. "Across Space and Time: Conversion, Community, and Cultural Change Among South Carolina Slaves." Ph.D. diss., University of North Carolina at Chapel Hill, 1985.

Stuckey, Sterling. *Slave Culture: Nationalist Theory and the Foundations of Black America.* New York: Oxford University Press, 1987.

Sweet, William Warren. "The Churches as Moral Courts of the Frontier." *Church History* 2 (1933): 2–21.

———. *Men of Zeal: The Romance of American Methodist Beginnings.* New York: Abingdon Press, 1935.

———. *Methodism in American History.* New York: Methodist Book Concern, 1933.

Thickstun, Margaret Olofson. *Fictions of the Feminine: Puritan Doctrine and the Representation of Women.* Ithaca: Cornell University Press, 1988.

Thomas, Jr., Arthur Dicken. "The Second Great Awakening in Virginia and Slavery Reform, 1785–1837." Ph.D. diss., Union Theological Seminary, 1981.

Thomas, John L. "Romantic Reform in America, 1815–1865." *American Quarterly* 17:4 (Winter 1965): 656–81.

Thompson, E. P. *The Making of the English Working Class.* New York: Vintage Books, 1966.

Tise, Larry E. *Proslavery: A History of the Defense of Slavery in America, 1701–1840.* Athens: University of Georgia Press, 1987.

Tuttle, Robert G. *John Wesley: His Life and Theology.* Grand Rapids: Zondervan Publishing House, 1978.

Ulrich, Laurel Thatcher. *Good Wives: Image and Reality in the Lives of Women in Northern New England, 1650–1750.* New York: Vintage Books, 1980.

Valenze, Deborah. *Prophetic Sons and Daughters: Female Preaching and Popular Religion in Industrial England.* Princeton: Princeton University Press, 1985.

Vandemeer, Philip R., and Robert P. Sweirenga, eds. *Belief and Behavior: Essays in the New Religious History.* New Brunswick: Rutgers University Press, 1991.

Waldrep, Christopher. "The Making of a Border State Society: James McGready, the Great Revival, and the Prosecution of Profanity in Kentucky." *American Historical Review* 99:3 (June 1994): 767–84.

Wearmouth, Robert F. *Methodism and the Common People of the Eighteenth Century.* London: Epworth Press, 1945.

Weber, Max. *The Protestant Ethic and the Spirit of Capitalism.* Trans. Talcott Parsons. London: Unwin Hyman, 1930.

Weddle, David Leroy. "The New Man: A Study of the Significance of Conversion for the Theological Definition of the Self in Jonathan Edwards and Charles G. Finney." Ph.D. diss., Harvard University, 1973.

Welter, Barbara. "The Feminization of American Religion: 1800–1860." In *Clio's Consciousness Raised,* ed. by Marty Hartman and Lois Banner. New York: Harper Torchbooks, 1973.

Wigger, John H. "Taking Heaven by Storm: Enthusiasm and Early American Methodism, 1770–1820." *Journal of the Early Republic* 14:2 (Summer 1994): 167–94.

Williams, Samuel W. *Pictures of Early Methodism in Ohio.* Cincinnati: Jennings and Graham, 1909.

Williams, William H. "Delaware and the Methodist Revolution." *Delaware History* 22:4 (Fall/Winter 1987): 219–40.

———. *The Garden of Methodism: The Delmarva Peninsula, 1769–1820.* Wilmington, Del.: Scholarly Resources, 1984.

Wilson, Charles Reagan. *Baptized in Blood: The Religion of the Lost Cause, 1865–1920.* Athens: University of Georgia Press, 1980.

Wood, Gordon S. *The Creation of the American Republic, 1776–1787.* Chapel Hill: University of North Carolina Press, 1969.

———. *The Radicalism of the American Revolution.* New York: Alfred A. Knopf, 1992.

Wood, Peter H. " 'Jesus Christ Has Got Thee at Last': Afro-American Conversion as a Forgotten

Chapter in Eighteenth-Century Southern Intellectual History." *The Bulletin for the Study of Southern Culture and Religion* 3:3 (November 1979): 1–7.

Wroten, Jr., William H. "The Protestant Episcopal Church in Dorchester County, 1692–1860." *Maryland Historical Magazine* 45:2 (June 1950): 104–25.

Wyatt-Brown, Bertram. *Southern Honor: Ethics and Behavior in the Old South.* New York: Oxford University Press, 1982.

Index